Beat

ORESAMA TEACHER

LAZY

Vol. 16
Story & Art by
Izumi Tsubaki

ORESAMA TEACHER

CHARACTERS AND THE STORY THUS FAR

◉PUBLIC MORALS CLUB◉

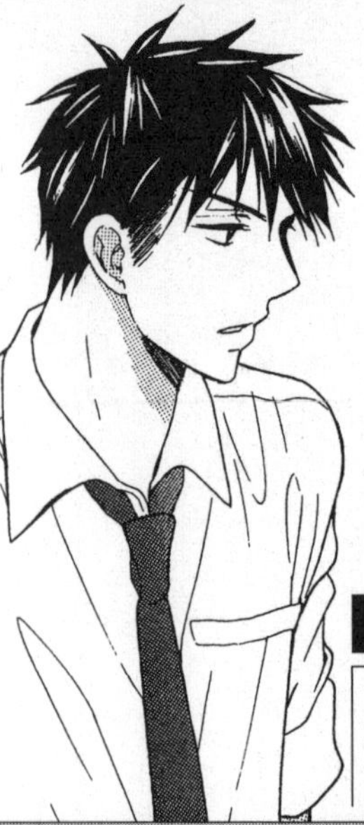

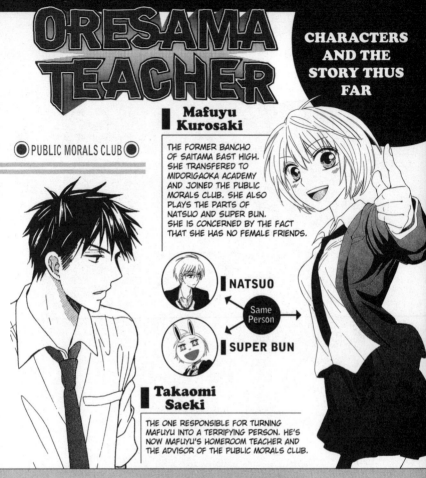

Mafuyu Kurosaki

THE FORMER BANCHO OF SAITAMA EAST HIGH. SHE TRANSFERED TO MIDORIGAOKA ACADEMY AND JOINED THE PUBLIC MORALS CLUB. SHE ALSO PLAYS THE PARTS OF NATSUO AND SUPER BUN. SHE IS CONCERNED BY THE FACT THAT SHE HAS NO FEMALE FRIENDS.

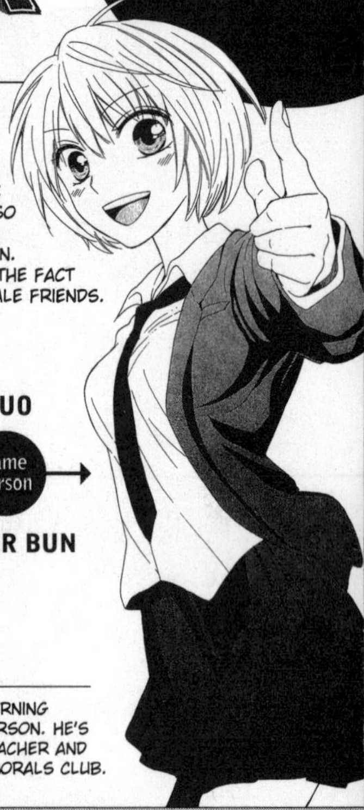

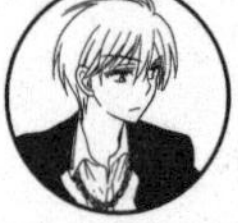

NATSUO

Same Person

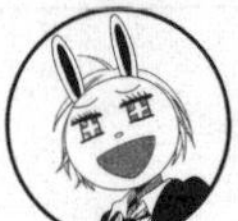

SUPER BUN

Takaomi Saeki

THE ONE RESPONSIBLE FOR TURNING MAFUYU INTO A TERRIFYING PERSON. HE'S NOW MAFUYU'S HOMEROOM TEACHER AND THE ADVISOR OF THE PUBLIC MORALS CLUB.

PUBLIC MORALS CLUB

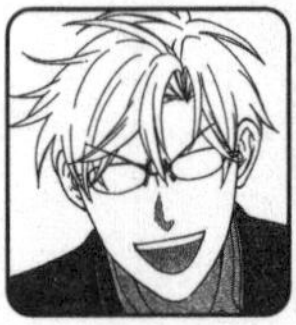

Shinobu Yui

A FORMER MEMBER OF THE STUDENT COUNCIL AND A SELF-PROCLAIMED NINJA. HE JOINED THE PUBLIC MORALS CLUB TO SPY ON THEM.

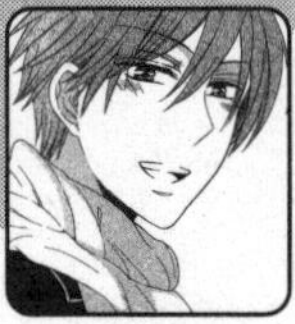

Hayasaka

MAFUYU'S CLASSMATE. HE ADMIRES SUPER BUN. HE IS A PLAIN AND SIMPLE DELINQUENT.

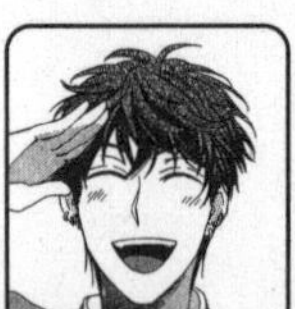

Aki Shibuya

A TALKATIVE AND WOMANIZING UNDERCLASSMAN. HIS NICKNAME IS AKKI. HE'S NOT GOOD AT FIGHTING.

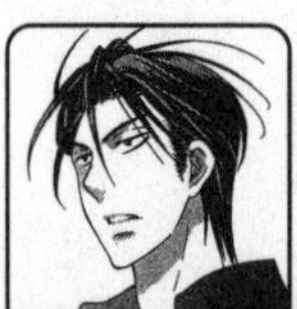

Kyotaro Okegawa

THE BANCHO OF MIDORIGAOKA. HE FLUNKED A YEAR, SO HE'S A SUPER SENIOR THIS YEAR. HE JOINED THE PUBLIC MORALS CLUB TO HELP MAFUYU AND HER FRIENDS.

From the animation studio that brought you Fullmetal Alchemist.

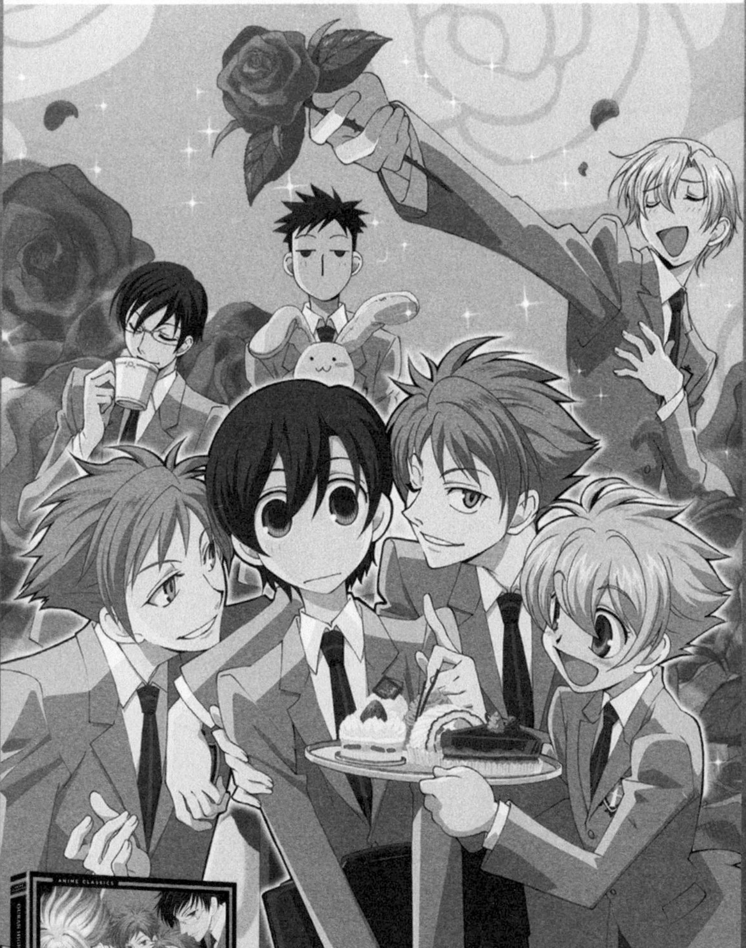

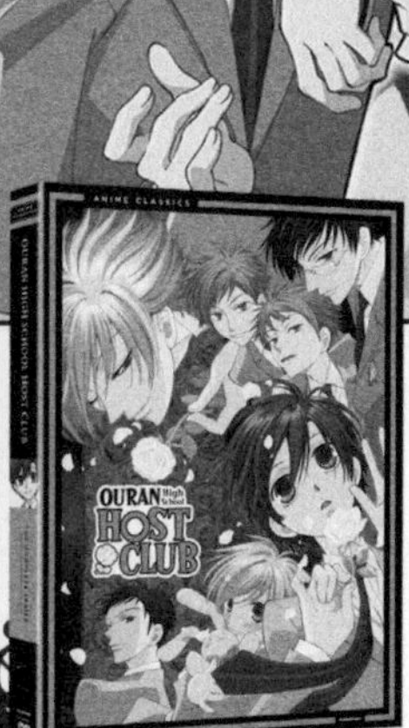
ANIME CLASSICS
OURAN High School HOST CLUB

See the Host Club brought to life!

Take the boys home on DVD or Blu-ray today!

YOU SHOULD BE WATCHING
FUNIMATION.COM/OURAN-HIGH-SCHOOL-HOST-CLUB

FUNIMATION

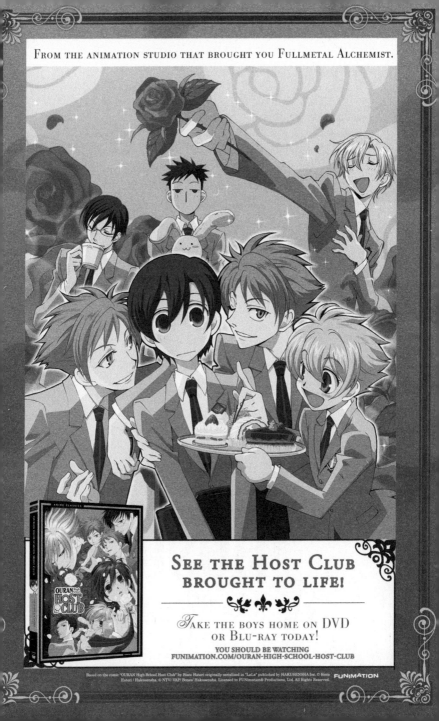

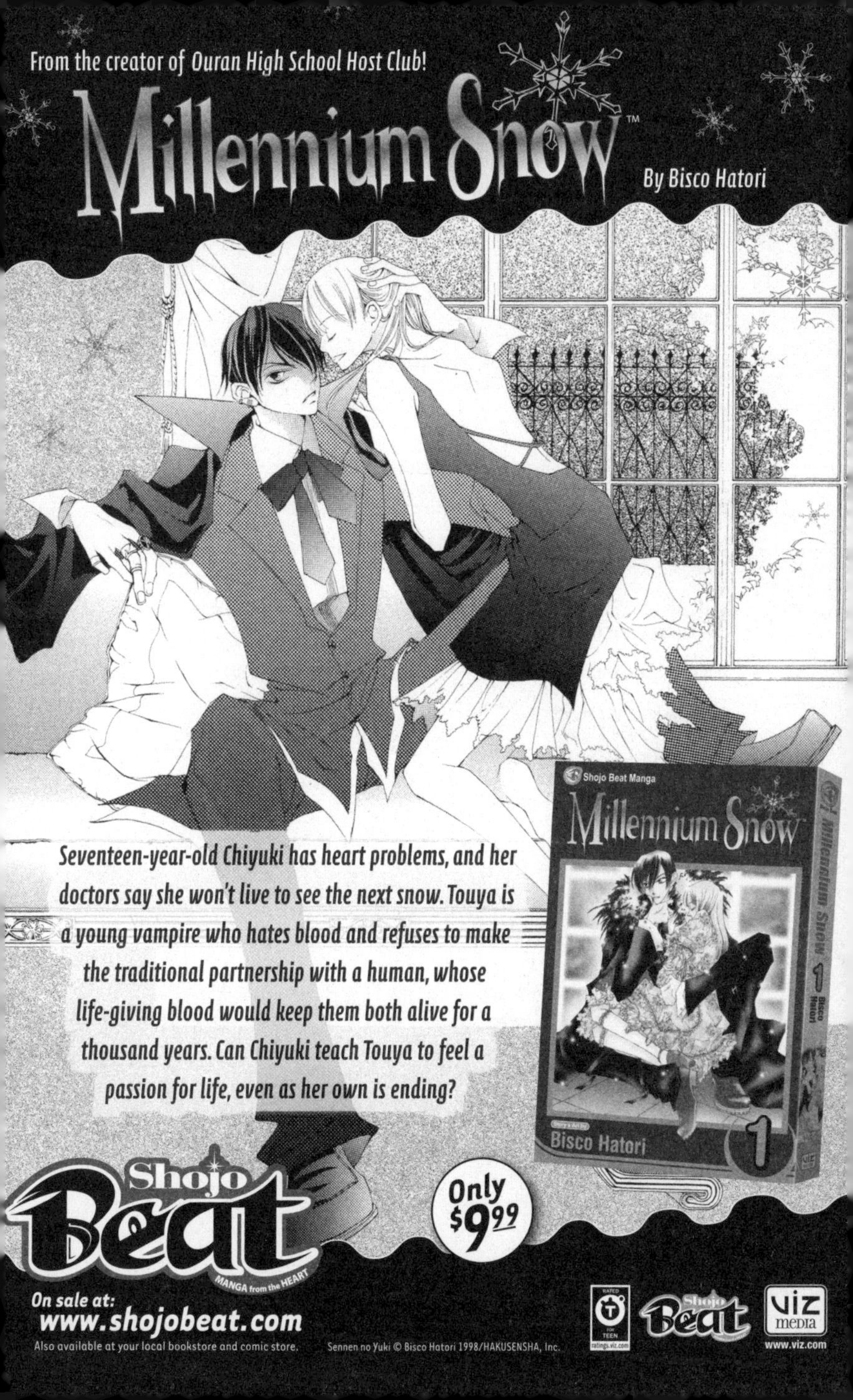
From the creator of Ouran High School Host Club!
Millennium Snow™
By Bisco Hatori
Shojo Beat Manga
Millennium Snow
Bisco Hatori
1
Seventeen-year-old Chiyuki has heart problems, and her doctors say she won't live to see the next snow. Touya is a young vampire who hates blood and refuses to make the traditional partnership with a human, whose life-giving blood would keep them both alive for a thousand years. Can Chiyuki teach Touya to feel a passion for life, even as her own is ending?
Shojo Beat
MANGA from the HEART
Only $9.99
On sale at:
www.shojobeat.com
Also available at your local bookstore and comic store.
Sennen no Yuki © Bisco Hatori 1998/HAKUSENSHA, Inc.
RATED T FOR TEEN
ratings.viz.com
VIZ media
www.viz.com

ORESAMA TEACHER
Vol. 16
Shojo Beat Edition

STORY AND ART BY
Izumi Tsubaki

English Translation & Adaptation/JN Productions
Touch-up Art & Lettering/Eric Erbes
Design/Yukiko Whitley
Editor/Pancha Diaz

Printed in the U.S.A.

Published by VIZ Media, LLC
P.O. Box 77010
San Francisco, CA 94107

10 9 8 7 6 5 4 3 2 1
First printing, March 2014

www.viz.com   www.shojobeat.com

STUDENT COUNCIL

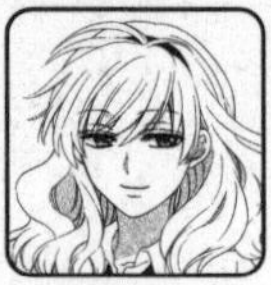

Runa Momochi

THIRD YEAR, CLASS THREE. HANABUSA'S CLASSMATE.

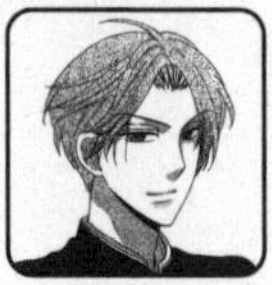

Shuntaro Kosaka

HE'S OBSESSED WITH MANUALS. HE DOES NOT HANDLE UNEXPECTED EVENTS WELL.

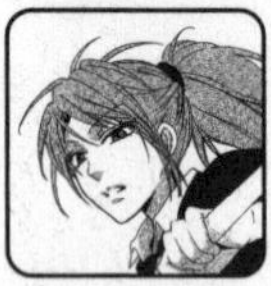

Wakana Hojo

SHE HAS A STOIC ATTITUDE AND WATCHES OVER HANABUSA. SHE HAS FEELINGS FOR YUI.

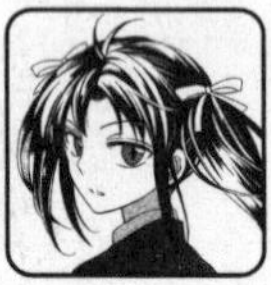

Kanon Nonoguchi

SHE HATES MEN. HER FAMILY RUNS A DOJO, SO SHE'S STRONG. SHE PLANS TO DESTROY THE PUBLIC MORALS CLUB OUT OF GRATITUDE TOWARDS MIYABI.

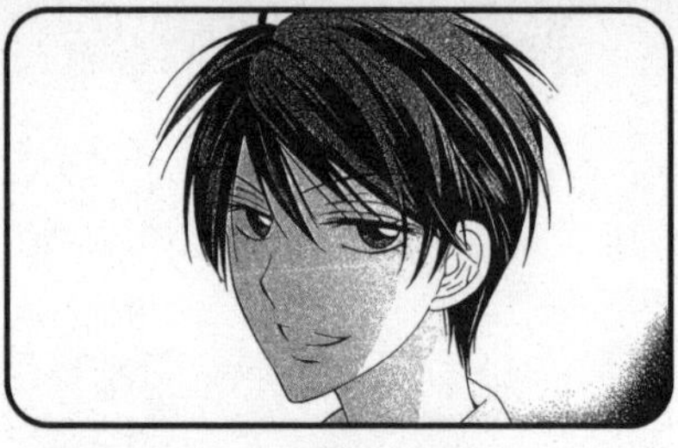

Miyabi Hanabusa

THE SCHOOL DIRECTOR'S SON AND THE PRESIDENT OF THE STUDENT COUNCIL.

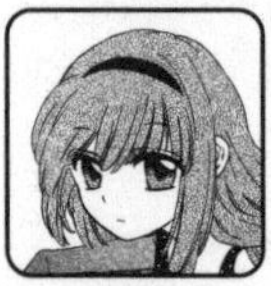

Komari Yukioka

USING HER CUTE LOOKS, SHE CONTROLS THOSE AROUND HER WITHOUT THE NEED FOR WORDS. BUT INSIDE, SHE'S LIKE A DIRTY OLD MAN.

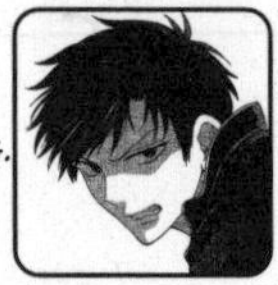

Reito Ayabe

HE LOVES CLEANING. HE GETS STRONGER IN DIRTY PLACES. HE IS A STUDENT COUNCIL OFFICER, BUT HE'S ALSO FRIENDS WITH MAFUYU.

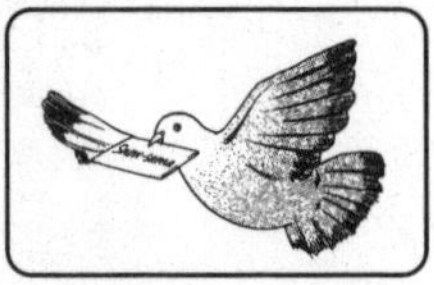

Torikichi / Josephine

THE MESSENGER PIGEON THAT MIDORIGAOKA BANCHO OKEGAWA LOVES VERY MUCH. SHE CARRIES LETTERS TO AND FROM MAFUYU (A.K.A. SNOW).

story

★ MAFUYU KUROSAKI WAS ONCE THE BANCHO WHO CONTROLLED ALL OF SAITAMA, BUT WHEN SHE WAS TRANSFERRED TO MIDORIGAOKA ACADEMY, SHE CHANGED COMPLETELY AND BECAME A NORMAL (BUT SPIRITED) HIGH SCHOOL GIRL...OR AT LEAST SHE WAS SUPPOSED TO! TAKAOMI SAEKI, MAFUYU'S CHILDHOOD FRIEND AND HOMEROOM TEACHER, FORCED HER TO JOIN THE PUBLIC MORALS CLUB, THUS MAKING SURE HER LIFE CONTINUED TO BE FAR FROM AVERAGE.

★ THE PUBLIC MORALS CLUB IS FIGHTING THE STUDENT COUNCIL FOR CONTROL OF MIDORIGAOKA ACADEMY, AND HAS ALREADY BESTED STUDENT COUNCIL MEMBERS KOSAKA AND AYABE. AND NOW THE PUBLIC MORALS CLUB HAS A NEW MEMBER NAMED SHIBUYA. THEIR CLASH WITH KANON NONOGUCHI, THE NEXT STUDENT COUNCIL MEMBER TO OPPOSE THEM, TURNED INTO A HUGE RIOT INVOLVING THE INFAMOUS KIYAMA HIGH SCHOOL. BUT BANCHO OKEGAWA JOINED THE PUBLIC MORALS CLUB AND THEY WERE ABLE TO OVERCOME THE THREAT.

★ MAFUYU AND THE OTHER SECOND-YEAR STUDENTS WENT ON A SCHOOL TRIP! EVEN THOUGH THEY RAN INTO WEST HIGH STUDENTS, THEY MANAGED TO HAVE A FUN TIME. MEANWHILE, WITH MAFUYU AND HER FRIENDS GONE, SHIBUYA WAS TARGETED BY KOMARI YUKIOKA OF THE STUDENT COUNCIL! KOMARI DECEIVES EVERYONE AROUND HER WITH HER TERRIFYING CUTENESS, BUT SHIBUYA SENSED HER TRUE NATURE!

ORESAMA TEACHER

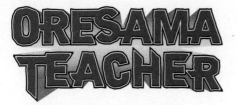

Volume 16
CONTENTS

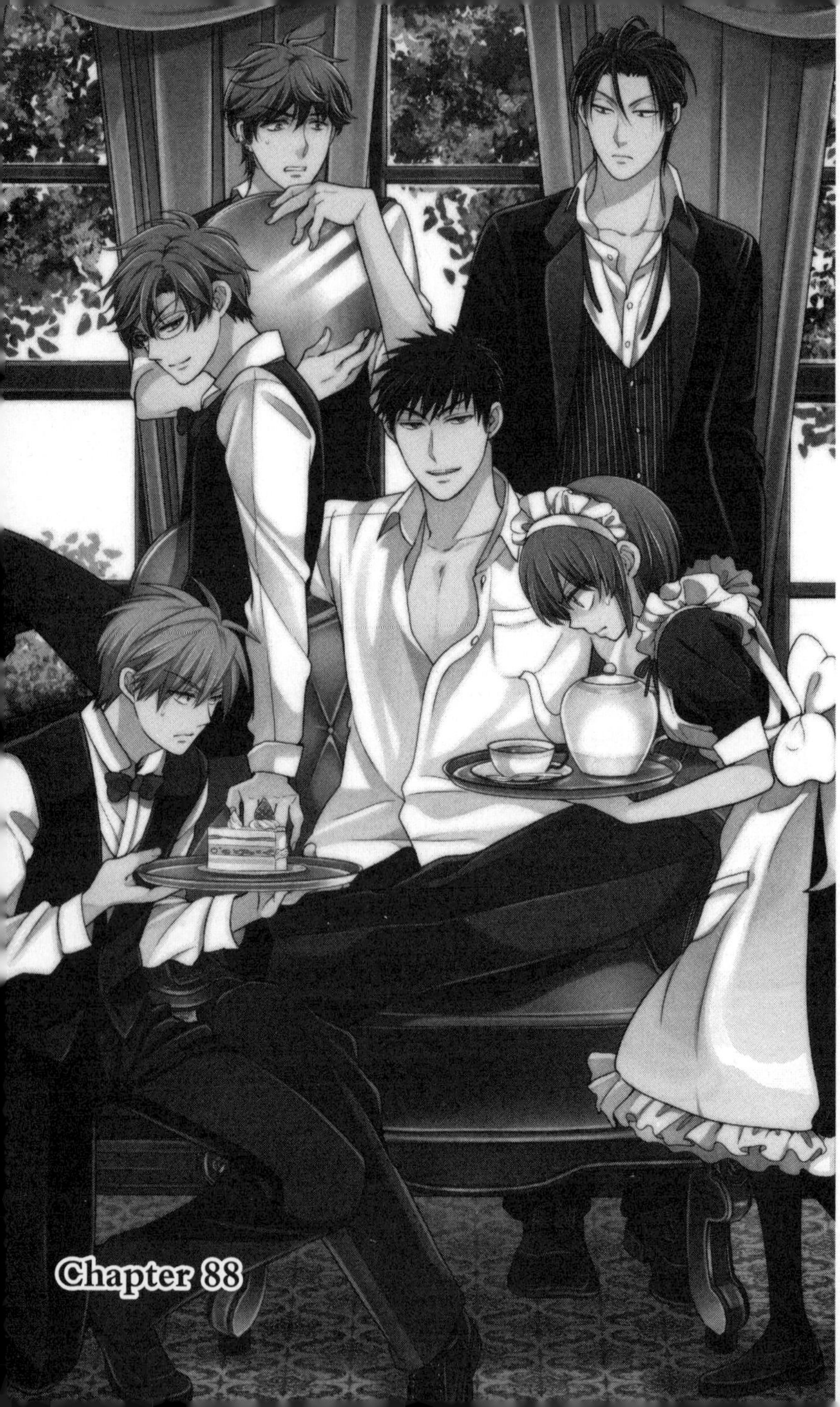
Chapter 88

SEEING HIS FRIEND

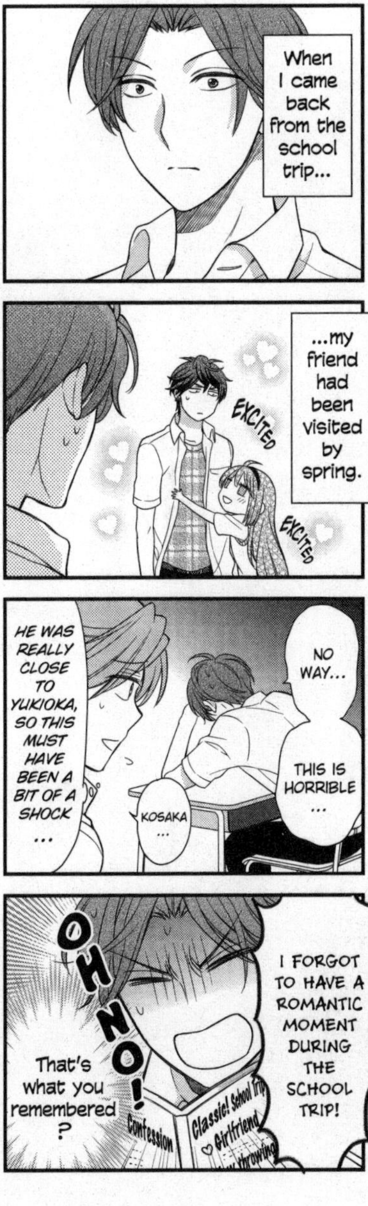
When I came back from the school trip...
...my friend had been visited by spring.
EXCITED
EXCITED
NO WAY...
THIS IS HORRIBLE...
KOSAKA...
HE WAS REALLY CLOSE TO YUKIOKA, SO THIS MUST HAVE BEEN A BIT OF A SHOCK...
I FORGOT TO HAVE A ROMANTIC MOMENT DURING THE SCHOOL TRIP!
OH NO!
That's what you remembered?
Classic! School Trip
Girlfriend
Confession

SPECIAL EVENT

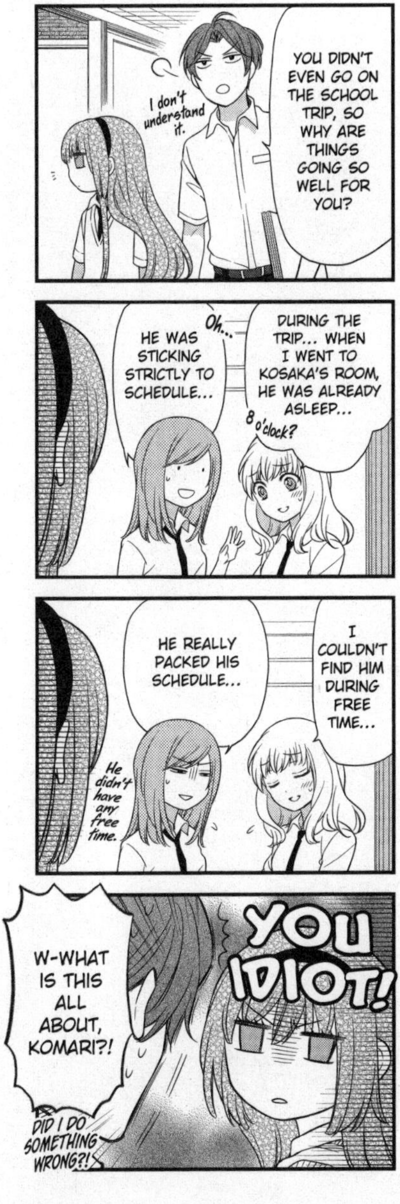
YOU DIDN'T EVEN GO ON THE SCHOOL TRIP, SO WHY ARE THINGS GOING SO WELL FOR YOU?
I don't understand it.
DURING THE TRIP... WHEN I WENT TO KOSAKA'S ROOM, HE WAS ALREADY ASLEEP...
8 o'clock?
Oh...
HE WAS STICKING STRICTLY TO SCHEDULE...
I COULDN'T FIND HIM DURING FREE TIME...
HE REALLY PACKED HIS SCHEDULE...
He didn't have any free time.
YOU IDIOT!
W-WHAT IS THIS ALL ABOUT, KOMARI?!
DID I DO SOMETHING WRONG?!

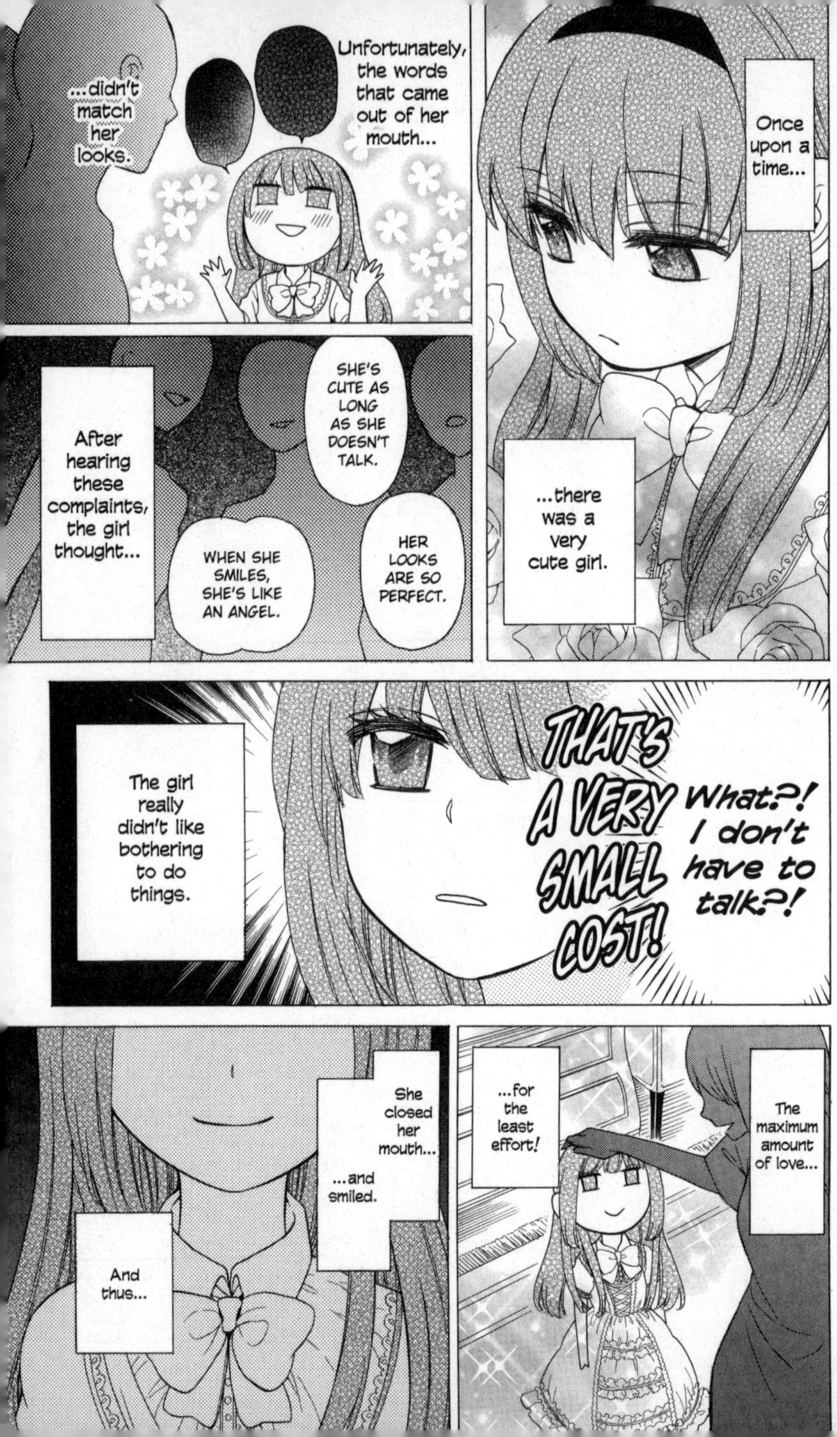
Once upon a time...
...there was a very cute girl.
Unfortunately, the words that came out of her mouth...
...didn't match her looks.
SHE'S CUTE AS LONG AS SHE DOESN'T TALK.
HER LOOKS ARE SO PERFECT.
WHEN SHE SMILES, SHE'S LIKE AN ANGEL.
After hearing these complaints, the girl thought...
What?! I don't have to talk?!
THAT'S A VERY SMALL COST!
The girl really didn't like bothering to do things.
The maximum amount of love...
...for the least effort!
She closed her mouth...
...and smiled.
And thus...

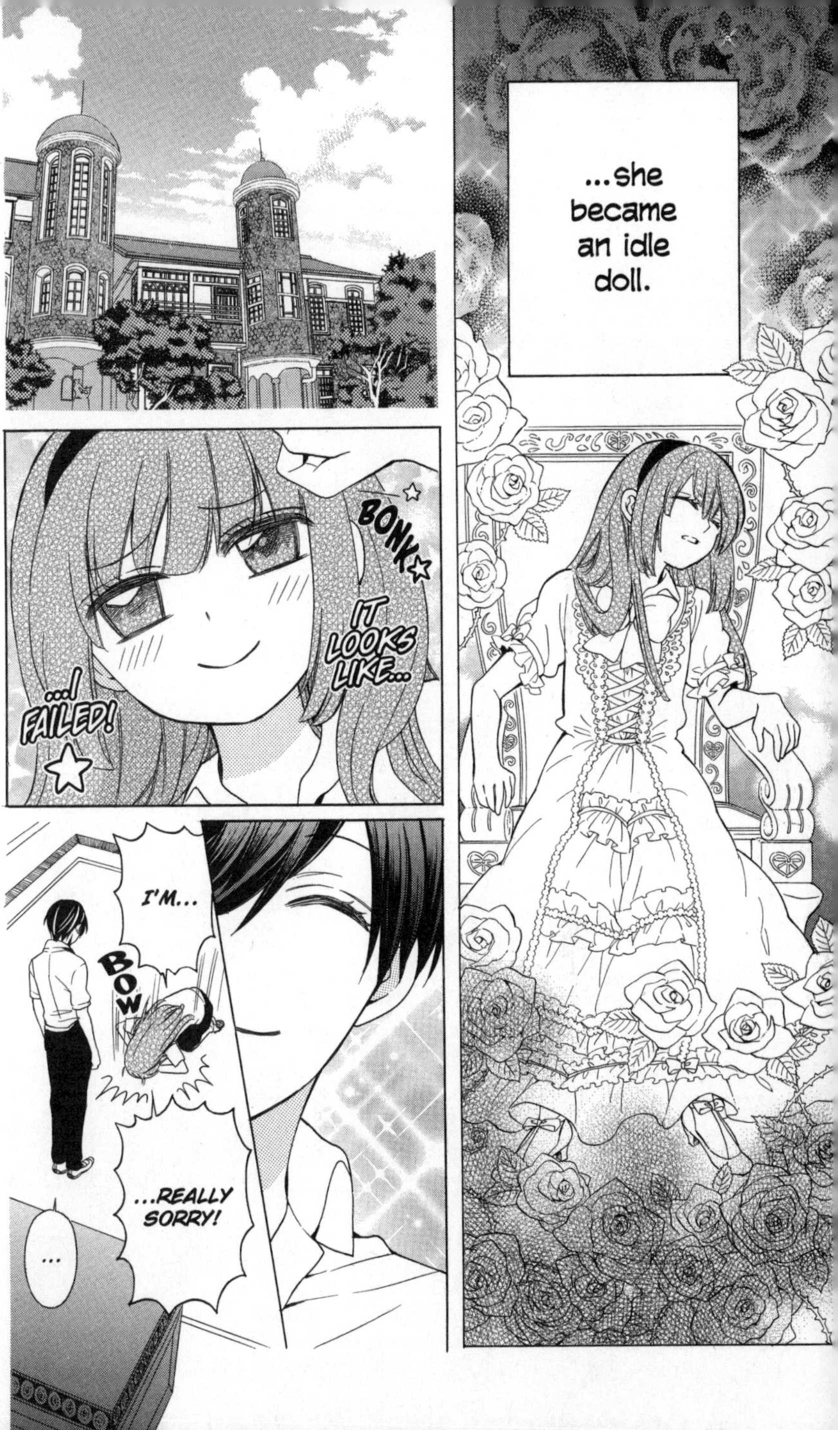
...she became an idle doll.
BONK☆
IT LOOKS LIKE...
...I FAILED!
I'M...
BOW
...REALLY SORRY!
...

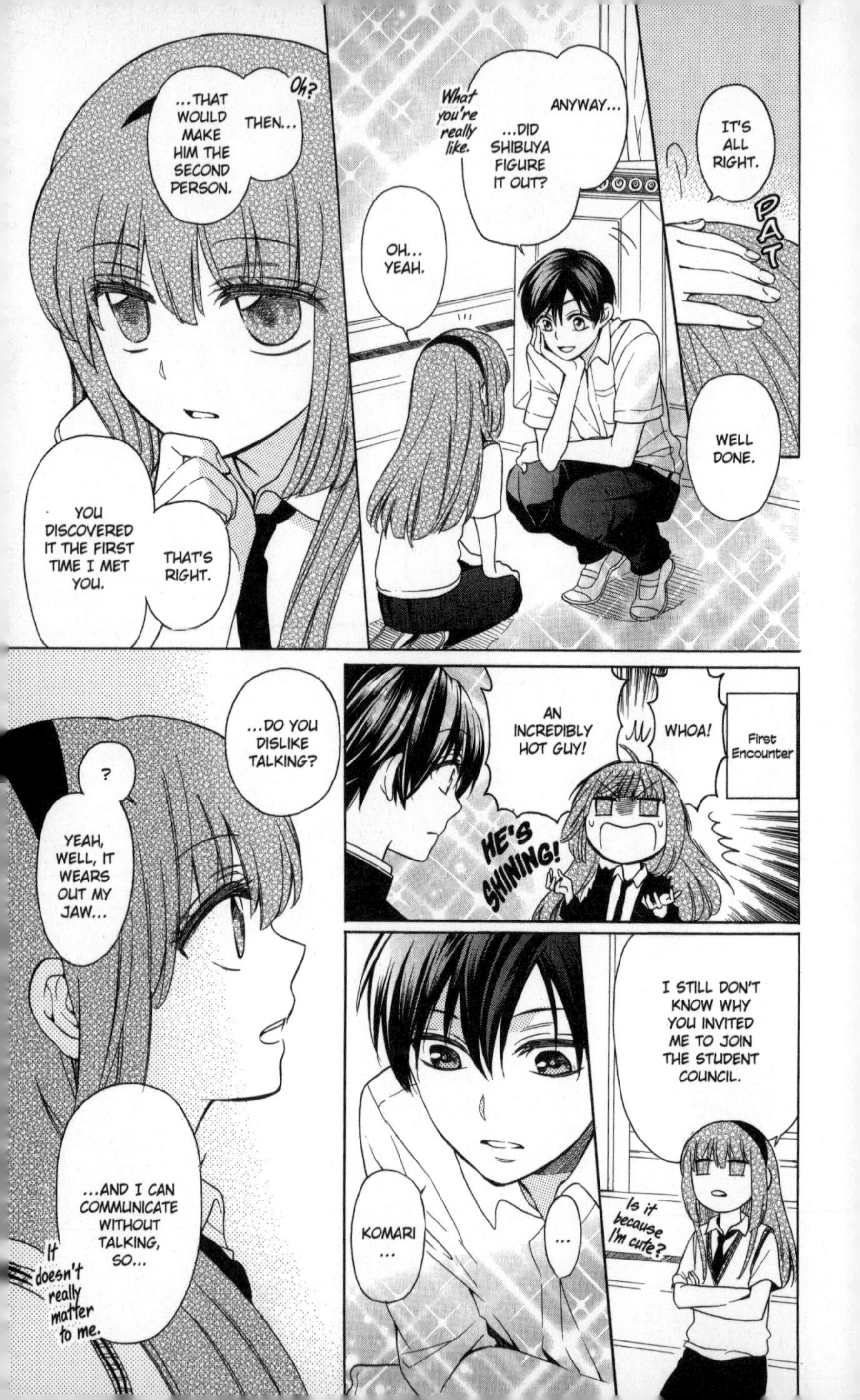
IT'S ALL RIGHT.
PAT
WELL DONE.
ANYWAY...
...DID SHIBUYA FIGURE IT OUT?
What you're really like.
OH... YEAH.
Oh?
THEN...
...THAT WOULD MAKE HIM THE SECOND PERSON.
THAT'S RIGHT.
YOU DISCOVERED IT THE FIRST TIME I MET YOU.
First Encounter
WHOA!
AN INCREDIBLY HOT GUY!
HE'S SHINING!
I STILL DON'T KNOW WHY YOU INVITED ME TO JOIN THE STUDENT COUNCIL.
Is it because I'm cute?
...
KOMARI...
...DO YOU DISLIKE TALKING?
?
YEAH, WELL, IT WEARS OUT MY JAW...
...AND I CAN COMMUNICATE WITHOUT TALKING, SO...
It doesn't really matter to me.

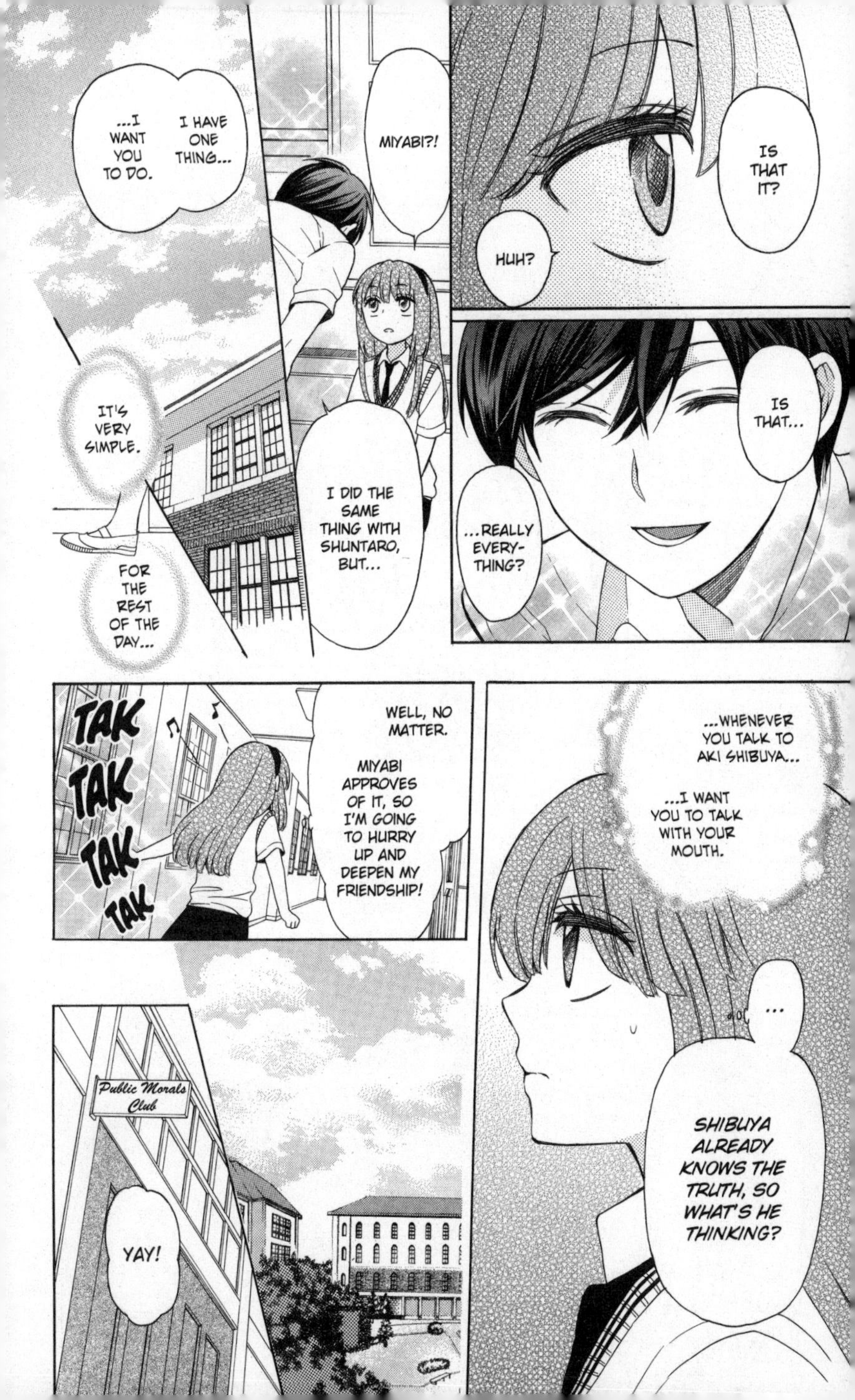
IS THAT IT?
HUH?
IS THAT...
...REALLY EVERYTHING?
MIYABI?!
I DID THE SAME THING WITH SHUNTARO, BUT...
I HAVE ONE THING...
...I WANT YOU TO DO.
IT'S VERY SIMPLE.
FOR THE REST OF THE DAY...
...WHENEVER YOU TALK TO AKI SHIBUYA...
...I WANT YOU TO TALK WITH YOUR MOUTH.
...
SHIBUYA ALREADY KNOWS THE TRUTH, SO WHAT'S HE THINKING?
WELL, NO MATTER.
MIYABI APPROVES OF IT, SO I'M GOING TO HURRY UP AND DEEPEN MY FRIENDSHIP!
TAK TAK TAK TAK
Public Morals Club
YAY!

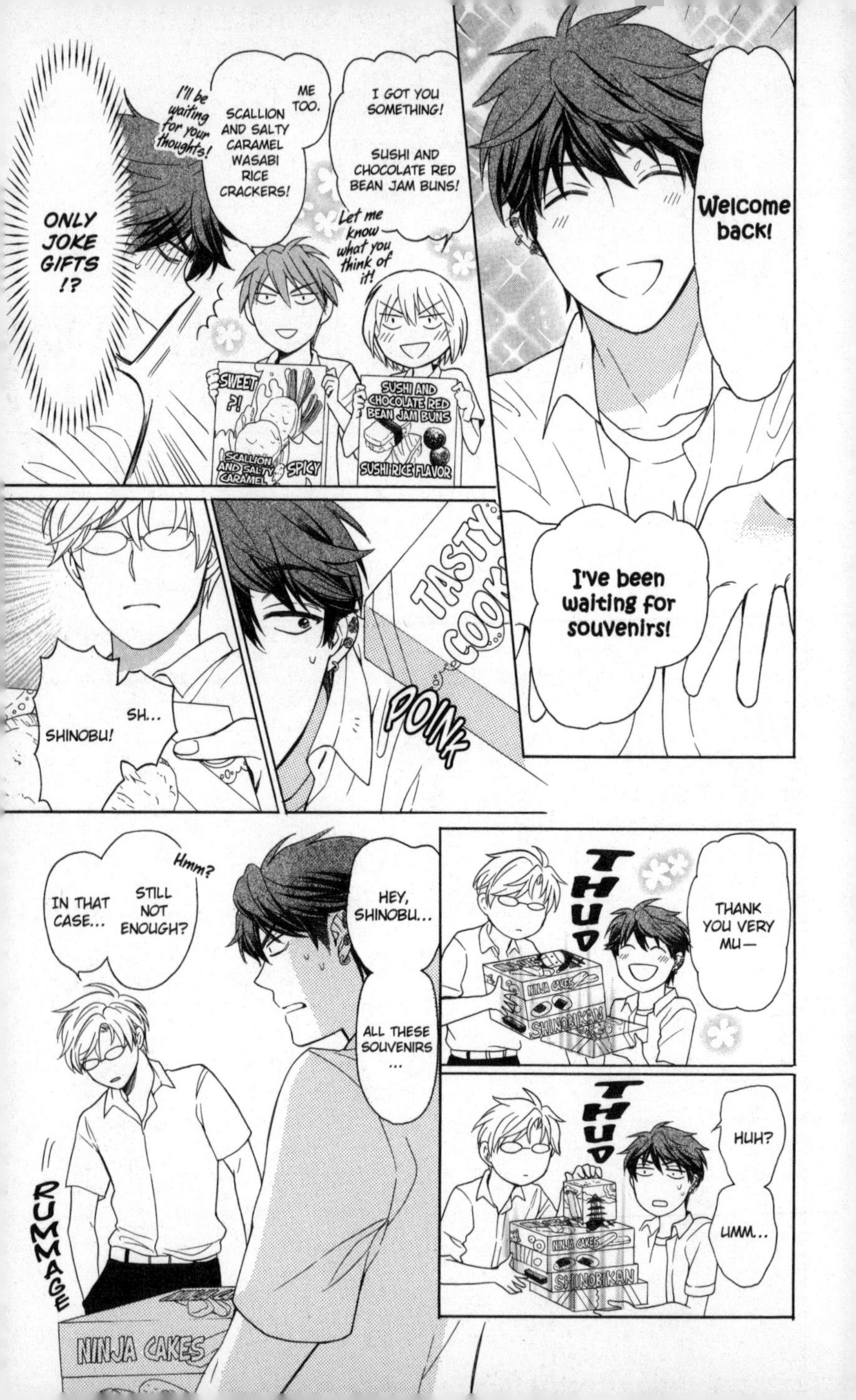
Welcome back!
I've been waiting for souvenirs!
I GOT YOU SOMETHING!
SUSHI AND CHOCOLATE RED BEAN JAM BUNS!
Let me know what you think of it!
SUSHI AND CHOCOLATE RED BEAN JAM BUNS
SUSHI RICE FLAVOR
ME TOO.
SCALLION AND SALTY CARAMEL WASABI RICE CRACKERS!
I'll be waiting for your thoughts!
SWEET ?!
SCALLION AND SALTY CARAMEL
SPICY
ONLY JOKE GIFTS !?
TASTY COOK
POINK
SH...
SHINOBU!
THANK YOU VERY MU—
THUD
NINJA CAKES
SHINOBIKAN
HUH?
UMM...
THUD
NINJA CAKES
SHINOBIKAN
HEY, SHINOBU...
ALL THESE SOUVENIRS ...
Hmm?
STILL NOT ENOUGH?
IN THAT CASE...
RUMMAGE
NINJA CAKES

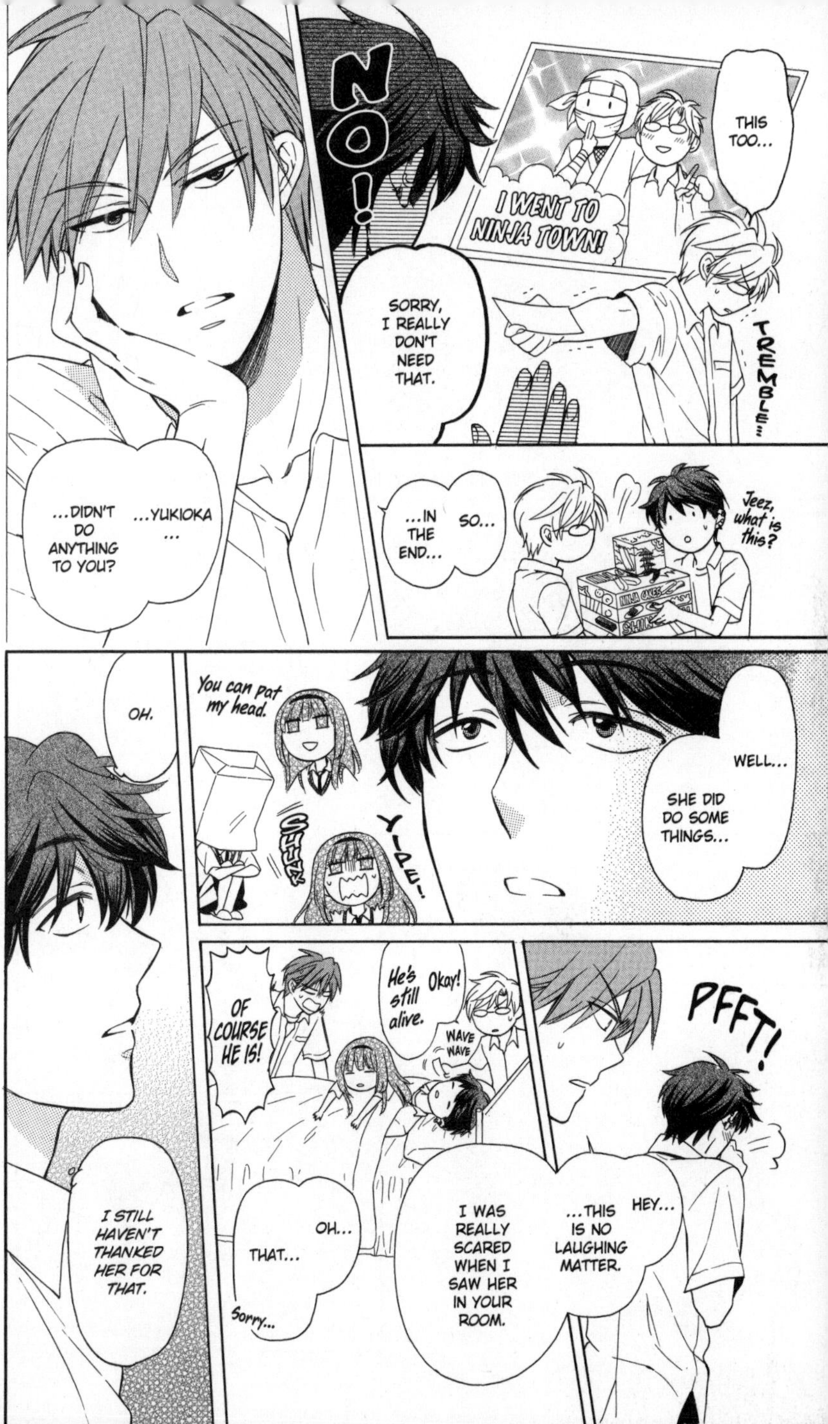
THIS TOO...
I WENT TO NINJA TOWN!
NO!
TREMBLE...
SORRY, I REALLY DON'T NEED THAT.
Jeez, what is this?
NINJA CAKES
SO...
...IN THE END...
...YUKIOKA...
...DIDN'T DO ANYTHING TO YOU?
WELL...
SHE DID DO SOME THINGS...
You can pat my head.
SHUNK
YIPE!
PFFT!
HEY...
...THIS IS NO LAUGHING MATTER.
I WAS REALLY SCARED WHEN I SAW HER IN YOUR ROOM.
Okay!
He's still alive.
OF COURSE HE IS!
WAVE WAVE
OH...
THAT...
Sorry...
OH.
I STILL HAVEN'T THANKED HER FOR THAT.

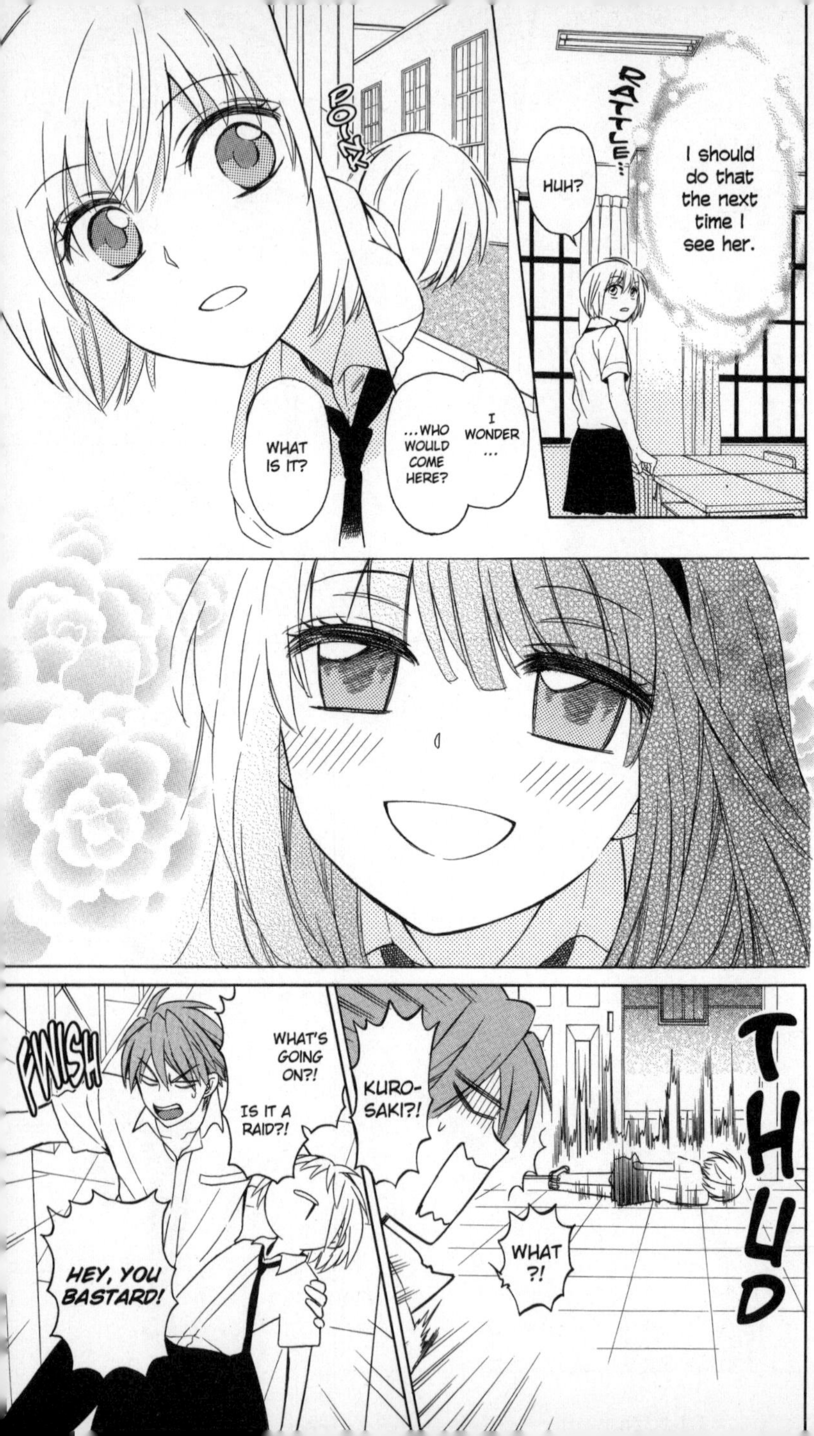

I should do that the next time I see her.
RATTLE...
HUH?
POKE
I WONDER...
...WHO WOULD COME HERE?
WHAT IS IT?
THUD
WHAT?!
KURO-SAKI?!
WHAT'S GOING ON?!
IS IT A RAID?!
FINISH
HEY, YOU BASTARD!

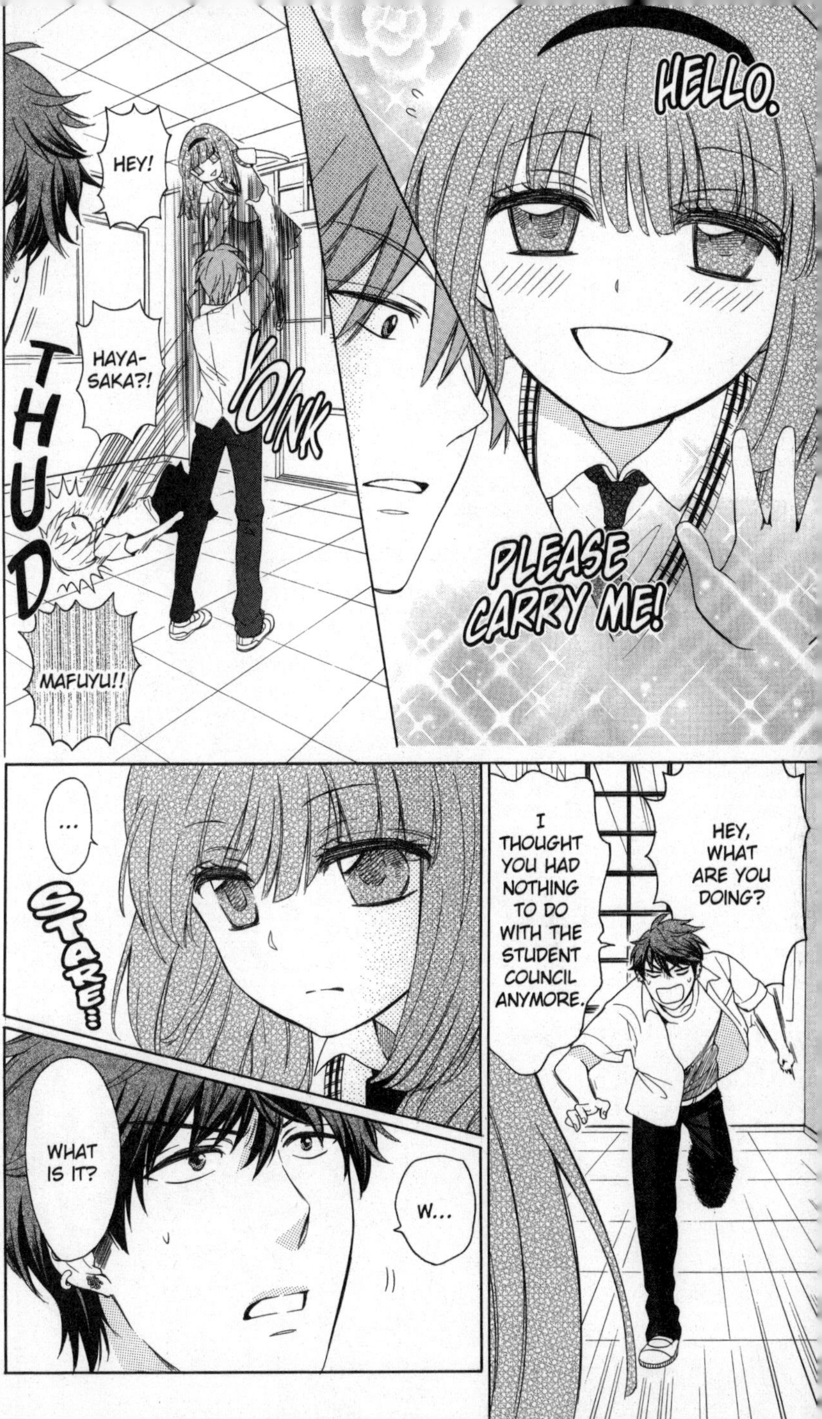

HELLO.
PLEASE CARRY ME!
HEY!
HAYA-SAKA?!
YOINK
THUD
MAFUYU!!
HEY, WHAT ARE YOU DOING?
I THOUGHT YOU HAD NOTHING TO DO WITH THE STUDENT COUNCIL ANYMORE.
...
STARE...
W...
WHAT IS IT?

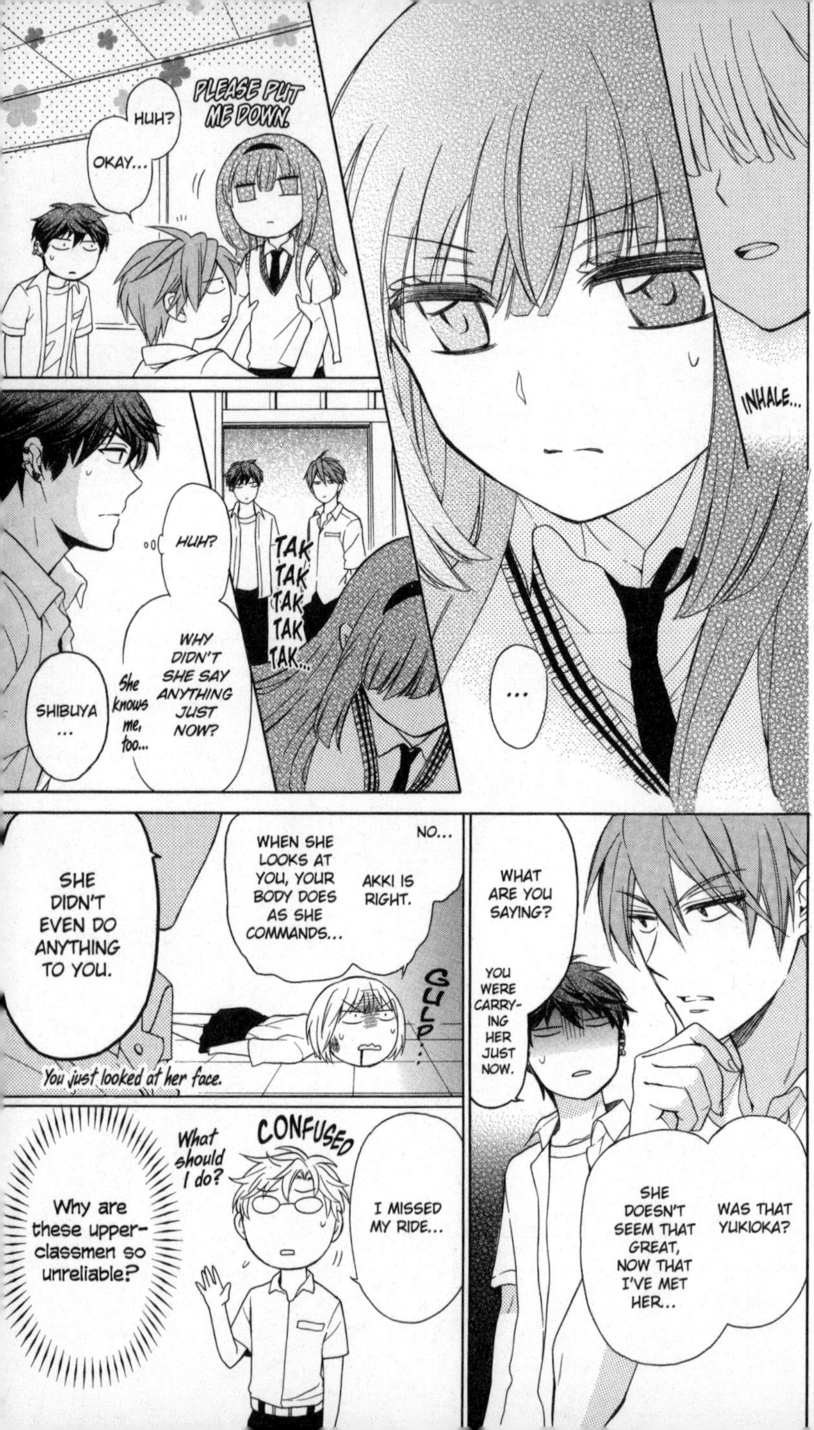
INHALE...
...
PLEASE PUT ME DOWN.
HUH?
OKAY...
HUH?
TAK TAK TAK TAK TAK...
WHY DIDN'T SHE SAY ANYTHING JUST NOW?
She knows me, too...
SHIBUYA ...
WHAT ARE YOU SAYING?
YOU WERE CARRYING HER JUST NOW.
WAS THAT YUKIOKA?
SHE DOESN'T SEEM THAT GREAT, NOW THAT I'VE MET HER..
NO...
AKKI IS RIGHT.
WHEN SHE LOOKS AT YOU, YOUR BODY DOES AS SHE COMMANDS...
SHE DIDN'T EVEN DO ANYTHING TO YOU.
GULP...
You just looked at her face.
I MISSED MY RIDE...
CONFUSED
What should I do?
Why are these upper-classmen so unreliable?

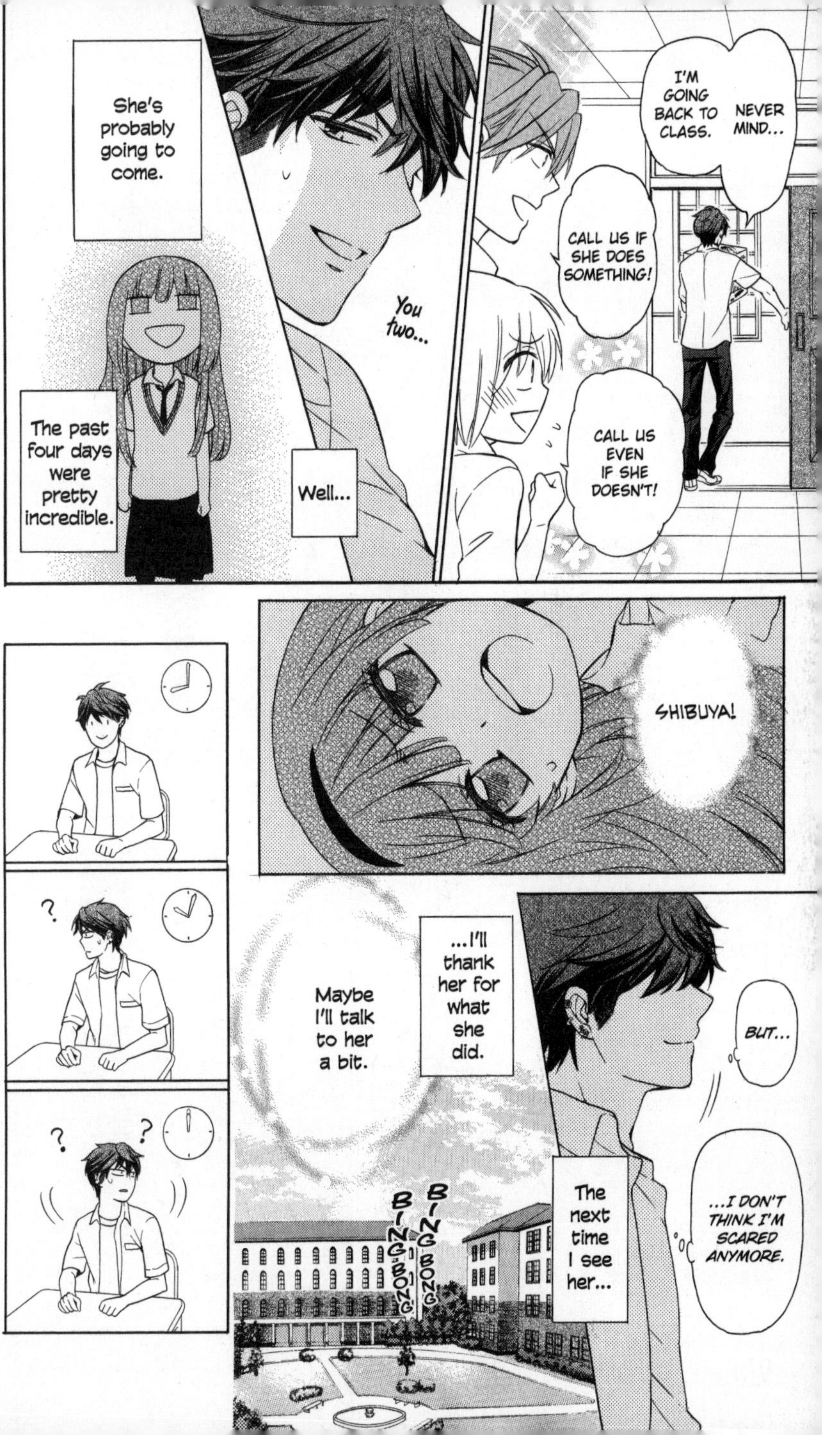
NEVER MIND...
I'M GOING BACK TO CLASS.
CALL US IF SHE DOES SOMETHING!
CALL US EVEN IF SHE DOESN'T!
You two...
Well...
She's probably going to come.
The past four days were pretty incredible.
SHIBUYA!
BUT...
...I DON'T THINK I'M SCARED ANYMORE.
The next time I see her...
...I'll thank her for what she did.
Maybe I'll talk to her a bit.
BING-BONG BING-BONG
?
? ?

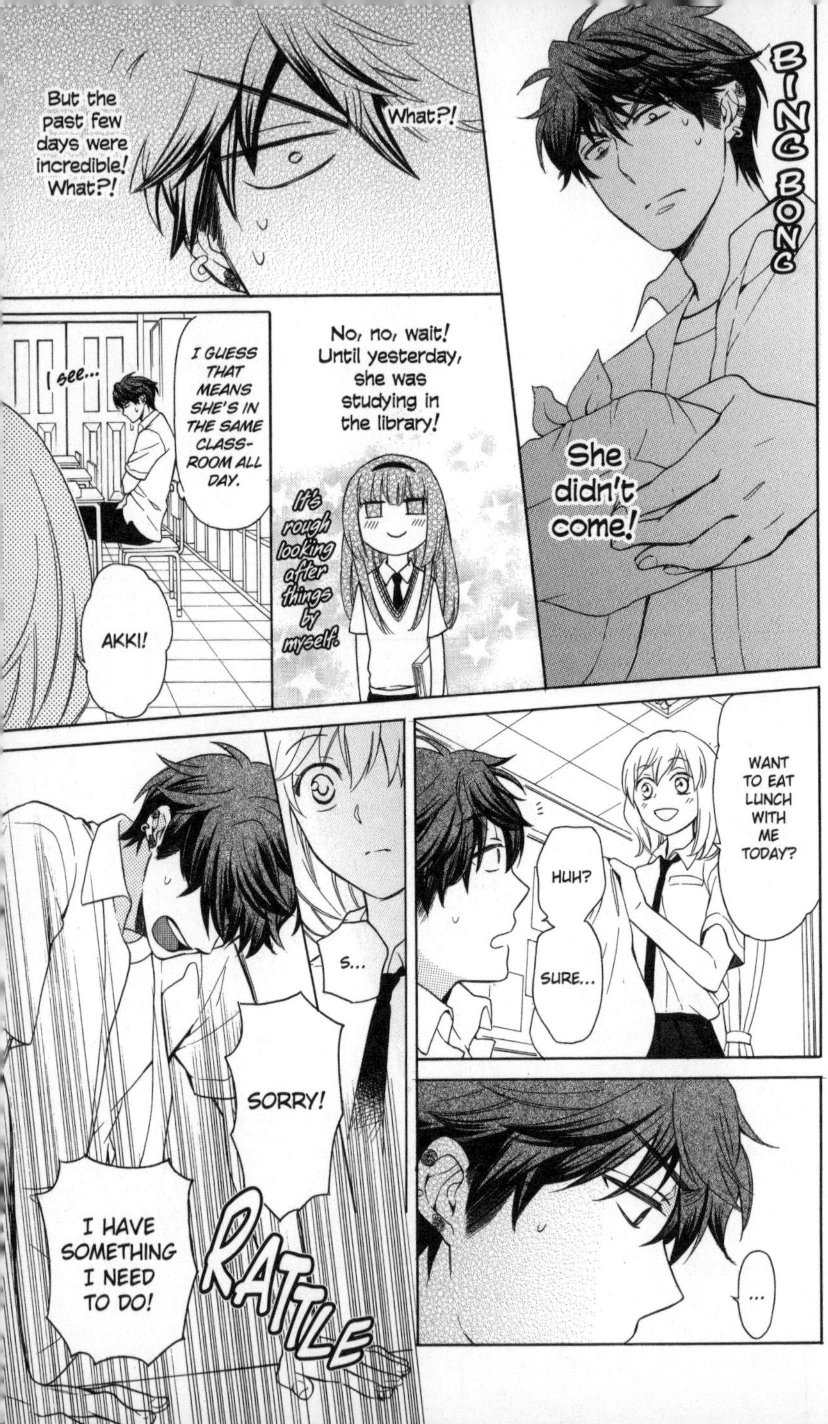
BING BONG
She didn't come!
What?!
But the past few days were incredible! What?!
No, no, wait! Until yesterday, she was studying in the library!
It's rough looking after things by myself.
I GUESS THAT MEANS SHE'S IN THE SAME CLASSROOM ALL DAY.
I see...
AKKI!
WANT TO EAT LUNCH WITH ME TODAY?
HUH?
SURE...
...
S...
SORRY!
I HAVE SOMETHING I NEED TO DO!
RATTLE

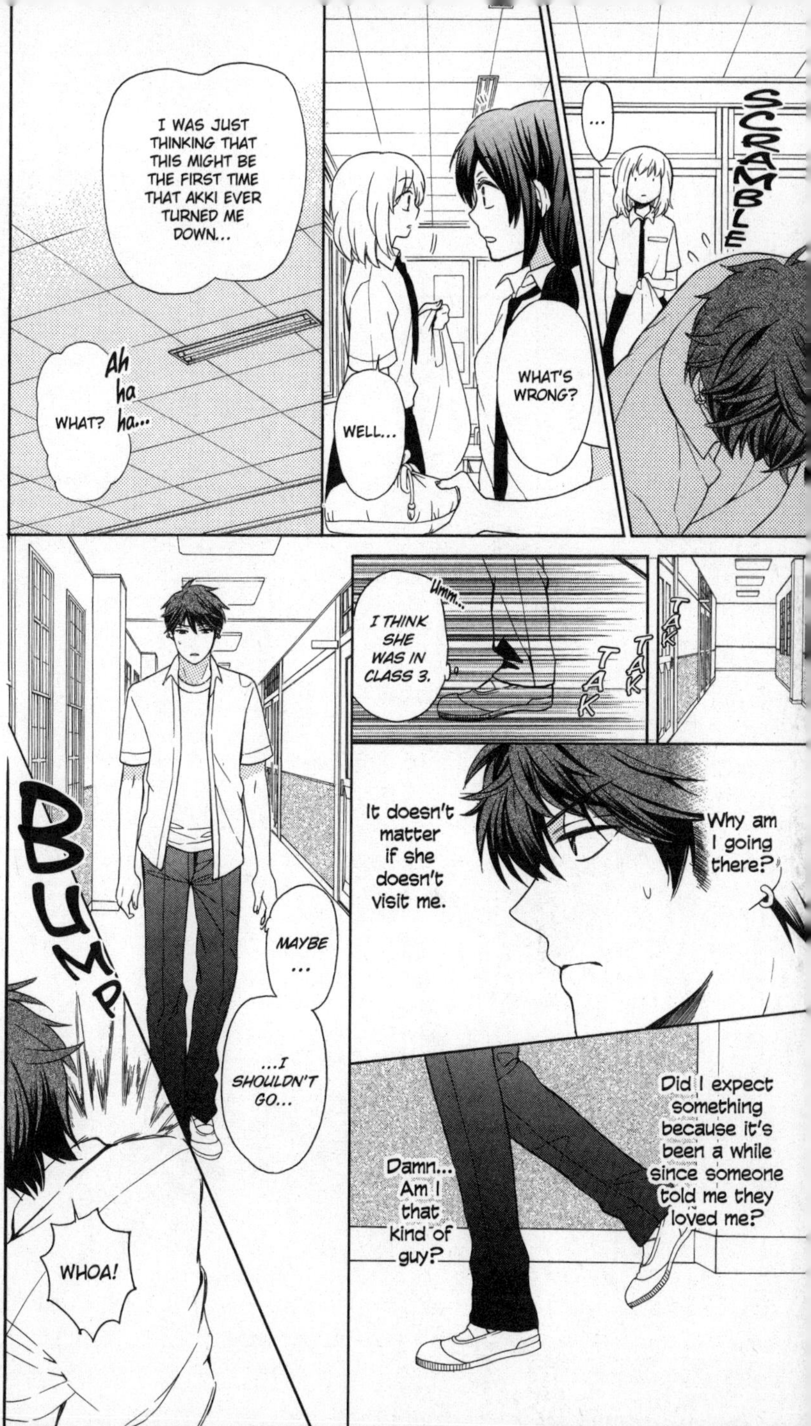
...
SCRAMBLE
WHAT'S WRONG?
WELL...
I WAS JUST THINKING THAT THIS MIGHT BE THE FIRST TIME THAT AKKI EVER TURNED ME DOWN...
Ah ha ha...
WHAT?
TAK TAK TAK
Umm...
I THINK SHE WAS IN CLASS 3.
Why am I going there?
It doesn't matter if she doesn't visit me.
Did I expect something because it's been a while since someone told me they loved me?
Damn... Am I that kind of guy?
MAYBE...
...I SHOULDN'T GO...
BUMP
WHOA!

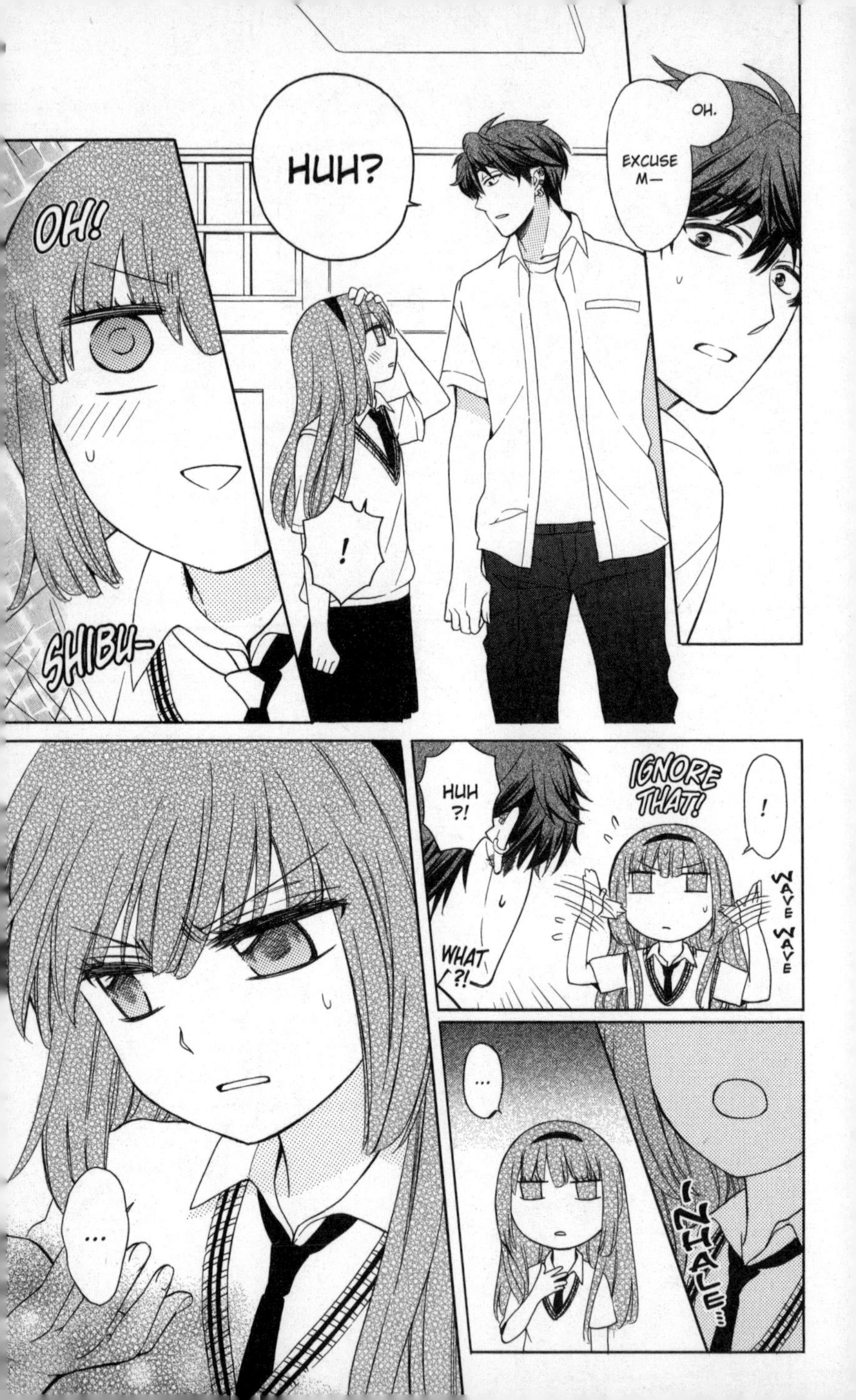
OH.
EXCUSE M—
HUH?
!
OH!
SHIBU-
!
IGNORE THAT!
WAVE WAVE
HUH ?!
WHAT ?!
...
INHALE...
...

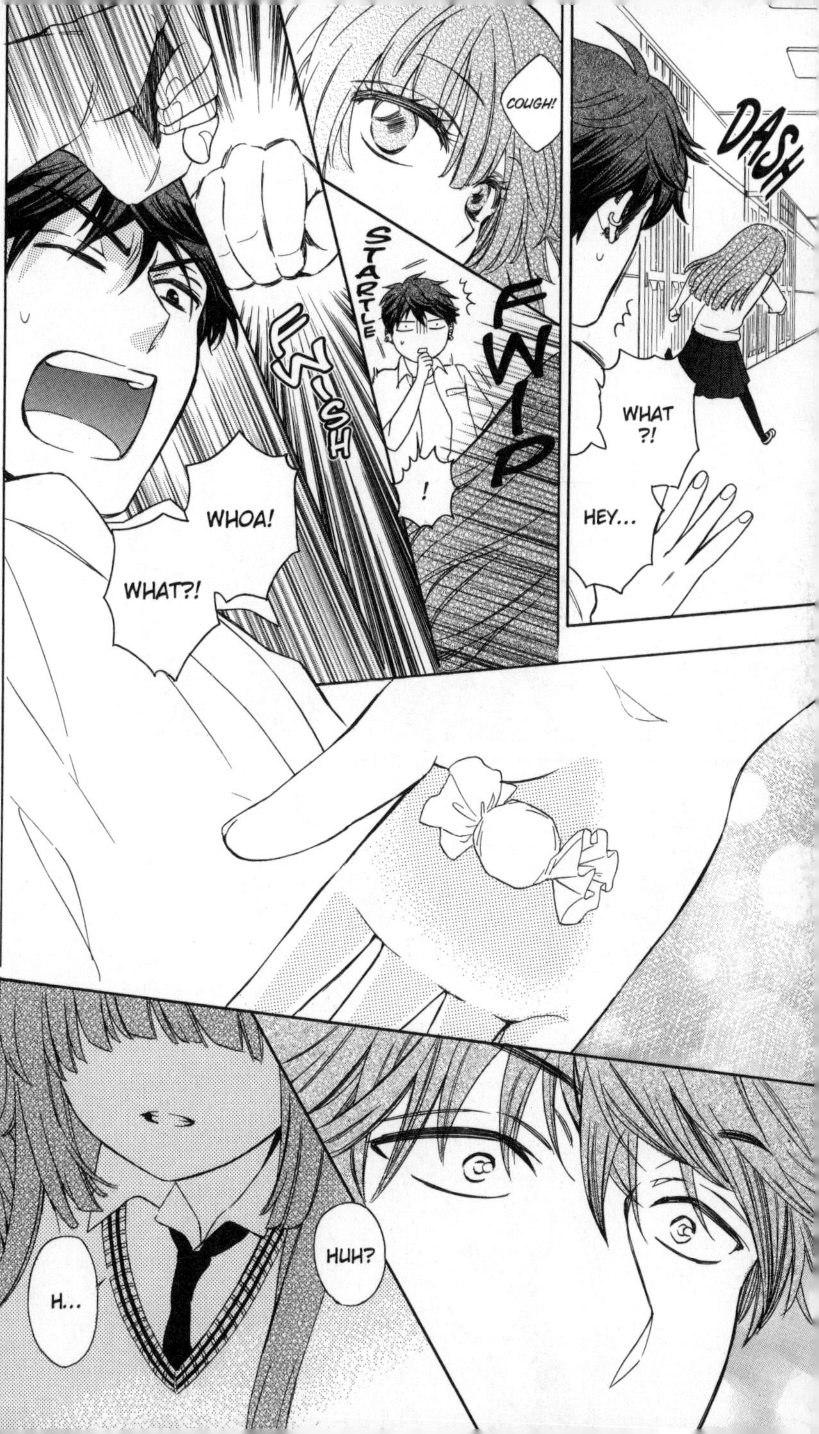
DASH
WHAT ?!
HEY...
COUGH!
STARTLE
FWIP
!
FWISH
WHOA!
WHAT?!
HUH?
H...

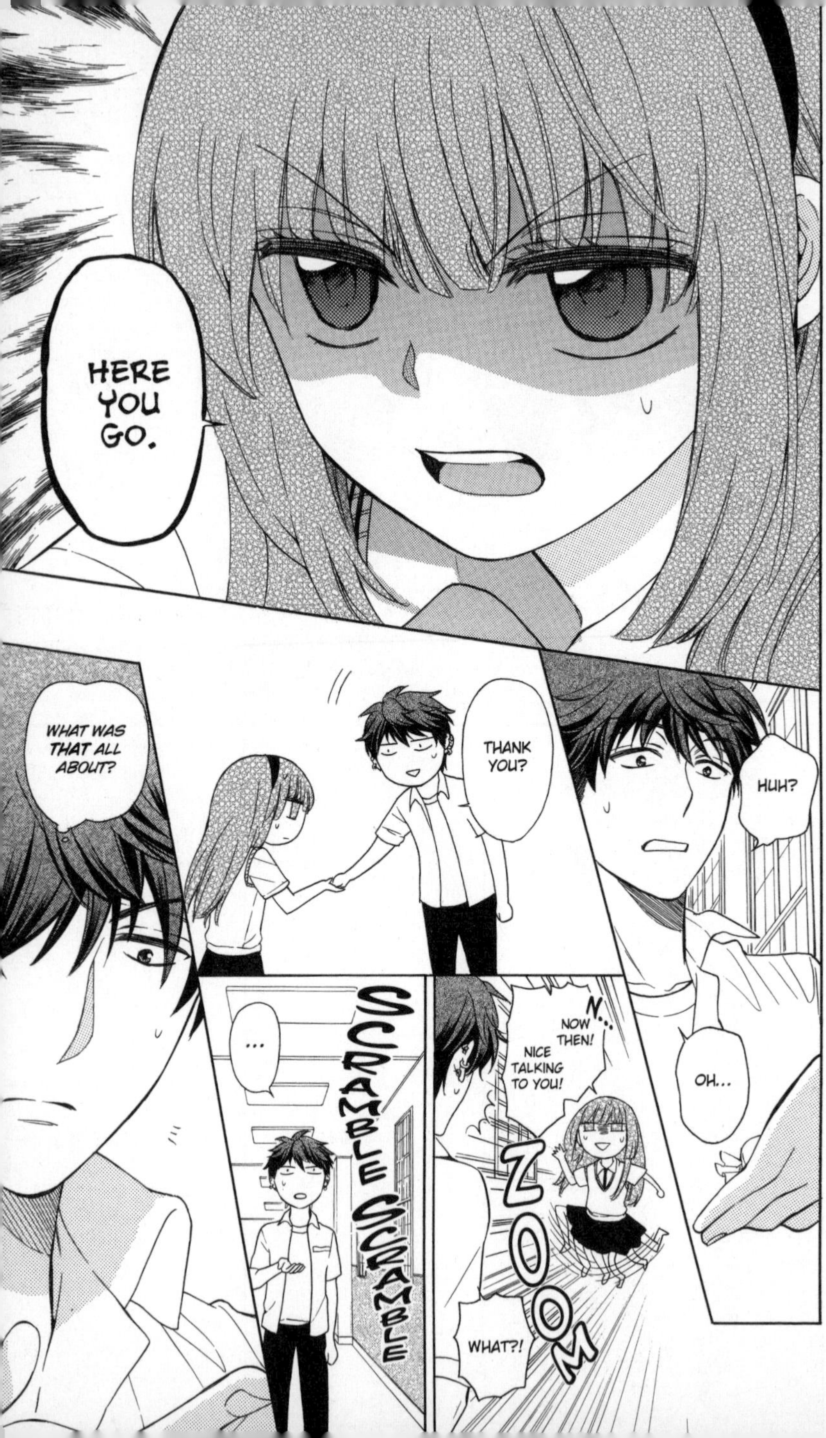
HERE YOU GO.
HUH?
THANK YOU?
OH...
N... NOW THEN! NICE TALKING TO YOU!
ZOOM
WHAT?!
...
SCRAMBLE SCRAMBLE
WHAT WAS THAT ALL ABOUT?

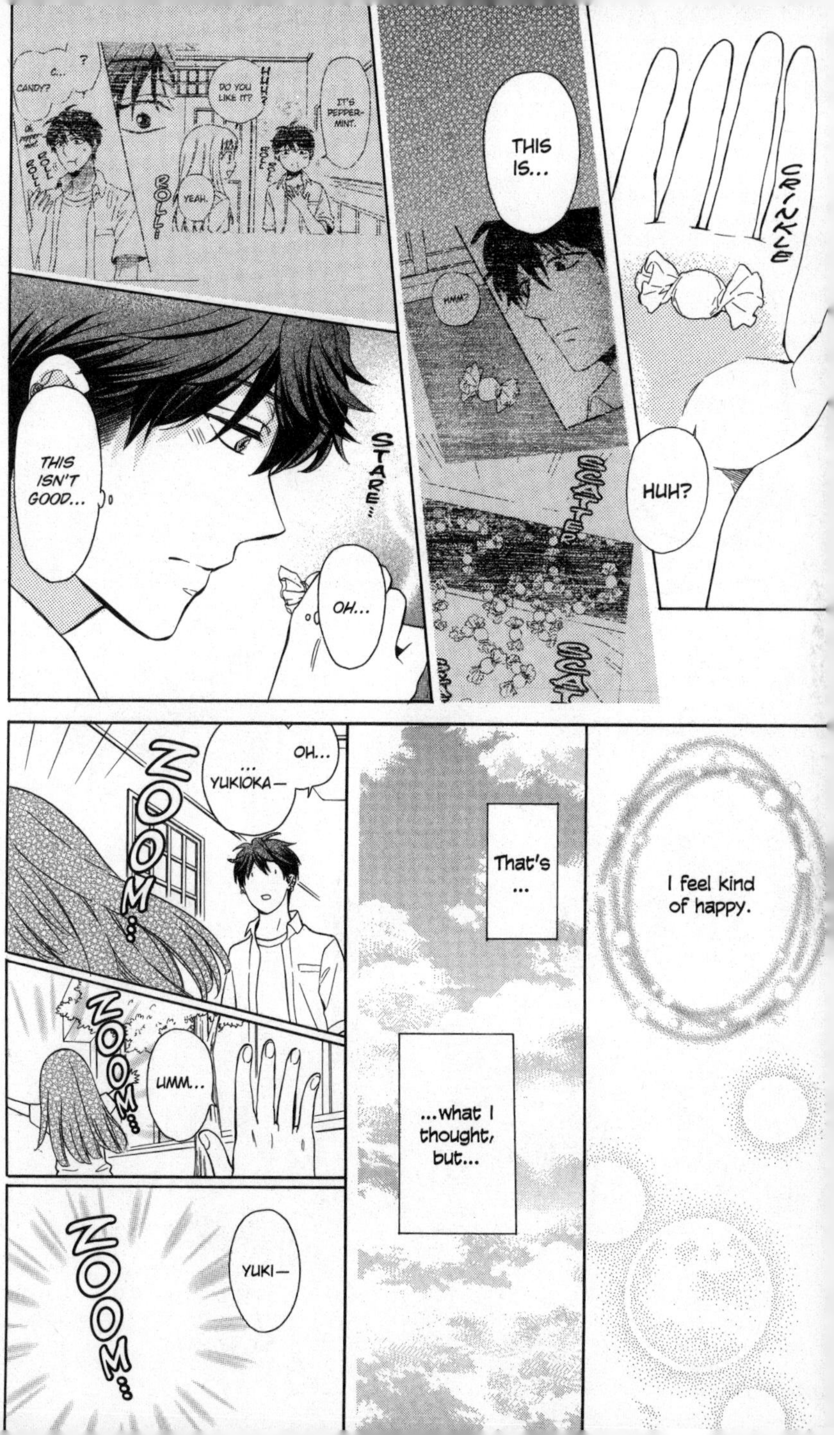
CRINKLE
HUH?
THIS IS...
HMM?
SCATTER
SCATTER
IT'S PEPPERMINT.
HUH?
DO YOU LIKE IT?
ROLL
ROLL
YEAH.
ROLL
C... CANDY?
?
OK, PEPPERMINT.
ROLL ROLL
STARE...
THIS ISN'T GOOD...
OH...
I feel kind of happy.
That's...
...what I thought, but...
OH... ...YUKIOKA—
ZOOM...
UMM...
ZOOM ZOOM...
YUKI—
ZOOM ZOOM...

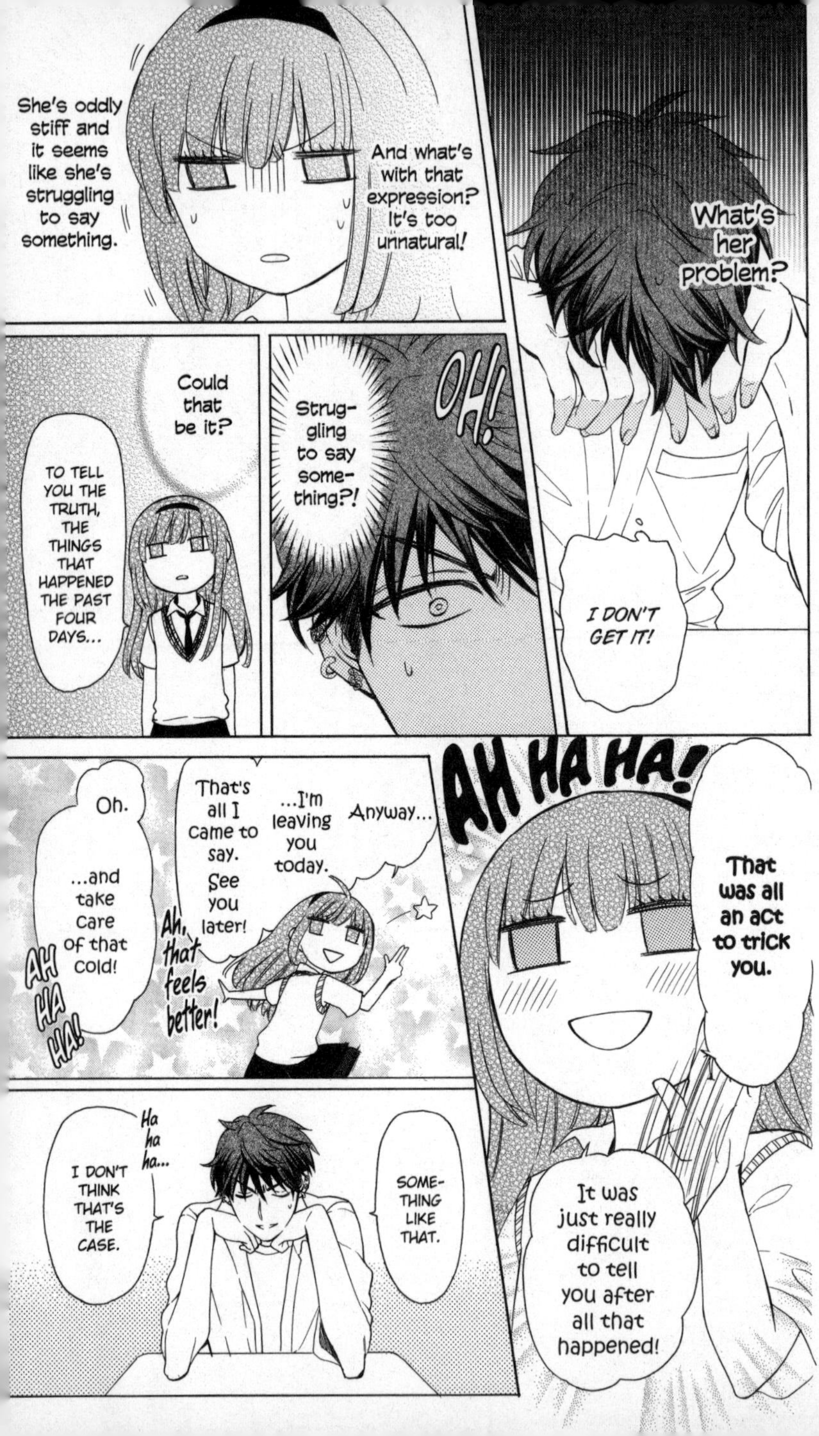
What's her problem?
I DON'T GET IT!
And what's with that expression? It's too unnatural!
She's oddly stiff and it seems like she's struggling to say something.
OH!
Strug-gling to say some-thing?!
Could that be it?
TO TELL YOU THE TRUTH, THE THINGS THAT HAPPENED THE PAST FOUR DAYS...
AH HA HA!
That was all an act to trick you.
It was just really difficult to tell you after all that happened!
Anyway...
...I'm leaving you today.
That's all I came to say. See you later!
Ah, that feels better!
Oh.
...and take care of that cold!
AH HA HA!
SOME-THING LIKE THAT.
Ha ha ha...
I DON'T THINK THAT'S THE CASE.

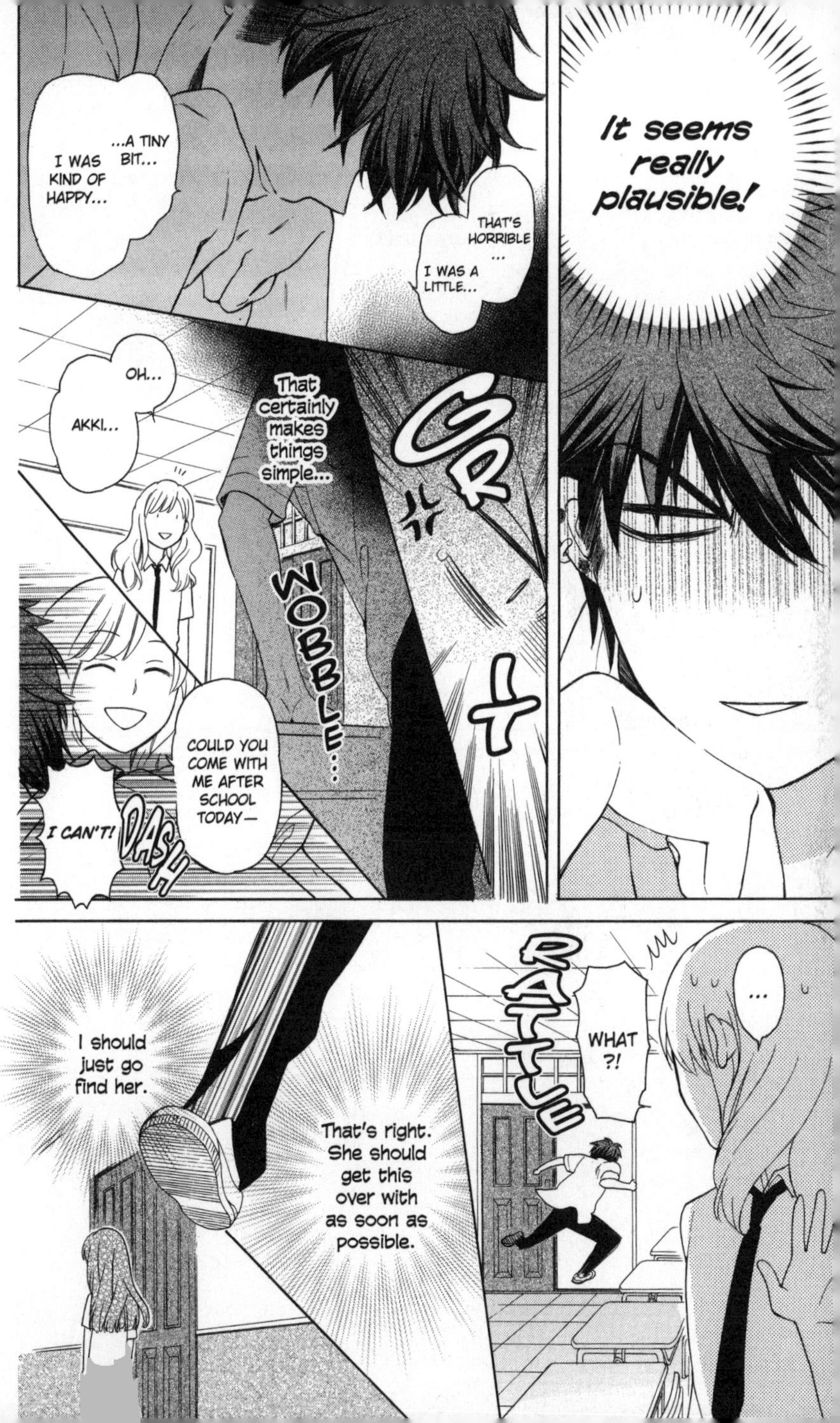
It seems really plausible!
THAT'S HORRIBLE ... I WAS A LITTLE...
...A TINY BIT... I WAS KIND OF HAPPY...
OH... AKKI...
That certainly makes things simple...
WOBBLE...
COULD YOU COME WITH ME AFTER SCHOOL TODAY—
I CAN'T!
DASH
...
WHAT?!
RATTLE
That's right. She should get this over with as soon as possible.
I should just go find her.

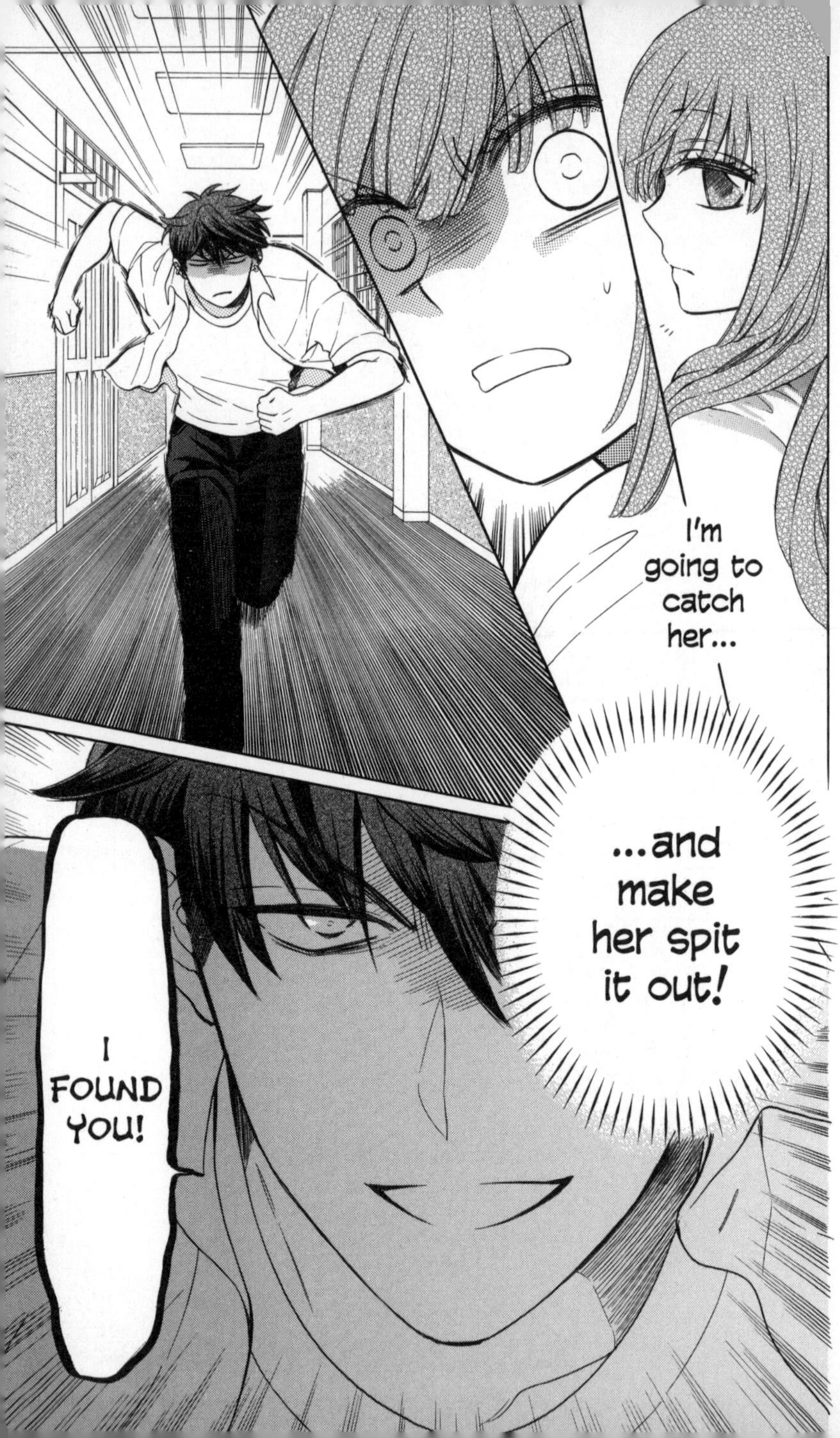
I'm going to catch her...
...and make her spit it out!
I FOUND YOU!

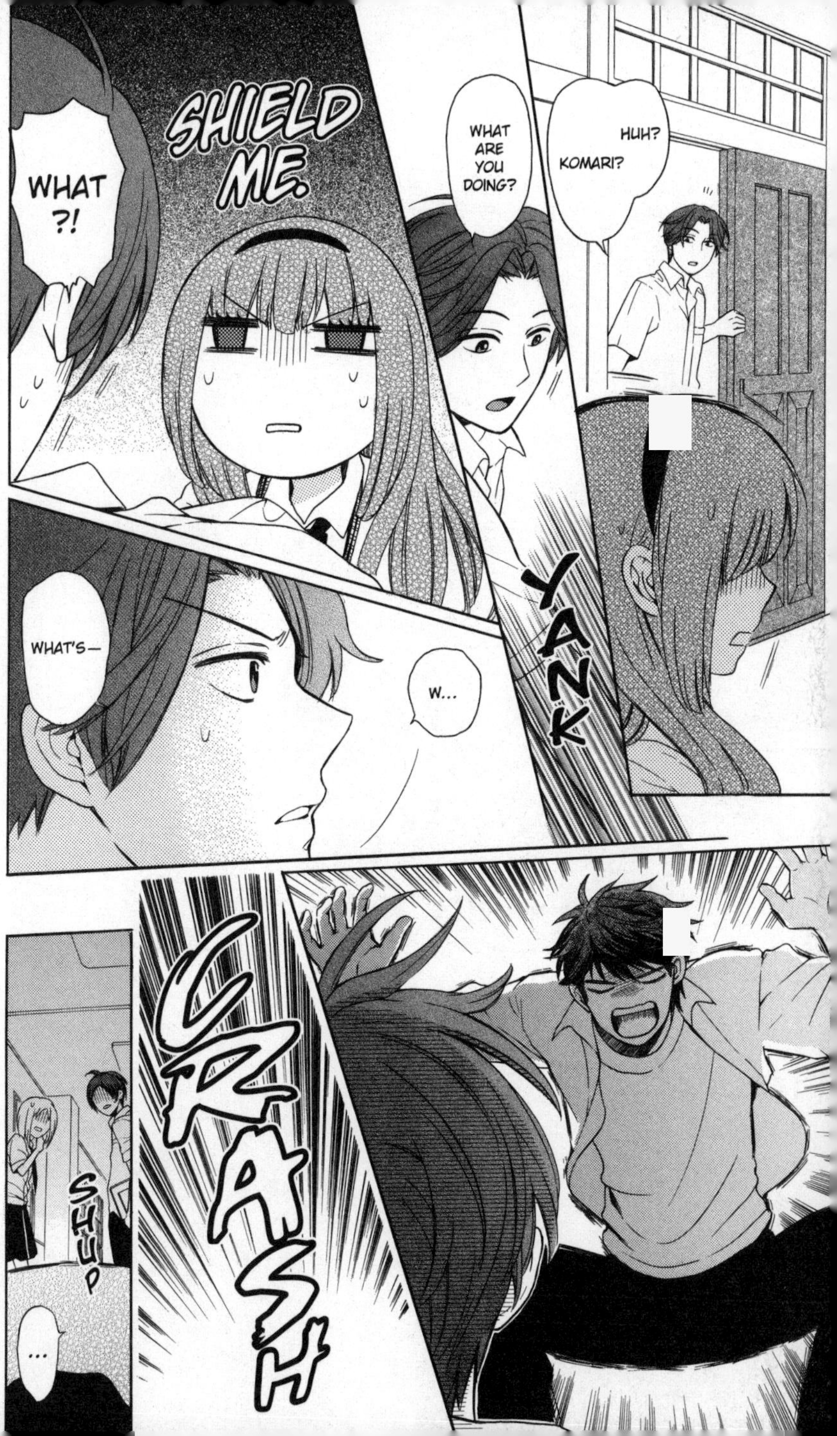
HUH? KOMARI?
WHAT ARE YOU DOING?
SHIELD ME.
WHAT ?!
YANK
W...
WHAT'S—
CRASH
SHUP
...

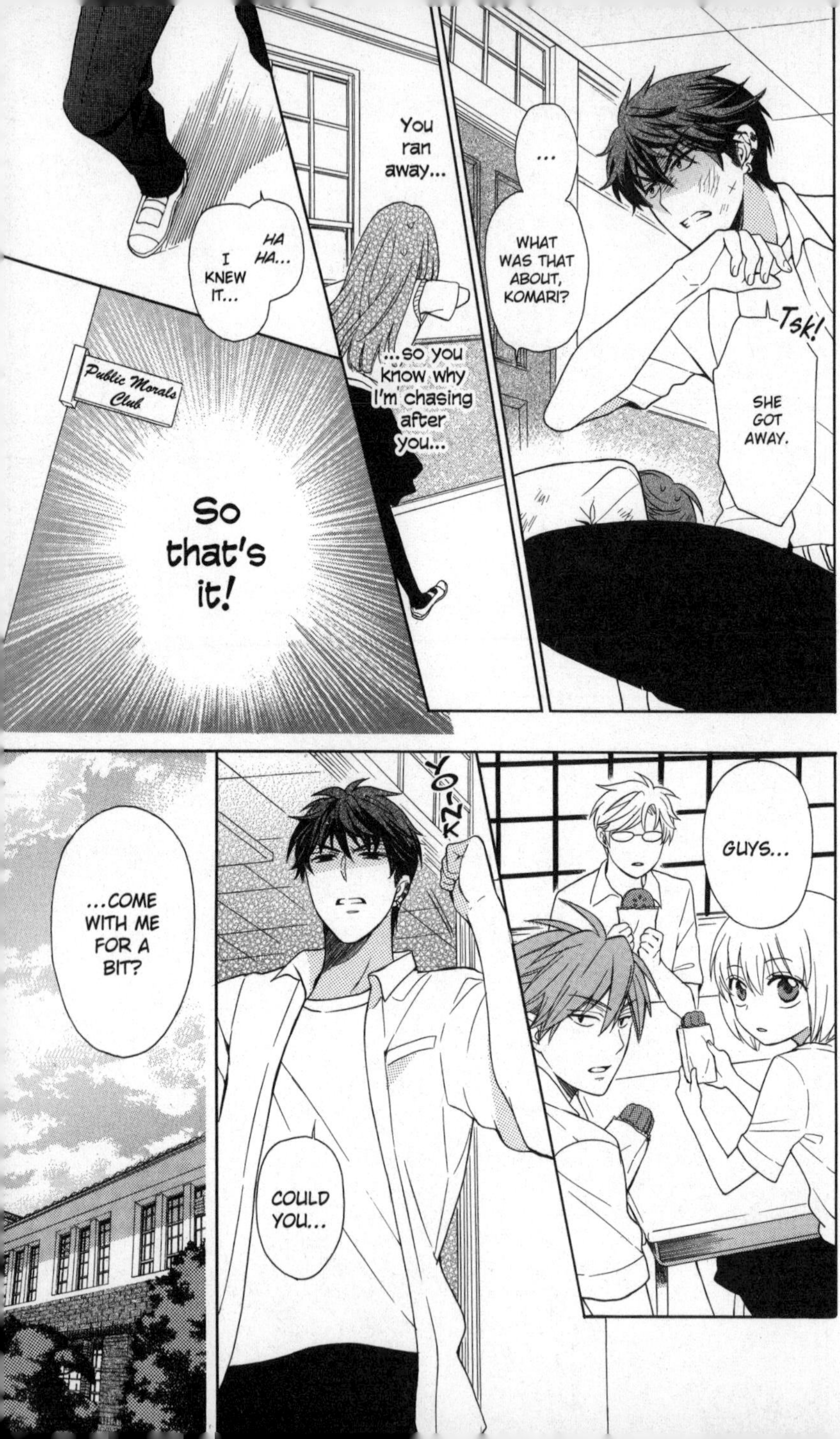
...
WHAT WAS THAT ABOUT, KOMARI?
Tsk!
SHE GOT AWAY.
You ran away...
...so you know why I'm chasing after you...
HA HA...
I KNEW IT...
Public Morals Club
So that's it!
GUYS...
YOINK
COULD YOU...
...COME WITH ME FOR A BIT?

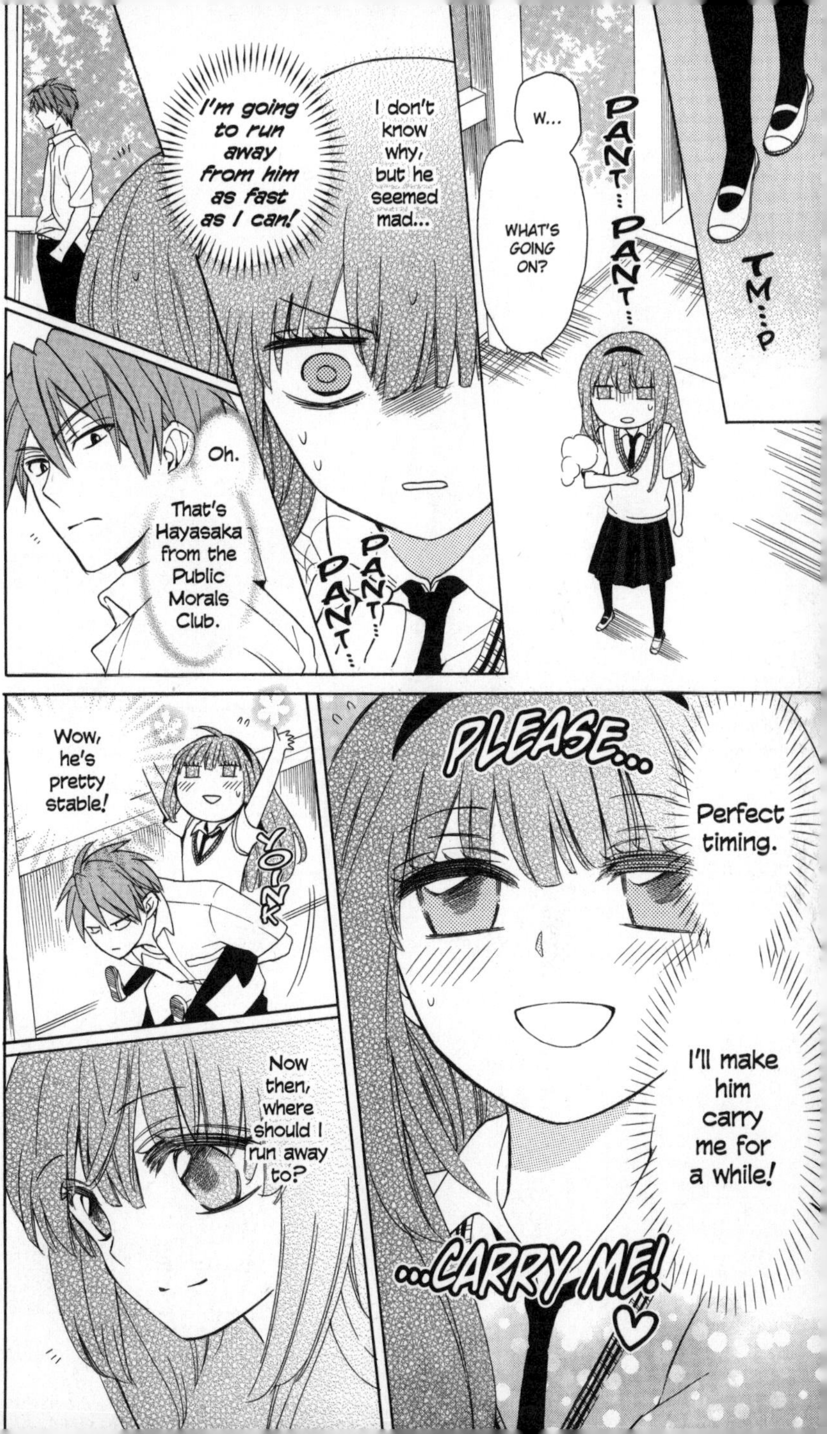
TM...P
PANT... PANT...
W...
WHAT'S GOING ON?
I don't know why, but he seemed mad...
I'm going to run away from him as fast as I can!
PANT... PANT...
Oh.
That's Hayasaka from the Public Morals Club.
PLEASE...
Perfect timing.
I'll make him carry me for a while!
...CARRY ME!
Wow, he's pretty stable!
YOINK
Now then, where should I run away to?

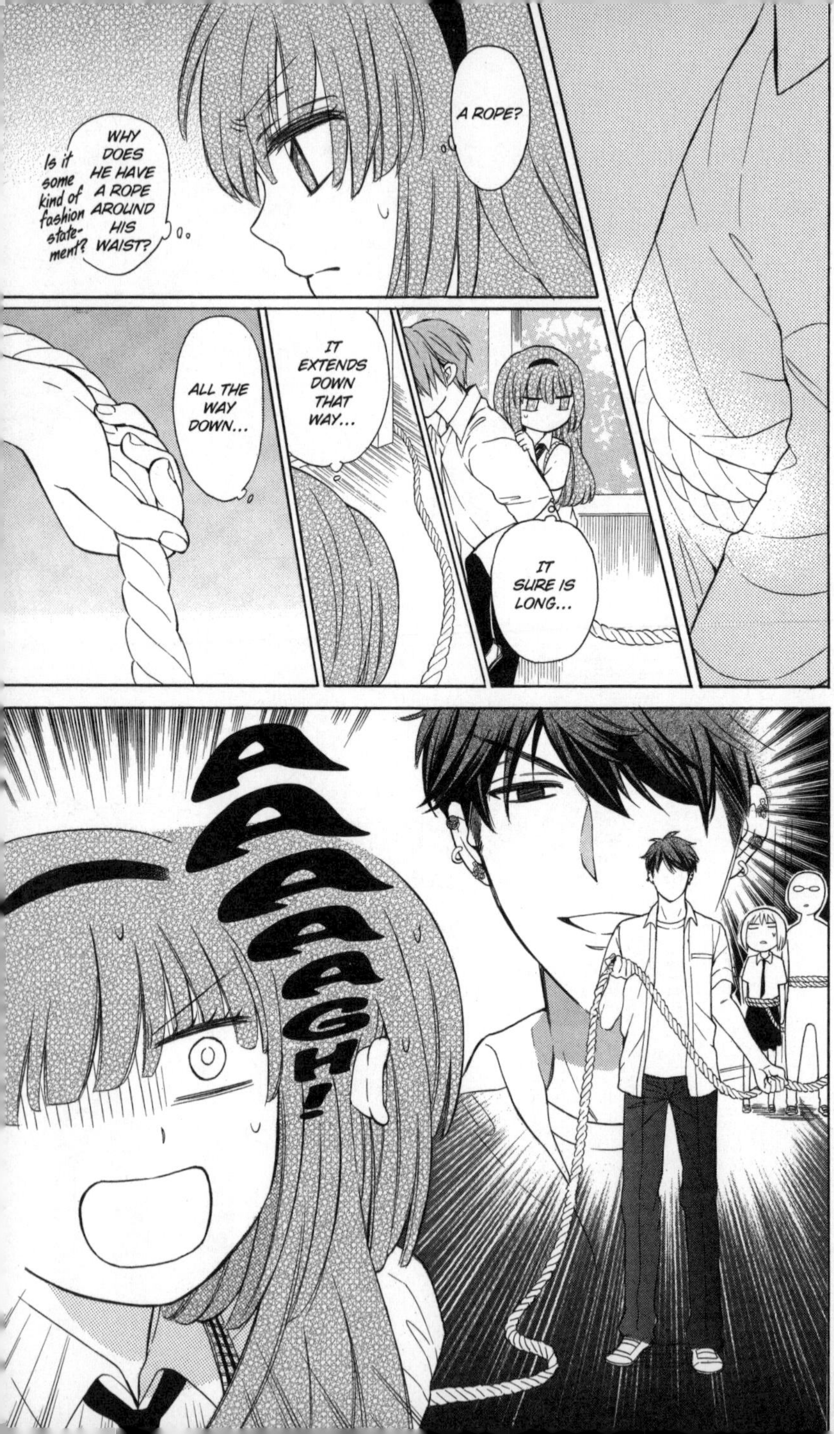
A ROPE?
WHY DOES HE HAVE A ROPE AROUND HIS WAIST?
Is it some kind of fashion state-ment?
IT SURE IS LONG...
IT EXTENDS DOWN THAT WAY...
ALL THE WAY DOWN...
AAAAAGH!

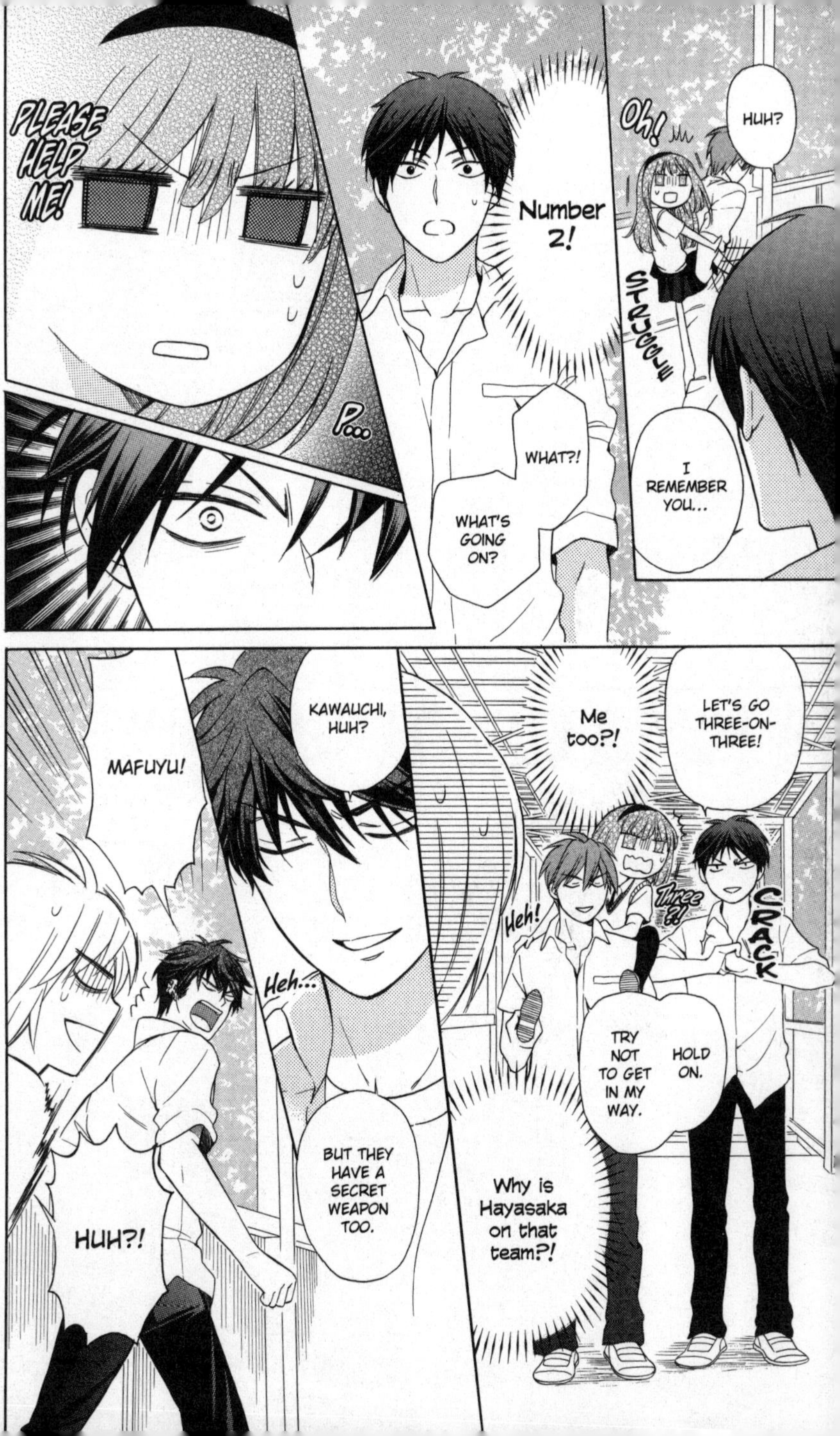
HUH?
Oh!
STRUGGLE
I REMEMBER YOU...
Number 2!
WHAT?!
WHAT'S GOING ON?
PLEASE HELP ME!
P...
LET'S GO THREE-ON-THREE!
Me too?!
Three?!
CRACK
Heh!
HOLD ON.
TRY NOT TO GET IN MY WAY.
Why is Hayasaka on that team?!
KAWAUCHI, HUH?
Heh...
BUT THEY HAVE A SECRET WEAPON TOO.
MAFUYU!
HUH?!

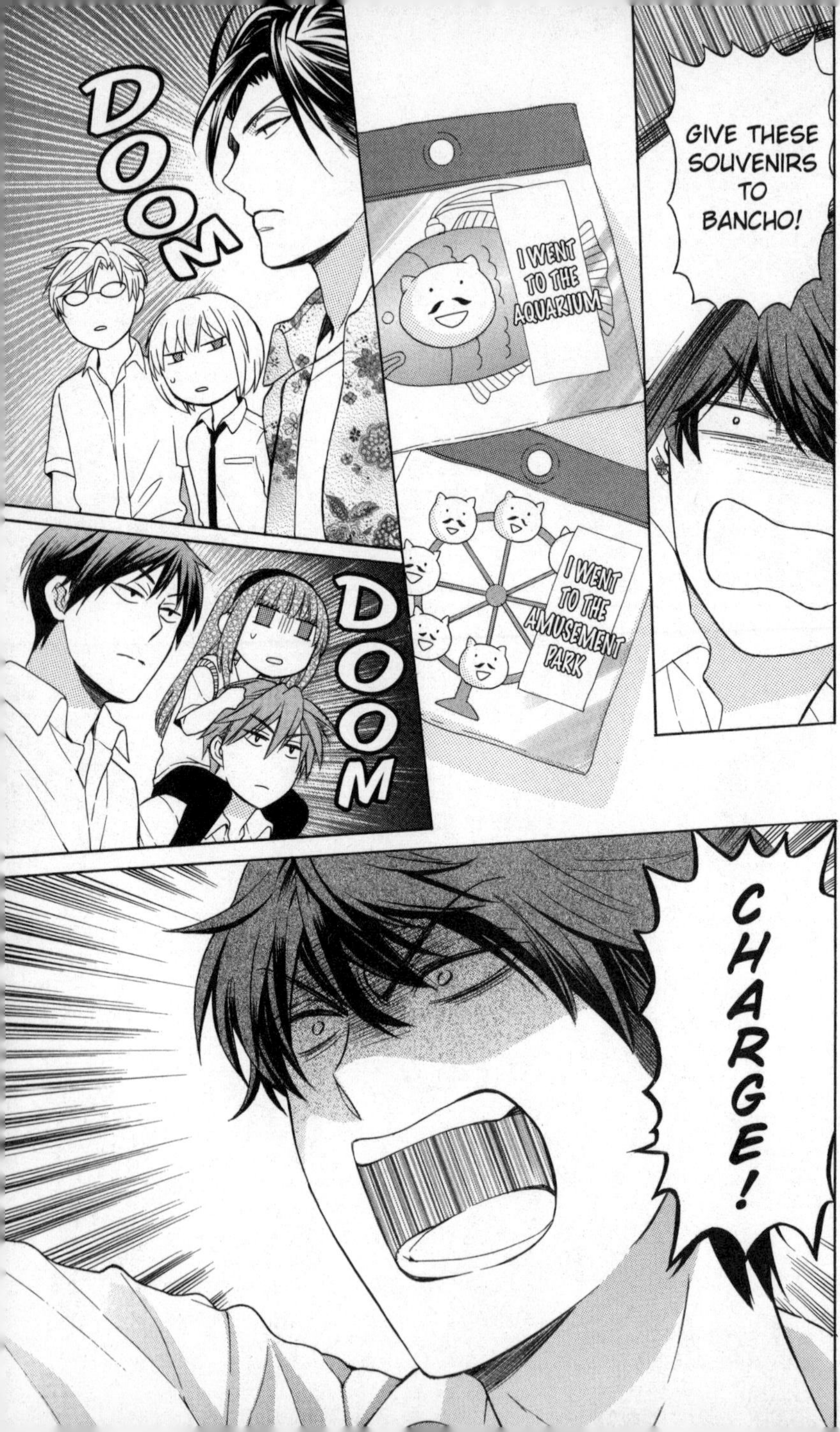
GIVE THESE SOUVENIRS TO BANCHO!
I WENT TO THE AQUARIUM
I WENT TO THE AMUSEMENT PARK
DOOM
DOOM
CHARGE!

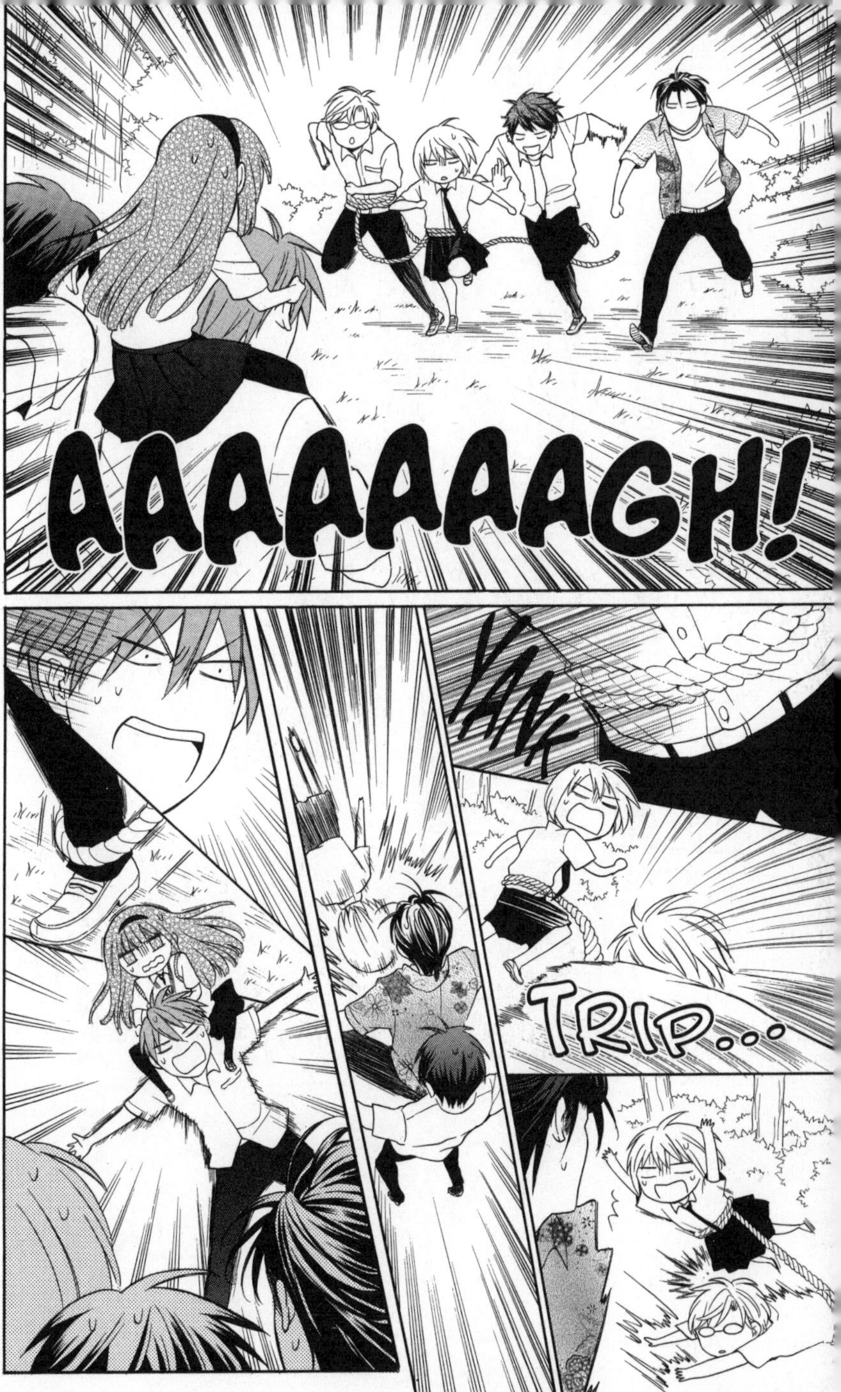
AAAAAAAAGH!
YANK
TRIP...

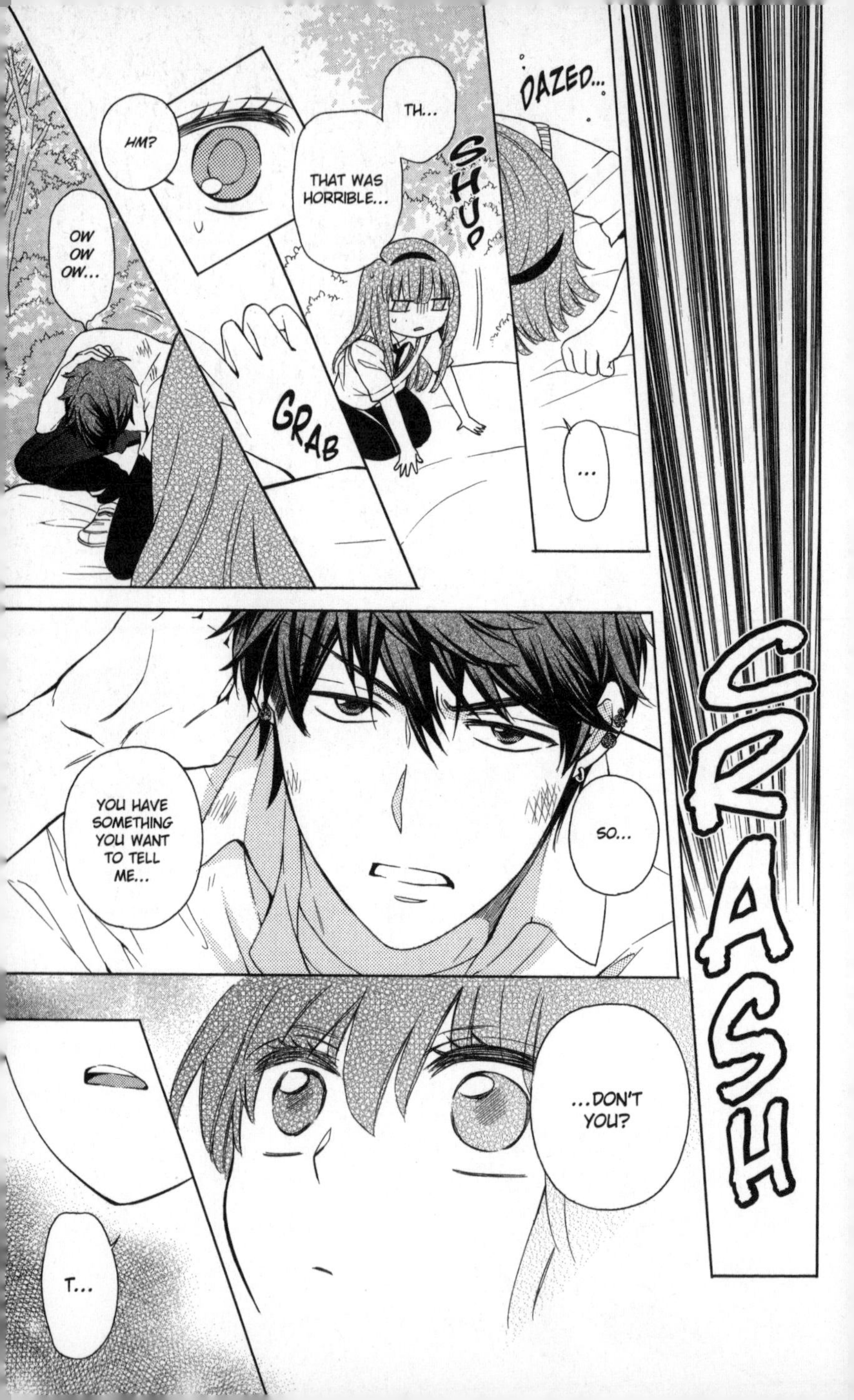
DAZED...
SHUP
...
TH...
THAT WAS HORRIBLE...
GRAB
HM?
OW OW OW...
CRASH
SO...
YOU HAVE SOMETHING YOU WANT TO TELL ME...
...DON'T YOU?
T...

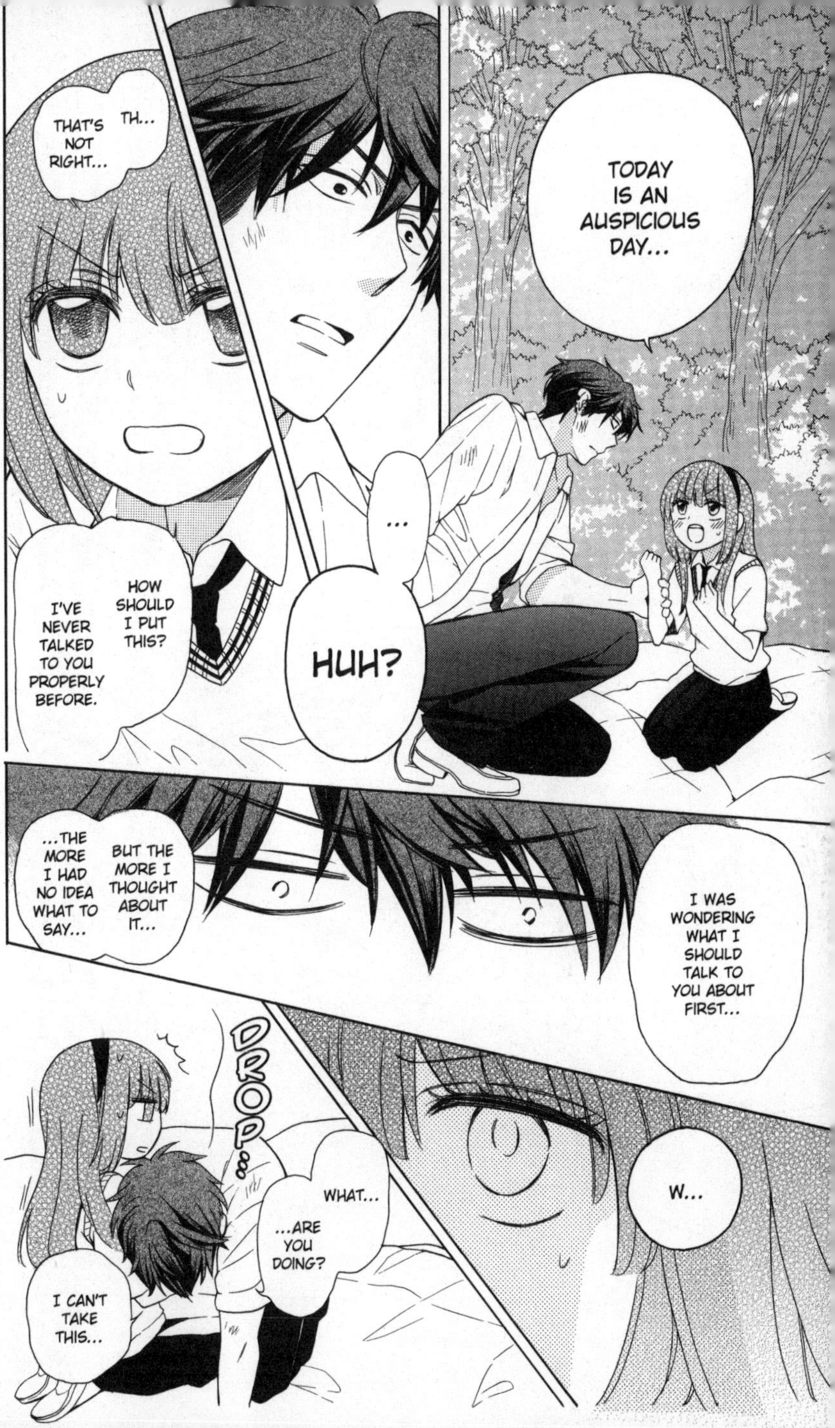
TODAY IS AN AUSPICIOUS DAY...
...
HUH?
TH...
THAT'S NOT RIGHT...
HOW SHOULD I PUT THIS?
I'VE NEVER TALKED TO YOU PROPERLY BEFORE.
I WAS WONDERING WHAT I SHOULD TALK TO YOU ABOUT FIRST...
BUT THE MORE I THOUGHT ABOUT IT...
...THE MORE I HAD NO IDEA WHAT TO SAY...
W...
WHAT...
...ARE YOU DOING?
DROP...
I CAN'T TAKE THIS...

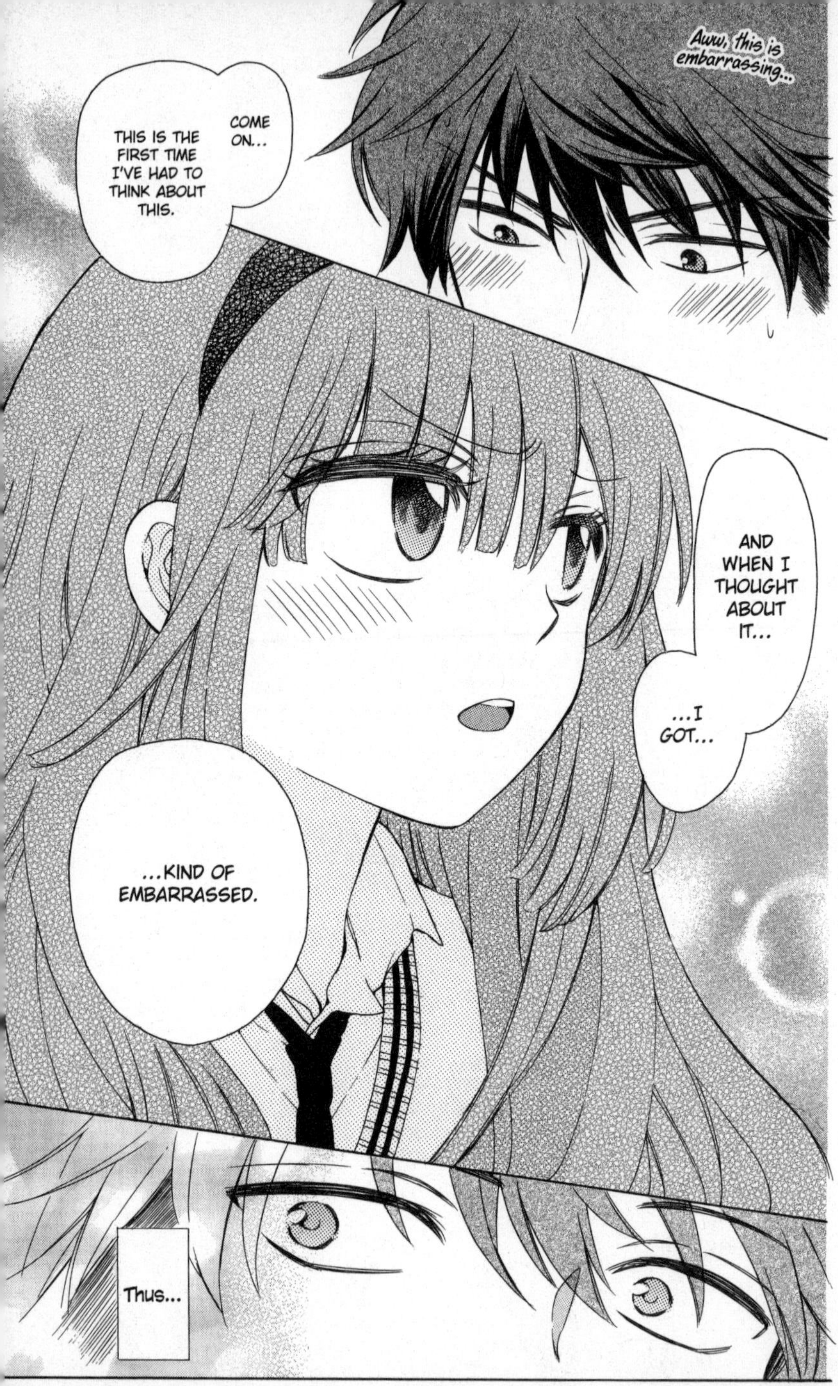
Aww, this is embarrassing...
COME ON...
THIS IS THE FIRST TIME I'VE HAD TO THINK ABOUT THIS.
AND WHEN I THOUGHT ABOUT IT...
...I GOT...
...KIND OF EMBARRASSED.
Thus...

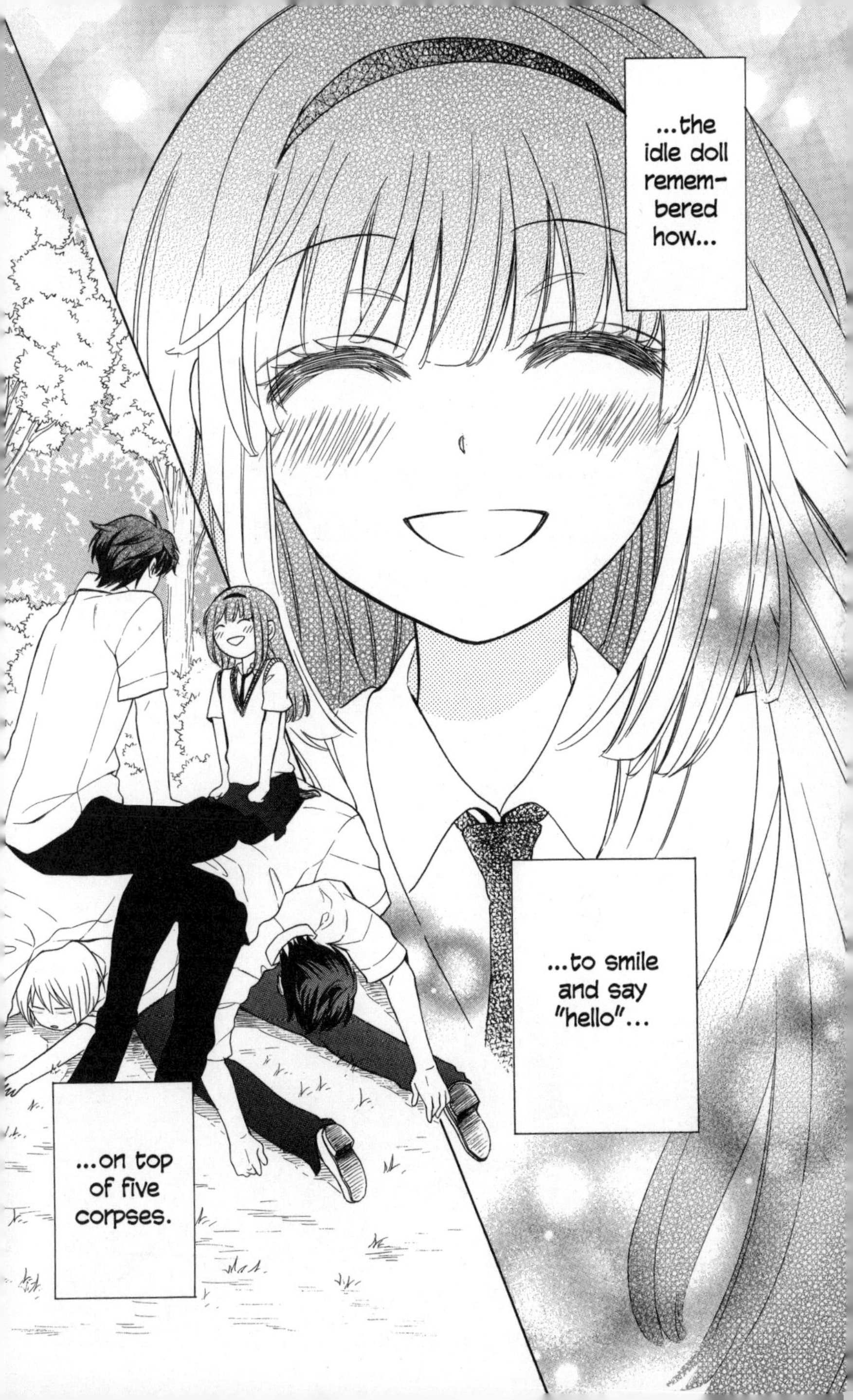
...the idle doll remem-bered how...
...to smile and say "hello"...
...on top of five corpses.

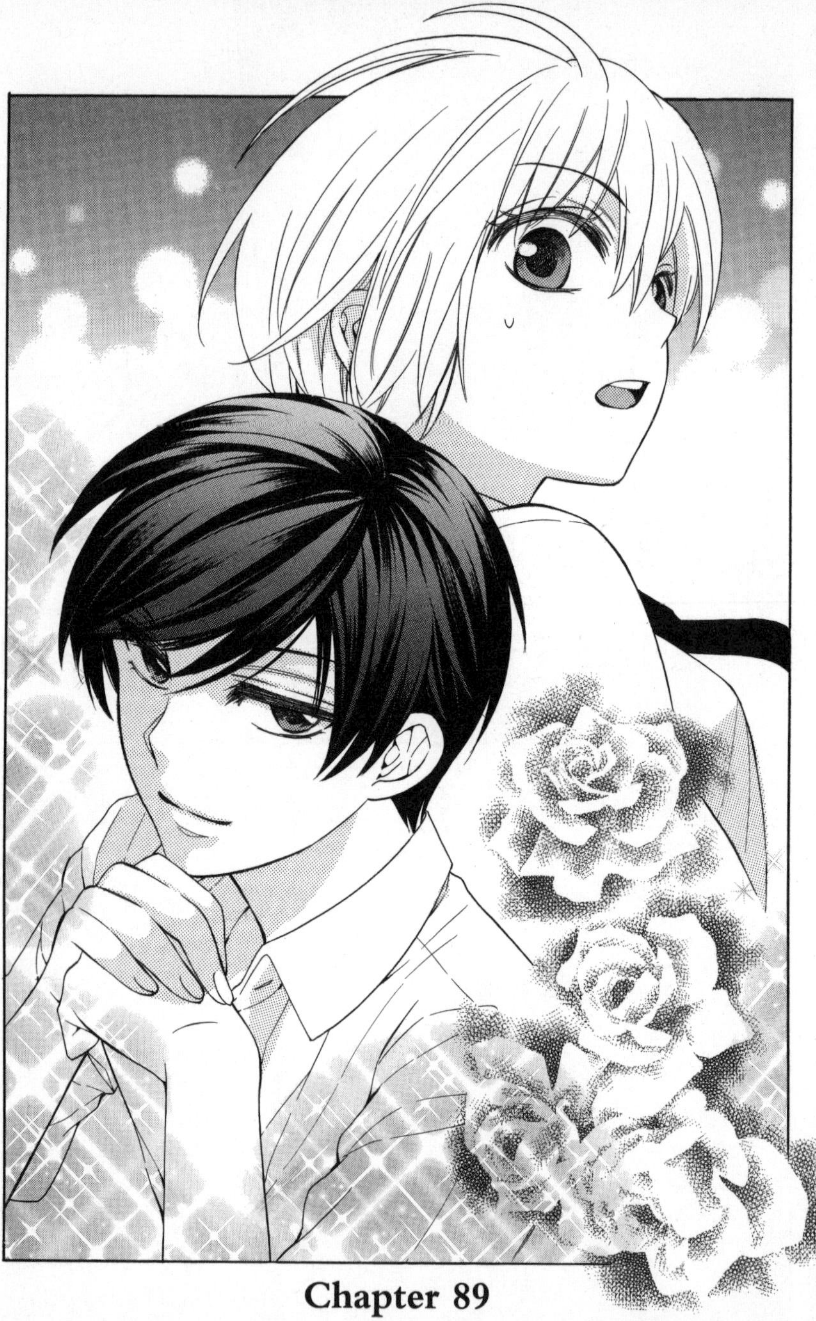

Chapter 89

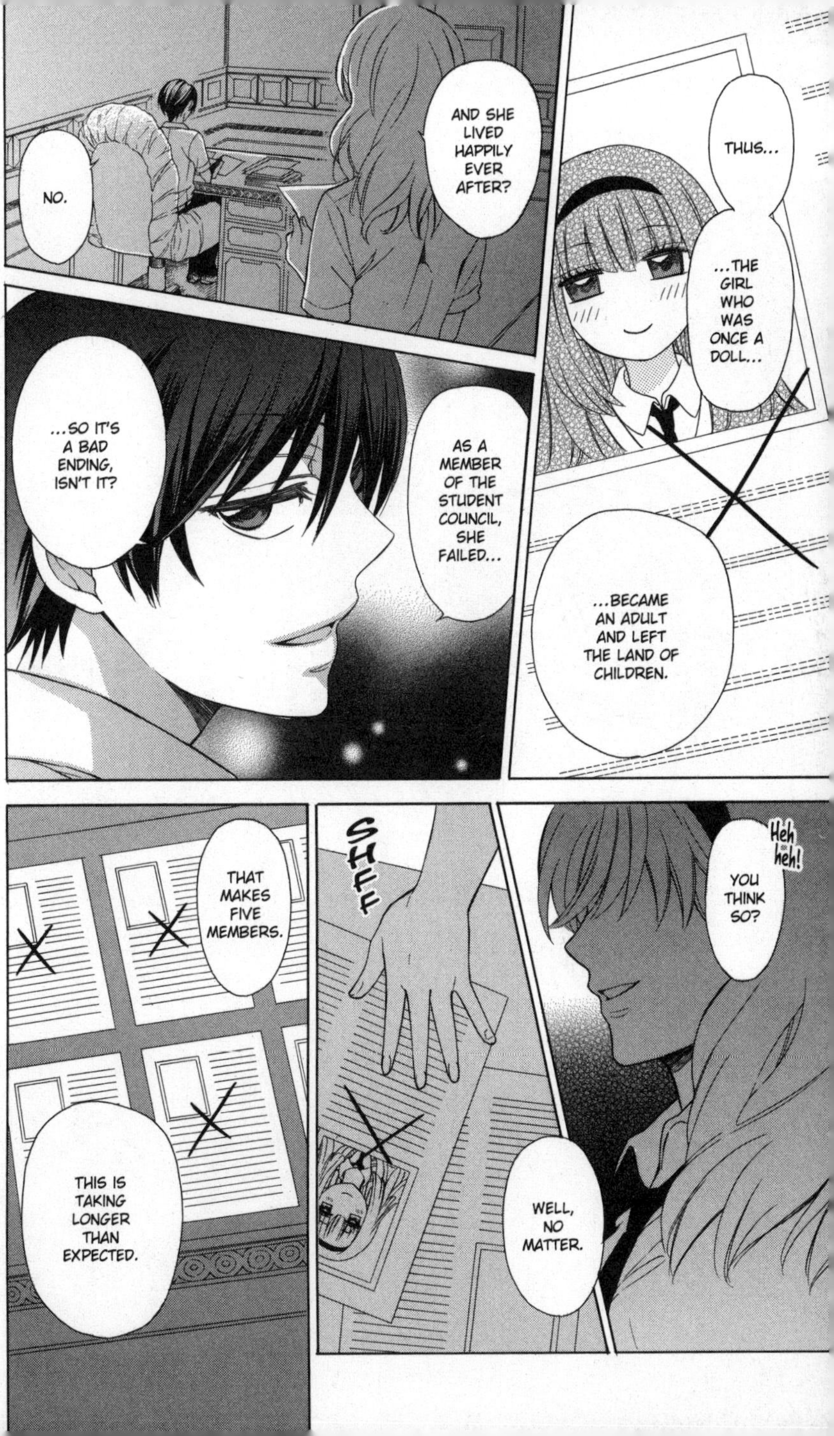
THUS...
...THE GIRL WHO WAS ONCE A DOLL...
...BECAME AN ADULT AND LEFT THE LAND OF CHILDREN.
AND SHE LIVED HAPPILY EVER AFTER?
NO.
AS A MEMBER OF THE STUDENT COUNCIL, SHE FAILED...
...SO IT'S A BAD ENDING, ISN'T IT?
Heh heh!
YOU THINK SO?
WELL, NO MATTER.
SHFF
THAT MAKES FIVE MEMBERS.
THIS IS TAKING LONGER THAN EXPECTED.

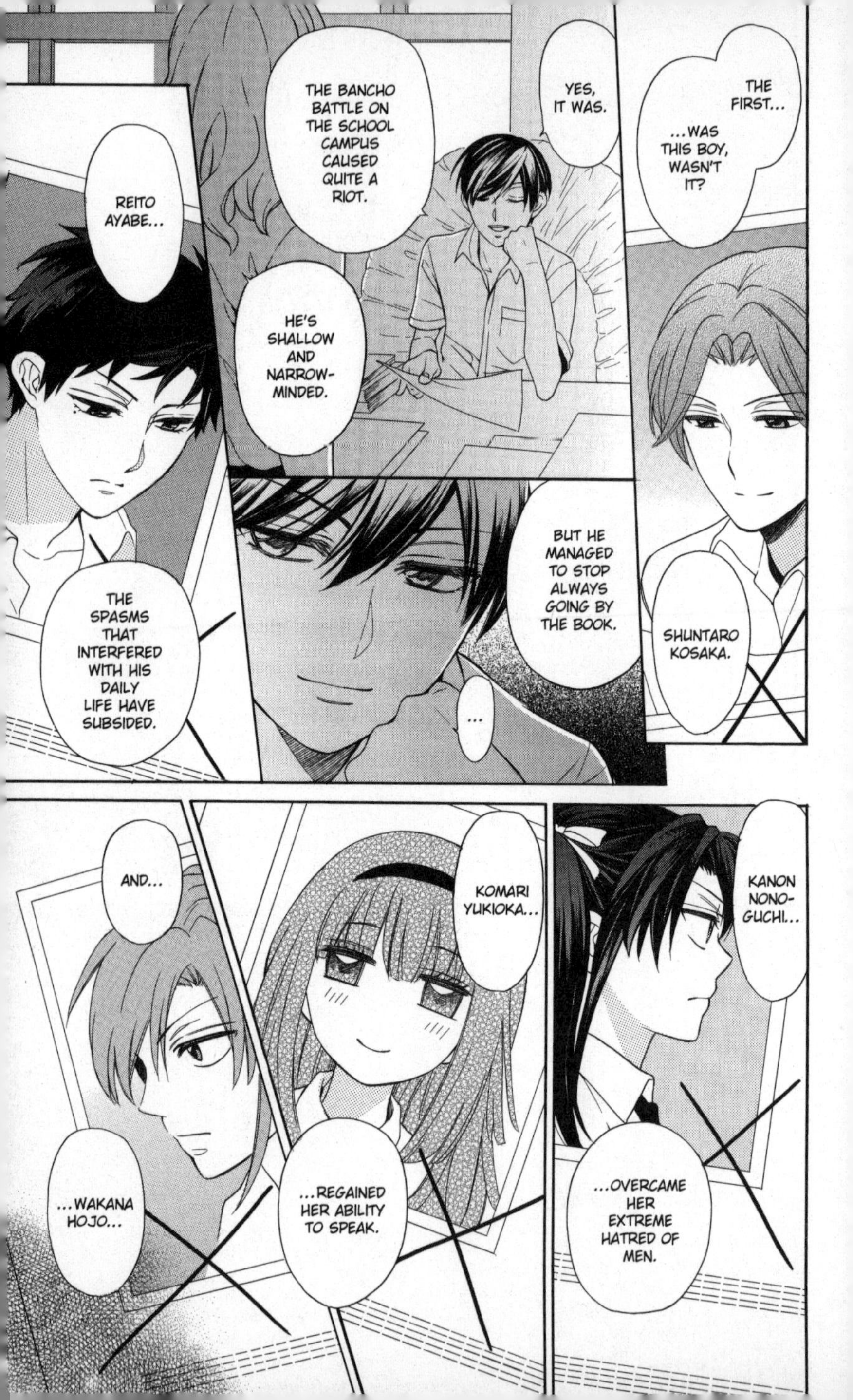
THE FIRST...
...WAS THIS BOY, WASN'T IT?
SHUNTARO KOSAKA.
YES, IT WAS.
THE BANCHO BATTLE ON THE SCHOOL CAMPUS CAUSED QUITE A RIOT.
HE'S SHALLOW AND NARROW-MINDED.
BUT HE MANAGED TO STOP ALWAYS GOING BY THE BOOK.
...
REITO AYABE...
THE SPASMS THAT INTERFERED WITH HIS DAILY LIFE HAVE SUBSIDED.
KANON NONO-GUCHI...
...OVERCAME HER EXTREME HATRED OF MEN.
KOMARI YUKIOKA...
...REGAINED HER ABILITY TO SPEAK.
AND...
...WAKANA HOJO...

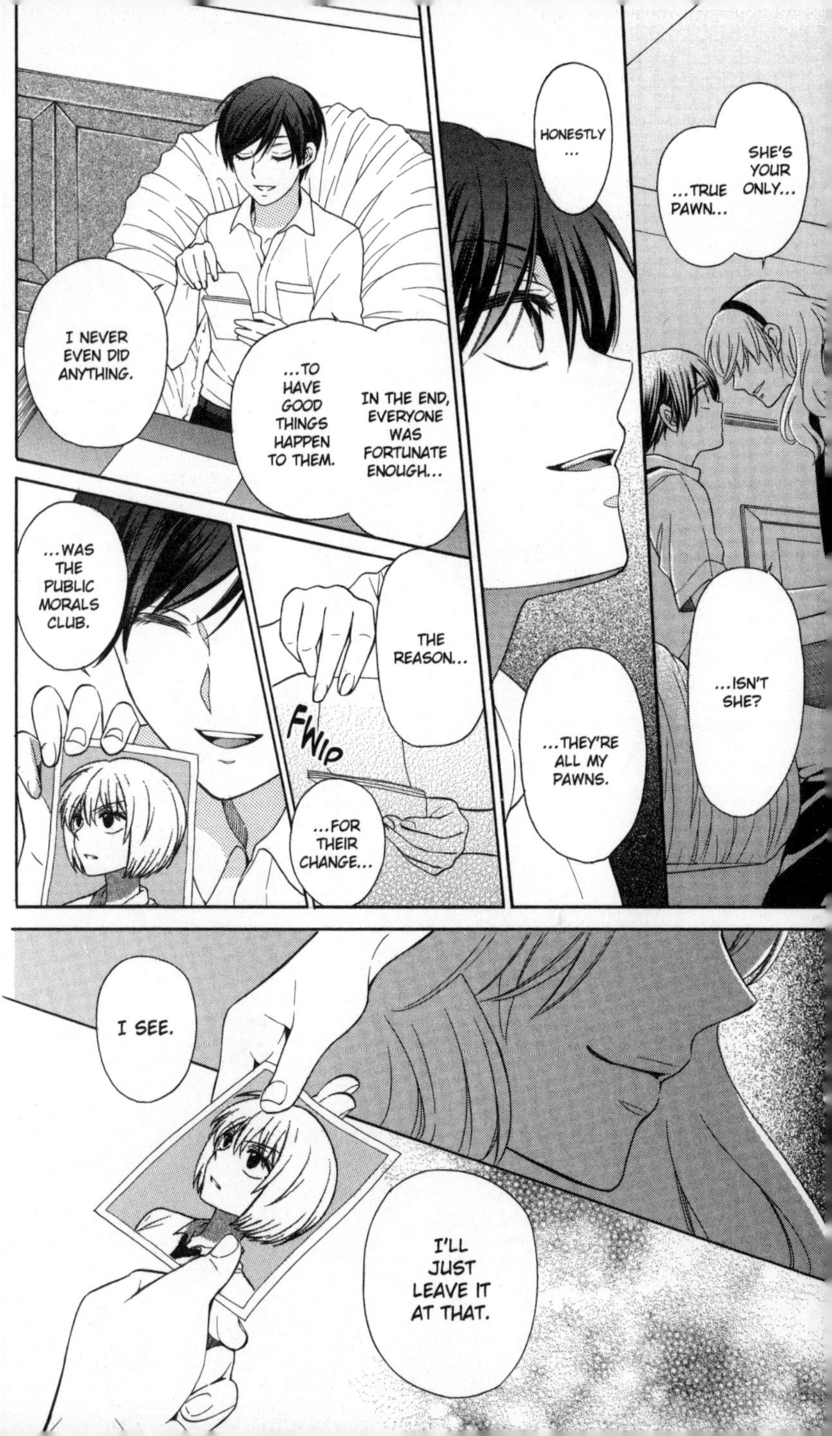
SHE'S YOUR ONLY...
...TRUE PAWN...
...ISN'T SHE?
HONESTLY...
...THEY'RE ALL MY PAWNS.
IN THE END, EVERYONE WAS FORTUNATE ENOUGH...
...TO HAVE GOOD THINGS HAPPEN TO THEM.
I NEVER EVEN DID ANYTHING.
THE REASON...
FWIP
...FOR THEIR CHANGE...
...WAS THE PUBLIC MORALS CLUB.
I SEE.
I'LL JUST LEAVE IT AT THAT.

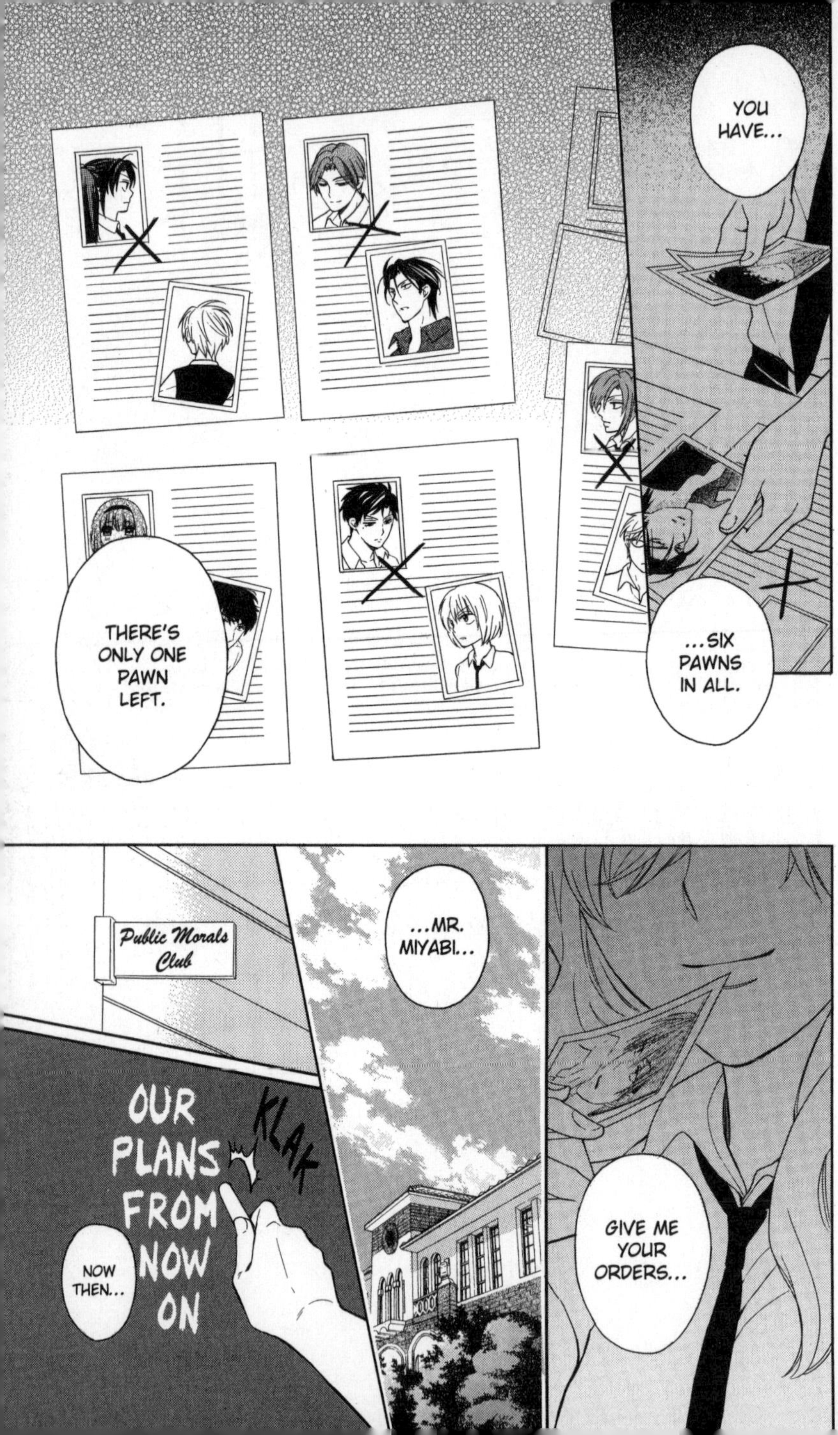
YOU HAVE...
...SIX PAWNS IN ALL.
THERE'S ONLY ONE PAWN LEFT.
GIVE ME YOUR ORDERS...
...MR. MIYABI...
Public Morals Club
OUR PLANS FROM NOW ON
KLAK
NOW THEN...

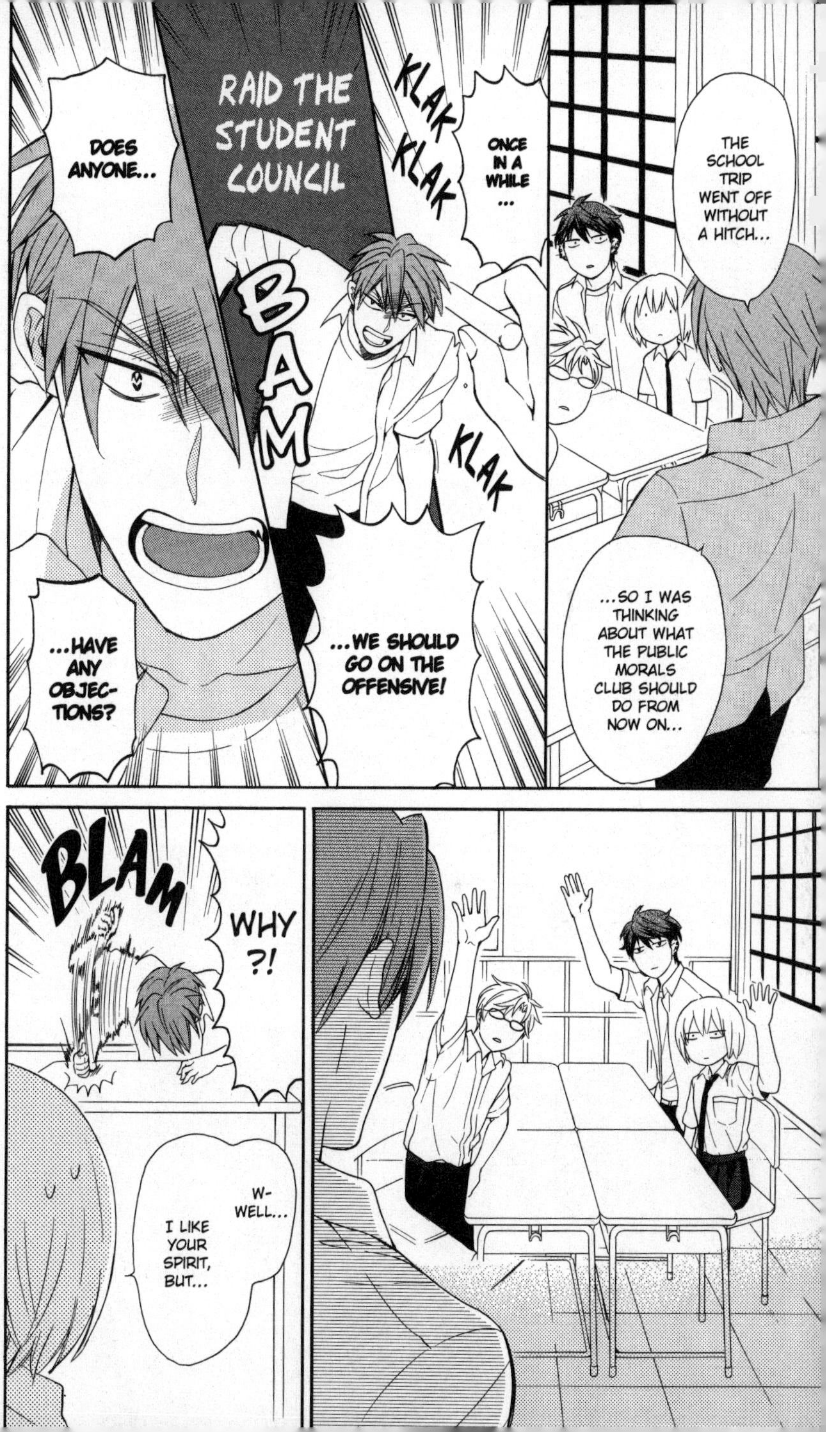
THE SCHOOL TRIP WENT OFF WITHOUT A HITCH...
...SO I WAS THINKING ABOUT WHAT THE PUBLIC MORALS CLUB SHOULD DO FROM NOW ON...
ONCE IN A WHILE...
KLAK KLAK
BAM
KLAK
...WE SHOULD GO ON THE OFFENSIVE!
RAID THE STUDENT COUNCIL
DOES ANYONE...
...HAVE ANY OBJEC-TIONS?
BLAM
WHY?!
W-WELL...
I LIKE YOUR SPIRIT, BUT...

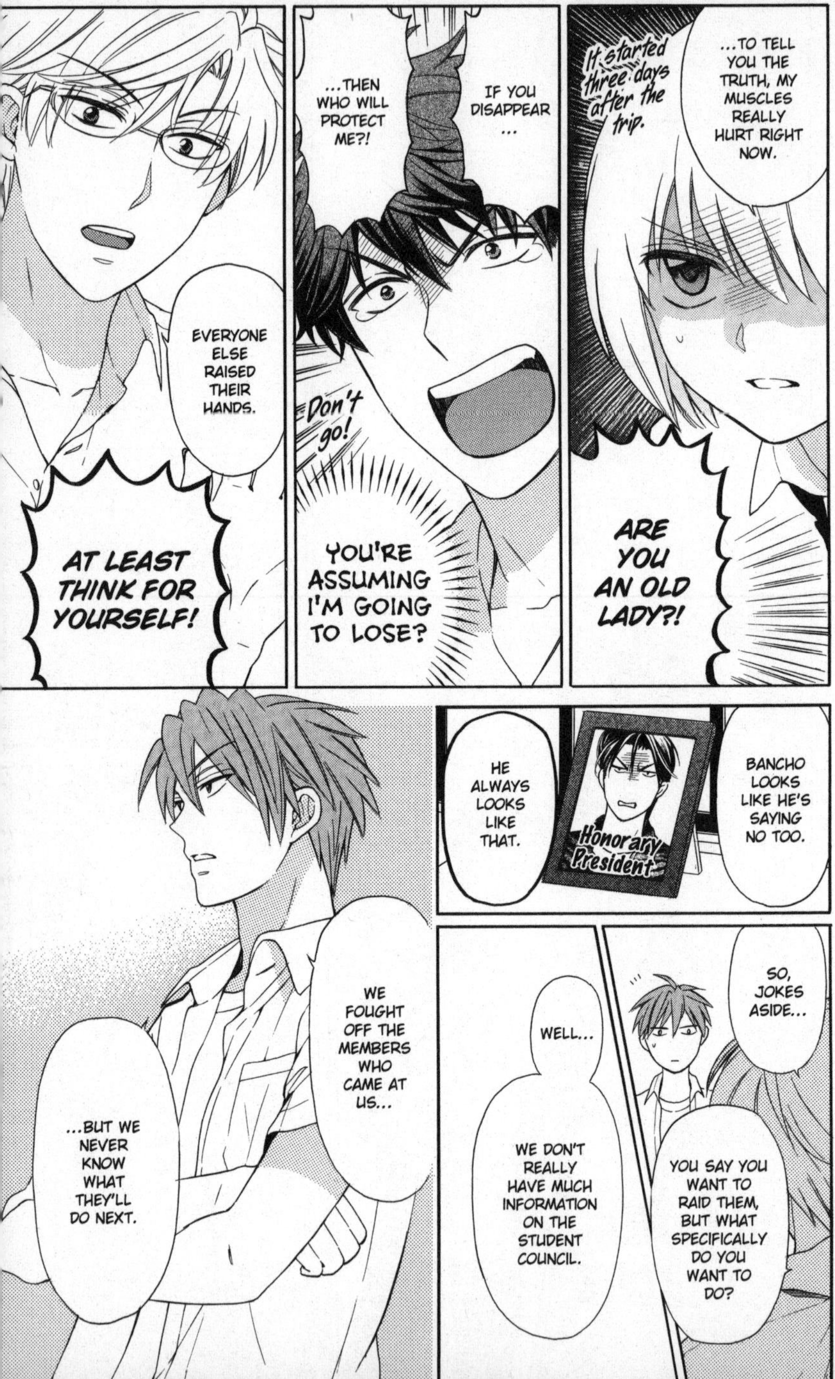
...TO TELL YOU THE TRUTH, MY MUSCLES REALLY HURT RIGHT NOW.
It started three days after the trip.
ARE YOU AN OLD LADY?!
IF YOU DISAPPEAR...
...THEN WHO WILL PROTECT ME?!
Don't go!
YOU'RE ASSUMING I'M GOING TO LOSE?
EVERYONE ELSE RAISED THEIR HANDS.
AT LEAST THINK FOR YOURSELF!
BANCHO LOOKS LIKE HE'S SAYING NO TOO.
Honorary President
HE ALWAYS LOOKS LIKE THAT.
SO, JOKES ASIDE...
YOU SAY YOU WANT TO RAID THEM, BUT WHAT SPECIFICALLY DO YOU WANT TO DO?
WELL...
WE DON'T REALLY HAVE MUCH INFORMATION ON THE STUDENT COUNCIL.
WE FOUGHT OFF THE MEMBERS WHO CAME AT US...
...BUT WE NEVER KNOW WHAT THEY'LL DO NEXT.

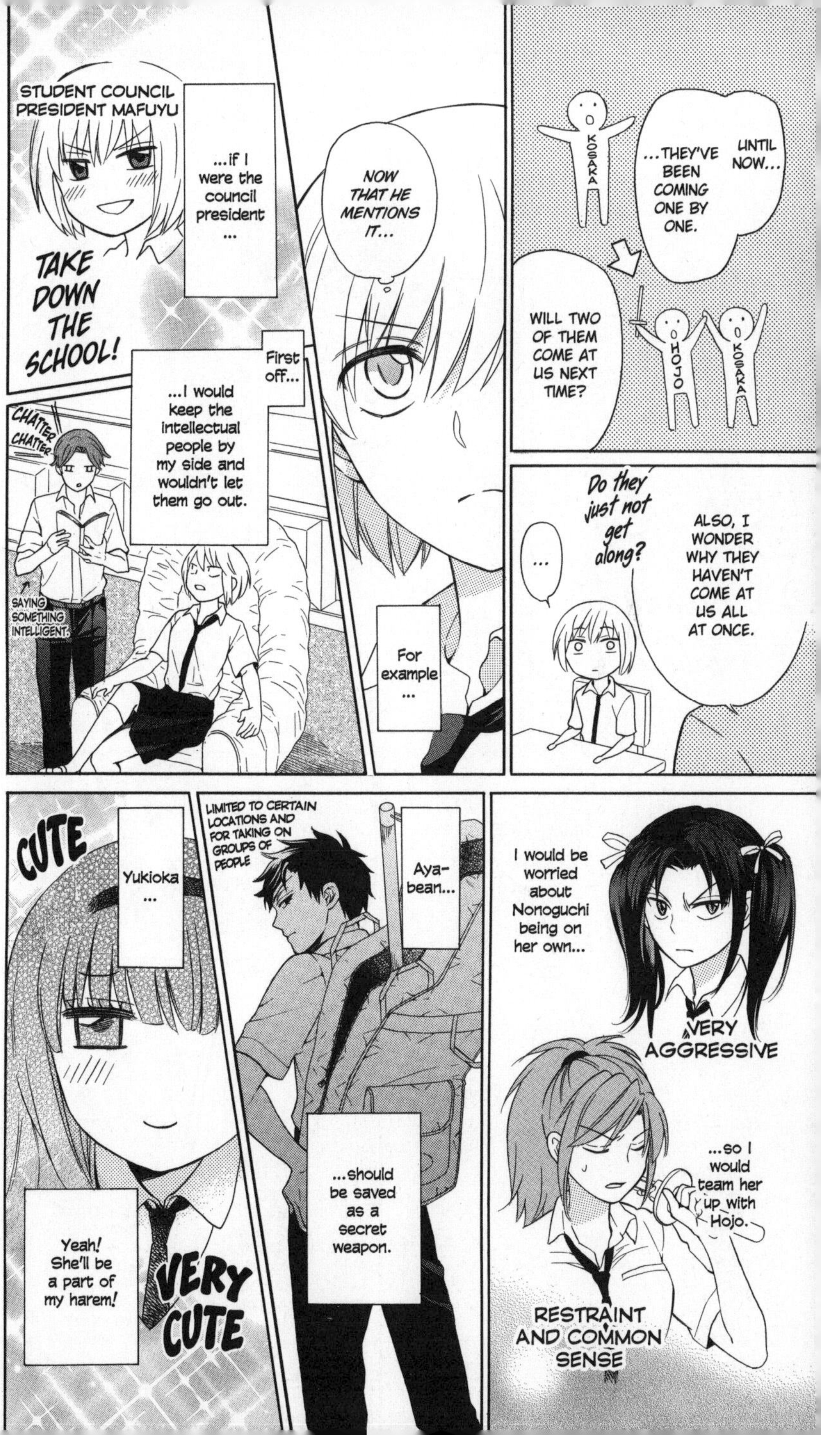
UNTIL NOW...
...THEY'VE BEEN COMING ONE BY ONE.
KOSAKA
WILL TWO OF THEM COME AT US NEXT TIME?
HOJO
KOSAKA
ALSO, I WONDER WHY THEY HAVEN'T COME AT US ALL AT ONCE.
Do they just not get along?
...
NOW THAT HE MENTIONS IT...
For example...
...if I were the council president...
STUDENT COUNCIL PRESIDENT MAFUYU
TAKE DOWN THE SCHOOL!
First off...
...I would keep the intellectual people by my side and wouldn't let them go out.
CHATTER CHATTER
SAYING SOMETHING INTELLIGENT.
I would be worried about Nonoguchi being on her own...
VERY AGGRESSIVE
...so I would team her up with Hojo.
RESTRAINT AND COMMON SENSE
Aya-bean...
LIMITED TO CERTAIN LOCATIONS AND FOR TAKING ON GROUPS OF PEOPLE
...should be saved as a secret weapon.
Yukioka...
CUTE
Yeah! She'll be a part of my harem!
VERY CUTE

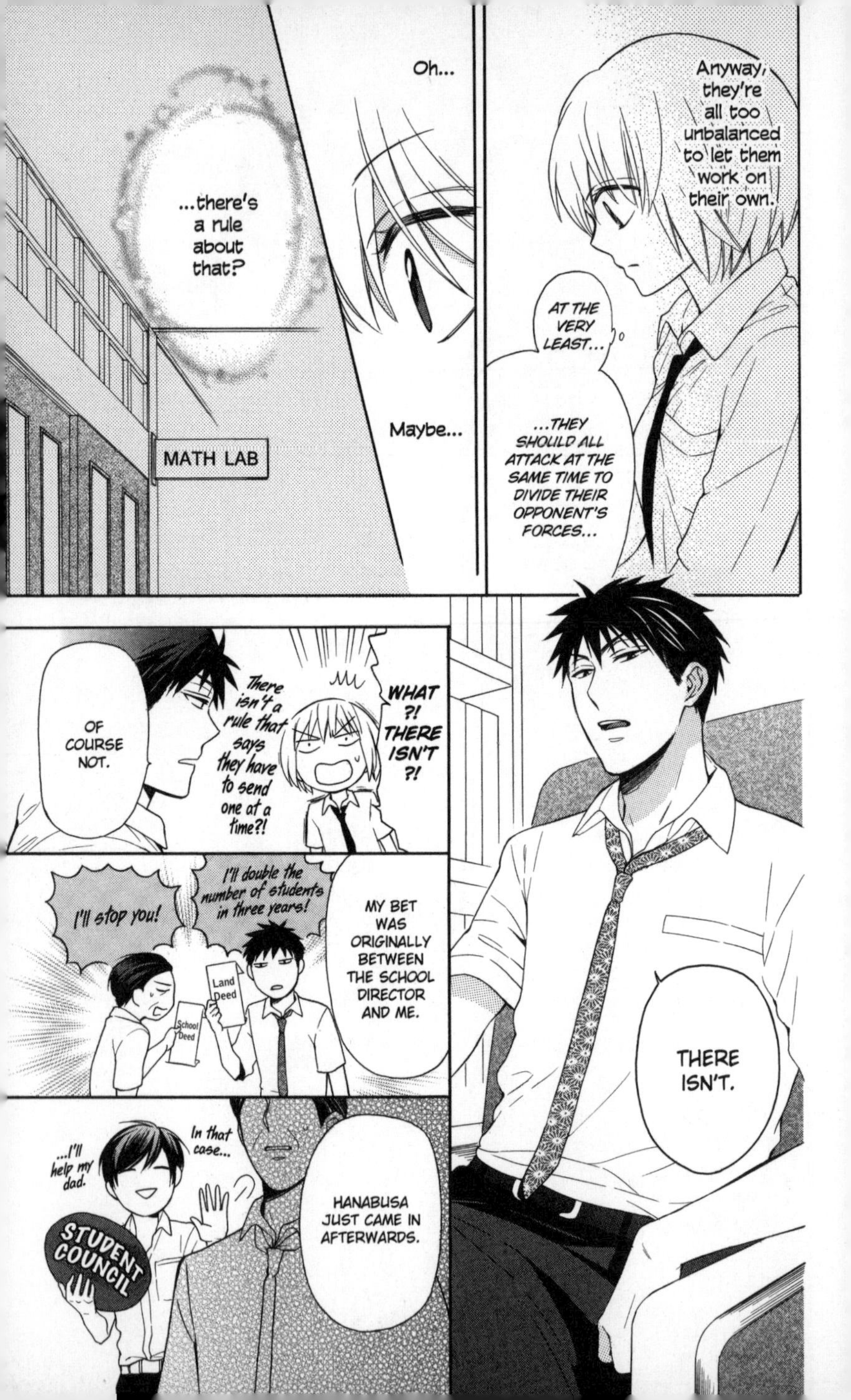
Anyway, they're all too unbalanced to let them work on their own.
AT THE VERY LEAST...
...THEY SHOULD ALL ATTACK AT THE SAME TIME TO DIVIDE THEIR OPPONENT'S FORCES...
Oh...
Maybe...
...there's a rule about that?
MATH LAB
THERE ISN'T.
WHAT?! THERE ISN'T?!
There isn't a rule that says they have to send one at a time?!
OF COURSE NOT.
MY BET WAS ORIGINALLY BETWEEN THE SCHOOL DIRECTOR AND ME.
I'll double the number of students in three years!
I'll stop you!
Land Deed
School Deed
HANABUSA JUST CAME IN AFTERWARDS.
In that case...
...I'll help my dad.
STUDENT COUNCIL

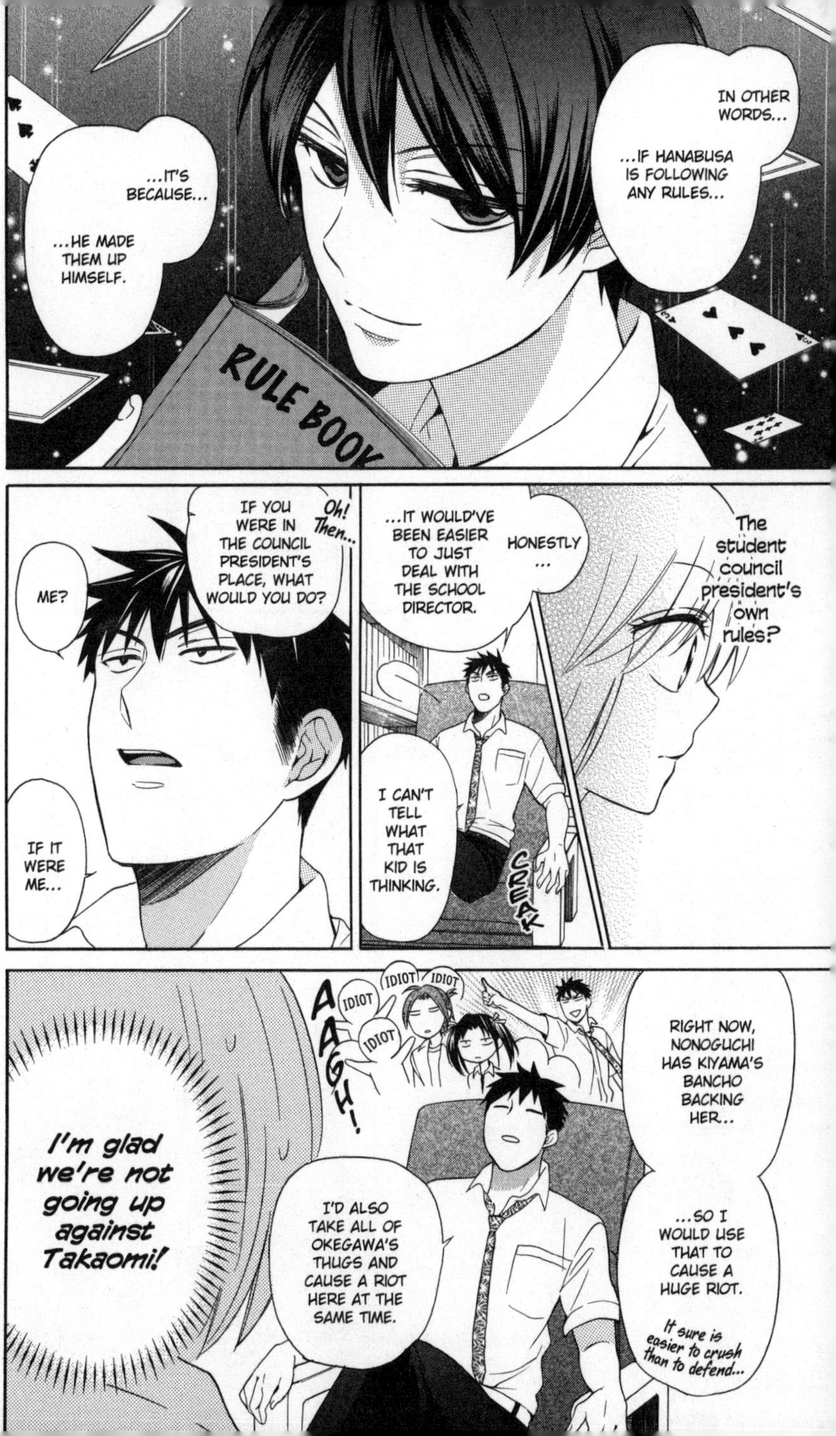
IN OTHER WORDS...
...IF HANABUSA IS FOLLOWING ANY RULES...
...IT'S BECAUSE...
...HE MADE THEM UP HIMSELF.
RULE BOOK
The student council president's own rules?
HONESTLY...
...IT WOULD'VE BEEN EASIER TO JUST DEAL WITH THE SCHOOL DIRECTOR.
I CAN'T TELL WHAT THAT KID IS THINKING.
CREAK
Oh! Then...
IF YOU WERE IN THE COUNCIL PRESIDENT'S PLACE, WHAT WOULD YOU DO?
ME?
IF IT WERE ME...
RIGHT NOW, NONOGUCHI HAS KIYAMA'S BANCHO BACKING HER..
...SO I WOULD USE THAT TO CAUSE A HUGE RIOT.
It sure is easier to crush than to defend...
I'D ALSO TAKE ALL OF OKEGAWA'S THUGS AND CAUSE A RIOT HERE AT THE SAME TIME.
IDIOT
IDIOT
IDIOT
IDIOT
AAGH!
I'm glad we're not going up against Takaomi!

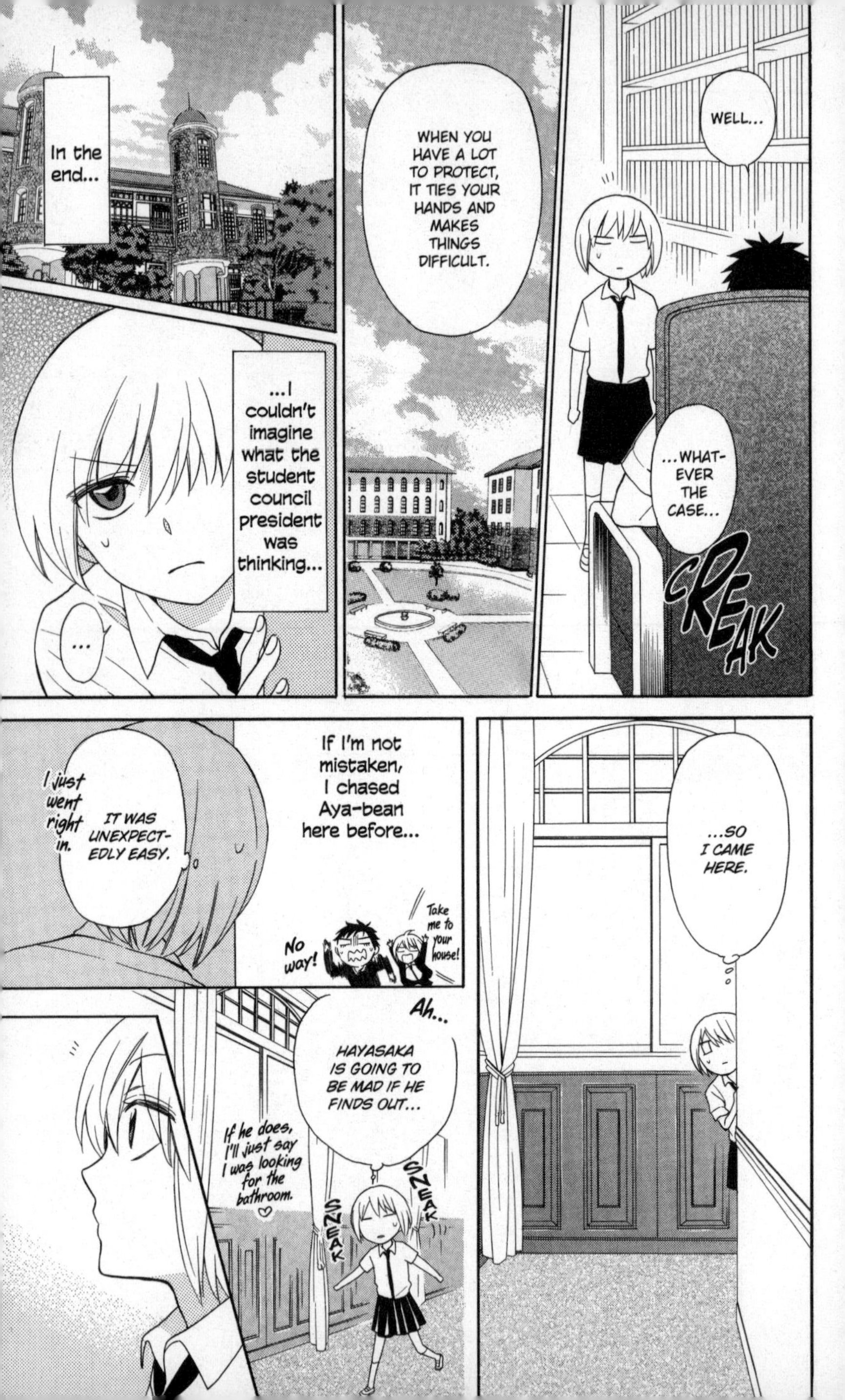
WELL...
...WHAT-EVER THE CASE...
CREAK
WHEN YOU HAVE A LOT TO PROTECT, IT TIES YOUR HANDS AND MAKES THINGS DIFFICULT.
In the end...
...I couldn't imagine what the student council president was thinking...
...
...SO I CAME HERE.
If I'm not mistaken, I chased Aya-bean here before...
Take me to your house!
No way!
IT WAS UNEXPECT-EDLY EASY.
I just went right in.
Ah...
HAYASAKA IS GOING TO BE MAD IF HE FINDS OUT...
If he does, I'll just say I was looking for the bathroom. ♡
SNEAK
SNEAK

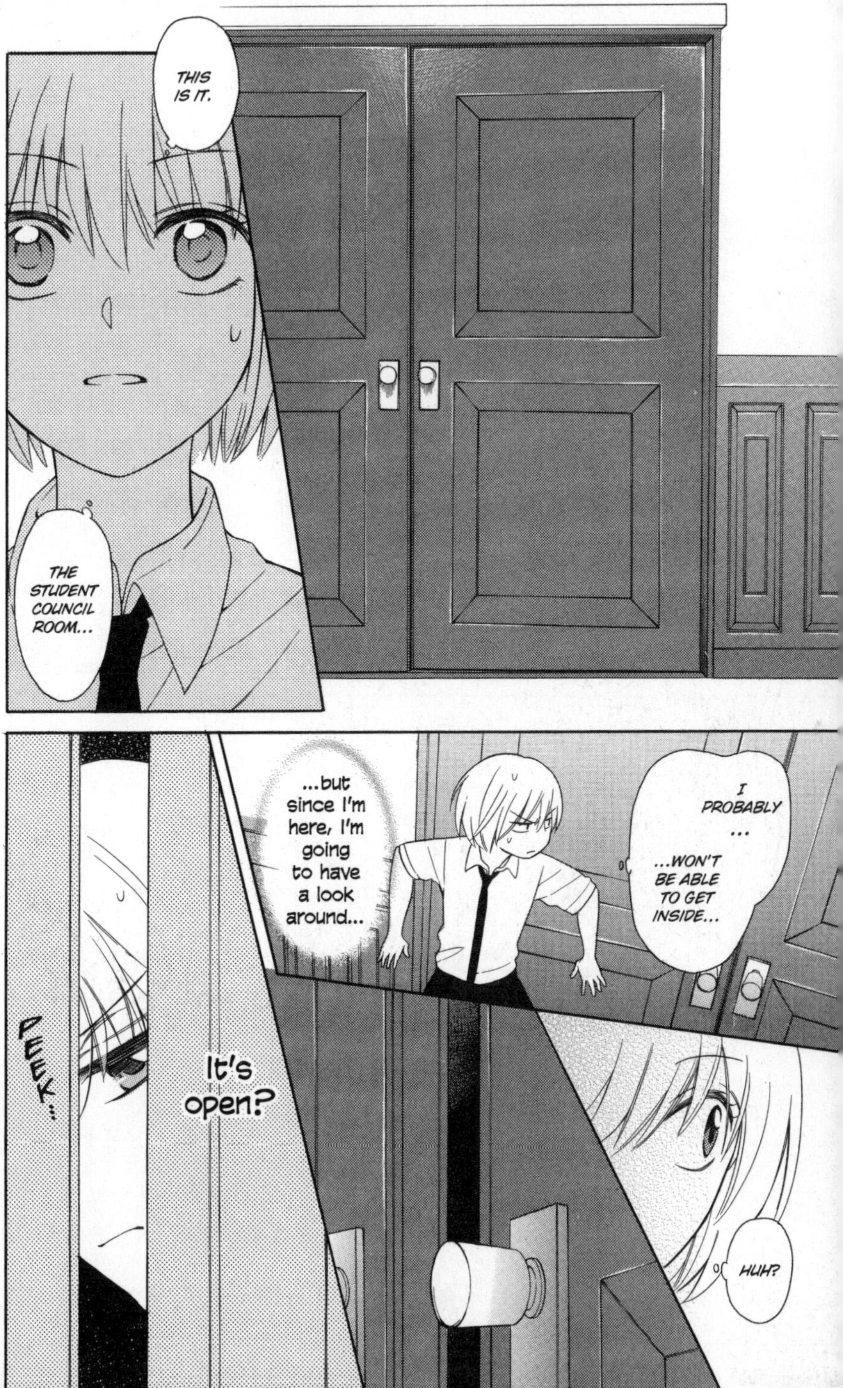
THIS IS IT.
THE STUDENT COUNCIL ROOM...
I PROBABLY ... ...WON'T BE ABLE TO GET INSIDE...
...but since I'm here, I'm going to have a look around...
HUH?
It's open?
PEEK...

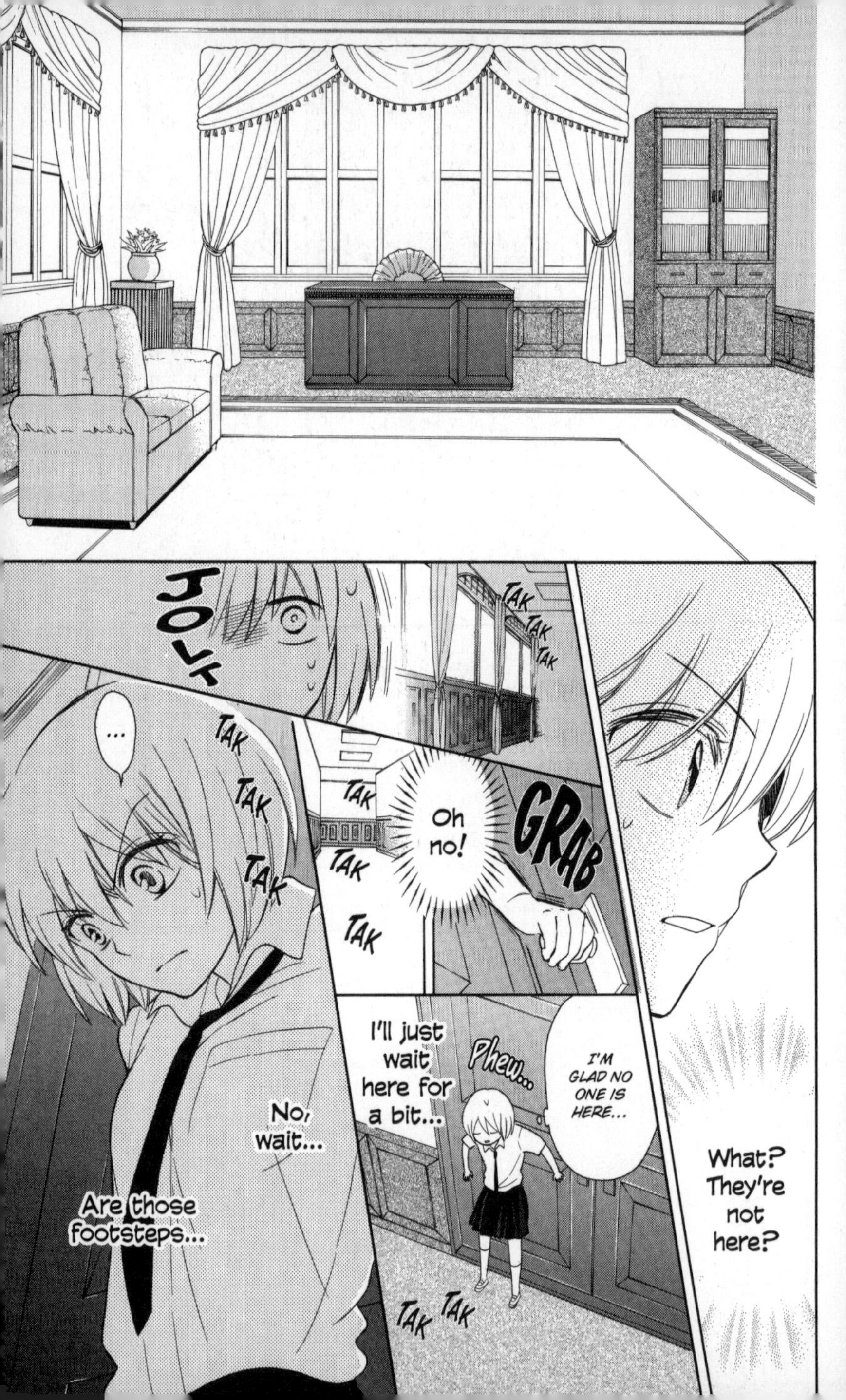
What? They're not here?
JOLT
TAK TAK TAK
Oh no!
GRAB
TAK
TAK
TAK
I'M GLAD NO ONE IS HERE...
Phew...
I'll just wait here for a bit...
TAK TAK
...
TAK
TAK
TAK
No, wait...
Are those footsteps...

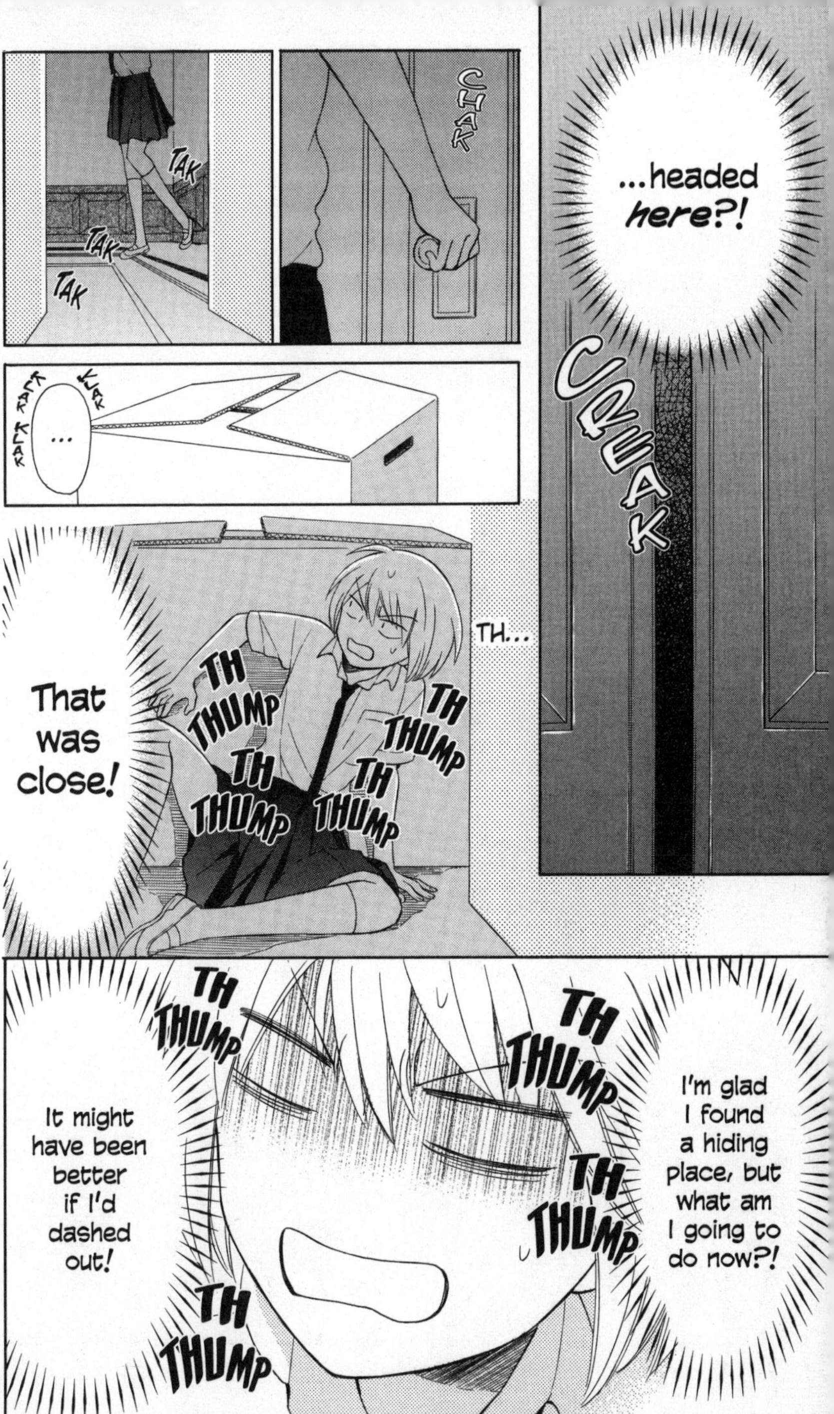
...headed *here?!*
CREAK
CHAK
TAK
TAK
TAK
KLAK
KLAK KLAK
...
TH...
That was close!
TH THUMP
TH THUMP
TH THUMP
TH THUMP
I'm glad I found a hiding place, but what am I going to do now?!
TH THUMP
TH THUMP
TH THUMP
It might have been better if I'd dashed out!
TH THUMP

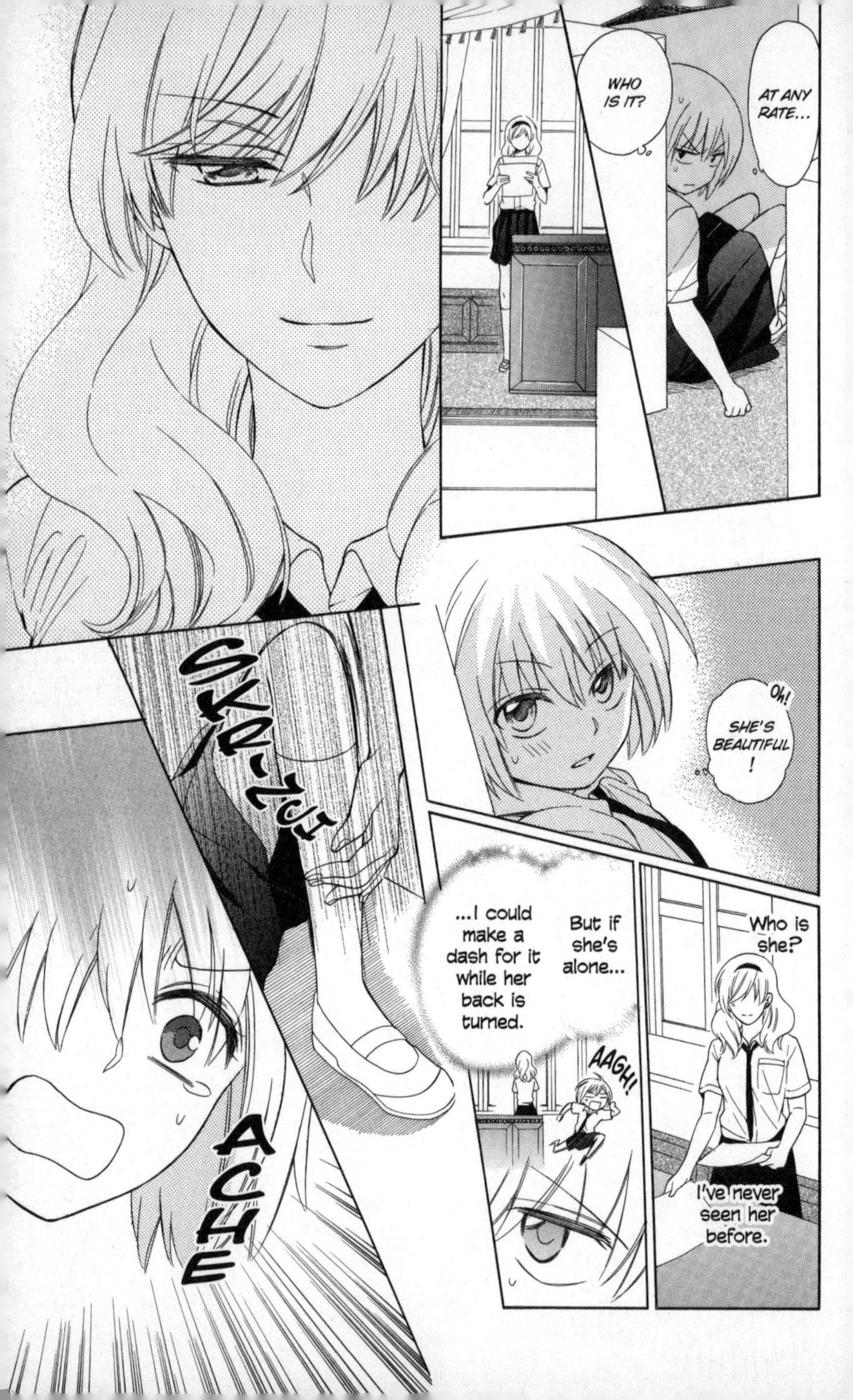

AT ANY RATE...
WHO IS IT?
Oh! SHE'S BEAUTIFUL!
Who is she?
I've never seen her before.
But if she's alone...
...I could make a dash for it while her back is turned.
AAGH!
SKR-ZUH
ACHE

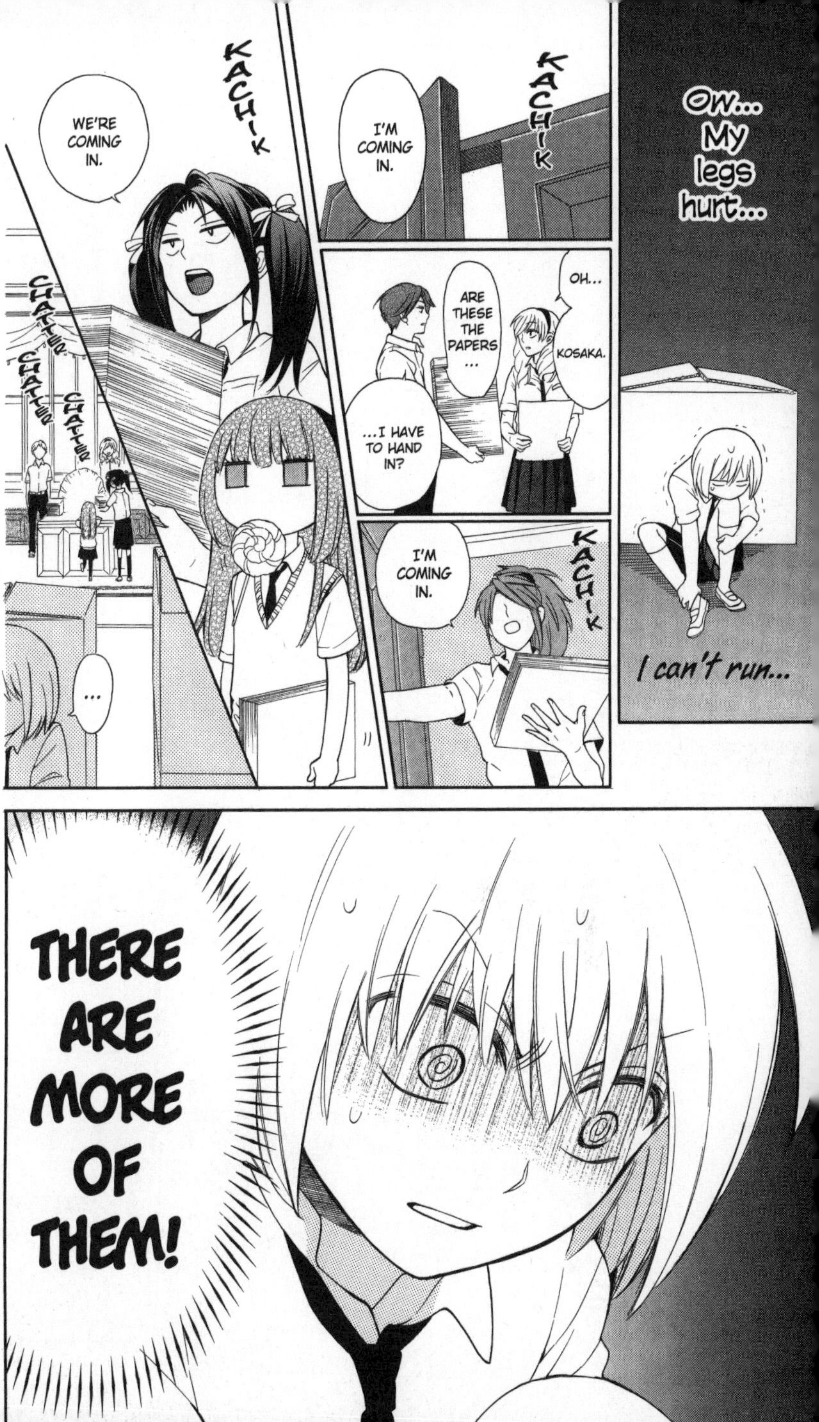
Ow... My legs hurt...
I can't run...
I'M COMING IN.
KACHIK
OH... KOSAKA.
ARE THESE THE PAPERS...
...I HAVE TO HAND IN?
I'M COMING IN.
KACHIK
WE'RE COMING IN.
KACHIK
CHATTER
CHATTER
CHATTER
...
THERE ARE MORE OF THEM!

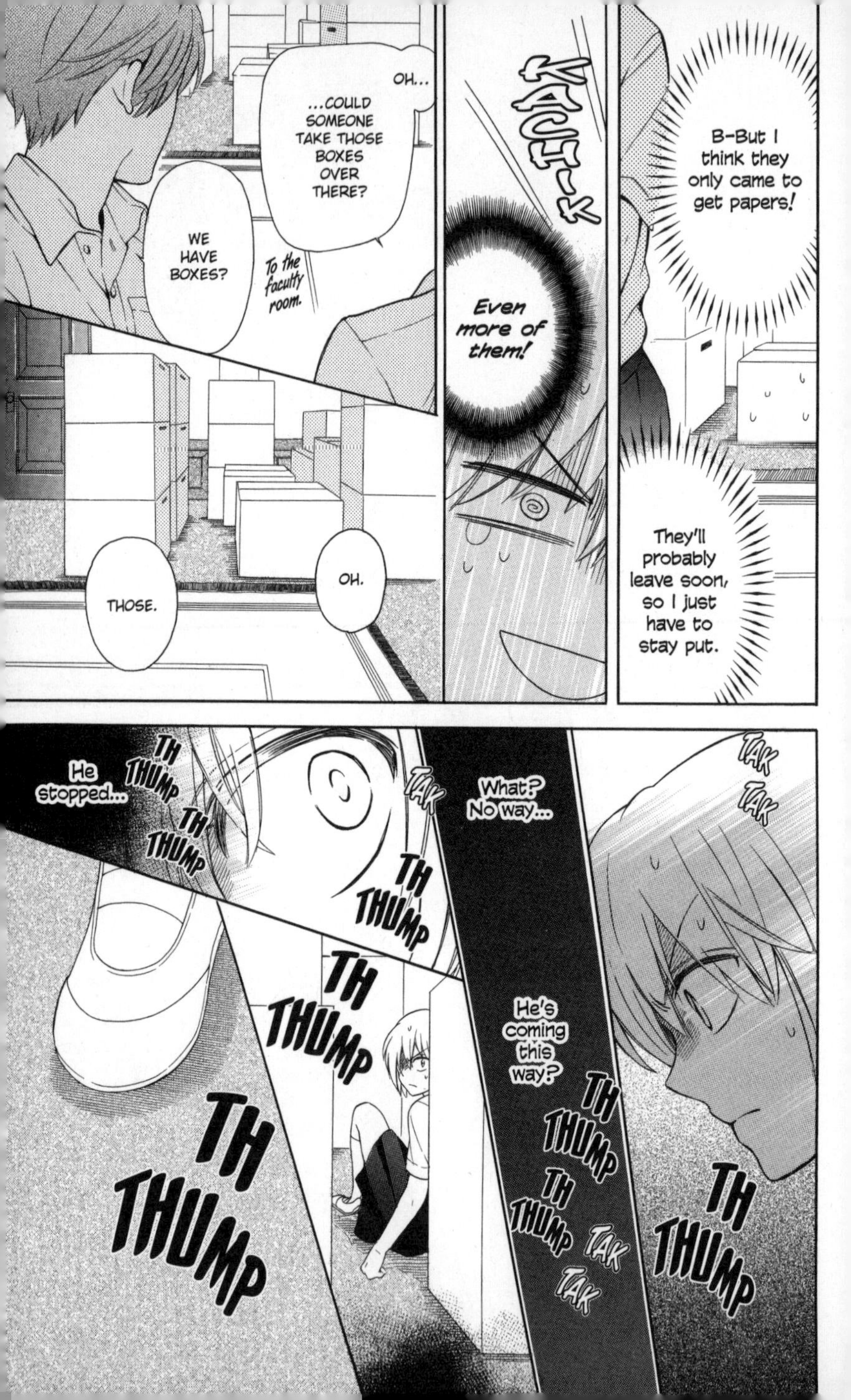
B-But I think they only came to get papers!
They'll probably leave soon, so I just have to stay put.
KACHI-K
Even more of them!
OH...
...COULD SOMEONE TAKE THOSE BOXES OVER THERE?
To the faculty room.
WE HAVE BOXES?
OH.
THOSE.
TAK TAK
TH THUMP
What? No way...
He's coming this way?
TH THUMP
TH THUMP
TAK
TAK
He stopped...
TH THUMP
TH THUMP
TAK
TH THUMP
TH THUMP
TH THUMP

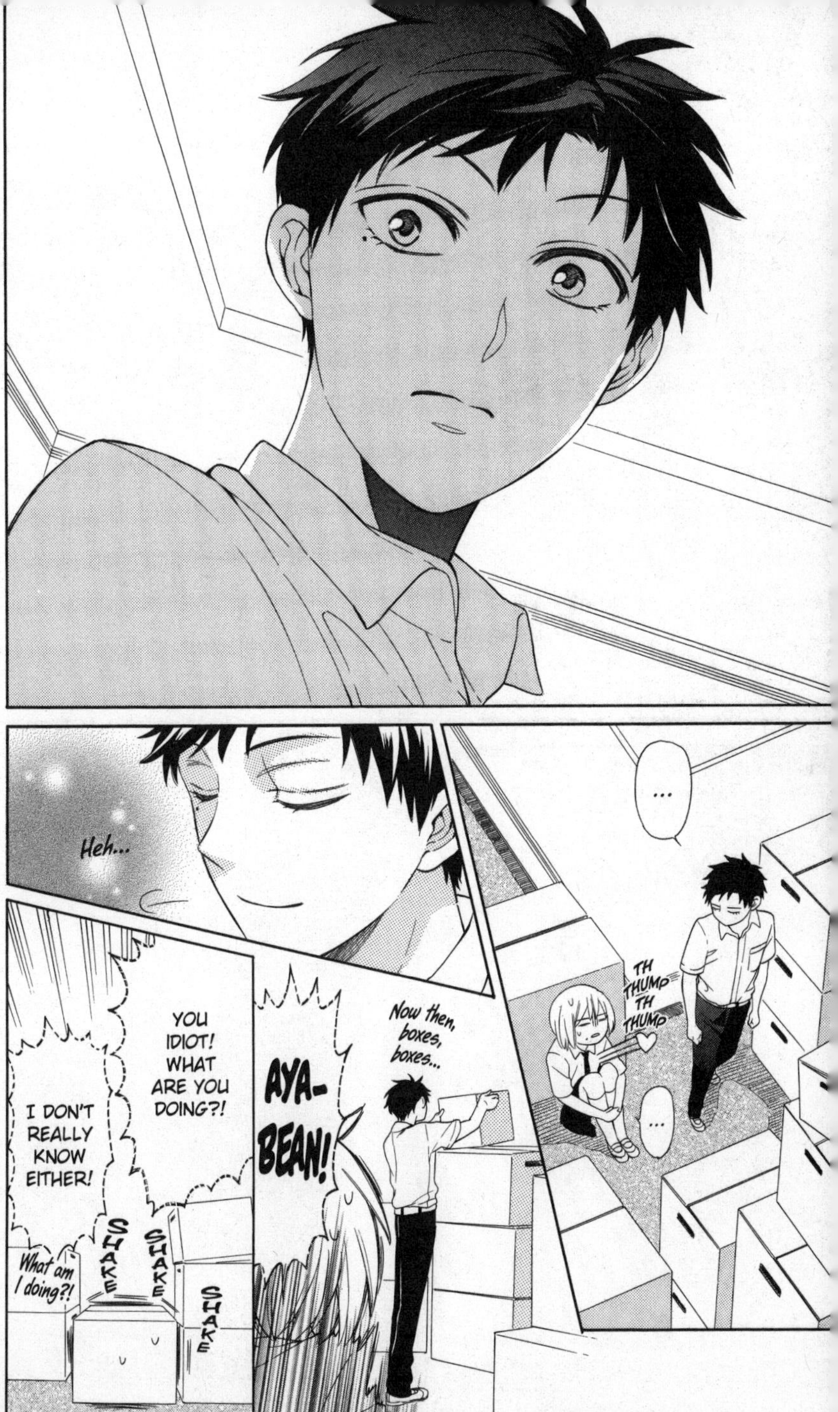
...
TH THUMP TH THUMP
...
Heh...
Now then, boxes, boxes...
AYA-BEAN!
YOU IDIOT! WHAT ARE YOU DOING?!
I DON'T REALLY KNOW EITHER!
SHAKE
SHAKE
SHAKE
What am I doing?!

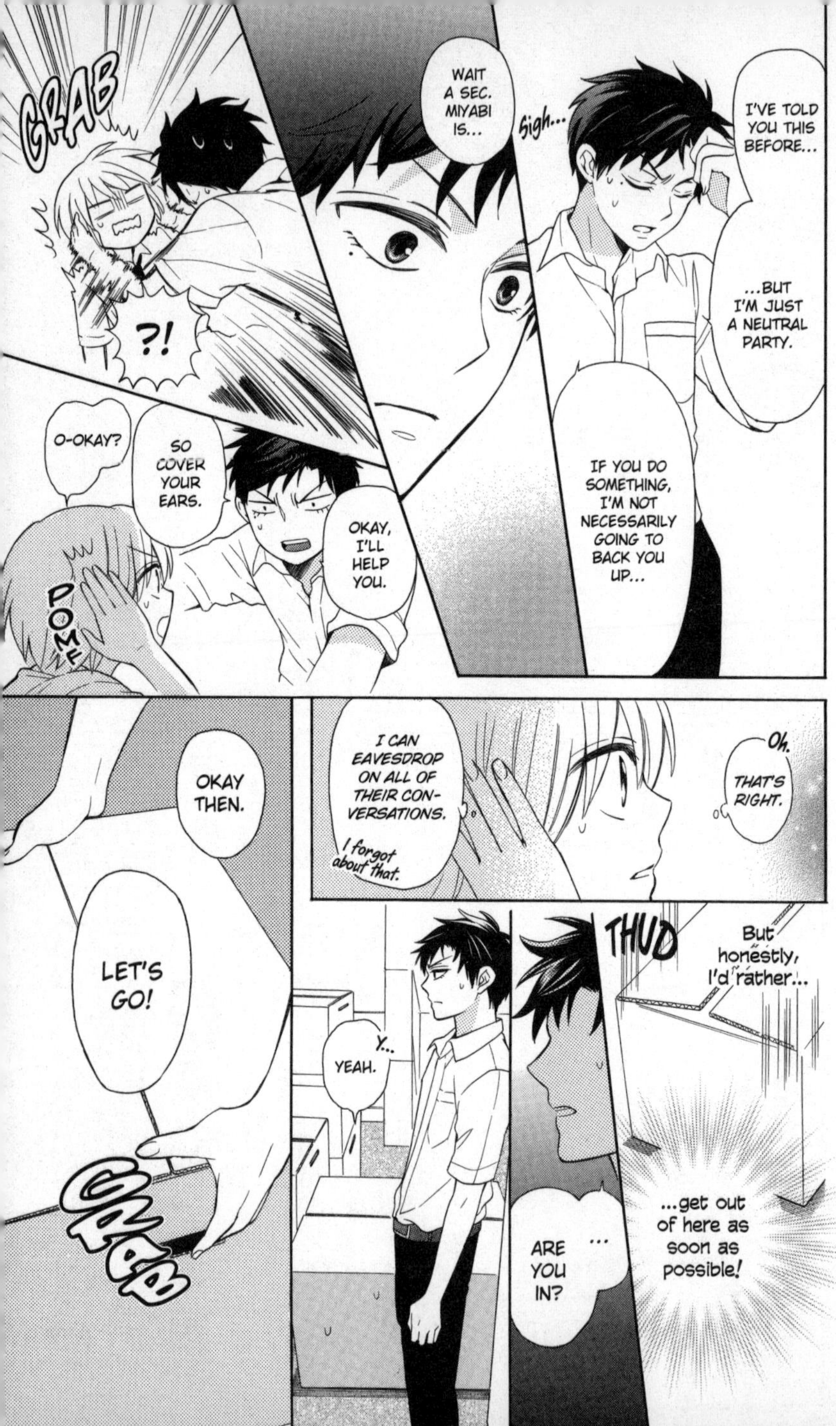
I'VE TOLD YOU THIS BEFORE...
Sigh...
...BUT I'M JUST A NEUTRAL PARTY.
IF YOU DO SOMETHING, I'M NOT NECESSARILY GOING TO BACK YOU UP...
WAIT A SEC. MIYABI IS...
GRAB
?!
OKAY, I'LL HELP YOU.
SO COVER YOUR EARS.
O-OKAY?
POMF
Oh. THAT'S RIGHT.
I CAN EAVESDROP ON ALL OF THEIR CON-VERSATIONS.
I forgot about that.
THUD
But honestly, I'd rather...
...get out of here as soon as possible!
...
ARE YOU IN?
Y... YEAH.
OKAY THEN.
LET'S GO!

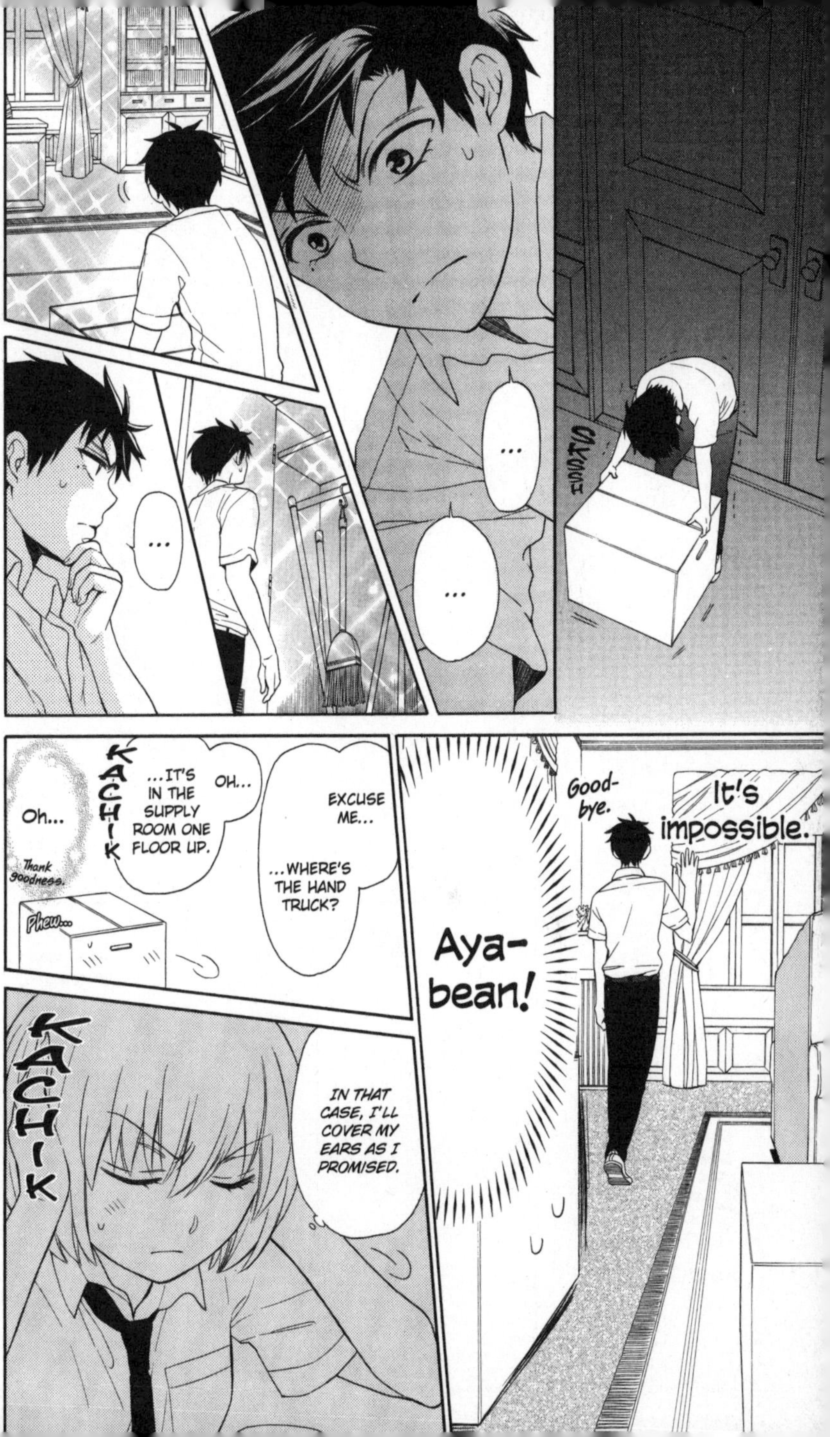
SKOOSH
...
...
...
It's impossible.
Good-bye.
Aya-bean!
EXCUSE ME...
...WHERE'S THE HAND TRUCK?
OH...
...IT'S IN THE SUPPLY ROOM ONE FLOOR UP.
KACHIK
Oh...
Thank goodness.
Phew...
KACHIK
IN THAT CASE, I'LL COVER MY EARS AS I PROMISED.

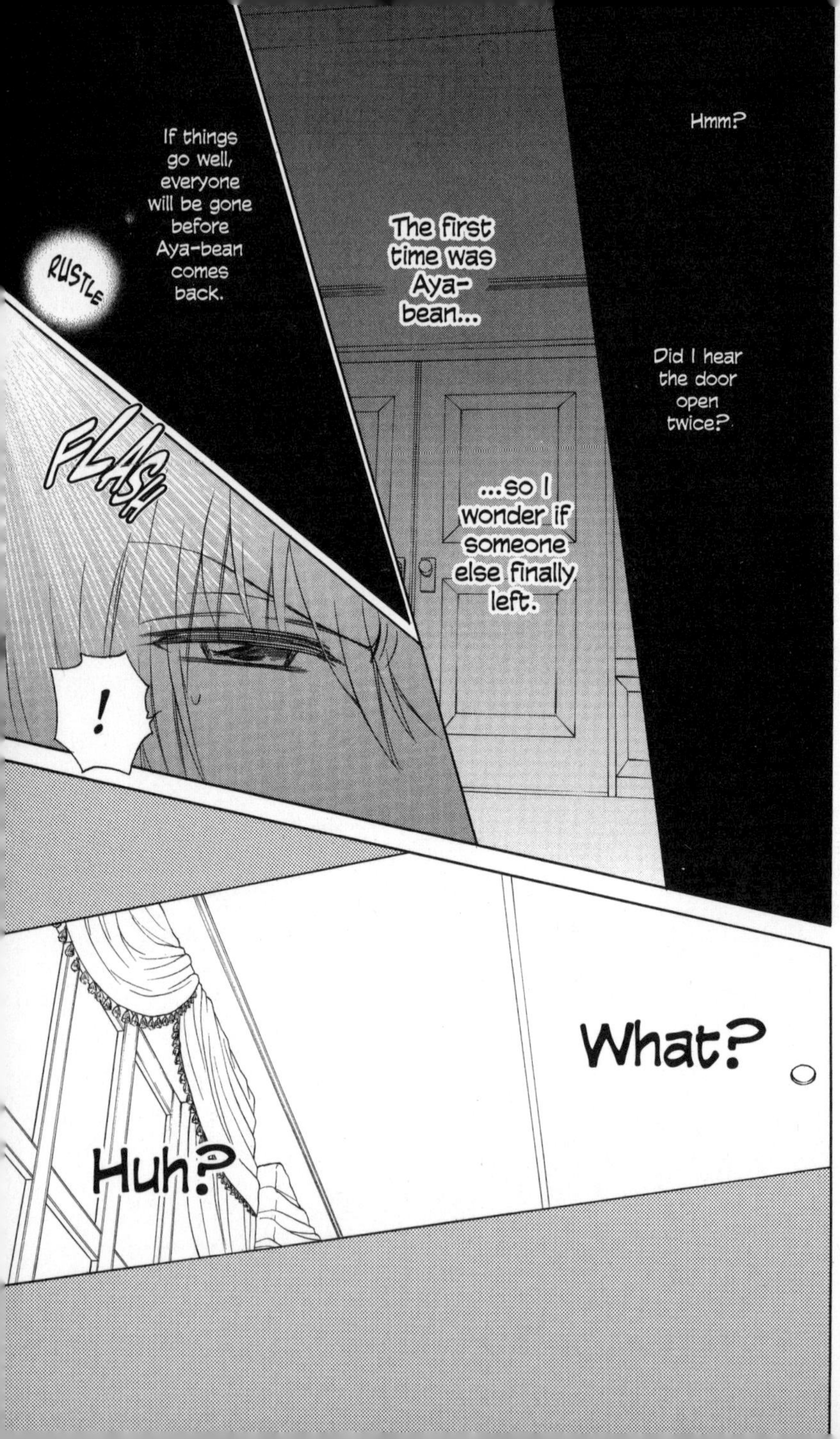
Hmm?
Did I hear the door open twice?
The first time was Aya-bean...
...so I wonder if someone else finally left.
If things go well, everyone will be gone before Aya-bean comes back.
RUSTLE
FLASH!!
!
What?
Huh?

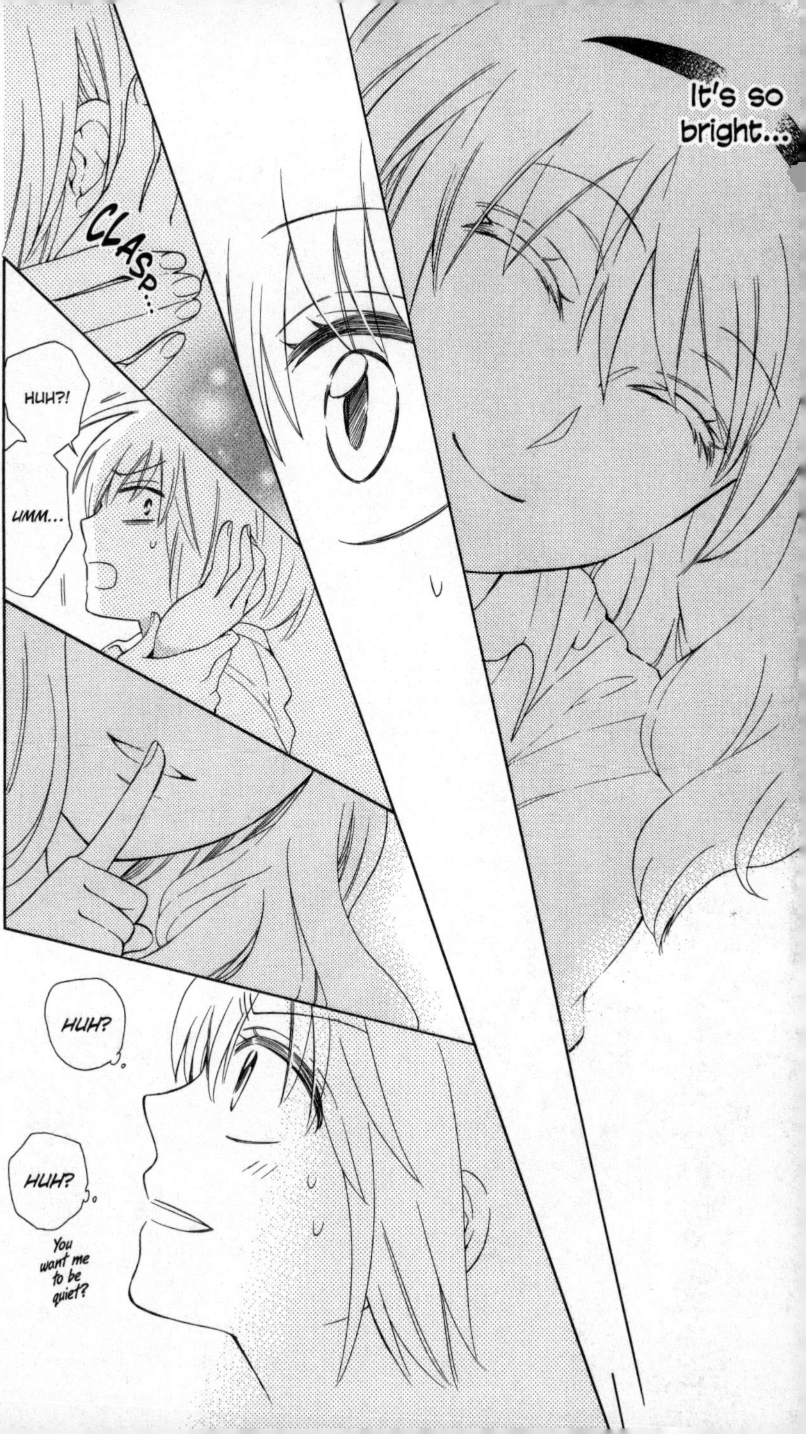
It's so bright...
CLASP...
HUH?!
UMM...
HUH?
HUH?
You want me to be quiet?

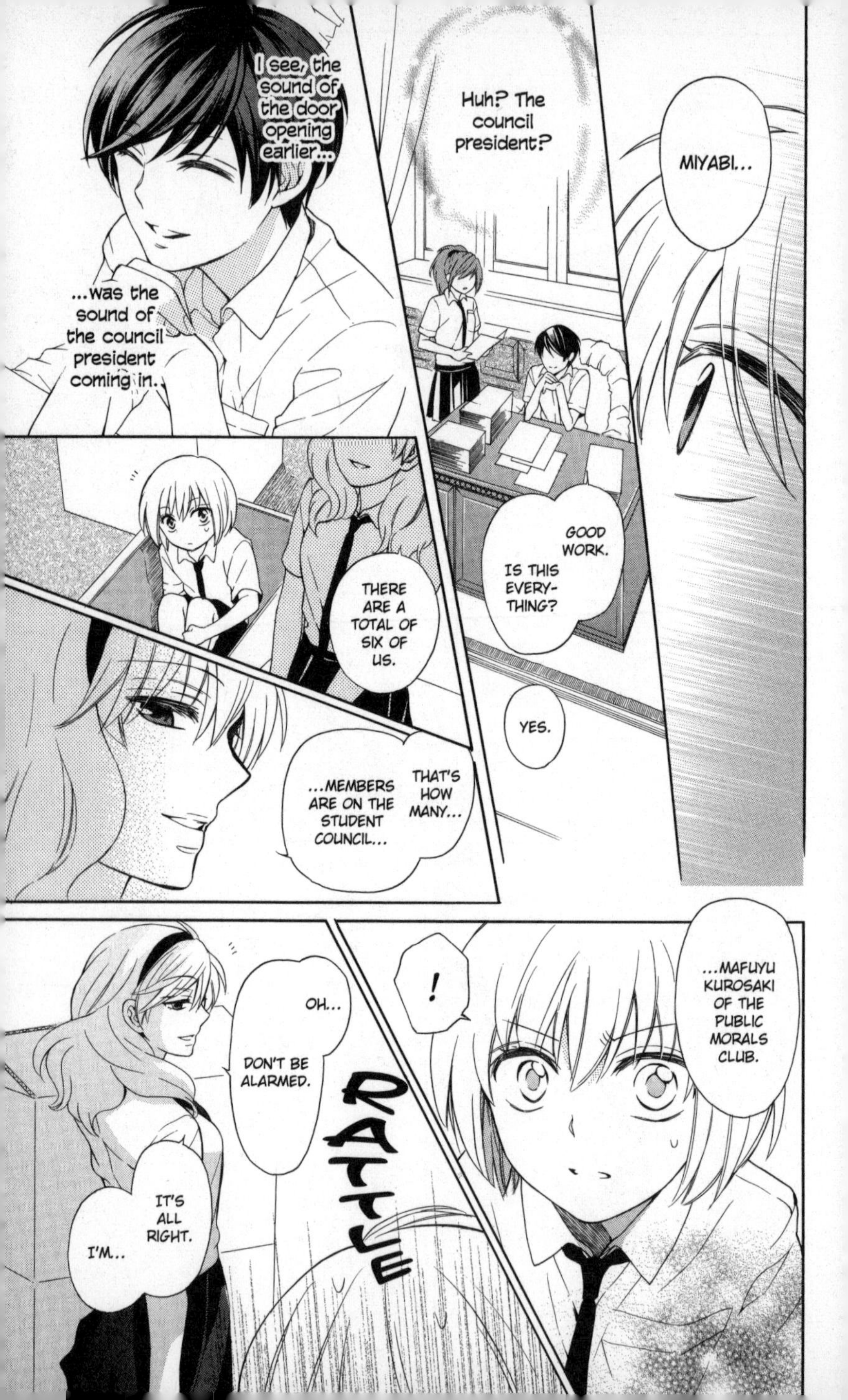
MIYABI...
Huh? The council president?
GOOD WORK. IS THIS EVERYTHING?
YES.
I see, the sound of the door opening earlier...
...was the sound of the council president coming in.
THERE ARE A TOTAL OF SIX OF US.
THAT'S HOW MANY...
...MEMBERS ARE ON THE STUDENT COUNCIL...
...MAFUYU KUROSAKI OF THE PUBLIC MORALS CLUB.
!
RATTLE
OH...
DON'T BE ALARMED.
IT'S ALL RIGHT.
I'M...

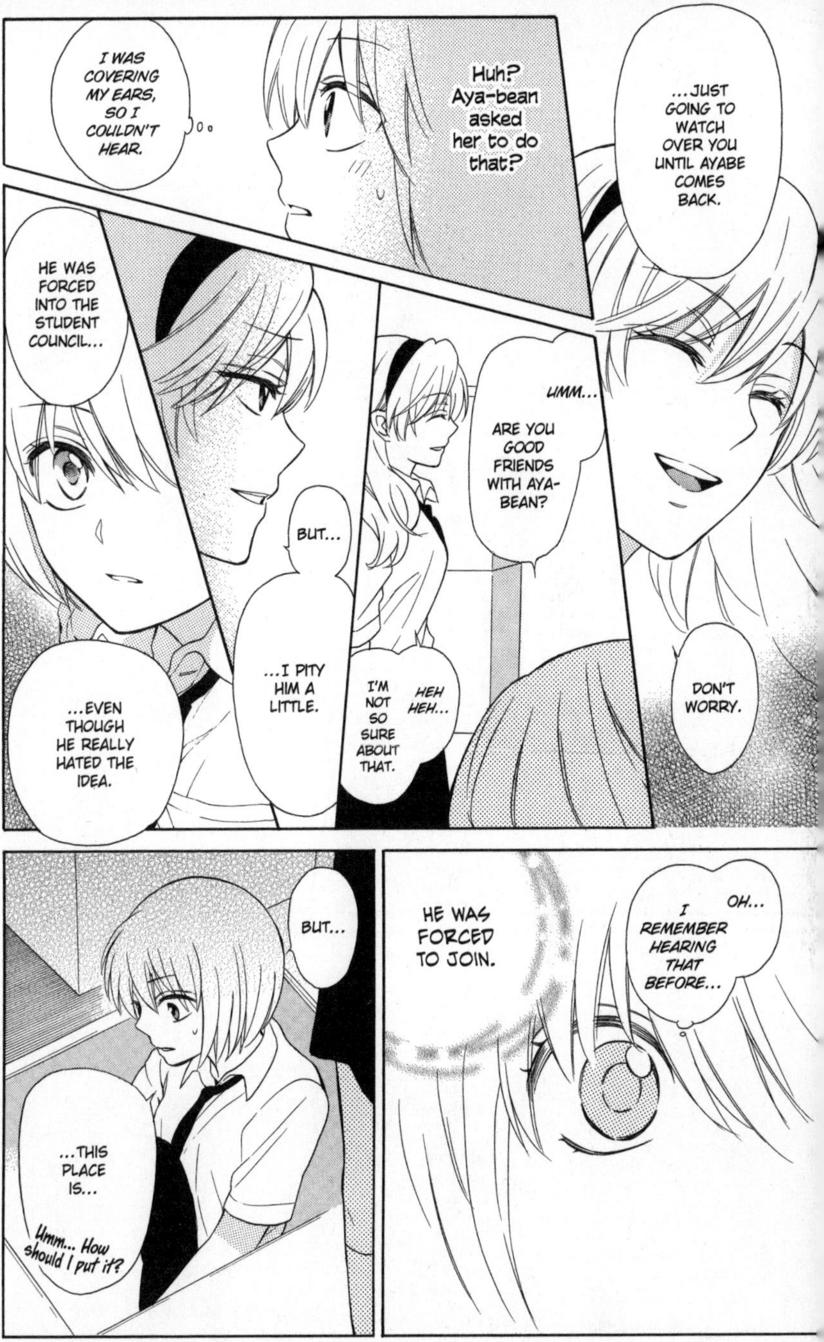
...JUST GOING TO WATCH OVER YOU UNTIL AYABE COMES BACK.
DON'T WORRY.
Huh? Aya-bean asked her to do that?
I WAS COVERING MY EARS, SO I COULDN'T HEAR.
UMM...
ARE YOU GOOD FRIENDS WITH AYA-BEAN?
HEH HEH...
I'M NOT SO SURE ABOUT THAT.
BUT...
...I PITY HIM A LITTLE.
HE WAS FORCED INTO THE STUDENT COUNCIL...
...EVEN THOUGH HE REALLY HATED THE IDEA.
OH...
I REMEMBER HEARING THAT BEFORE...
HE WAS FORCED TO JOIN.
BUT...
...THIS PLACE IS...
Umm... How should I put it?

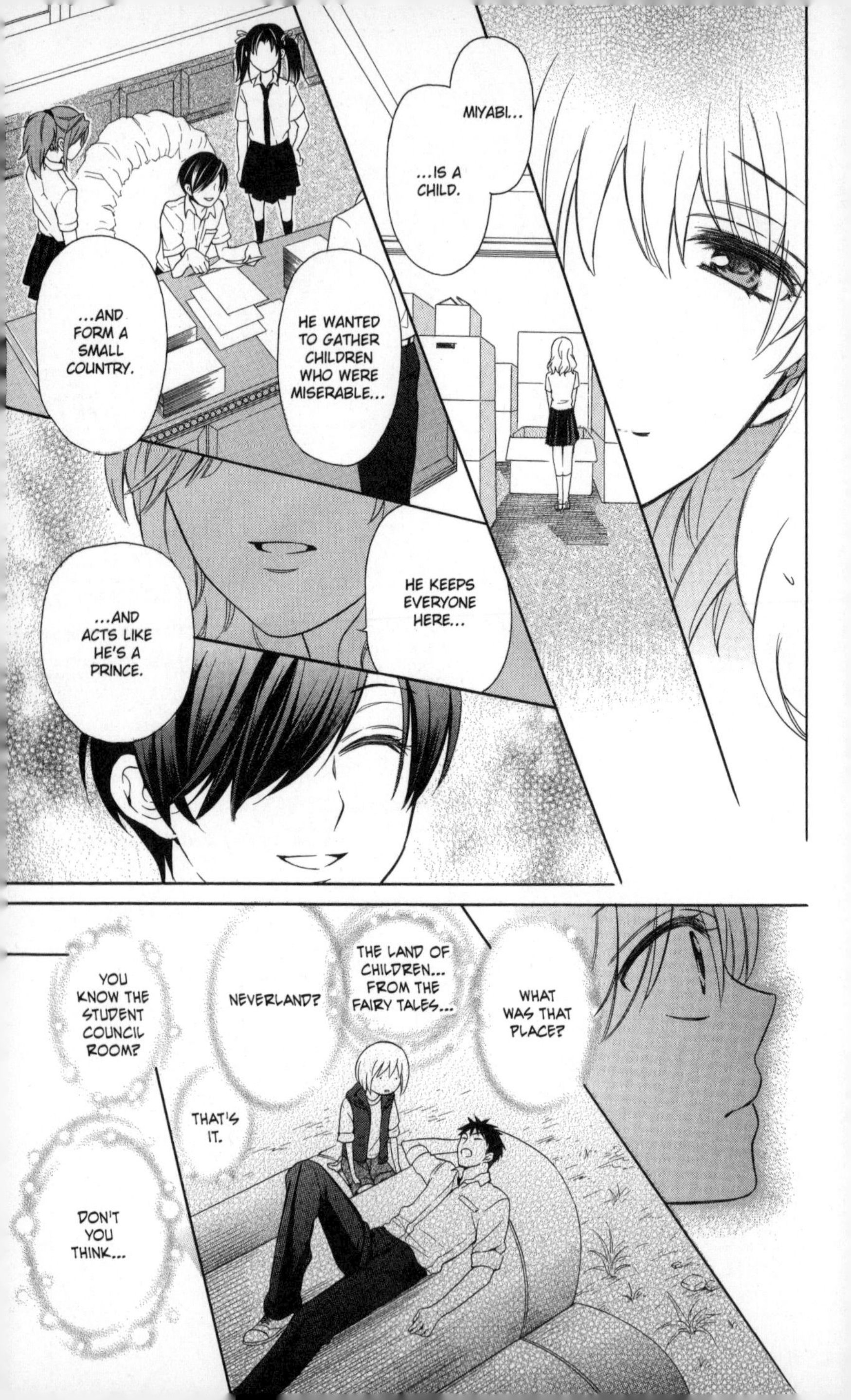
MIYABI...
...IS A CHILD.
HE WANTED TO GATHER CHILDREN WHO WERE MISERABLE...
...AND FORM A SMALL COUNTRY.
HE KEEPS EVERYONE HERE...
...AND ACTS LIKE HE'S A PRINCE.
WHAT WAS THAT PLACE?
THE LAND OF CHILDREN... FROM THE FAIRY TALES...
NEVERLAND?
YOU KNOW THE STUDENT COUNCIL ROOM?
THAT'S IT.
DON'T YOU THINK...

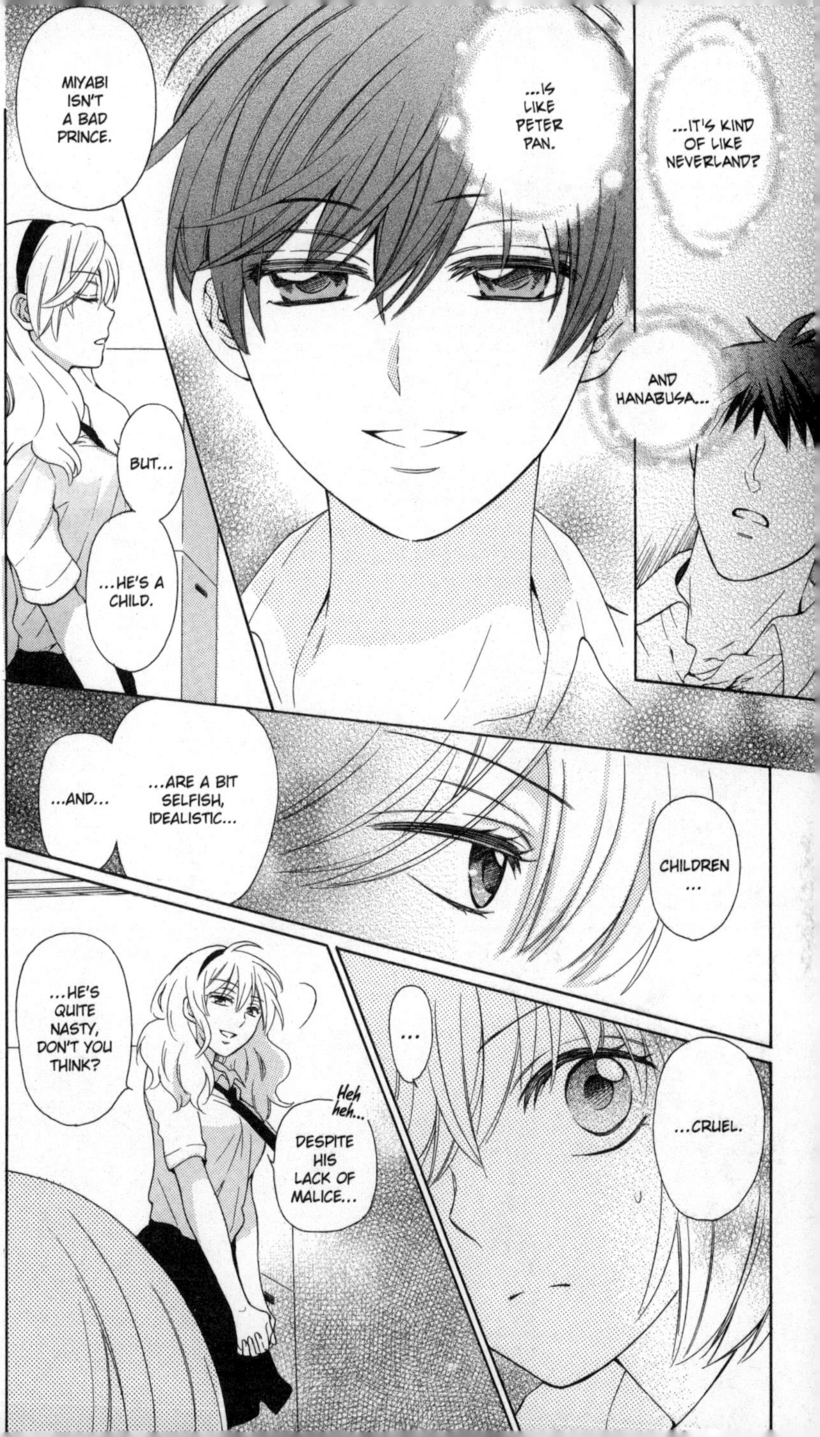
...IT'S KIND OF LIKE NEVERLAND?
AND HANABUSA...
...IS LIKE PETER PAN.
MIYABI ISN'T A BAD PRINCE.
BUT...
...HE'S A CHILD.
CHILDREN ...
...ARE A BIT SELFISH, IDEALISTIC...
...AND...
...
...CRUEL.
Heh heh...
DESPITE HIS LACK OF MALICE...
...HE'S QUITE NASTY, DON'T YOU THINK?

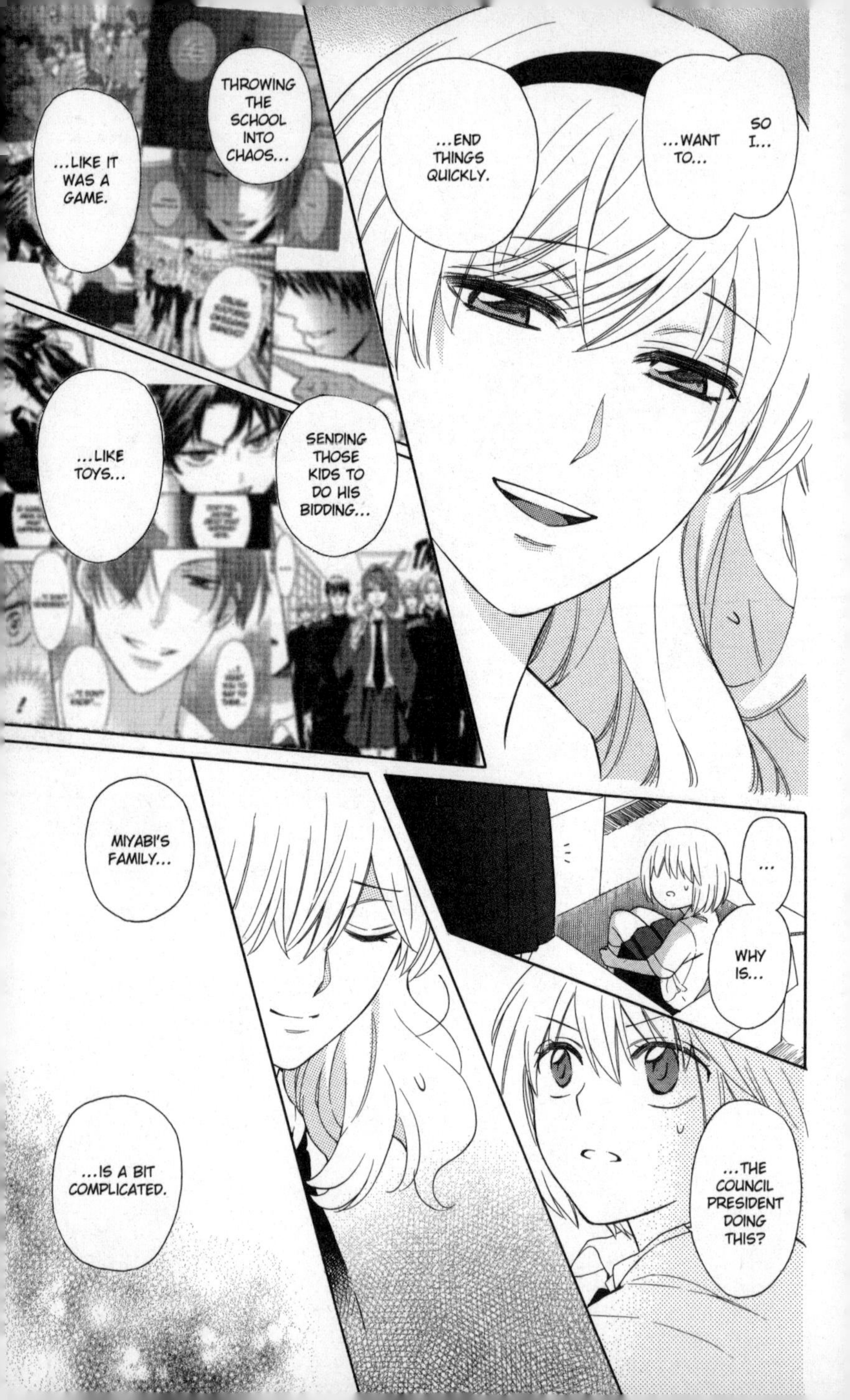
SO I...
...WANT TO...
...END THINGS QUICKLY.
THROWING THE SCHOOL INTO CHAOS...
...LIKE IT WAS A GAME.
SENDING THOSE KIDS TO DO HIS BIDDING...
...LIKE TOYS...
...
WHY IS...
...THE COUNCIL PRESIDENT DOING THIS?
MIYABI'S FAMILY...
...IS A BIT COMPLICATED.

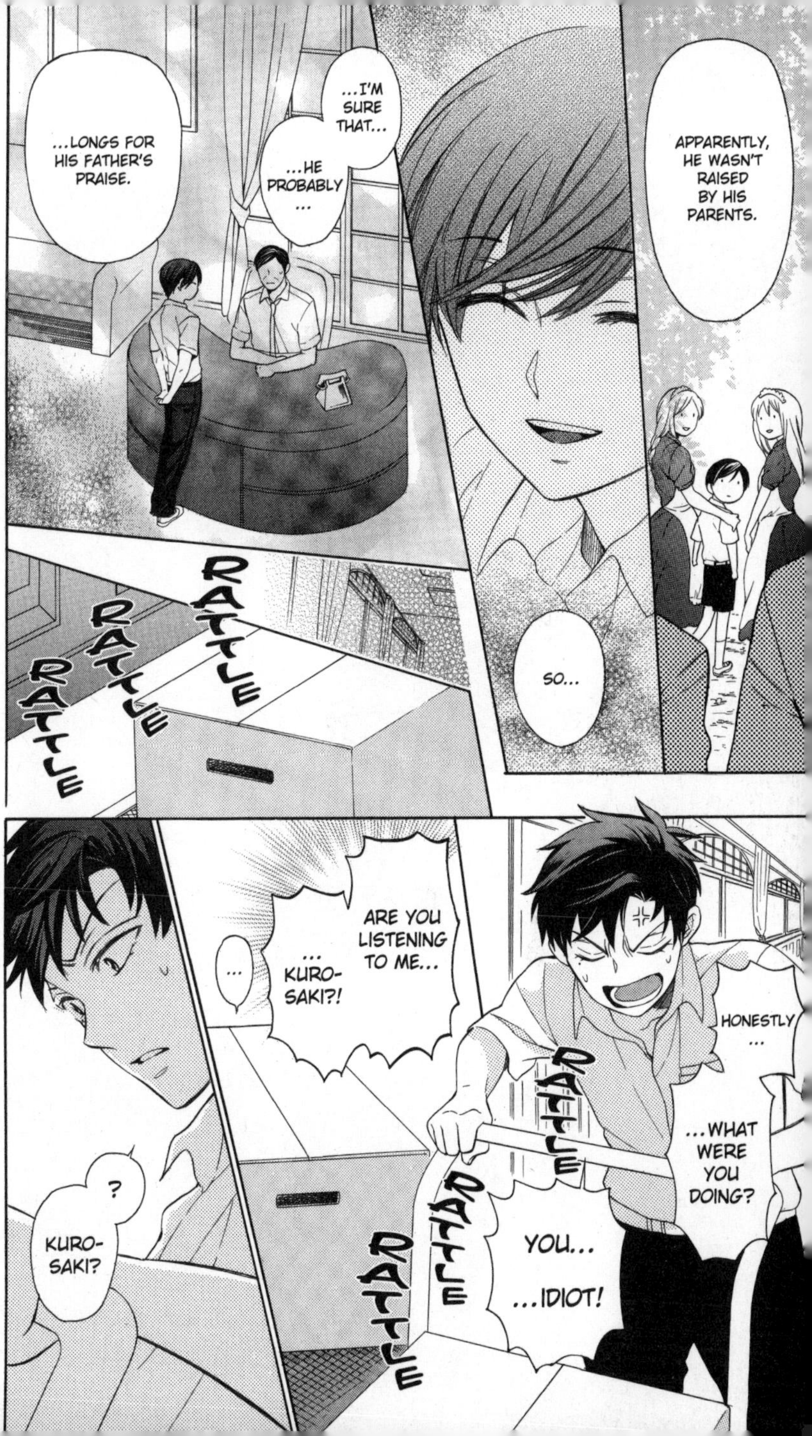
APPARENTLY, HE WASN'T RAISED BY HIS PARENTS.
SO...
...I'M SURE THAT...
...HE PROBABLY...
...LONGS FOR HIS FATHER'S PRAISE.
RATTLE
RATTLE
RATTLE
HONESTLY...
...WHAT WERE YOU DOING?
RATTLE
RATTLE
RATTLE
YOU...
...IDIOT!
ARE YOU LISTENING TO ME...
...KURO-SAKI?!
...
?
KURO-SAKI?

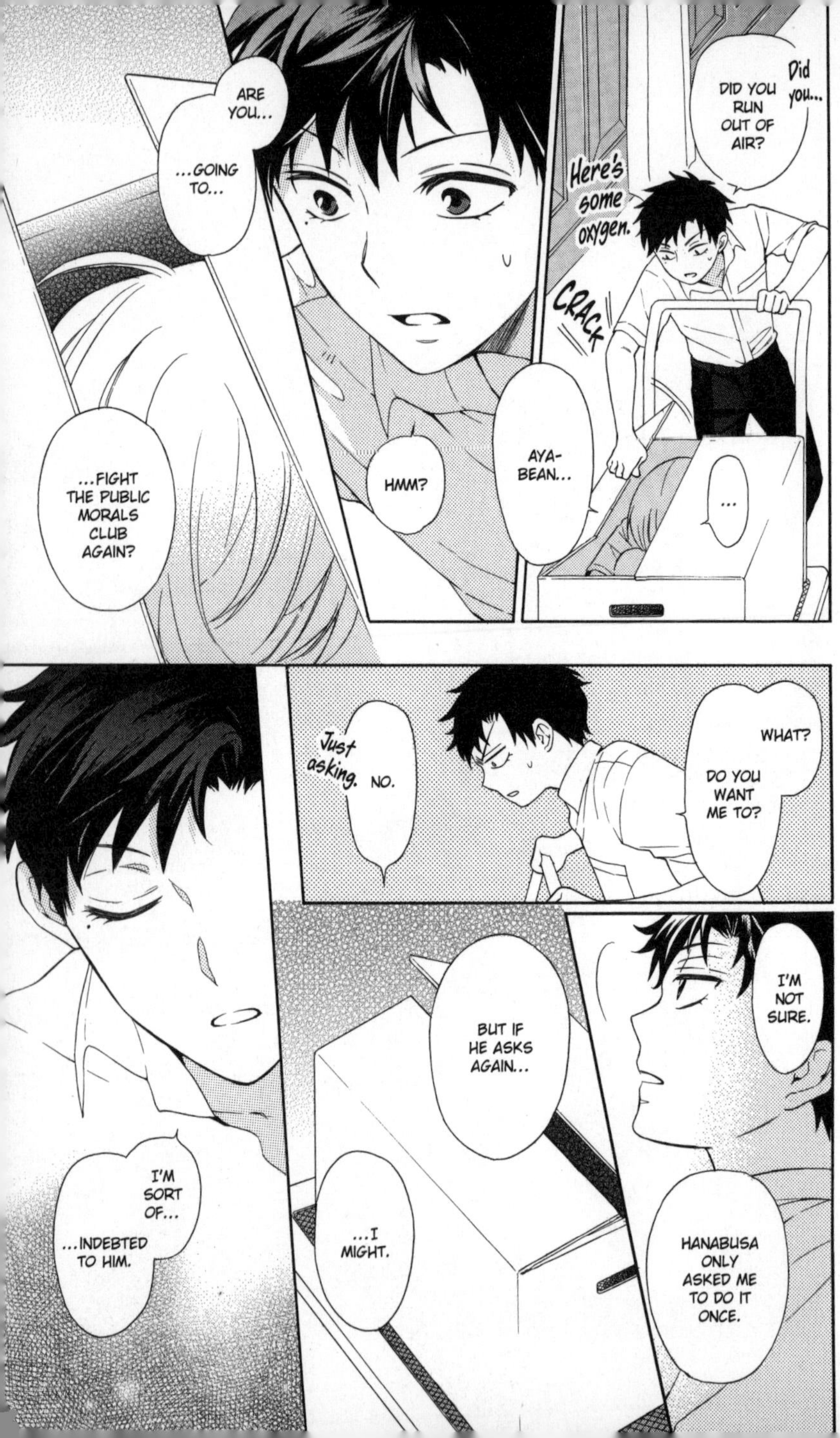
Did you...
DID YOU RUN OUT OF AIR?
Here's some oxygen.
CRACK
...
AYA-BEAN...
HMM?
ARE YOU...
...GOING TO...
...FIGHT THE PUBLIC MORALS CLUB AGAIN?
WHAT?
DO YOU WANT ME TO?
NO.
Just asking.
I'M NOT SURE.
HANABUSA ONLY ASKED ME TO DO IT ONCE.
BUT IF HE ASKS AGAIN...
...I MIGHT.
I'M SORT OF...
...INDEBTED TO HIM.

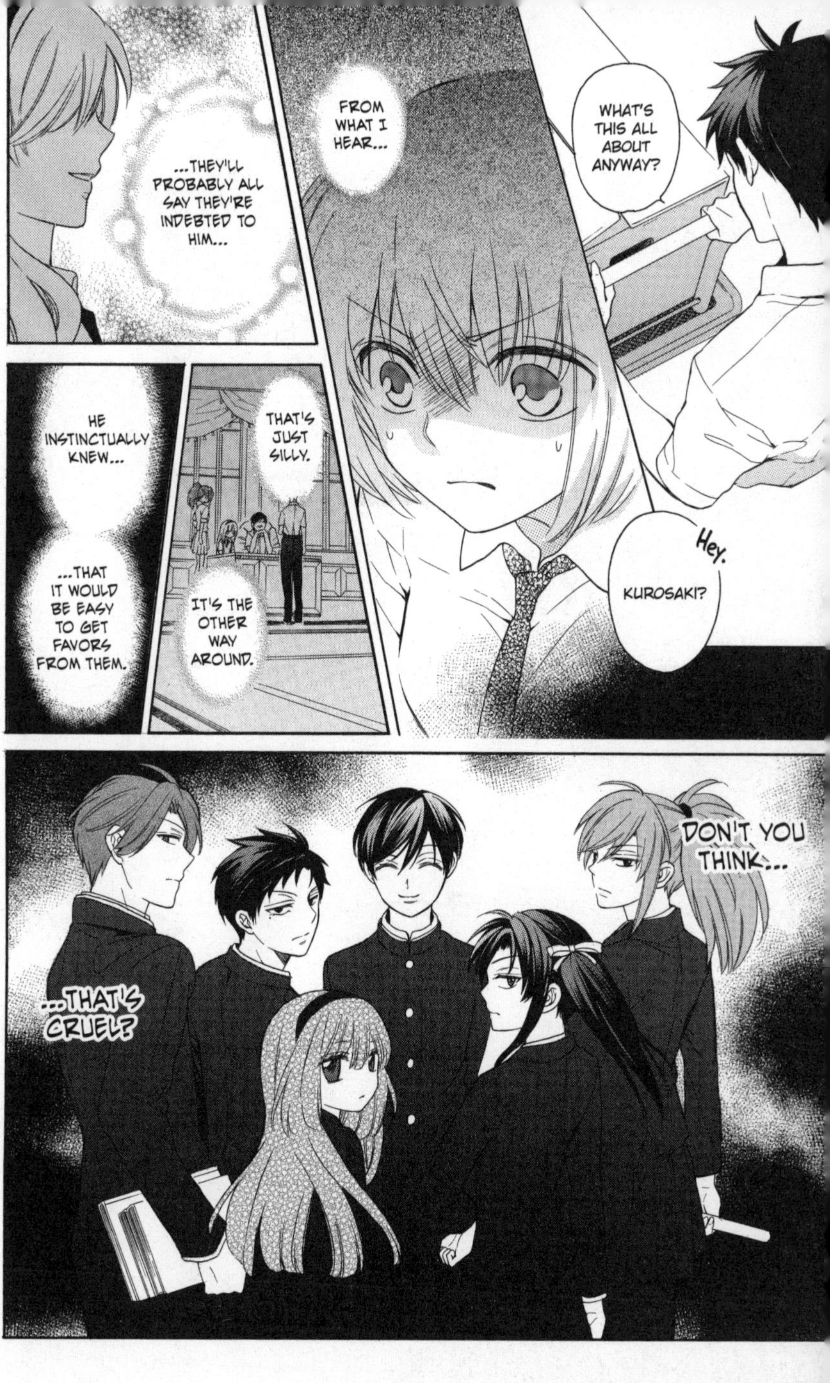
WHAT'S THIS ALL ABOUT ANYWAY?
FROM WHAT I HEAR...
Hey.
KUROSAKI?
...THEY'LL PROBABLY ALL SAY THEY'RE INDEBTED TO HIM...
THAT'S JUST SILLY.
IT'S THE OTHER WAY AROUND.
HE INSTINCTUALLY KNEW...
...THAT IT WOULD BE EASY TO GET FAVORS FROM THEM.
DON'T YOU THINK...
...THAT'S CRUEL?

Chapter 90

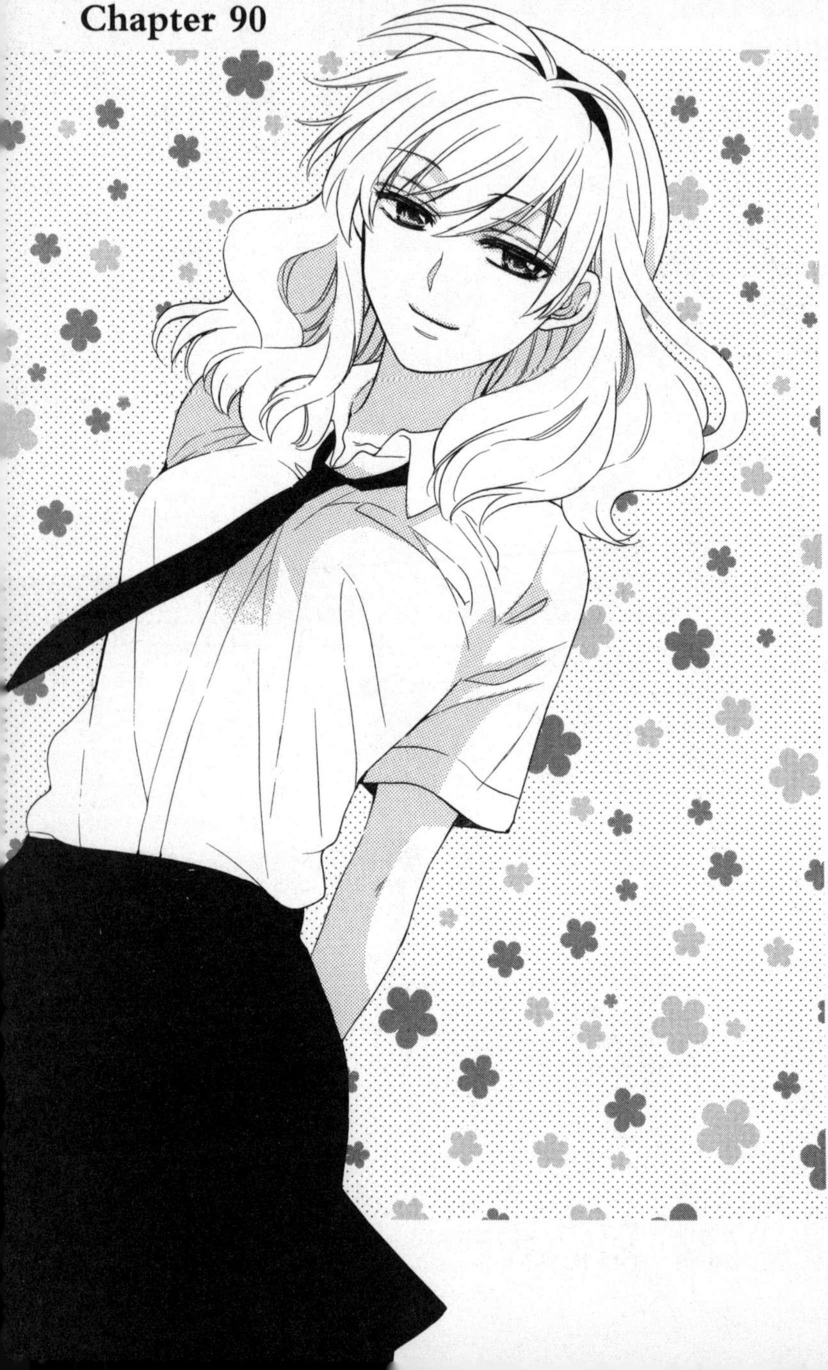

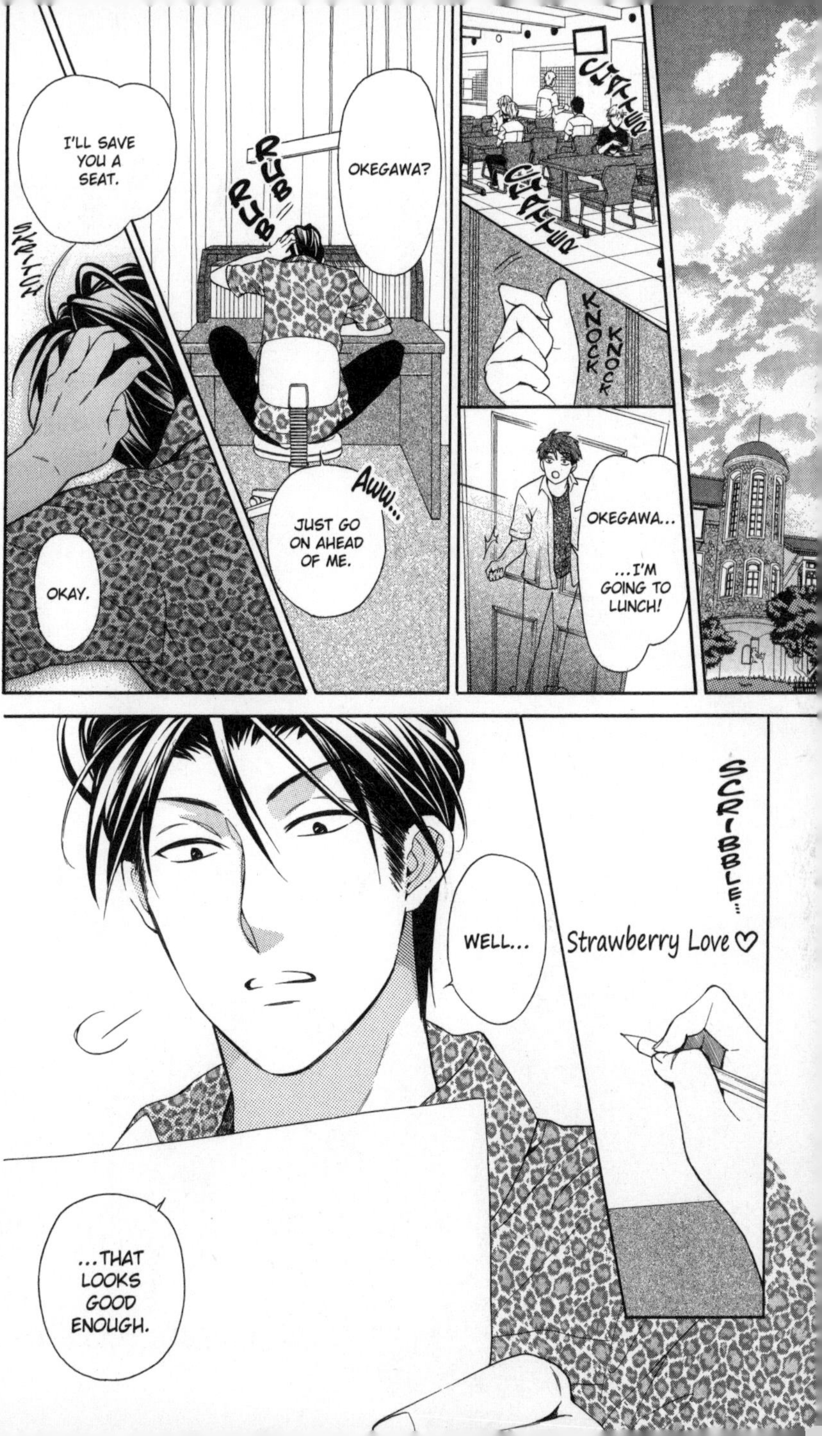
CLATTER
CLATTER
KNOCK KNOCK
OKEGAWA...
...I'M GOING TO LUNCH!
OKEGAWA?
RUB RUB
AWW...
JUST GO ON AHEAD OF ME.
I'LL SAVE YOU A SEAT.
SKRITCH
OKAY.
SCRIBBLE...
Strawberry Love ♡
WELL...
...THAT LOOKS GOOD ENOUGH.

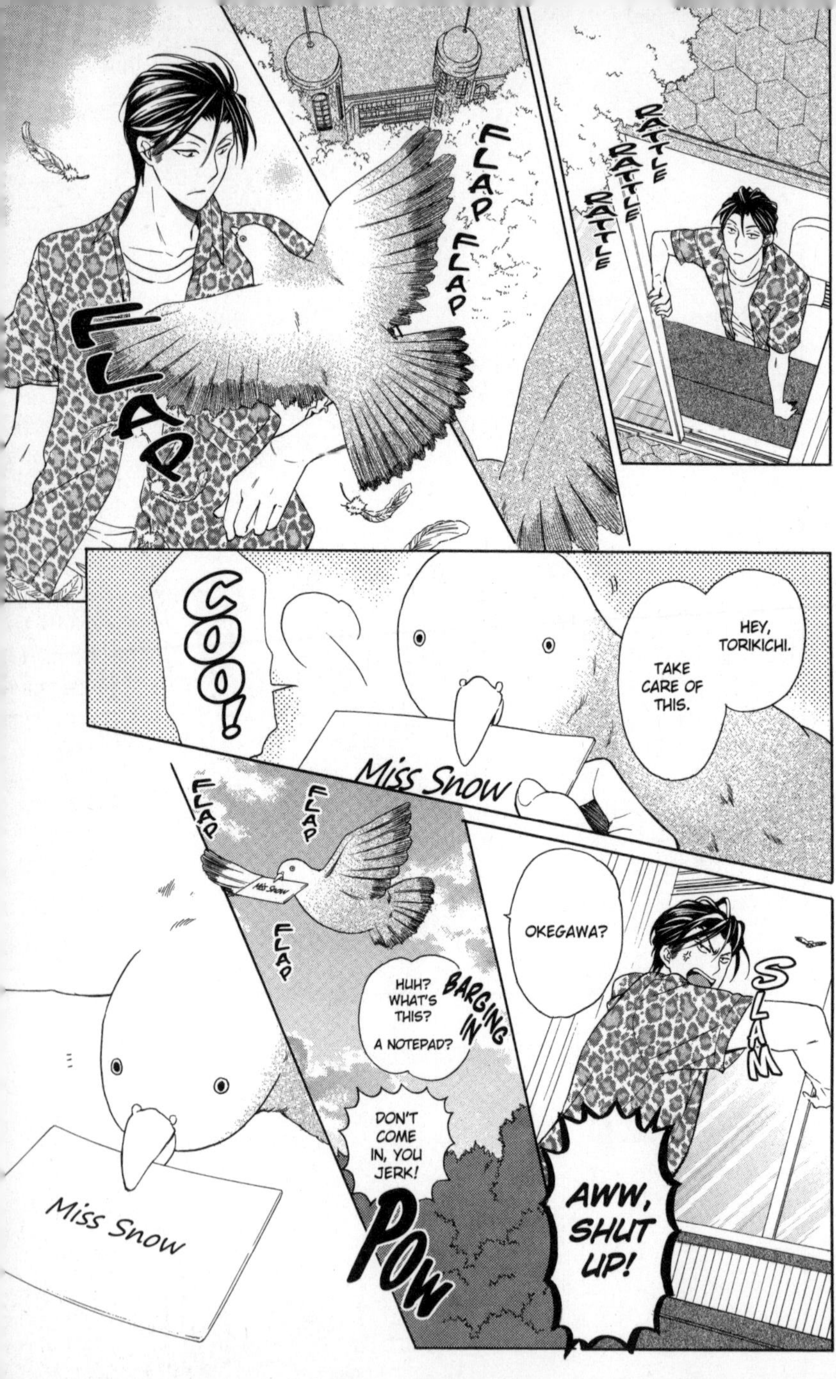
RATTLE
RATTLE
RATTLE
FLAP FLAP
FLAP
HEY, TORIKICHI.
TAKE CARE OF THIS.
COO!
Miss Snow
OKEGAWA?
SLAM
HUH? WHAT'S THIS?
A NOTEPAD?
BARGING IN
DON'T COME IN, YOU JERK!
AWW, SHUT UP!
POW
FLAP
FLAP
FLAP
Miss Snow
Miss Snow

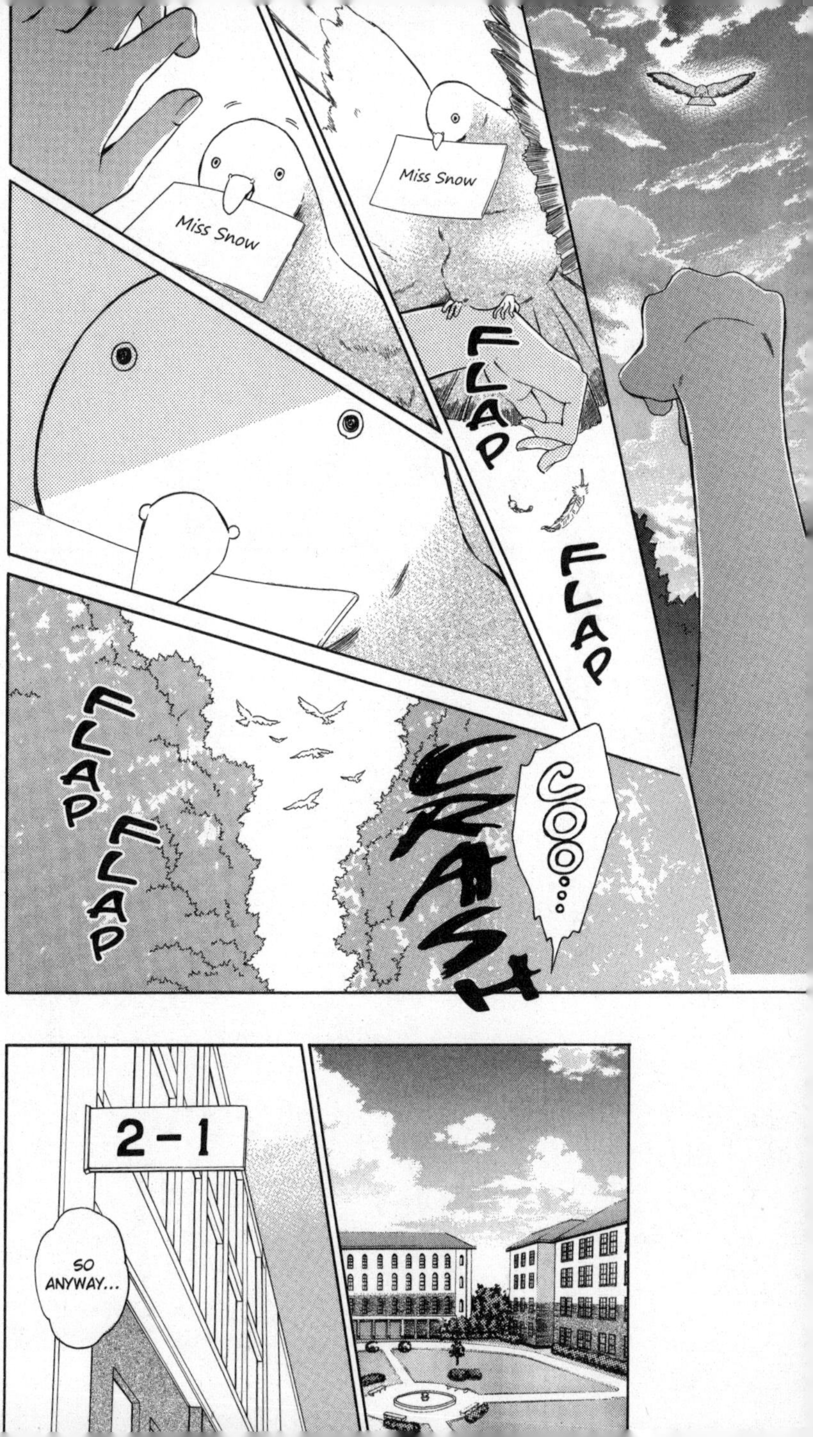
Miss Snow
FLAP
FLAP
Miss Snow
CRASH
COO...
FLAP
FLAP
FLAP
FLAP
2-1
SO ANYWAY...

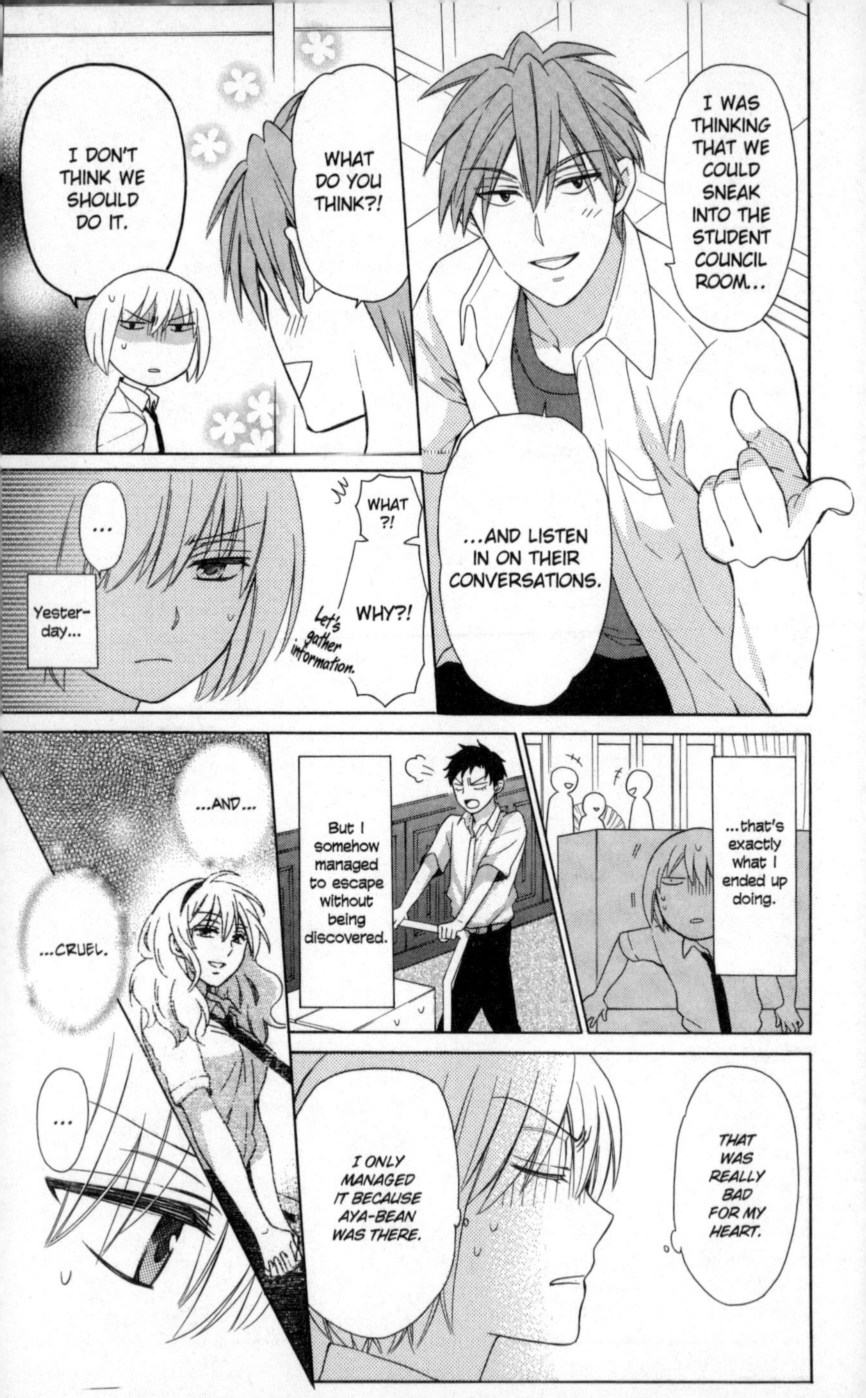
I WAS THINKING THAT WE COULD SNEAK INTO THE STUDENT COUNCIL ROOM...
WHAT DO YOU THINK?!
I DON'T THINK WE SHOULD DO IT.
...AND LISTEN IN ON THEIR CONVERSATIONS.
WHAT?!
WHY?!
Let's gather information.
...
Yester-day...
...that's exactly what I ended up doing.
But I somehow managed to escape without being discovered.
THAT WAS REALLY BAD FOR MY HEART.
I ONLY MANAGED IT BECAUSE AYA-BEAN WAS THERE.
...AND...
...CRUEL.
...

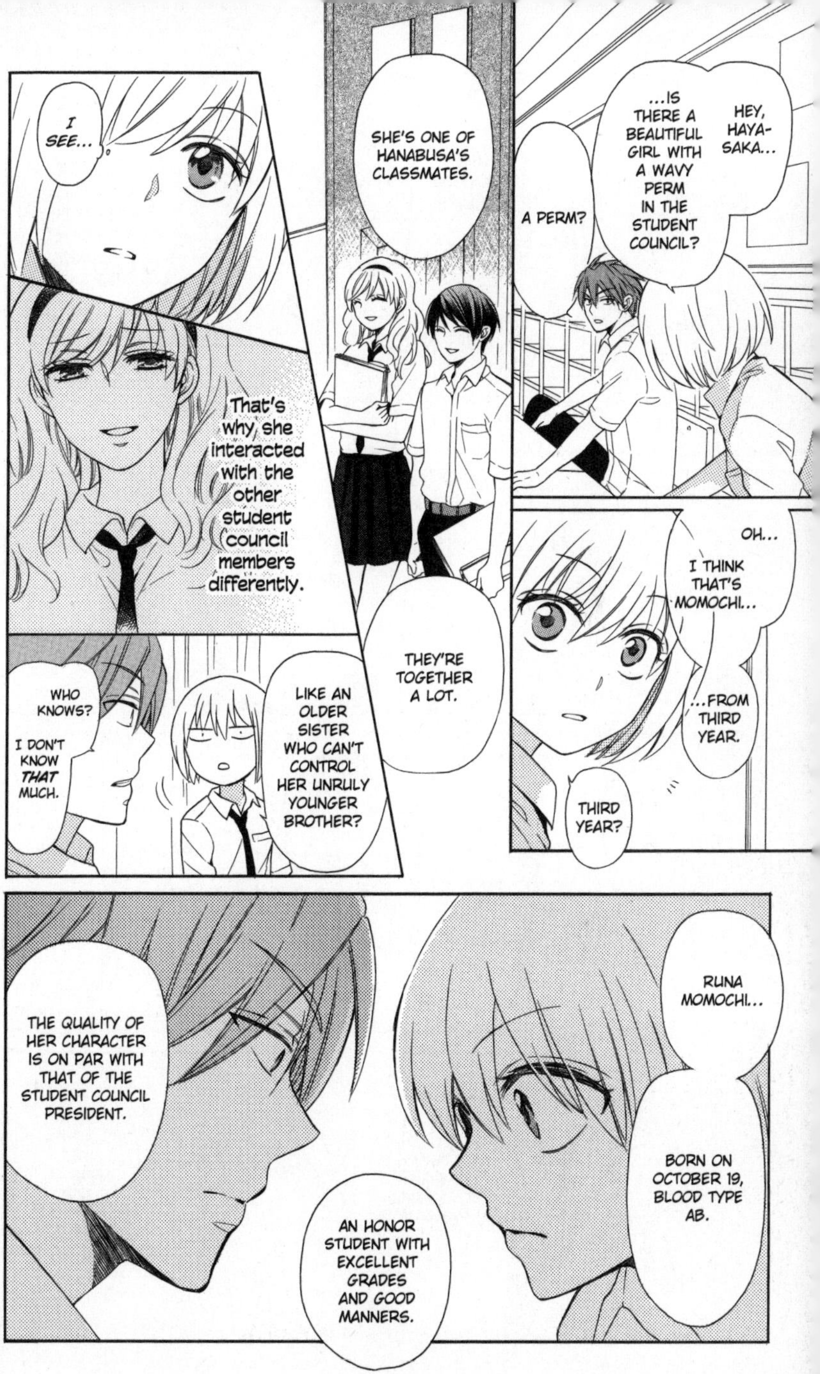
HEY, HAYA-SAKA...
...IS THERE A BEAUTIFUL GIRL WITH A WAVY PERM IN THE STUDENT COUNCIL?
A PERM?
OH...
I THINK THAT'S MOMOCHI...
...FROM THIRD YEAR.
THIRD YEAR?
SHE'S ONE OF HANABUSA'S CLASSMATES.
THEY'RE TOGETHER A LOT.
I SEE...
That's why she interacted with the other student council members differently.
LIKE AN OLDER SISTER WHO CAN'T CONTROL HER UNRULY YOUNGER BROTHER?
WHO KNOWS?
I DON'T KNOW *THAT* MUCH.
RUNA MOMOCHI...
BORN ON OCTOBER 19, BLOOD TYPE AB.
AN HONOR STUDENT WITH EXCELLENT GRADES AND GOOD MANNERS.
THE QUALITY OF HER CHARACTER IS ON PAR WITH THAT OF THE STUDENT COUNCIL PRESIDENT.

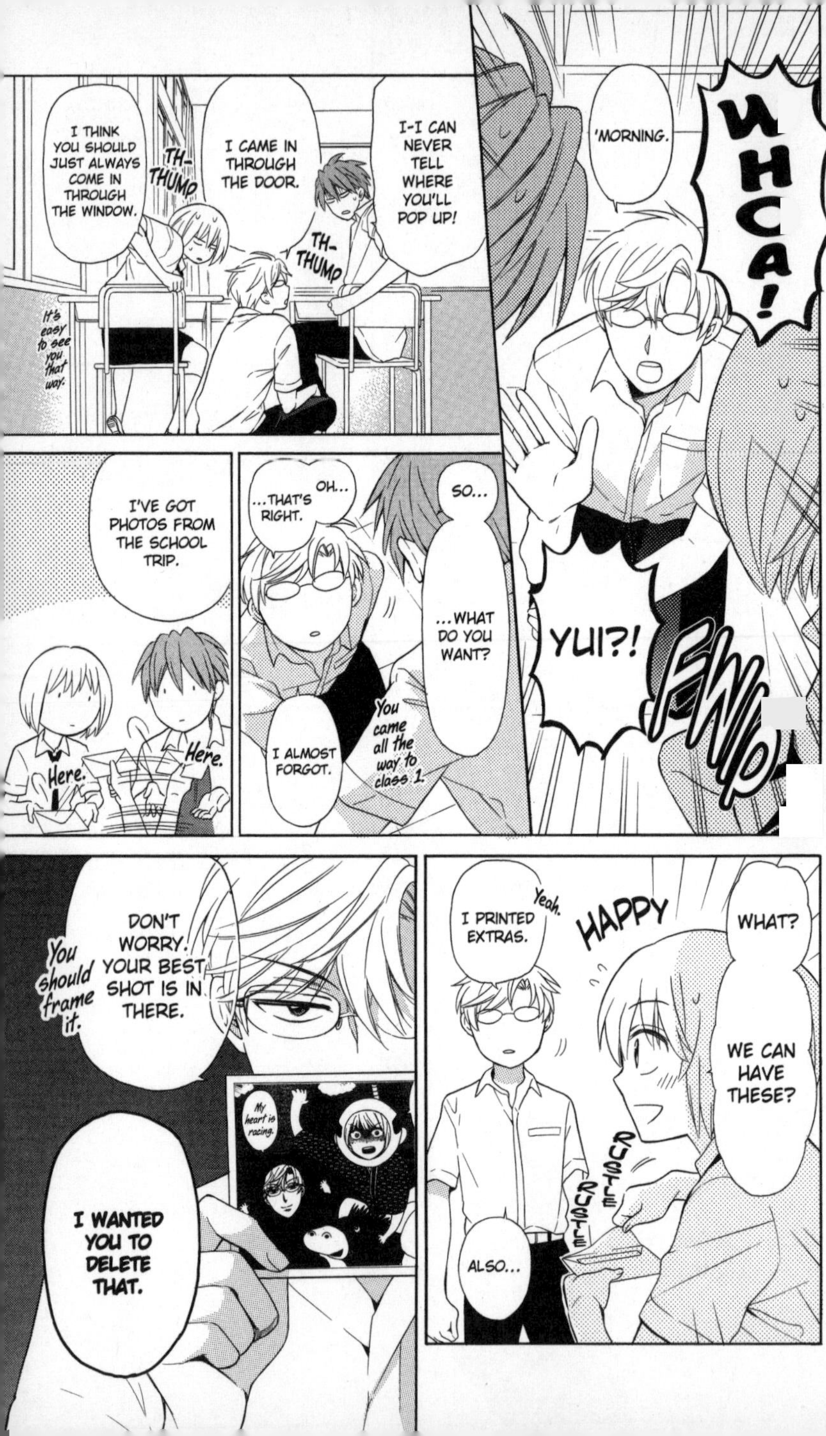
WHCA!
'MORNING.
YUI?!
FWIP
I-I CAN NEVER TELL WHERE YOU'LL POP UP!
TH-THUMP
I CAME IN THROUGH THE DOOR.
TH-THUMP
I THINK YOU SHOULD JUST ALWAYS COME IN THROUGH THE WINDOW.
It's easy to see you that way.
SO...
...WHAT DO YOU WANT?
OH... ...THAT'S RIGHT.
You came all the way to class 1.
I ALMOST FORGOT.
I'VE GOT PHOTOS FROM THE SCHOOL TRIP.
Here.
Here.
WHAT?
WE CAN HAVE THESE?
HAPPY
Yeah.
I PRINTED EXTRAS.
RUSTLE
RUSTLE
ALSO...
DON'T WORRY. YOUR BEST SHOT IS IN THERE.
You should frame it.
My heart is racing.
I WANTED YOU TO DELETE THAT.

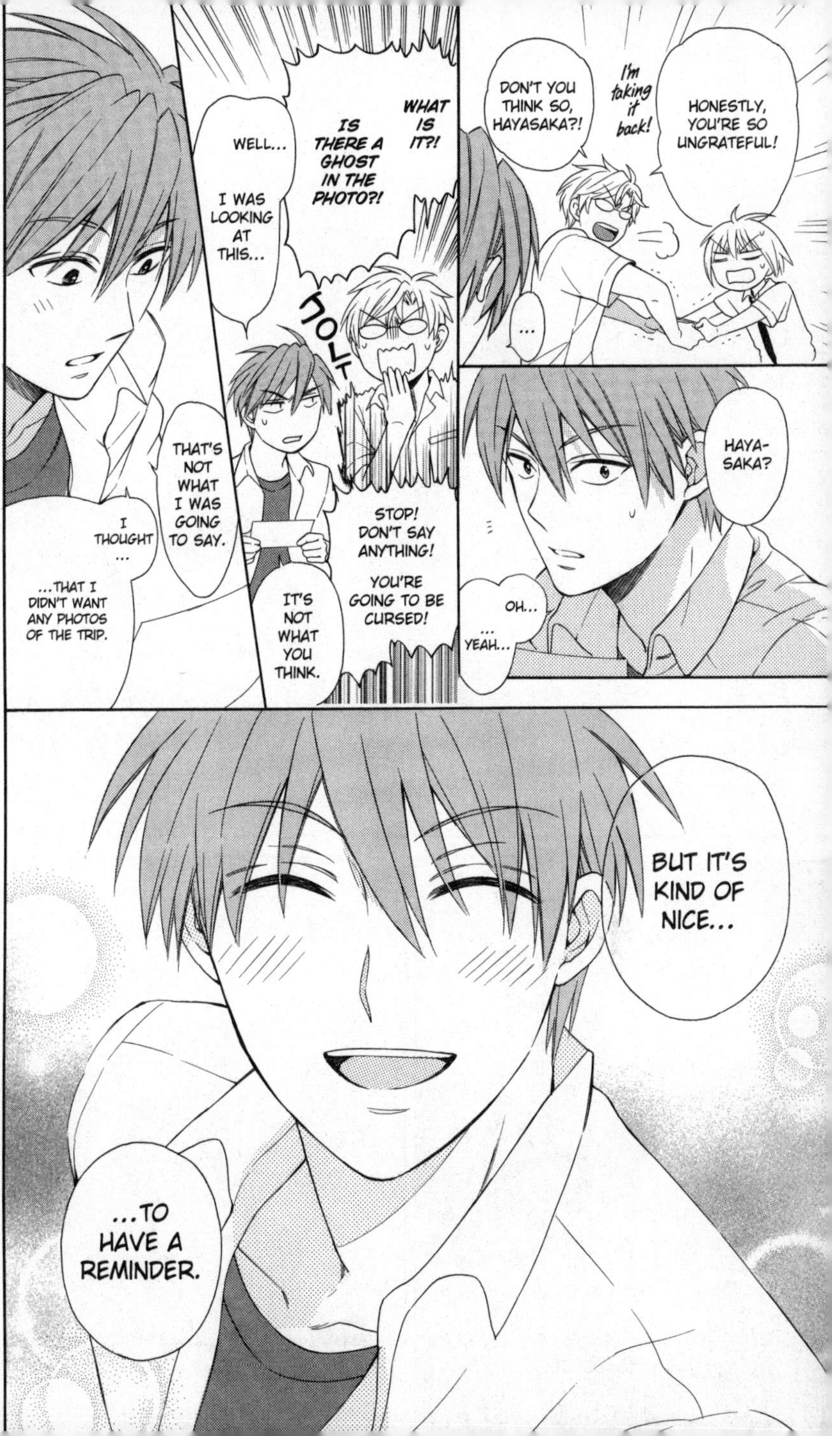
HONESTLY, YOU'RE SO UNGRATEFUL!
I'm taking it back!
DON'T YOU THINK SO, HAYASAKA?!
...
HAYA-SAKA?
OH...
...YEAH...
WHAT IS IT?!
IS THERE A GHOST IN THE PHOTO?!
WELL...
I WAS LOOKING AT THIS...
JOLT
STOP! DON'T SAY ANYTHING!
YOU'RE GOING TO BE CURSED!
IT'S NOT WHAT YOU THINK.
THAT'S NOT WHAT I WAS GOING TO SAY.
I THOUGHT...
...THAT I DIDN'T WANT ANY PHOTOS OF THE TRIP.
BUT IT'S KIND OF NICE...
...TO HAVE A REMINDER.

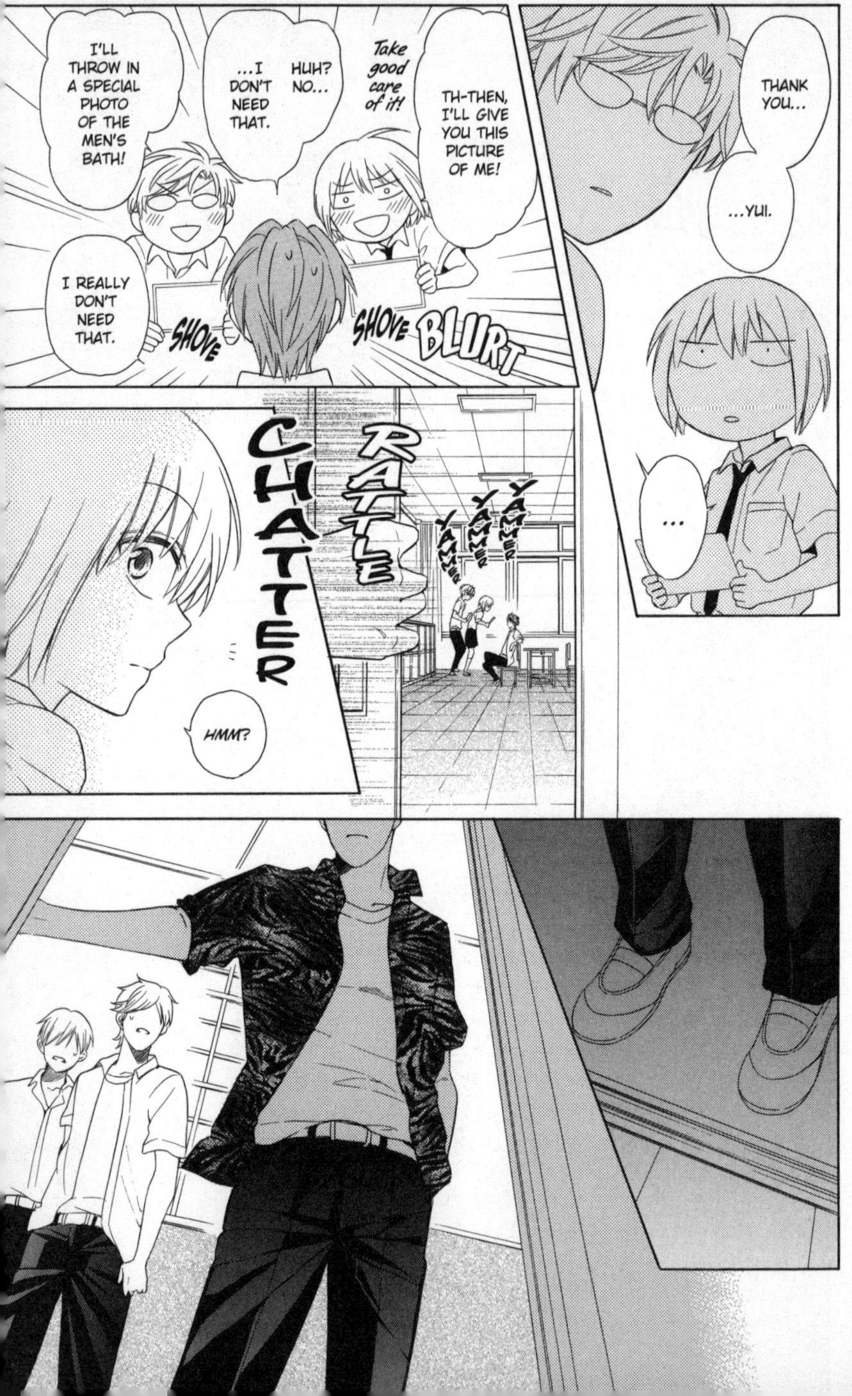
THANK YOU...
...YUI.
...
TH-THEN, I'LL GIVE YOU THIS PICTURE OF ME!
Take good care of it!
HUH? NO...
...I DON'T NEED THAT.
I'LL THROW IN A SPECIAL PHOTO OF THE MEN'S BATH!
BLURT
SHOVE
SHOVE
I REALLY DON'T NEED THAT.
YAMMER
YAMMER
YAMMER
RATTLE
CHATTER
HMM?

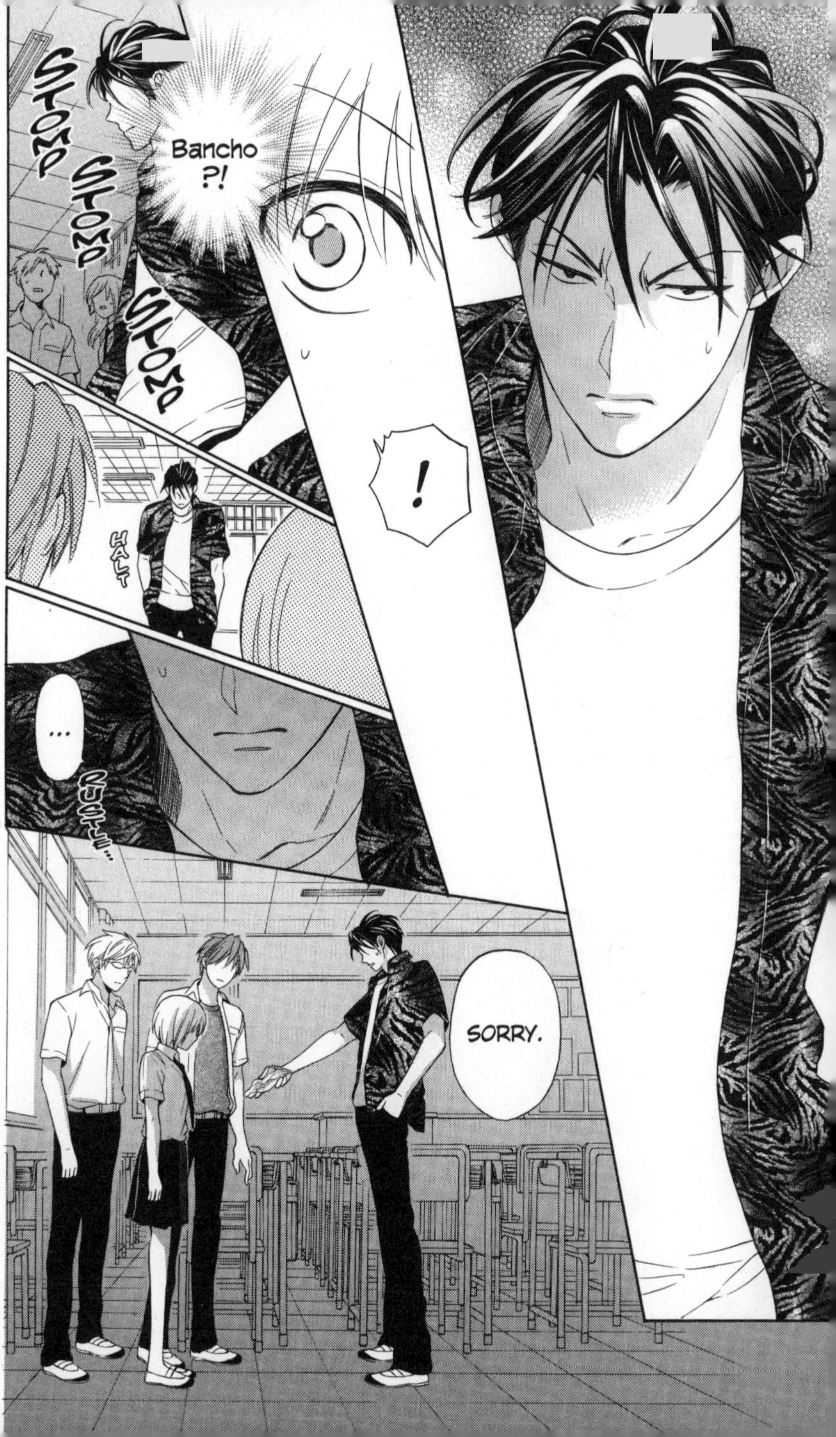

STOMP
STOMP
STOMP
STOMP
Bancho ?!
!
HALT
...
RUSTLE...
SORRY.

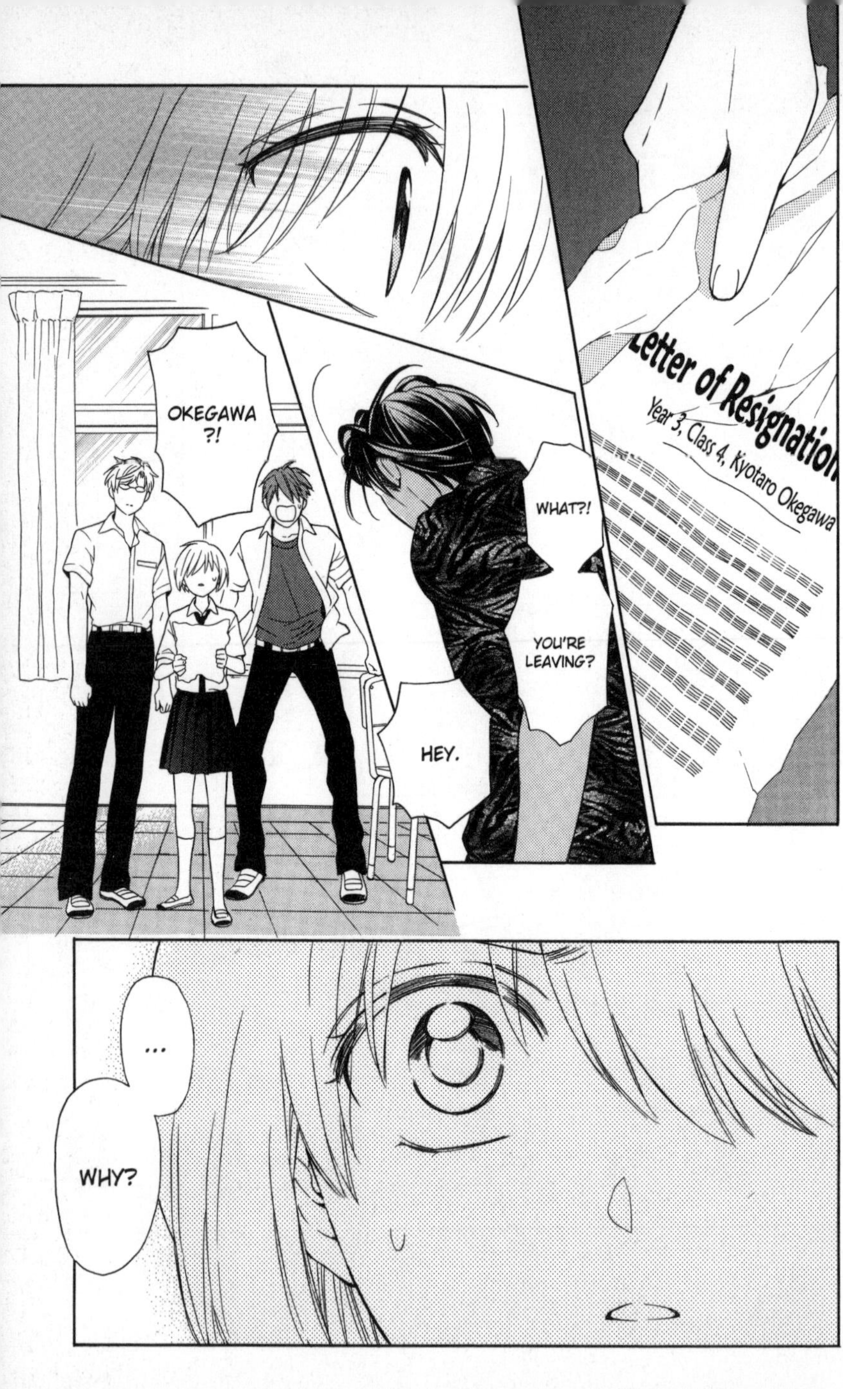
Letter of Resignation
Year 3, Class 4, Kyotaro Okegawa
WHAT?!
YOU'RE LEAVING?
HEY.
OKEGAWA ?!
...
WHY?

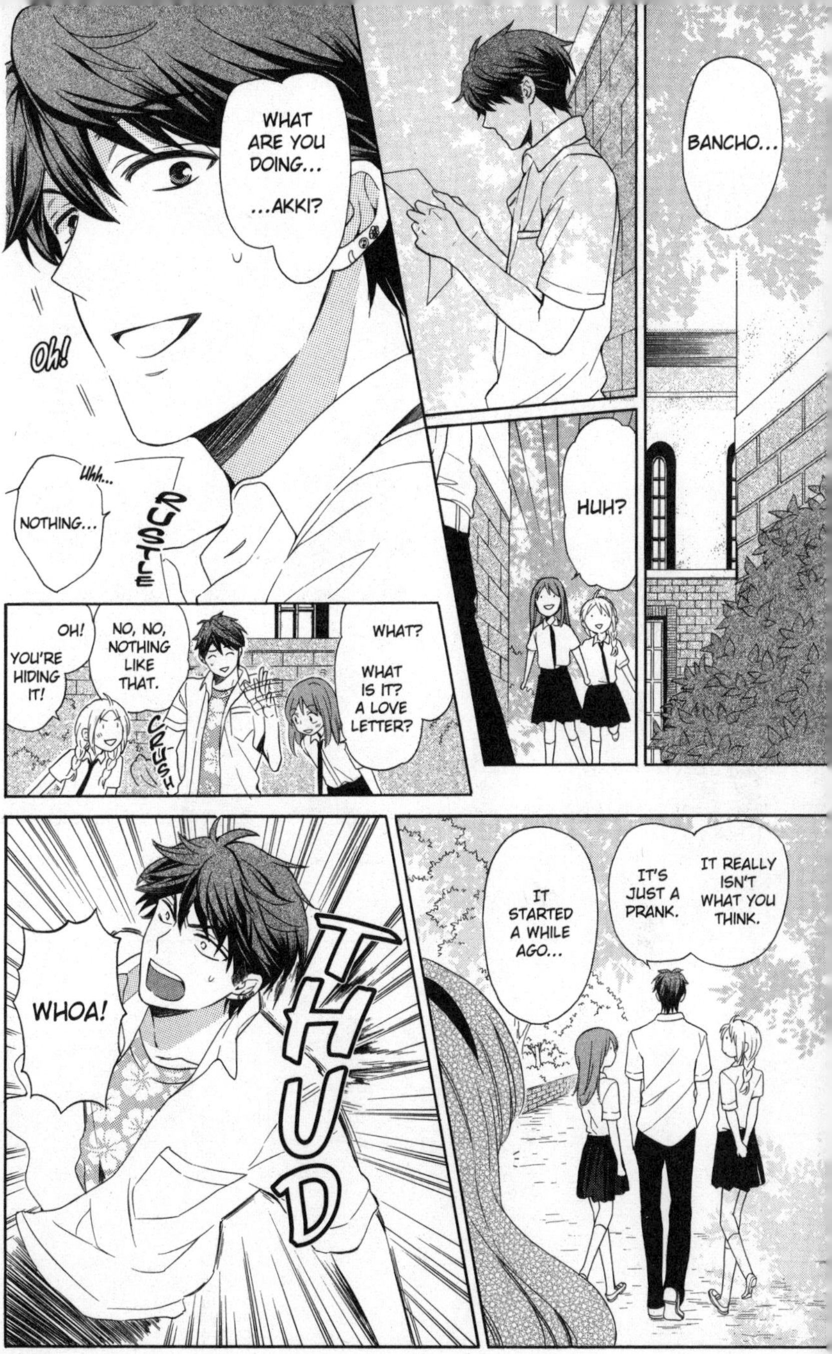
BANCHO...
HUH?
WHAT ARE YOU DOING... ...AKKI?
Oh!
Uhh... NOTHING...
RUSTLE
WHAT? WHAT IS IT? A LOVE LETTER?
NO, NO, NOTHING LIKE THAT.
OH! YOU'RE HIDING IT!
CRUSH
IT REALLY ISN'T WHAT YOU THINK.
IT'S JUST A PRANK.
IT STARTED A WHILE AGO...
WHOA!
THUD

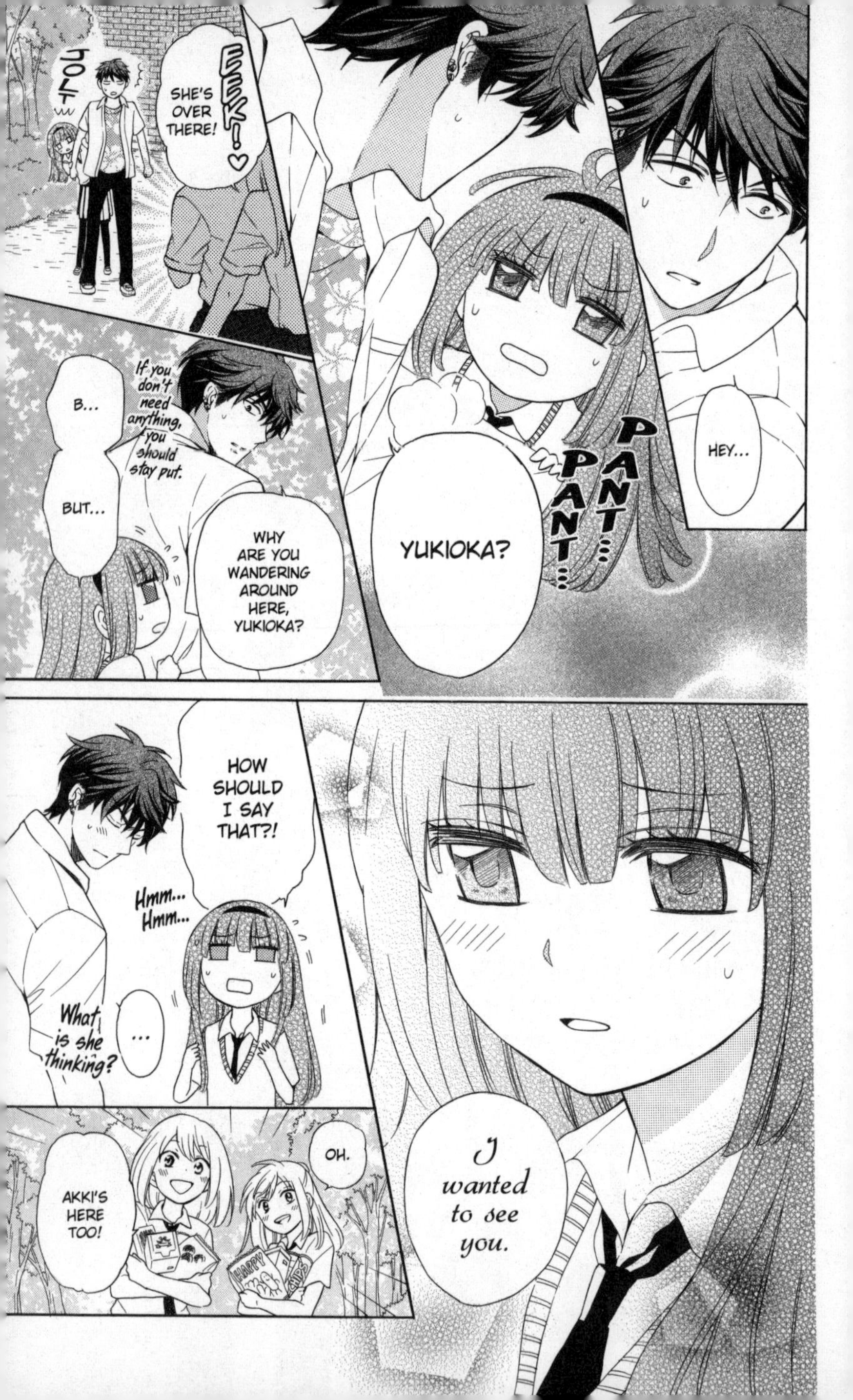
HEY...
YUKIOKA?
PANT PANT...
EEK! ♥
SHE'S OVER THERE!
JOLT
WHY ARE YOU WANDERING AROUND HERE, YUKIOKA?
If you don't need anything, you should stay put.
B...
BUT...
I wanted to see you.
HOW SHOULD I SAY THAT?!
Hmm... Hmm...
...
What is she thinking?
OH.
AKKI'S HERE TOO!
HAPPY CHIPS

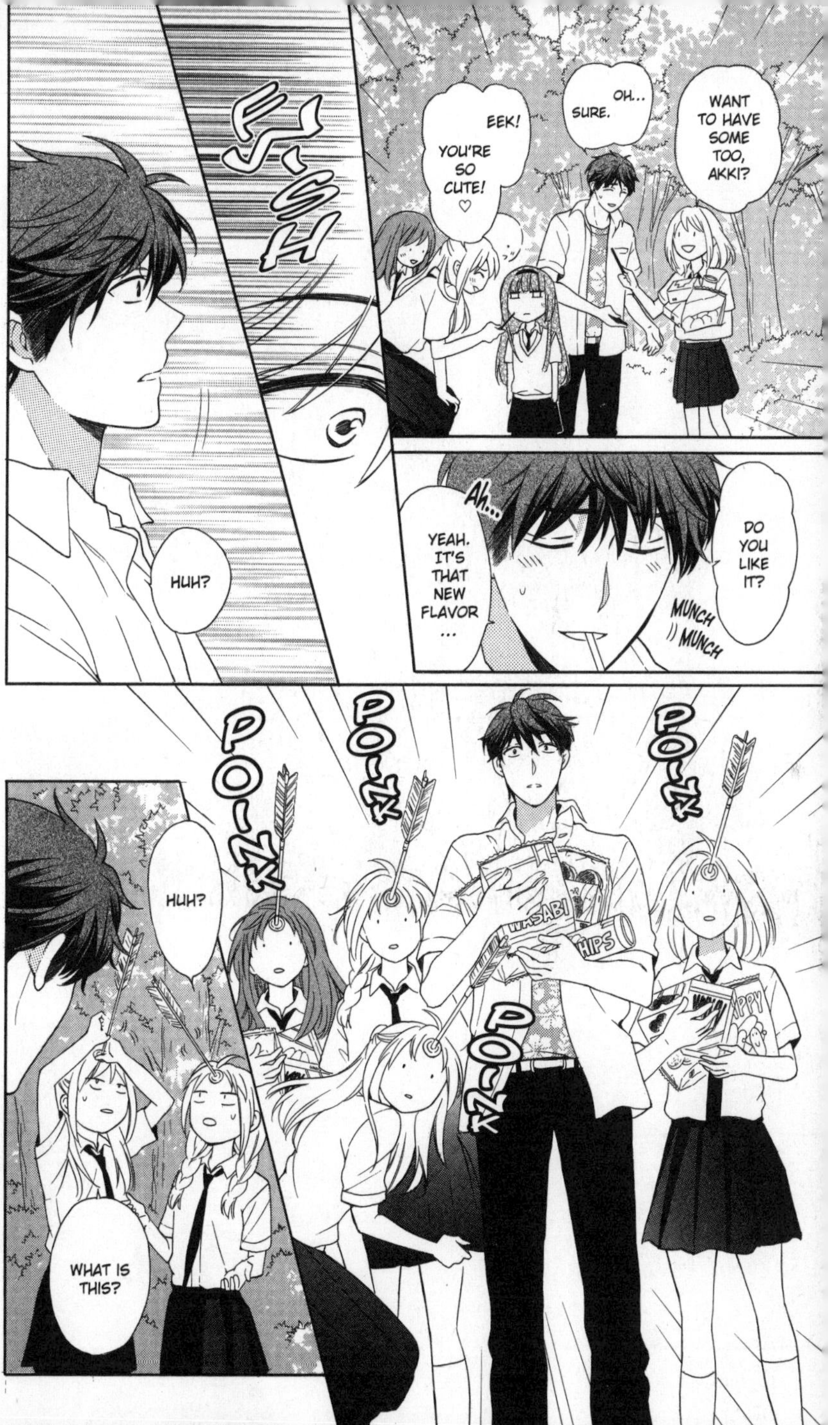
WANT TO HAVE SOME TOO, AKKI?
OH... SURE.
EEK! YOU'RE SO CUTE! ♡
DO YOU LIKE IT?
MUNCH MUNCH
YEAH. IT'S THAT NEW FLAVOR ...
Ah...
FWISH
HUH?
PO-INK
PO-INK
PO-INK
PO-INK
WASABI
HUH?
WHAT IS THIS?

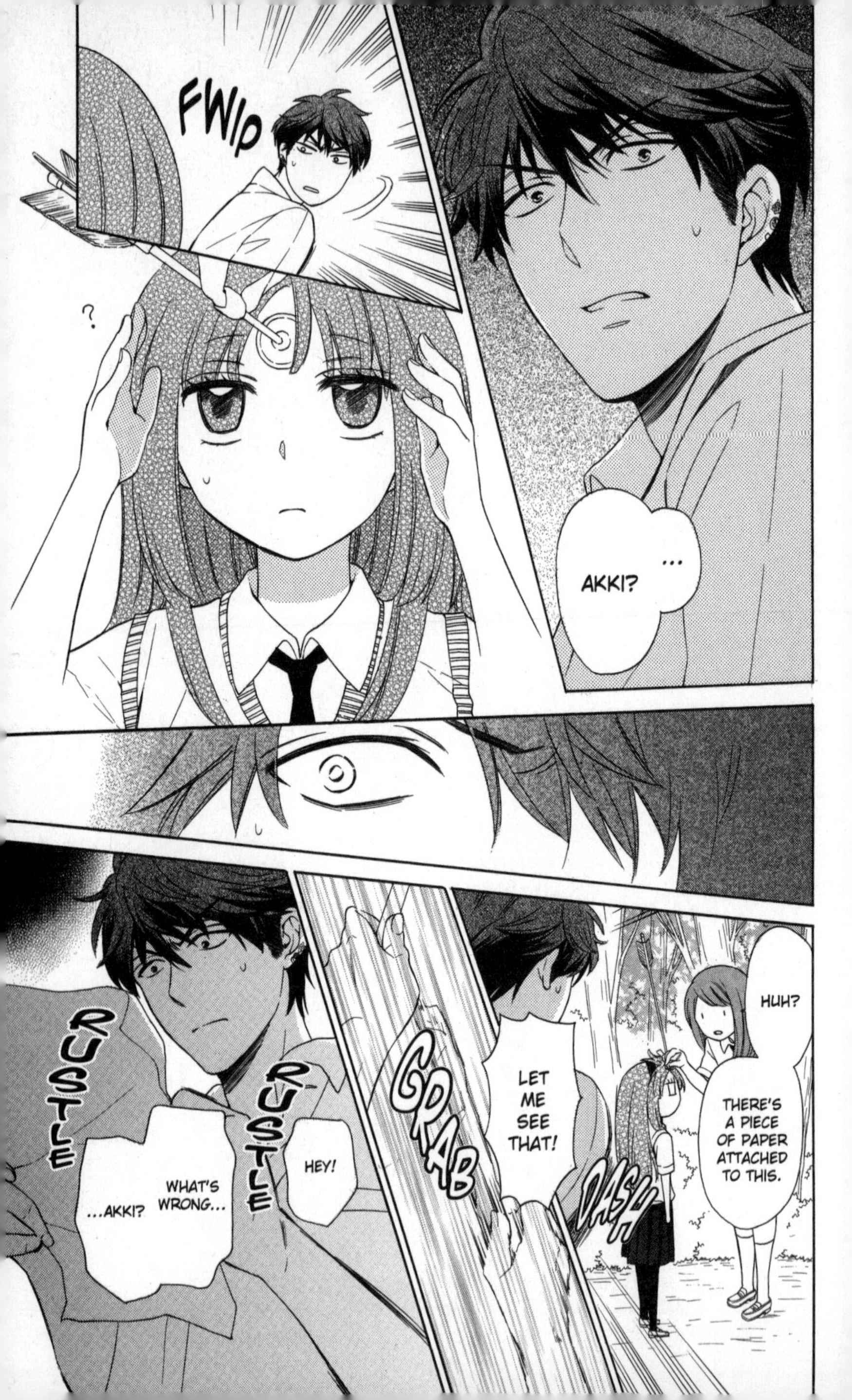
... AKKI?
FWIP
?
HUH?
THERE'S A PIECE OF PAPER ATTACHED TO THIS.
LET ME SEE THAT!
DASH
GRAB
HEY!
RUSTLE RUSTLE
WHAT'S WRONG... ...AKKI?

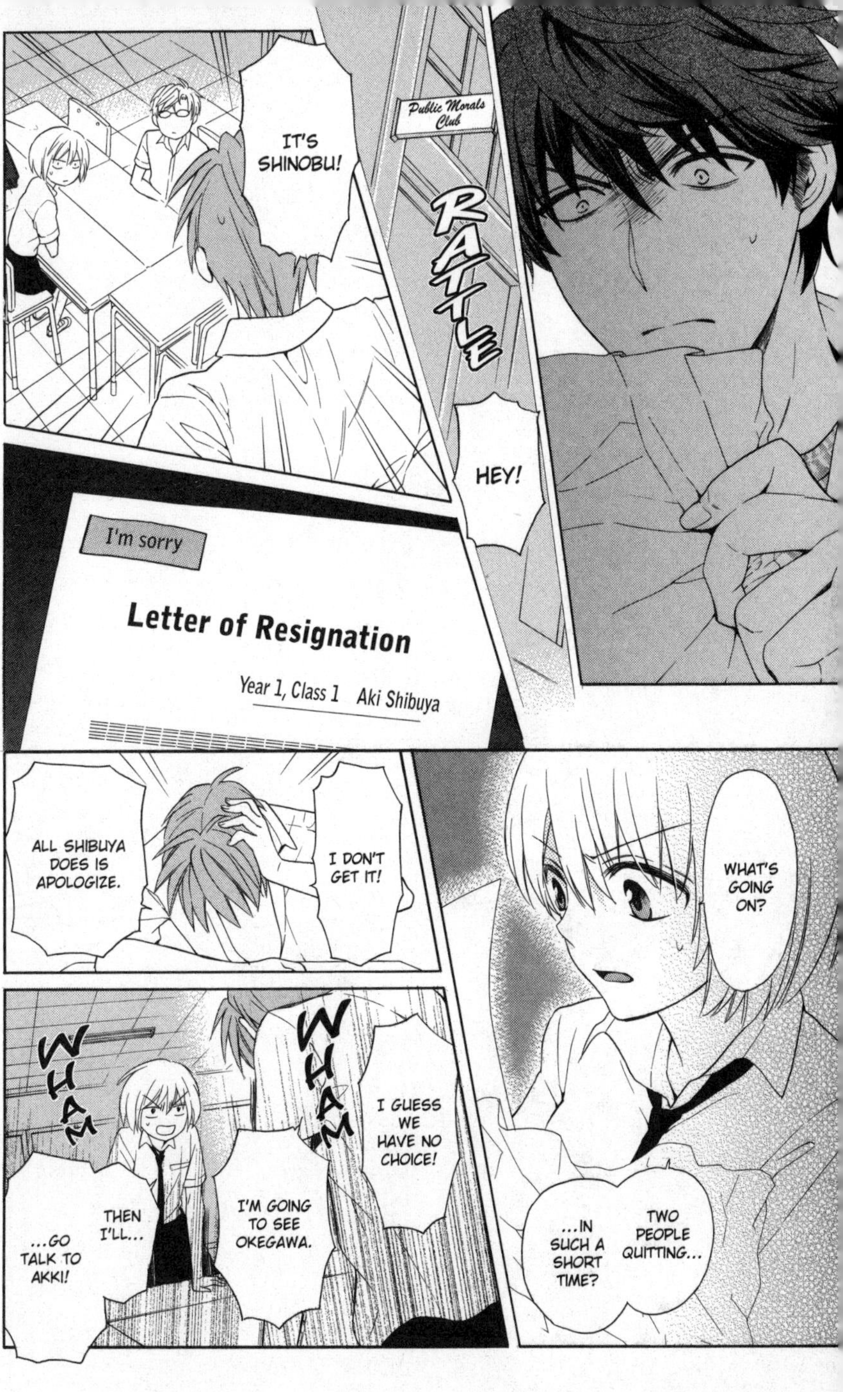
Public Morals Club
RATTLE
HEY!
IT'S SHINOBU!
I'm sorry
Letter of Resignation
Year 1, Class 1 Aki Shibuya
WHAT'S GOING ON?
TWO PEOPLE QUITTING...
...IN SUCH A SHORT TIME?
I DON'T GET IT!
ALL SHIBUYA DOES IS APOLOGIZE.
WHAM
I GUESS WE HAVE NO CHOICE!
I'M GOING TO SEE OKEGAWA.
WHAM
THEN I'LL...
...GO TALK TO AKKI!

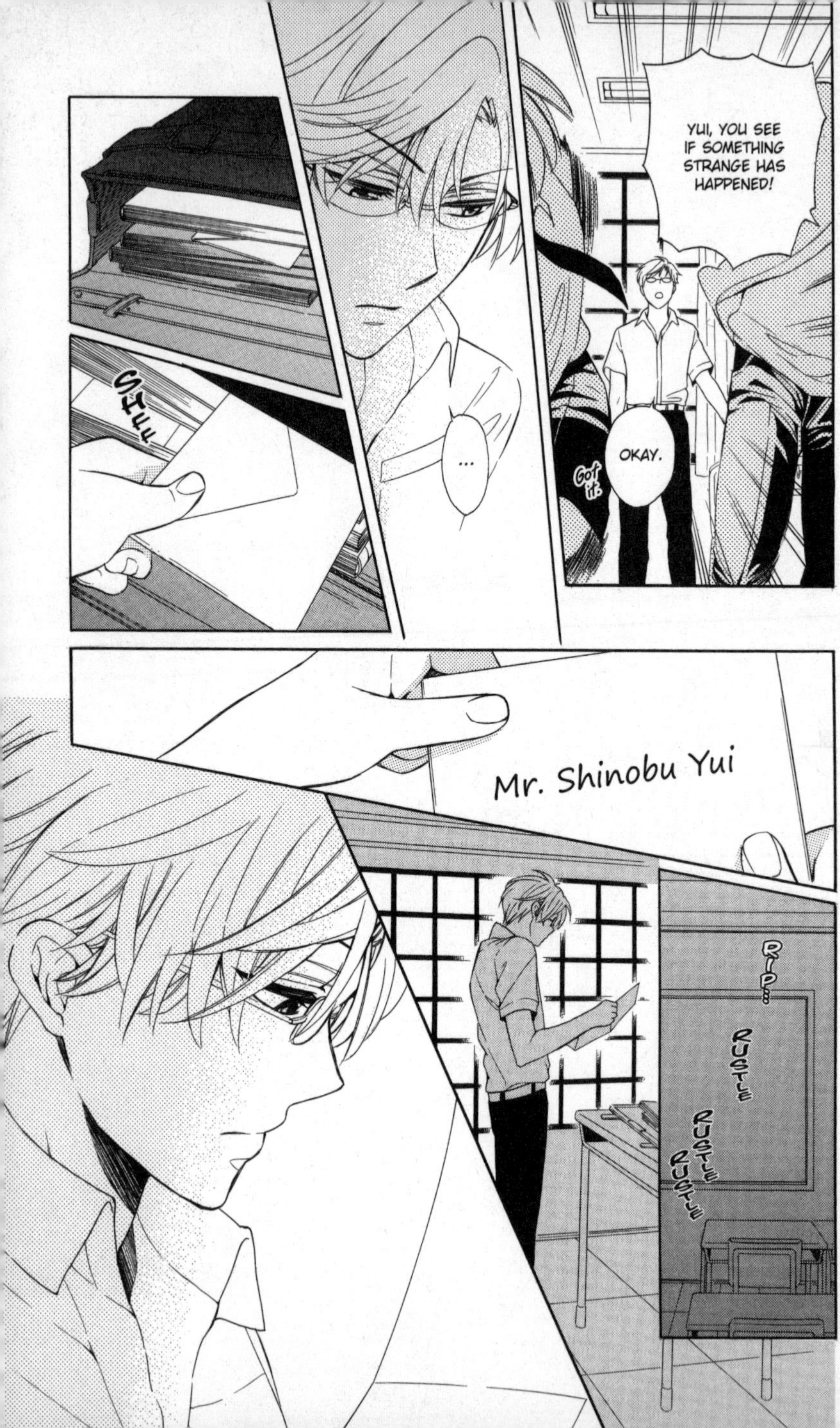
YUI, YOU SEE IF SOMETHING STRANGE HAS HAPPENED!
OKAY.
Got it.
...
SHFF
Mr. Shinobu Yui
RIP...
RUSTLE
RUSTLE
RUSTLE

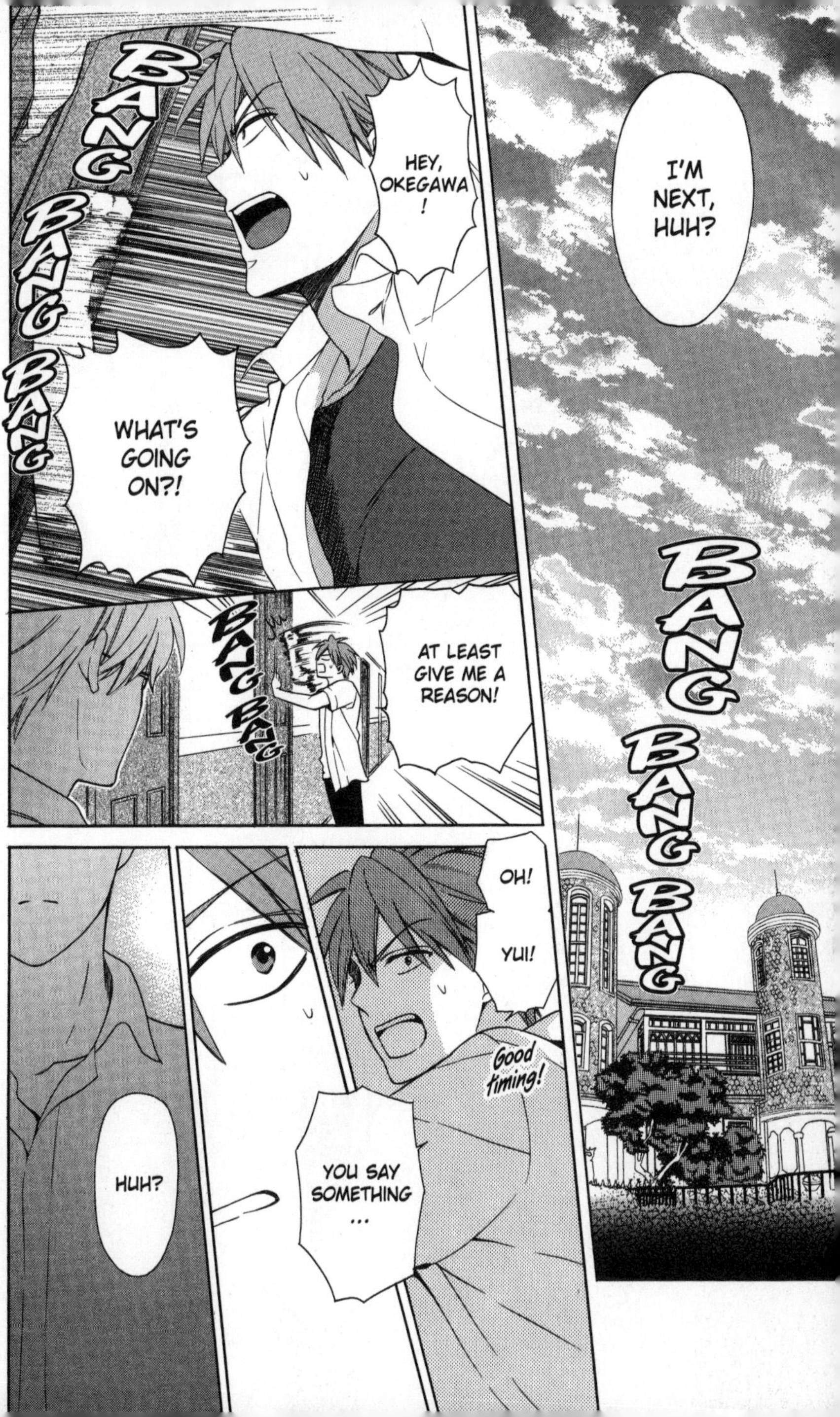
I'M NEXT, HUH?
BANG BANG BANG BANG
HEY, OKEGAWA!
WHAT'S GOING ON?!
BANG BANG BANG
AT LEAST GIVE ME A REASON!
BANG BANG
OH!
YUI!
Good timing!
YOU SAY SOMETHING...
HUH?

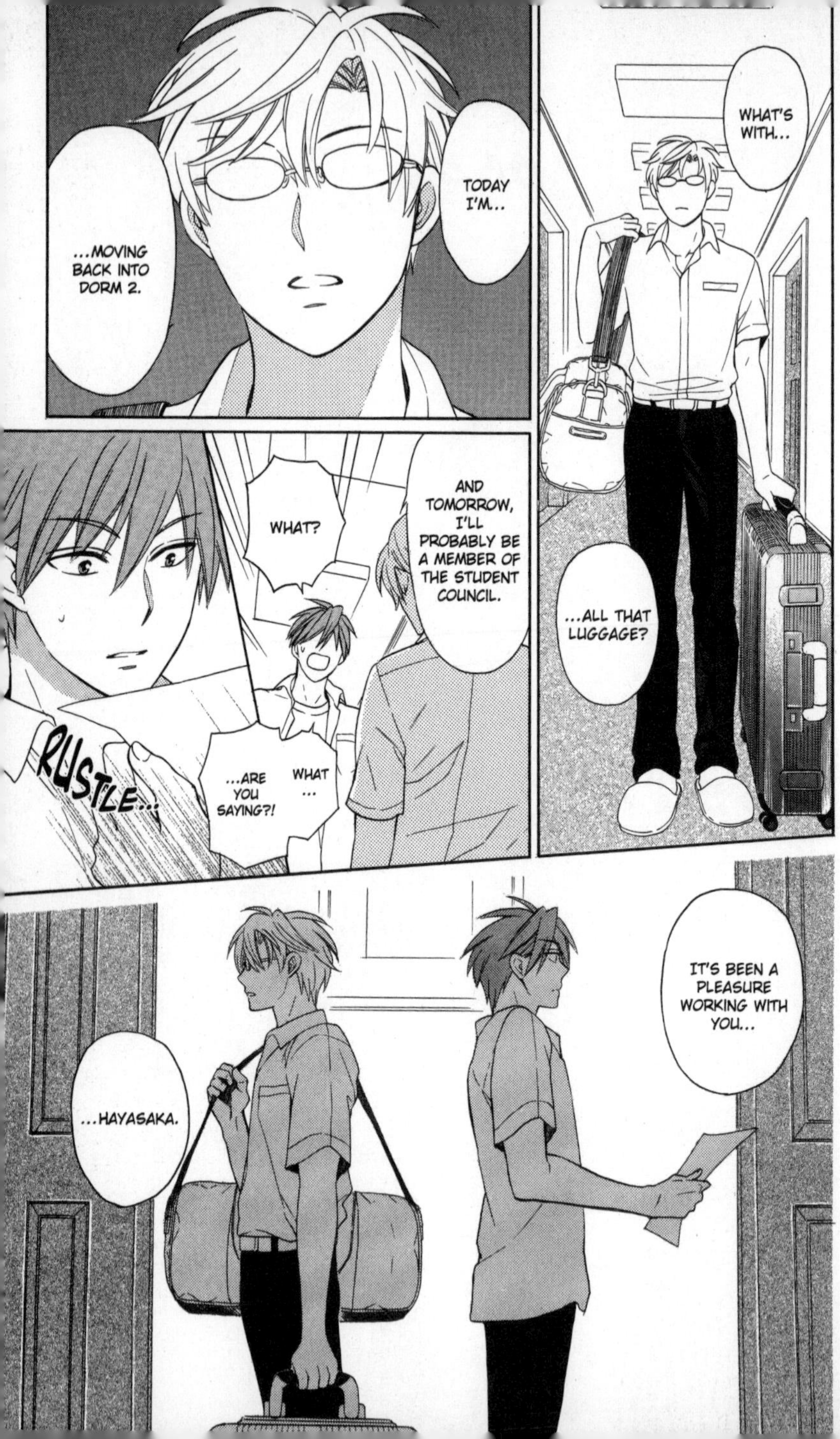
WHAT'S WITH...
...ALL THAT LUGGAGE?
TODAY I'M...
...MOVING BACK INTO DORM 2.
AND TOMORROW, I'LL PROBABLY BE A MEMBER OF THE STUDENT COUNCIL.
WHAT?
WHAT ...
...ARE YOU SAYING?!
RUSTLE...
IT'S BEEN A PLEASURE WORKING WITH YOU...
...HAYASAKA.

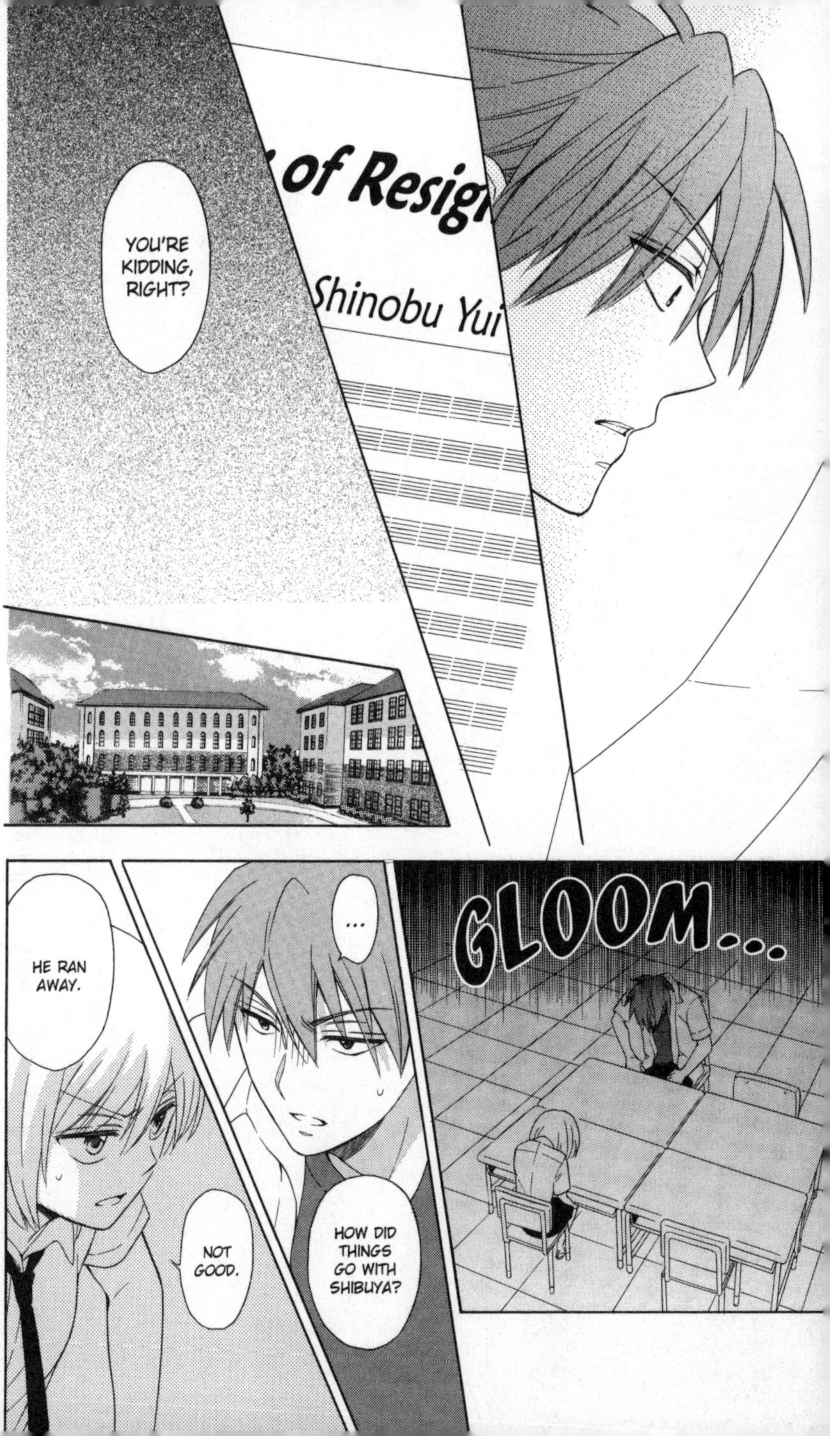
of Resig
Shinobu Yui
YOU'RE KIDDING, RIGHT?
GLOOM...
...
HOW DID THINGS GO WITH SHIBUYA?
HE RAN AWAY.
NOT GOOD.

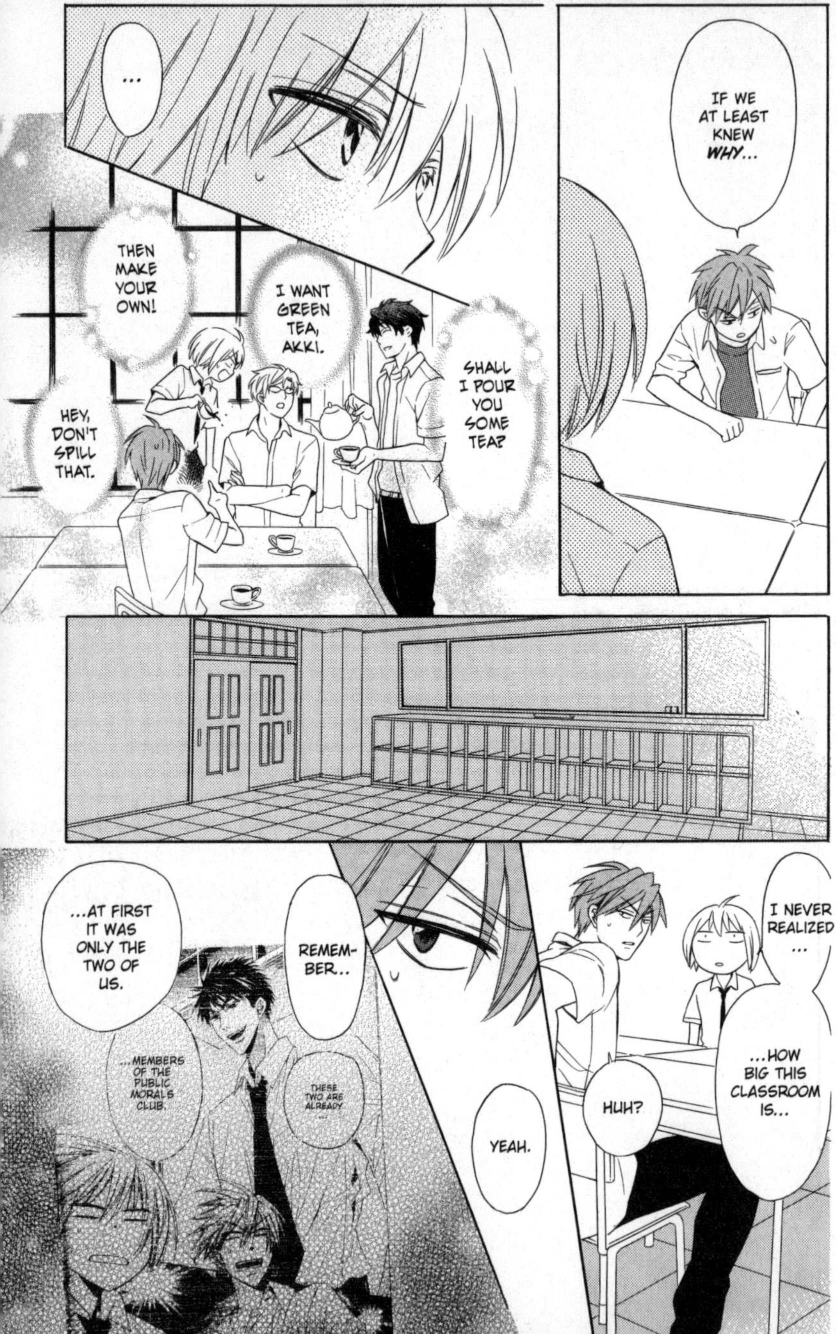
IF WE AT LEAST KNEW *WHY*...
...
SHALL I POUR YOU SOME TEA?
I WANT GREEN TEA, AKKI.
THEN MAKE YOUR OWN!
HEY, DON'T SPILL THAT.
I NEVER REALIZED...
...HOW BIG THIS CLASSROOM IS...
HUH?
REMEMBER...
YEAH.
...AT FIRST IT WAS ONLY THE TWO OF US.
THESE TWO ARE ALREADY...
...MEMBERS OF THE PUBLIC MORALS CLUB.

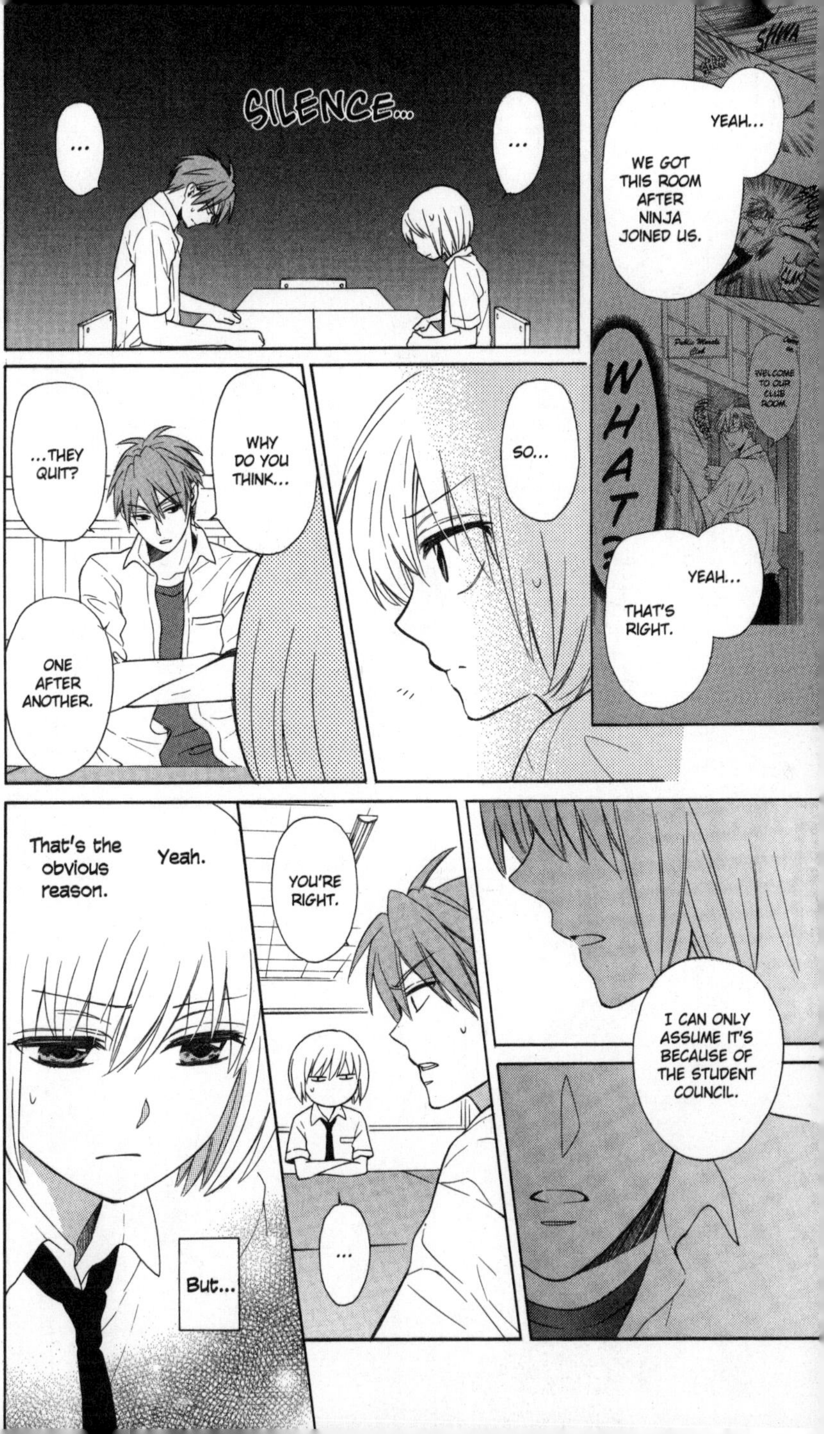
SHWA
YEAH...
WE GOT THIS ROOM AFTER NINJA JOINED US.
WELCOME TO OUR CLUB ROOM.
WHAT?
YEAH... THAT'S RIGHT.
...
SILENCE...
...
SO...
WHY DO YOU THINK...
...THEY QUIT?
ONE AFTER ANOTHER.
I CAN ONLY ASSUME IT'S BECAUSE OF THE STUDENT COUNCIL.
YOU'RE RIGHT.
...
Yeah.
That's the obvious reason.
But...

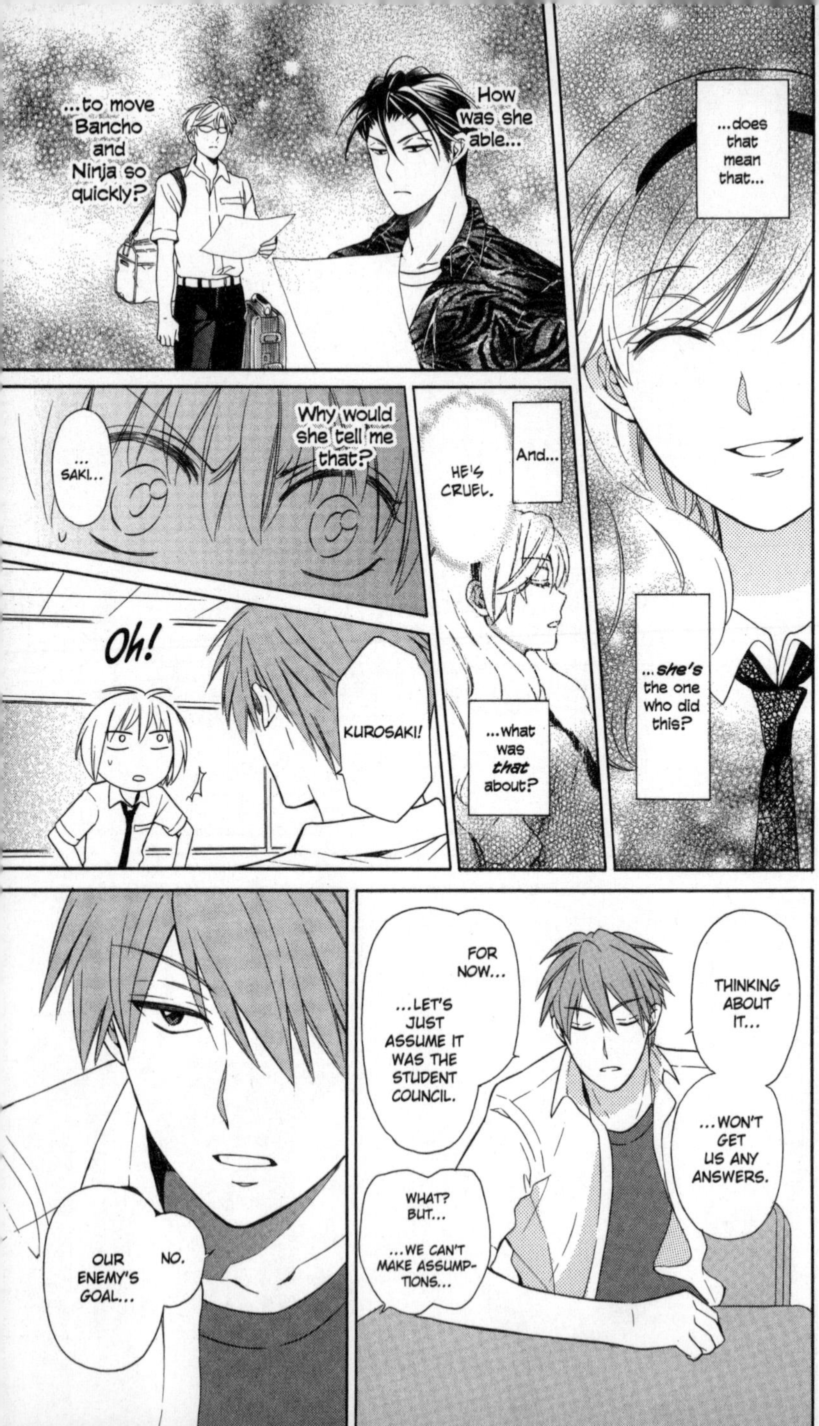
How was she able...
...to move Bancho and Ninja so quickly?
...does that mean that...
...she's the one who did this?
And...
HE'S CRUEL.
...what was that about?
Why would she tell me that?
...SAKI...
KUROSAKI!
Oh!
THINKING ABOUT IT...
...WON'T GET US ANY ANSWERS.
FOR NOW...
...LET'S JUST ASSUME IT WAS THE STUDENT COUNCIL.
WHAT? BUT...
...WE CAN'T MAKE ASSUMPTIONS...
NO.
OUR ENEMY'S GOAL...

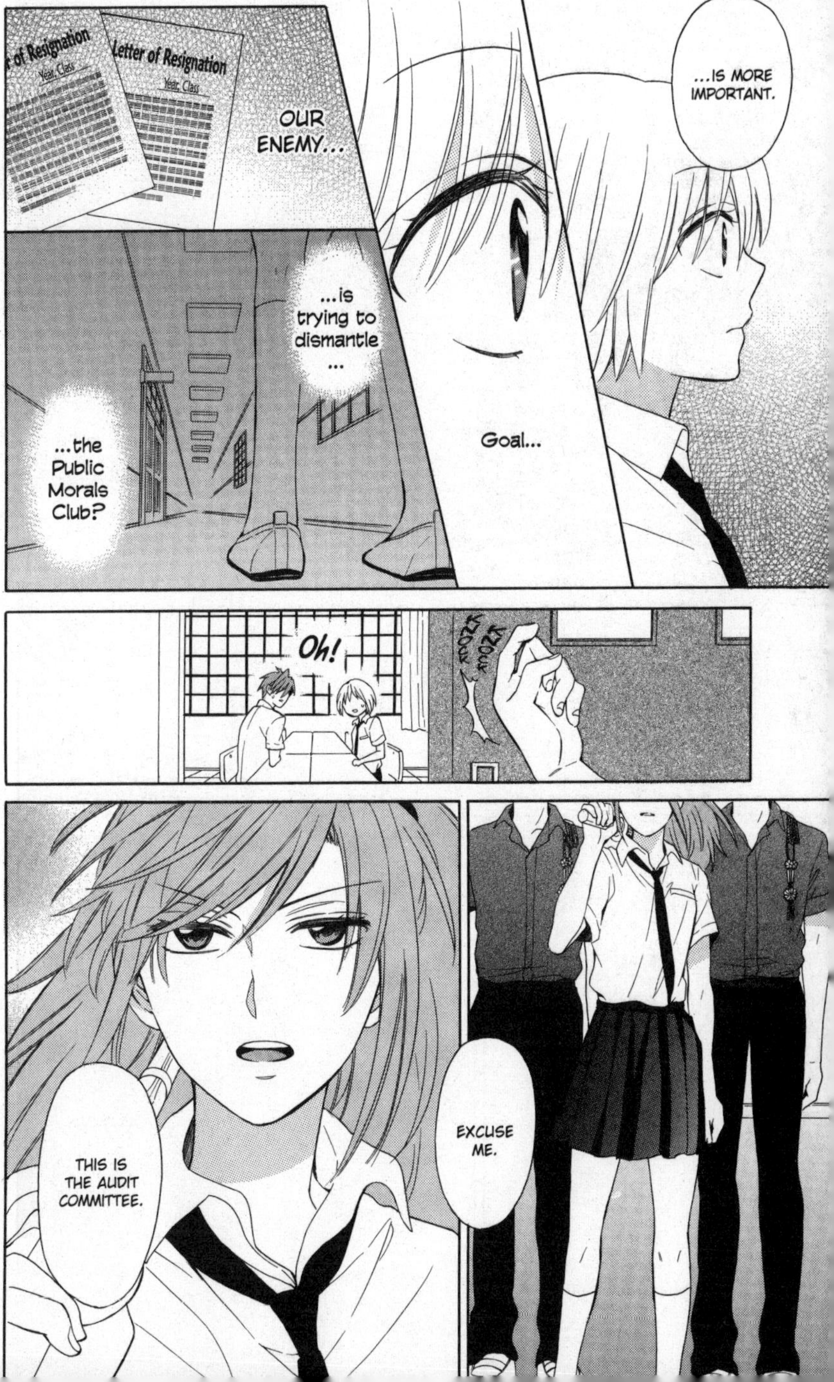
...IS MORE IMPORTANT.
Goal...
Letter of Resignation
Year, Class
OUR ENEMY...
...is trying to dismantle ...
...the Public Morals Club?
KNOCK KNOCK
Oh!
EXCUSE ME.
THIS IS THE AUDIT COMMITTEE.

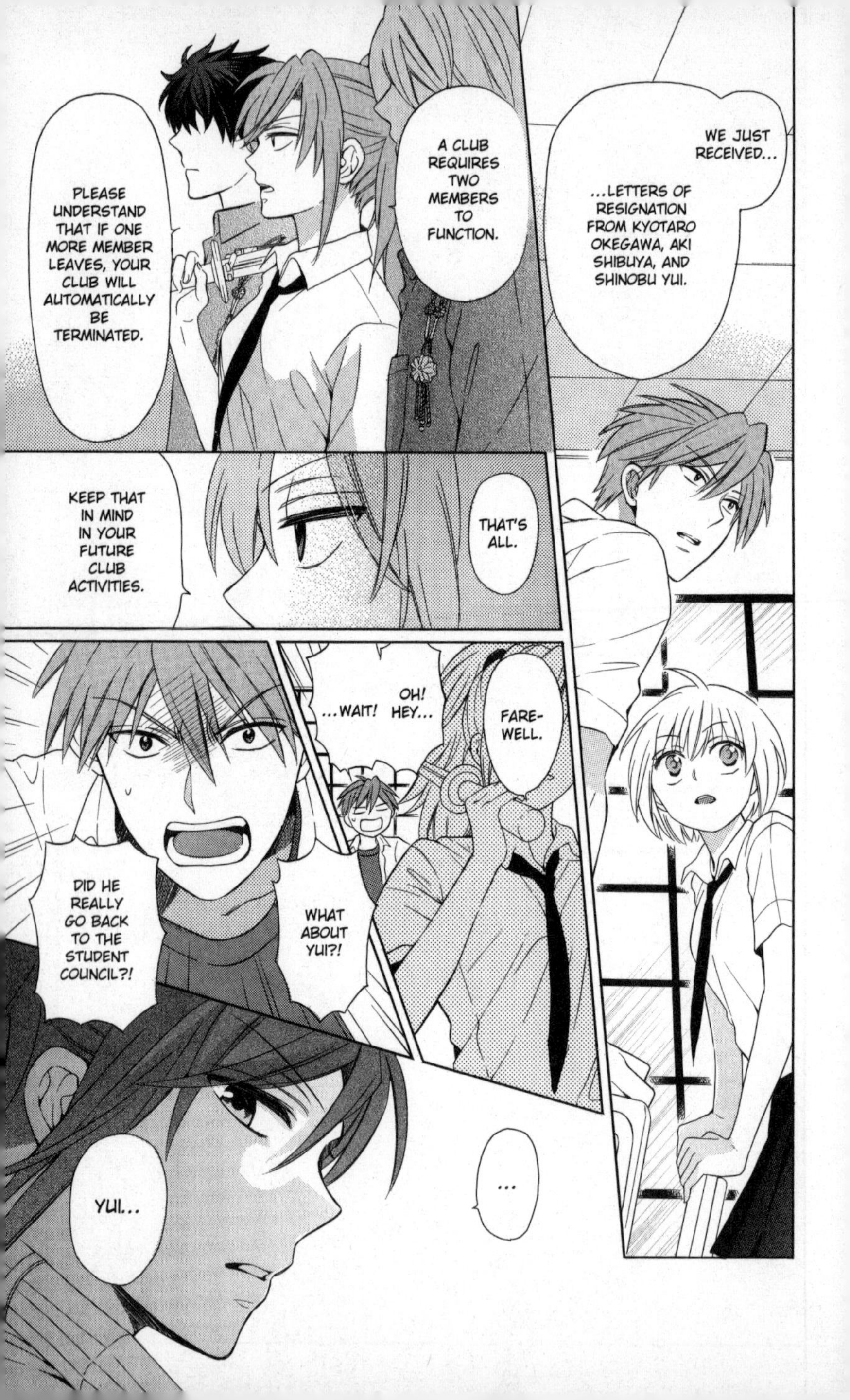
WE JUST RECEIVED...
...LETTERS OF RESIGNATION FROM KYOTARO OKEGAWA, AKI SHIBUYA, AND SHINOBU YUI.
A CLUB REQUIRES TWO MEMBERS TO FUNCTION.
PLEASE UNDERSTAND THAT IF ONE MORE MEMBER LEAVES, YOUR CLUB WILL AUTOMATICALLY BE TERMINATED.
THAT'S ALL.
KEEP THAT IN MIND IN YOUR FUTURE CLUB ACTIVITIES.
FARE-WELL.
OH! HEY...
...WAIT!
DID HE REALLY GO BACK TO THE STUDENT COUNCIL?!
WHAT ABOUT YUI?!
...
YUI...

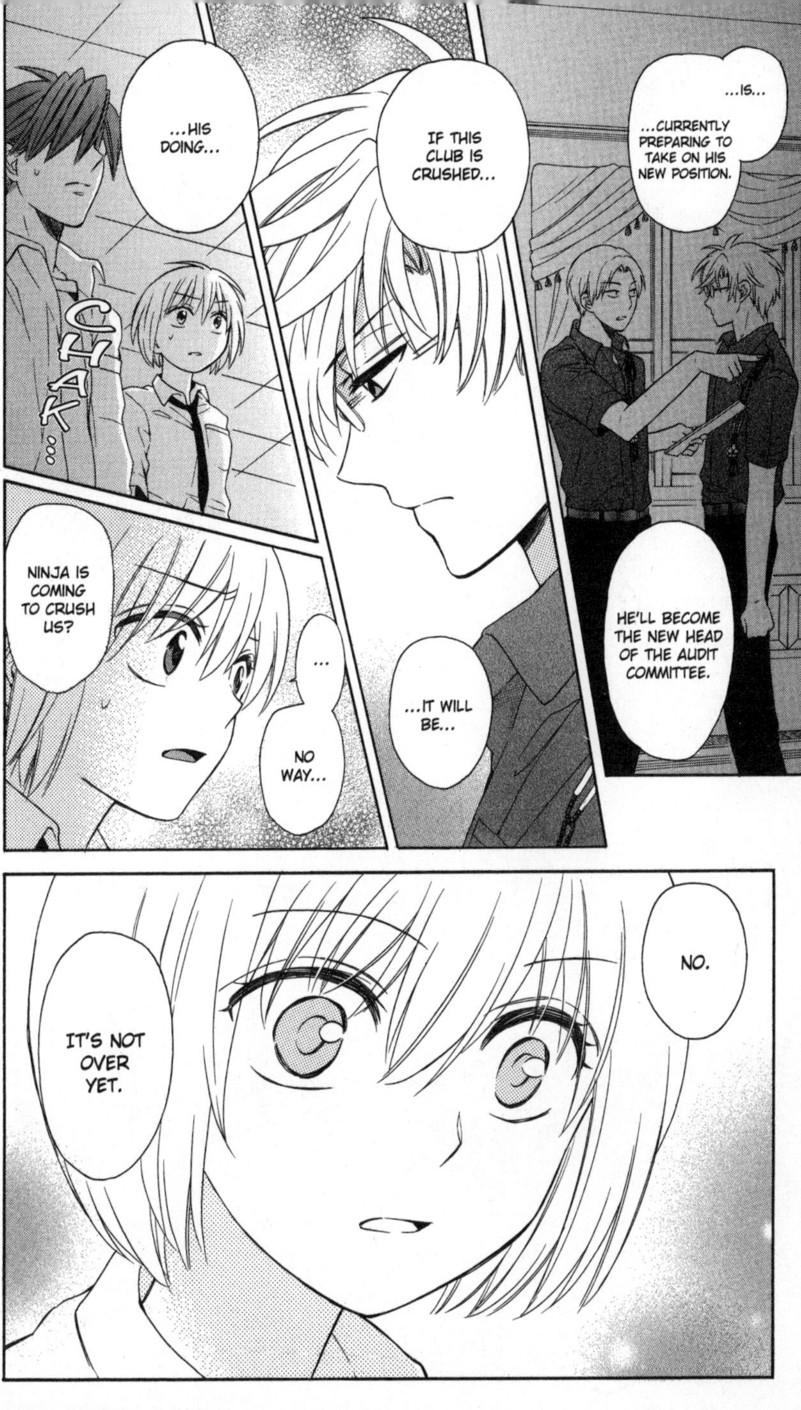
...IS...
...CURRENTLY PREPARING TO TAKE ON HIS NEW POSITION.
HE'LL BECOME THE NEW HEAD OF THE AUDIT COMMITTEE.
IF THIS CLUB IS CRUSHED...
...IT WILL BE...
...HIS DOING...
CHAK...
NINJA IS COMING TO CRUSH US?
...
NO WAY...
NO.
IT'S NOT OVER YET.

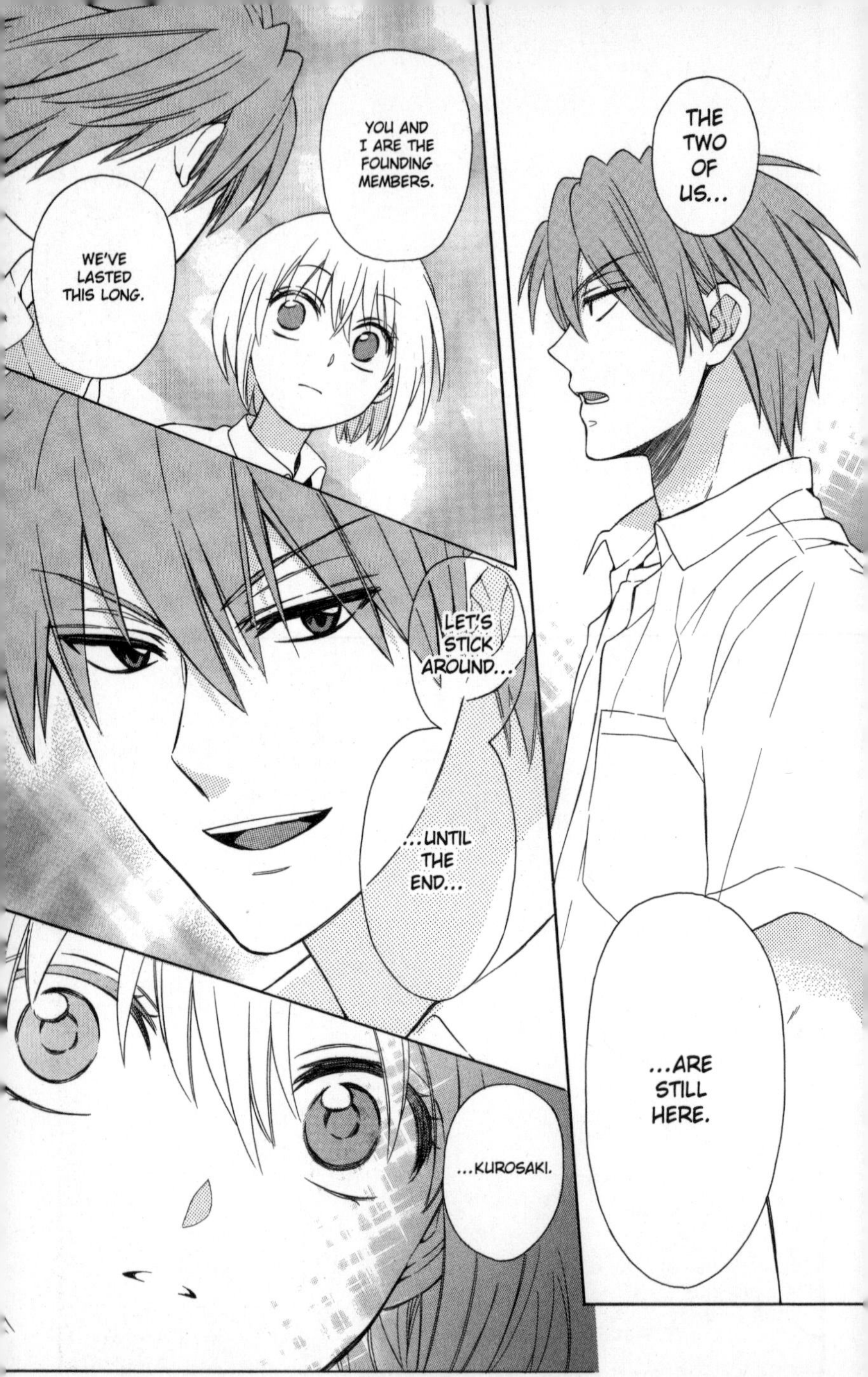
THE TWO OF US...
...ARE STILL HERE.
YOU AND I ARE THE FOUNDING MEMBERS.
WE'VE LASTED THIS LONG.
LET'S STICK AROUND...
...UNTIL THE END...
...KUROSAKI.

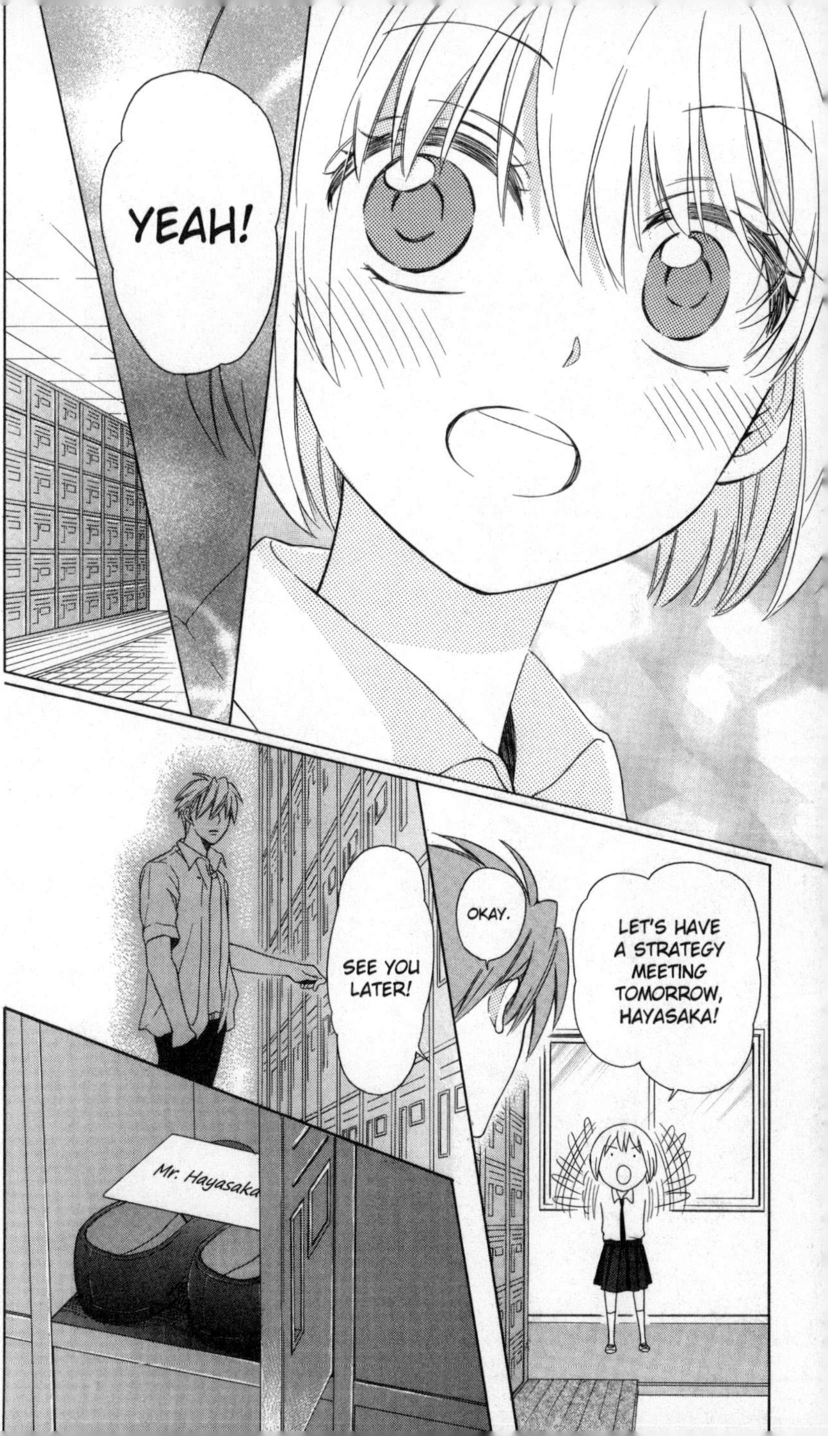
YEAH!
LET'S HAVE A STRATEGY MEETING TOMORROW, HAYASAKA!
OKAY.
SEE YOU LATER!
Mr. Hayasaka

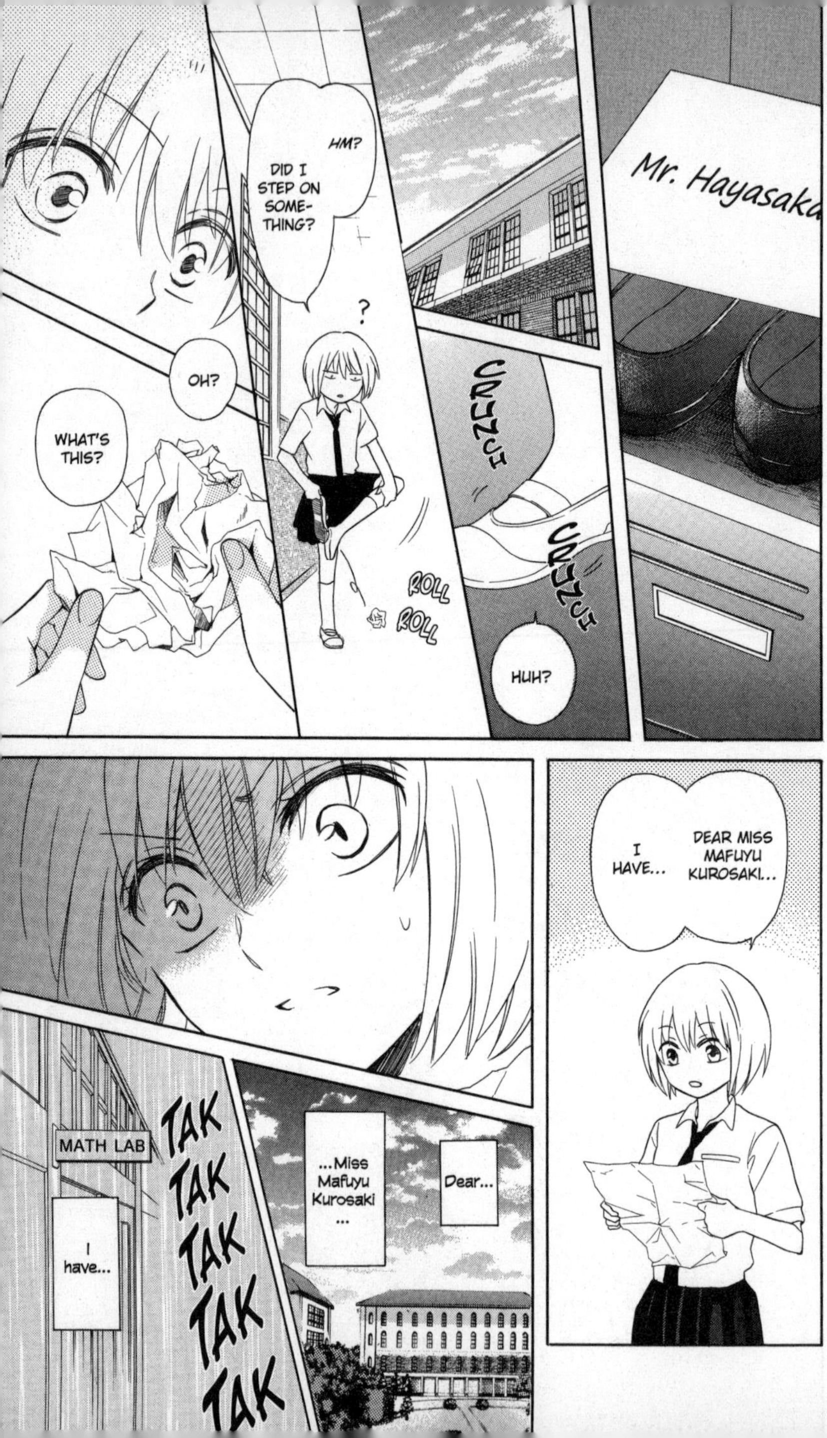
Mr. Hayasaka
CRUNCH
CRUNCH
HUH?
HM?
DID I STEP ON SOME-THING?
?
ROLL
ROLL
OH?
WHAT'S THIS?
DEAR MISS MAFUYU KUROSAKI...
I HAVE...
Dear...
...Miss Mafuyu Kurosaki ...
MATH LAB
I have...
TAK TAK TAK TAK TAK TAK

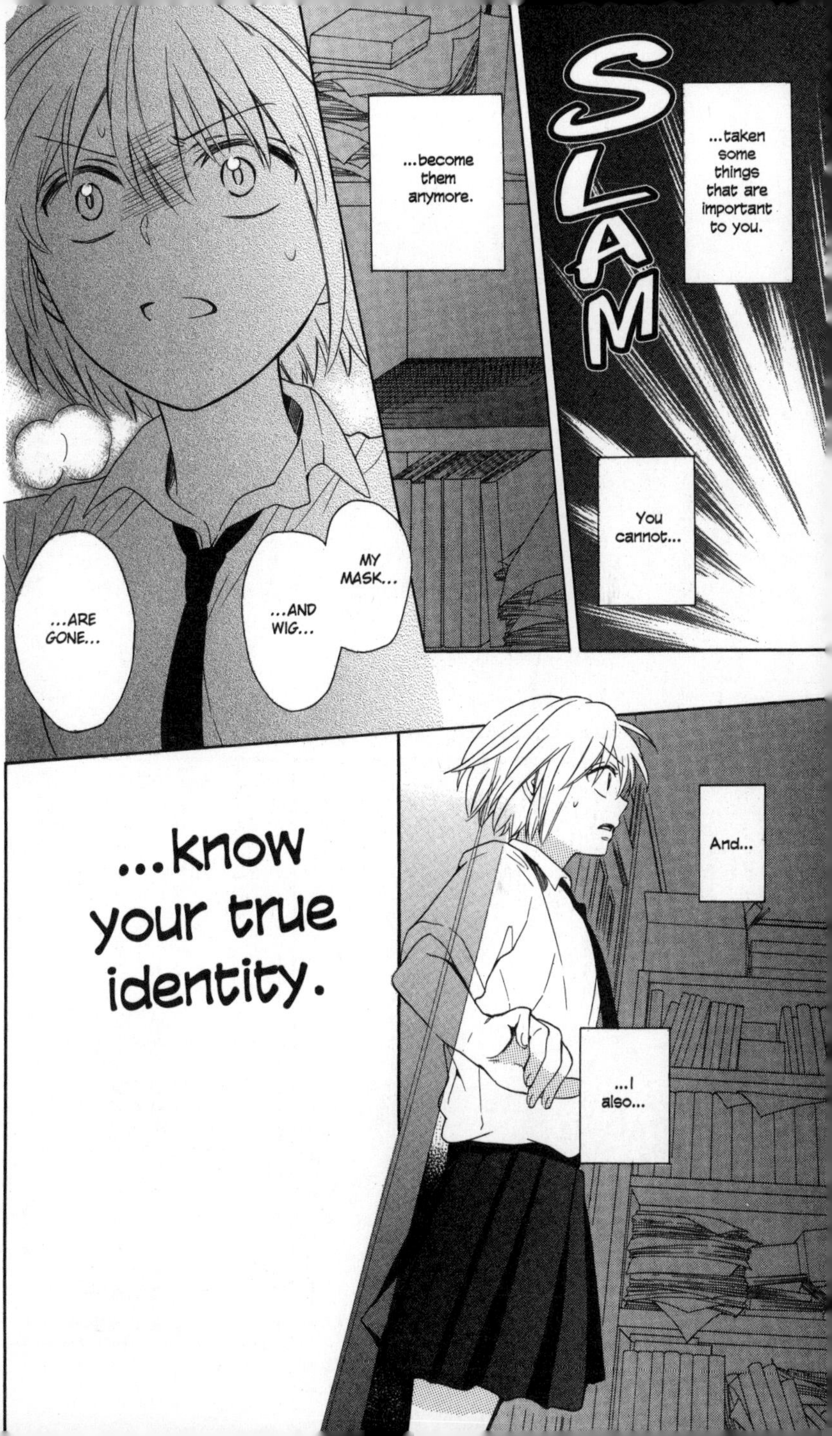
...taken some things that are important to you.
SLAM
You cannot...
...become them anymore.
MY MASK...
...AND WIG...
...ARE GONE...
And...
...I also...
...know your true identity.

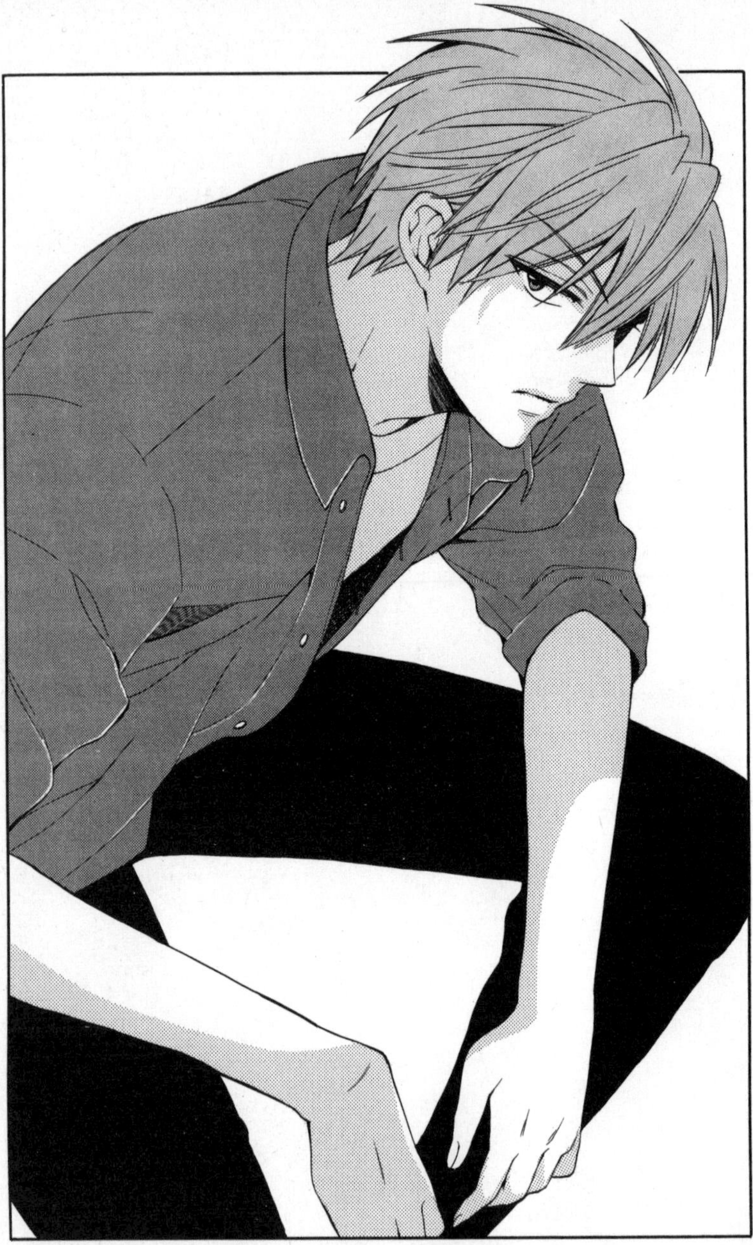

Chapter 91

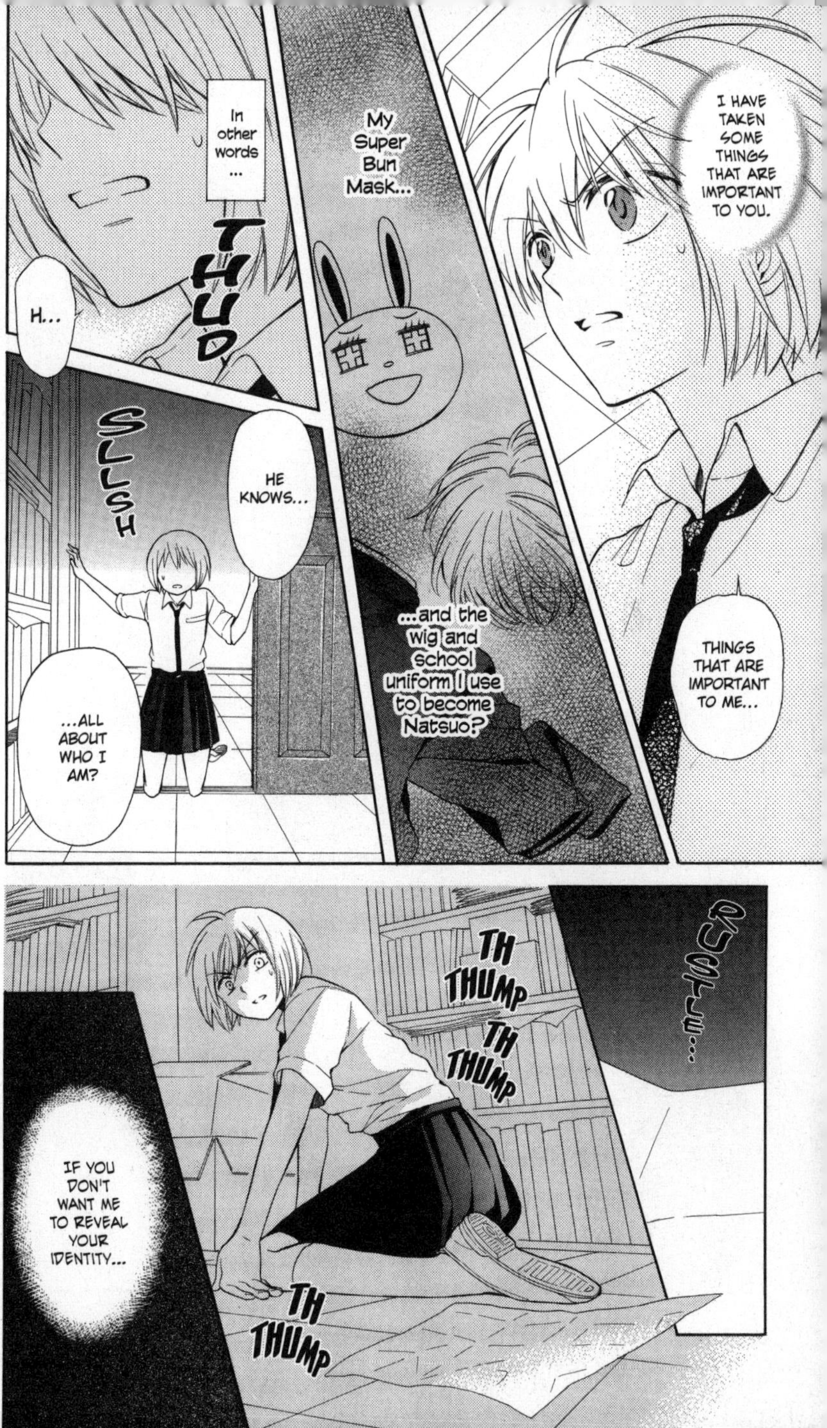
I HAVE TAKEN SOME THINGS THAT ARE IMPORTANT TO YOU.
THINGS THAT ARE IMPORTANT TO ME...
My Super Bun Mask...
...and the wig and school uniform I use to become Natsuo?
In other words...
THUD
H...
SLLSH
HE KNOWS...
...ALL ABOUT WHO I AM?
RUSTLE...
TH THUMP
TH THUMP
IF YOU DON'T WANT ME TO REVEAL YOUR IDENTITY...
TH THUMP

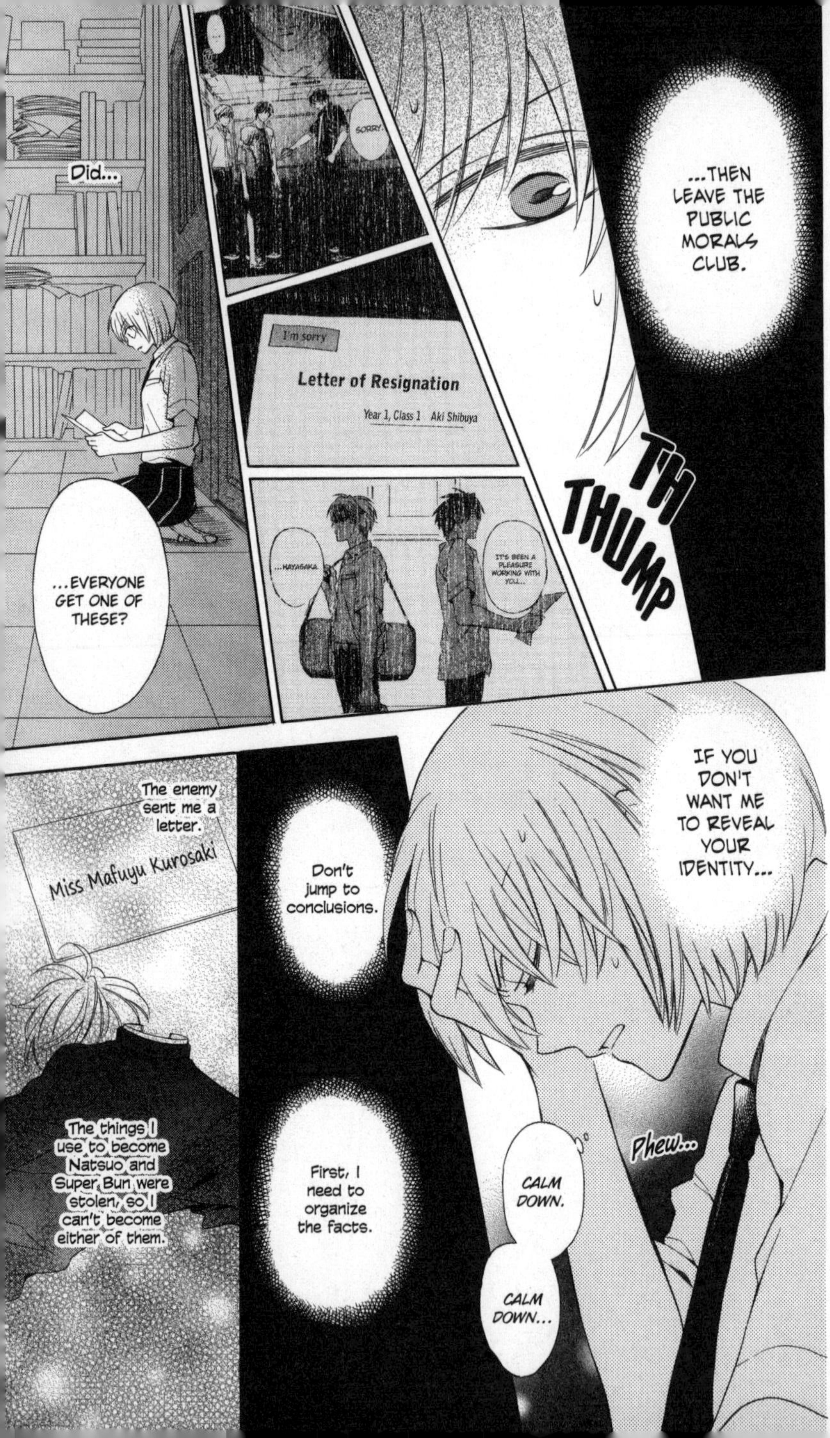
...THEN LEAVE THE PUBLIC MORALS CLUB.
TH THUMP
SORRY.
I'm sorry
Letter of Resignation
Year 1, Class 1 Aki Shibuya
IT'S BEEN A PLEASURE WORKING WITH YOU...
...HAYASAKA.
Did...
...EVERYONE GET ONE OF THESE?
IF YOU DON'T WANT ME TO REVEAL YOUR IDENTITY...
Phew...
CALM DOWN.
CALM DOWN...
Don't jump to conclusions.
First, I need to organize the facts.
The enemy sent me a letter.
Miss Mafuyu Kurosaki
The things I use to become Natsuo and Super Bun were stolen, so I can't become either of them.

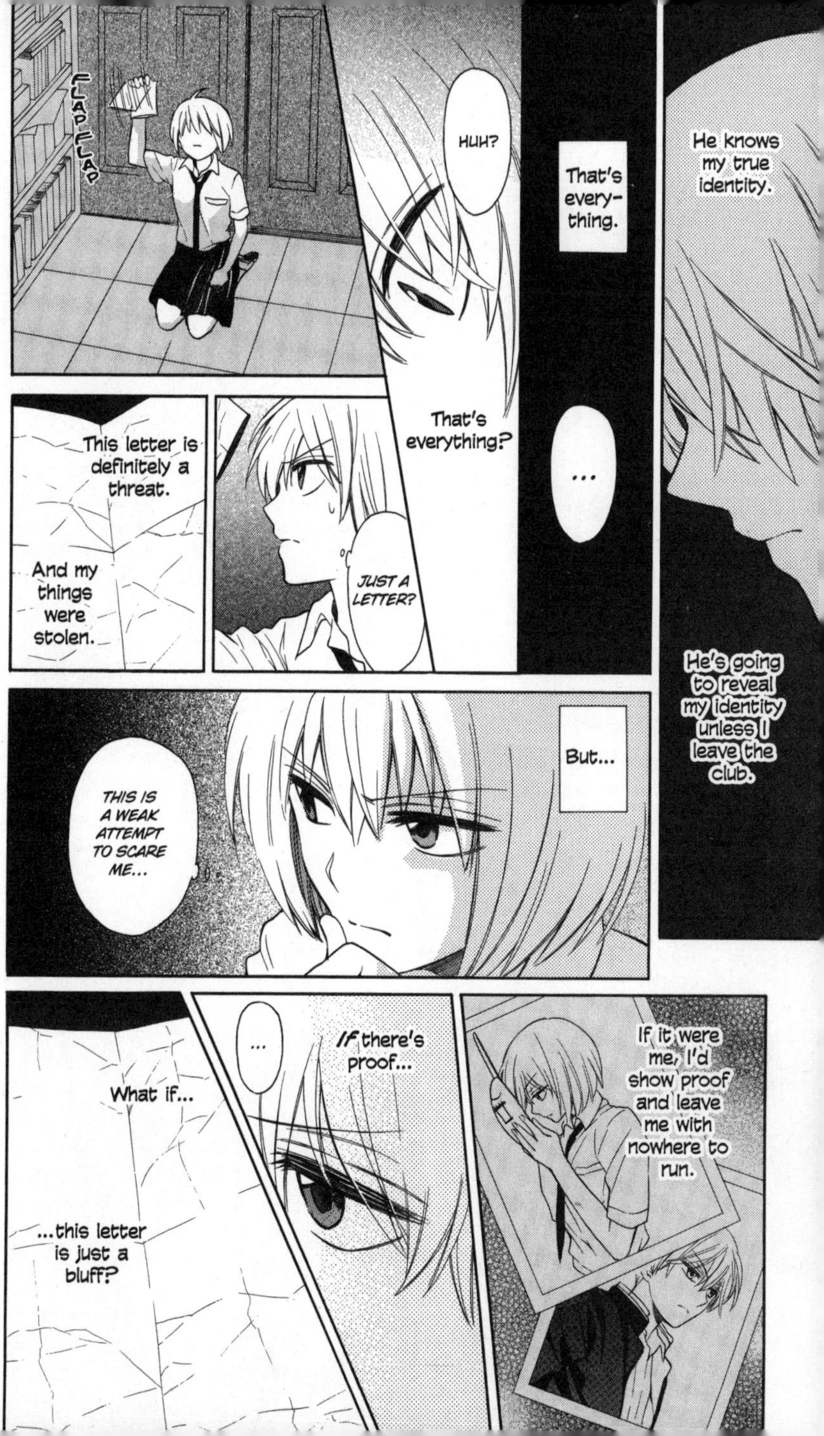
He knows my true identity.
He's going to reveal my identity unless I leave the club.
That's every-thing.
HUH?
FLAP FLAP
...
That's everything?
JUST A LETTER?
This letter is definitely a threat.
And my things were stolen.
But...
THIS IS A WEAK ATTEMPT TO SCARE ME...
If it were me, I'd show proof and leave me with nowhere to run.
If there's proof...
...
What if...
...this letter is just a bluff?

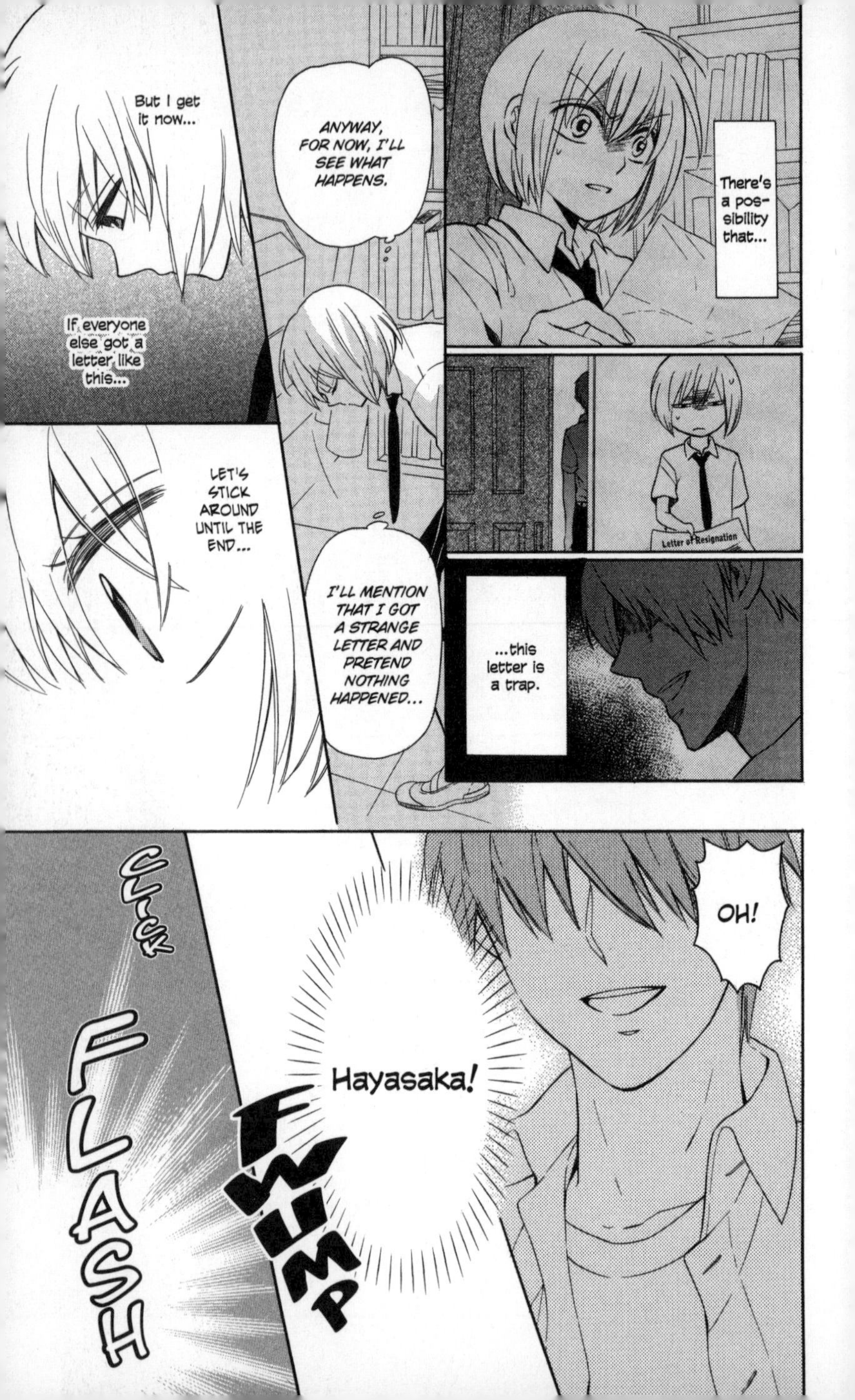
There's a pos-sibility that...
Letter of Resignation
...this letter is a trap.
ANYWAY, FOR NOW, I'LL SEE WHAT HAPPENS.
I'LL MENTION THAT I GOT A STRANGE LETTER AND PRETEND NOTHING HAPPENED...
But I get it now...
If everyone else got a letter like this...
LET'S STICK AROUND UNTIL THE END...
OH!
Hayasaka!
FWUMP
Click
FLASH

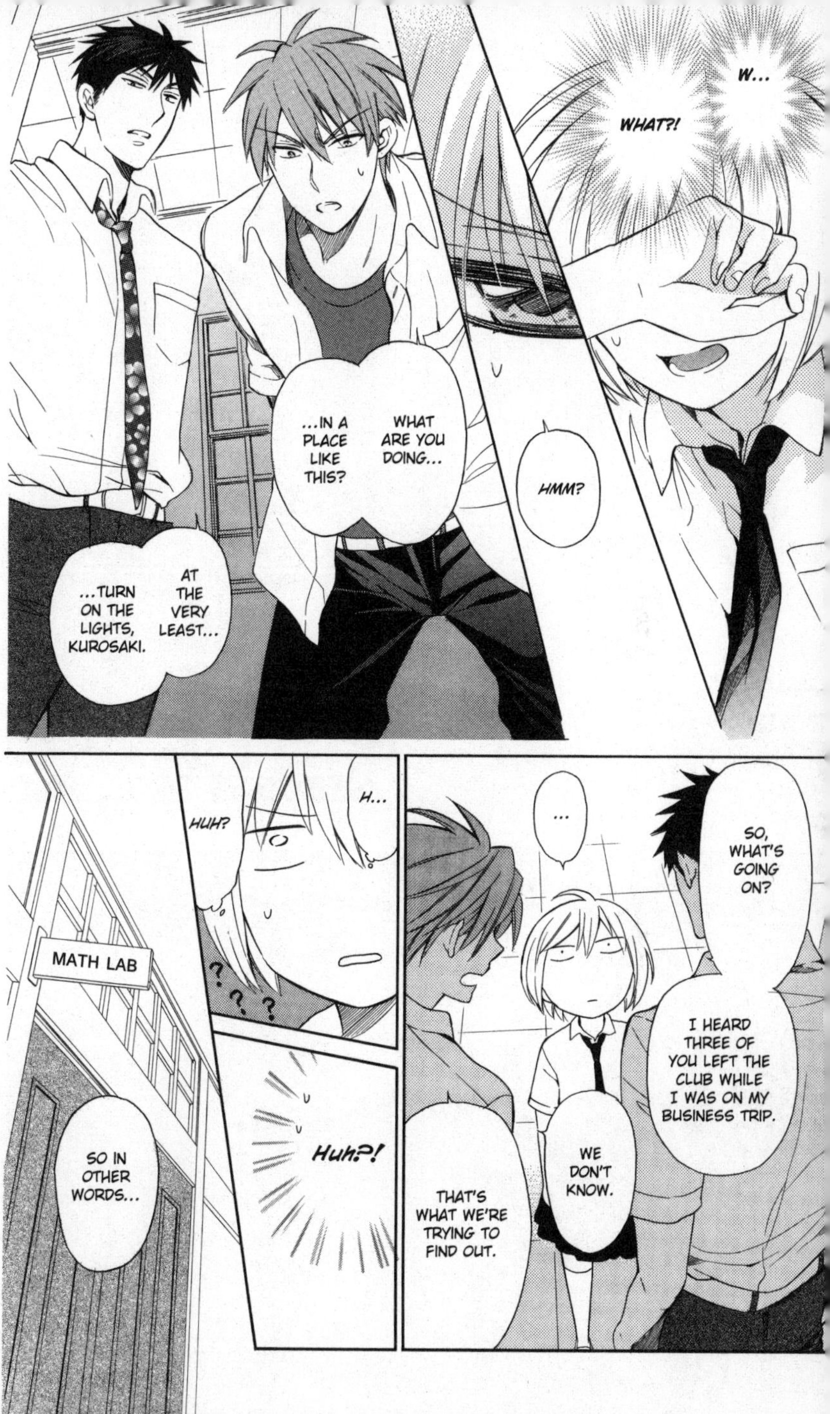
W...
WHAT?!
HMM?
WHAT ARE YOU DOING... ...IN A PLACE LIKE THIS?
AT THE VERY LEAST... ...TURN ON THE LIGHTS, KUROSAKI.
SO, WHAT'S GOING ON?
...
I HEARD THREE OF YOU LEFT THE CLUB WHILE I WAS ON MY BUSINESS TRIP.
WE DON'T KNOW.
THAT'S WHAT WE'RE TRYING TO FIND OUT.
H...
HUH?
Huh?!
MATH LAB
SO IN OTHER WORDS...

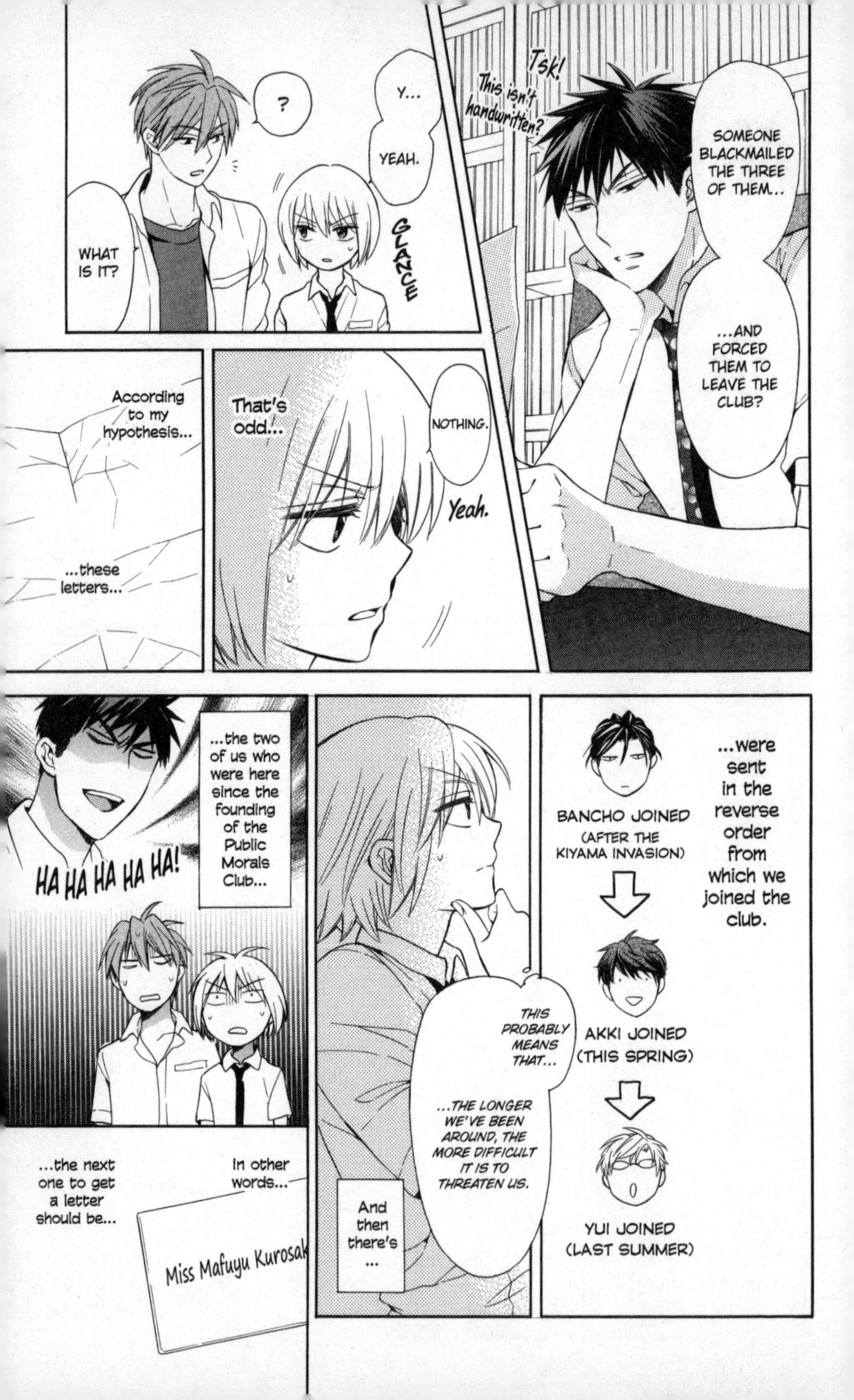
Tsk! This isn't handwritten?
SOMEONE BLACKMAILED THE THREE OF THEM...
...AND FORCED THEM TO LEAVE THE CLUB?
Y...
YEAH.
GLANCE
?
WHAT IS IT?
NOTHING.
Yeah.
That's odd...
According to my hypothesis...
...these letters...
...were sent in the reverse order from which we joined the club.
BANCHO JOINED (AFTER THE KIYAMA INVASION)
AKKI JOINED (THIS SPRING)
YUI JOINED (LAST SUMMER)
THIS PROBABLY MEANS THAT...
...THE LONGER WE'VE BEEN AROUND, THE MORE DIFFICULT IT IS TO THREATEN US.
And then there's ...
...the two of us who were here since the founding of the Public Morals Club...
HA HA HA HA HA!
In other words...
...the next one to get a letter should be...
Miss Mafuyu Kurosak

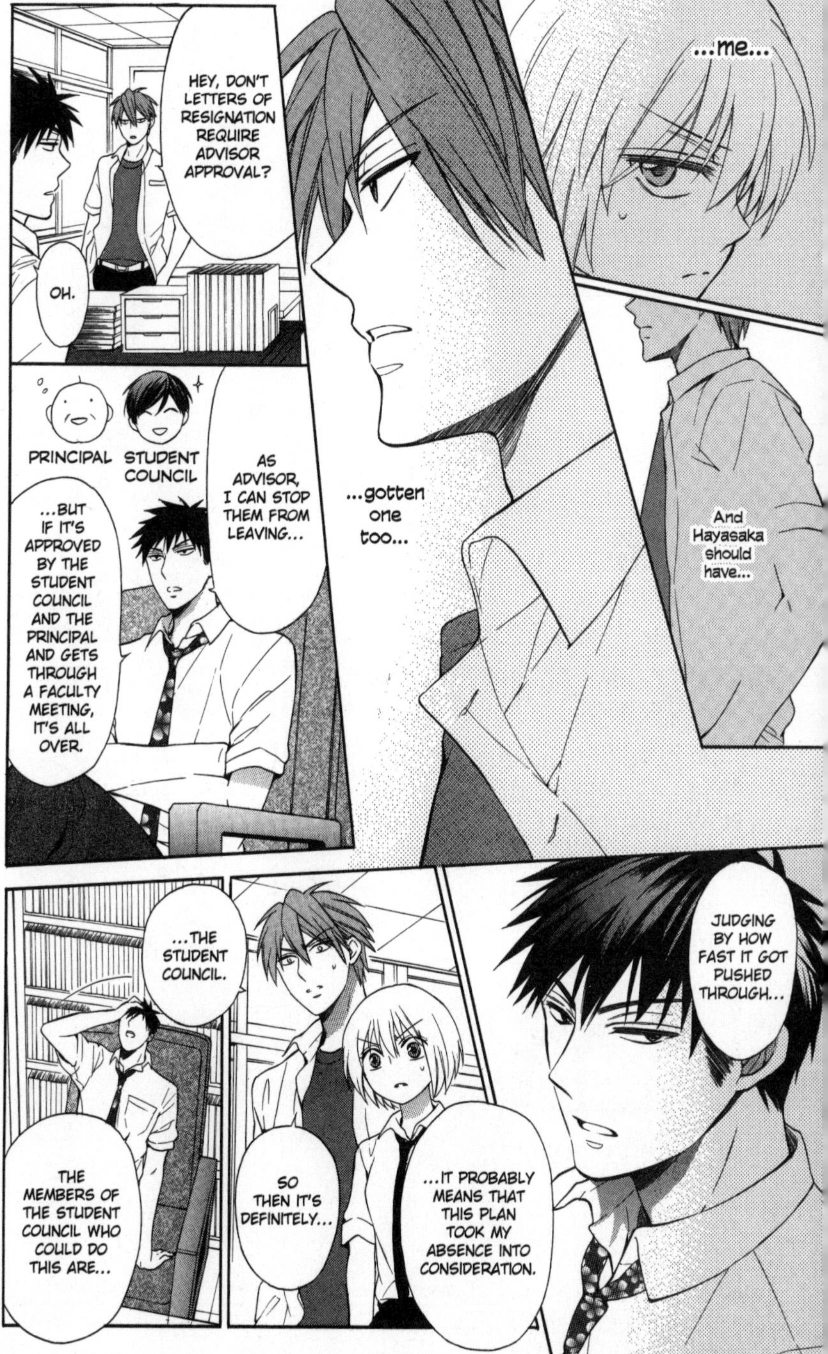
...me...
And Hayasaka should have...
...gotten one too...
HEY, DON'T LETTERS OF RESIGNATION REQUIRE ADVISOR APPROVAL?
OH.
AS ADVISOR, I CAN STOP THEM FROM LEAVING...
STUDENT COUNCIL
PRINCIPAL
...BUT IF IT'S APPROVED BY THE STUDENT COUNCIL AND THE PRINCIPAL AND GETS THROUGH A FACULTY MEETING, IT'S ALL OVER.
JUDGING BY HOW FAST IT GOT PUSHED THROUGH...
...IT PROBABLY MEANS THAT THIS PLAN TOOK MY ABSENCE INTO CONSIDERATION.
SO THEN IT'S DEFINITELY...
...THE STUDENT COUNCIL.
THE MEMBERS OF THE STUDENT COUNCIL WHO COULD DO THIS ARE...

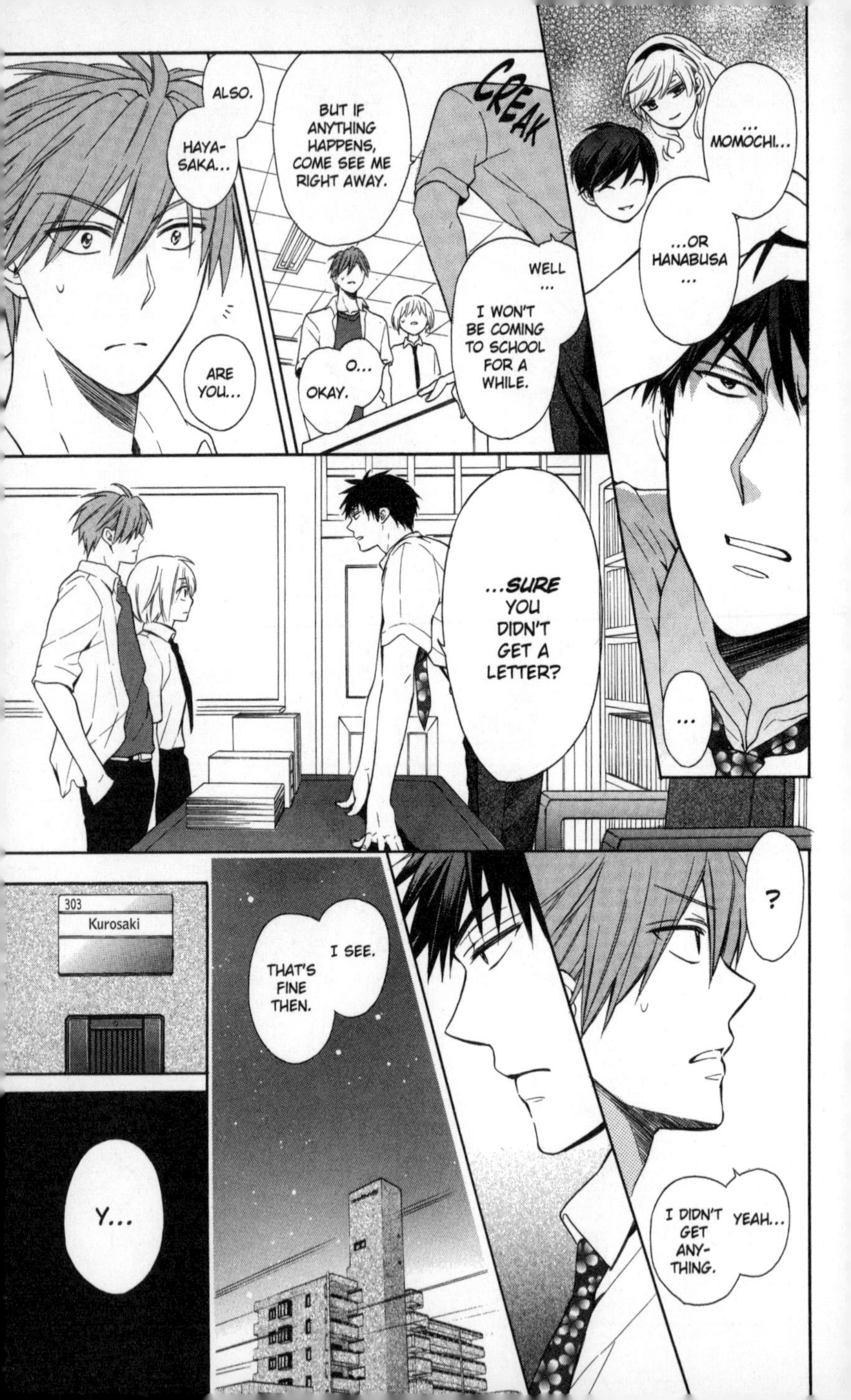
...MOMOCHI...
...OR HANABUSA...
...
CREAK
WELL... I WON'T BE COMING TO SCHOOL FOR A WHILE.
BUT IF ANYTHING HAPPENS, COME SEE ME RIGHT AWAY.
O... OKAY.
ALSO.
HAYA-SAKA...
ARE YOU...
...*SURE* YOU DIDN'T GET A LETTER?
...
?
YEAH...
I DIDN'T GET ANY-THING.
I SEE. THAT'S FINE THEN.
303
Kurosaki
Y...

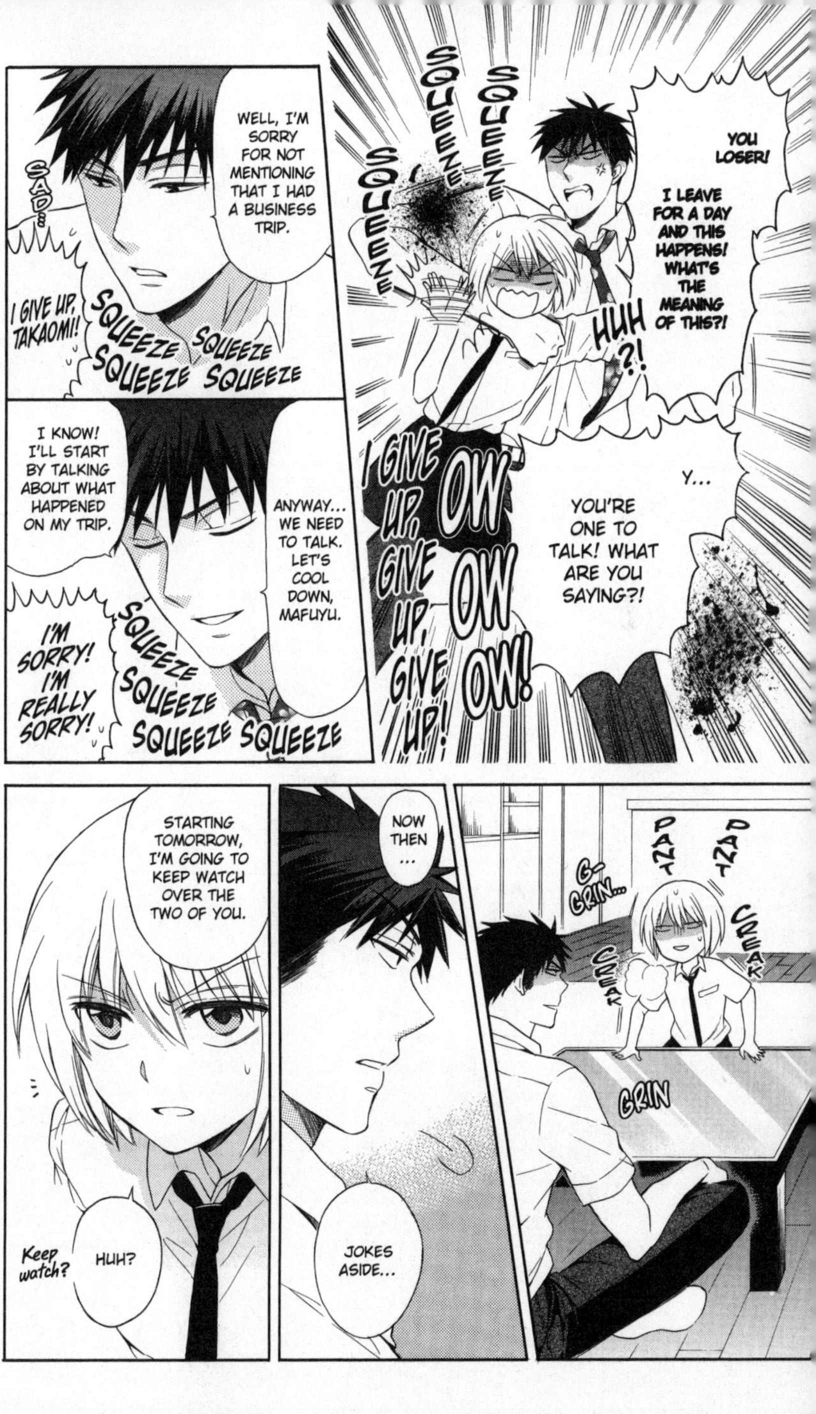
YOU LOSER!
I LEAVE FOR A DAY AND THIS HAPPENS! WHAT'S THE MEANING OF THIS?!
SQUEEZE SQUEEZE SQUEEZE
HUH?!
Y...
YOU'RE ONE TO TALK! WHAT ARE YOU SAYING?!
OW OW OW!
I GIVE UP, GIVE UP, GIVE UP!
WELL, I'M SORRY FOR NOT MENTIONING THAT I HAD A BUSINESS TRIP.
SAD...
I GIVE UP, TAKAOMI!
SQUEEZE SQUEEZE SQUEEZE SQUEEZE
ANYWAY... WE NEED TO TALK. LET'S COOL DOWN, MAFUYU.
I KNOW! I'LL START BY TALKING ABOUT WHAT HAPPENED ON MY TRIP.
I'M SORRY! I'M REALLY SORRY!
SQUEEZE SQUEEZE SQUEEZE SQUEEZE
PANT PANT
CREAK CREAK
G-GRIN...
GRIN
NOW THEN...
JOKES ASIDE...
STARTING TOMORROW, I'M GOING TO KEEP WATCH OVER THE TWO OF YOU.
HUH?
Keep watch?

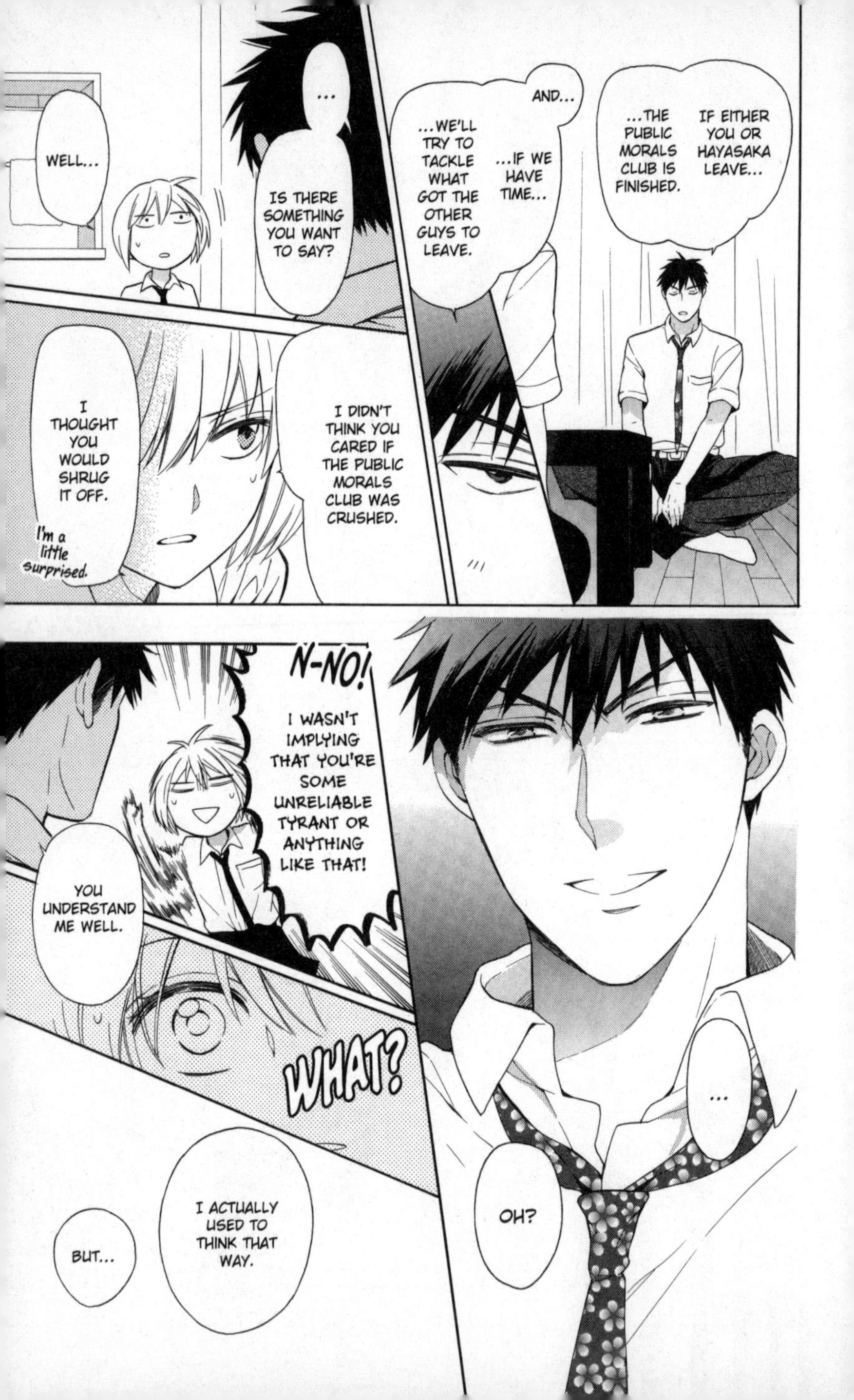
IF EITHER YOU OR HAYASAKA LEAVE...
...THE PUBLIC MORALS CLUB IS FINISHED.
AND...
...IF WE HAVE TIME...
...WE'LL TRY TO TACKLE WHAT GOT THE OTHER GUYS TO LEAVE.
...
IS THERE SOMETHING YOU WANT TO SAY?
WELL...
I DIDN'T THINK YOU CARED IF THE PUBLIC MORALS CLUB WAS CRUSHED.
I THOUGHT YOU WOULD SHRUG IT OFF.
I'm a little surprised.
...
OH?
N-NO!
I WASN'T IMPLYING THAT YOU'RE SOME UNRELIABLE TYRANT OR ANYTHING LIKE THAT!
YOU UNDERSTAND ME WELL.
WHAT?
I ACTUALLY USED TO THINK THAT WAY.
BUT...

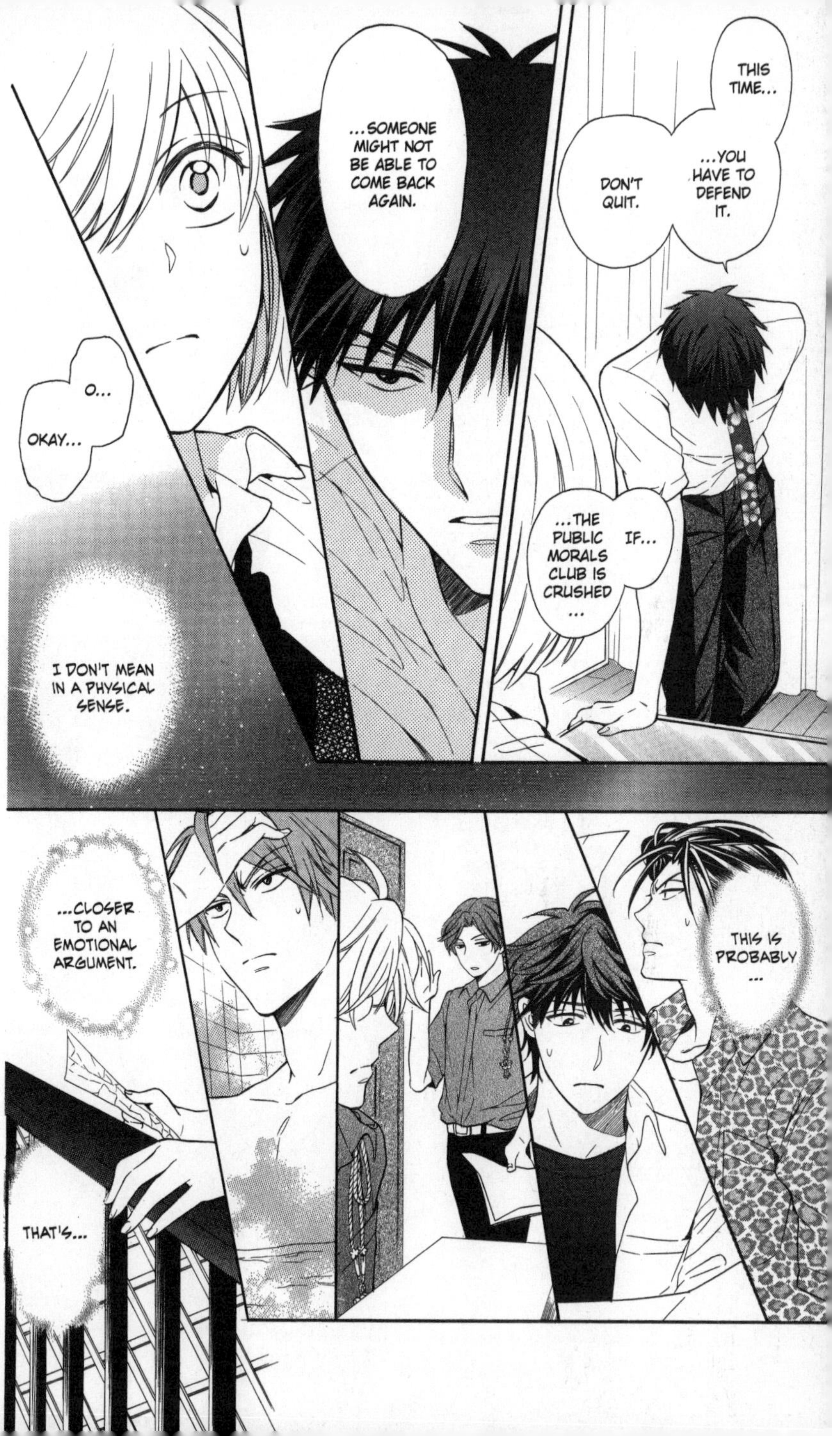
THIS TIME...
...YOU HAVE TO DEFEND IT.
DON'T QUIT.
IF...
...THE PUBLIC MORALS CLUB IS CRUSHED...
...SOMEONE MIGHT NOT BE ABLE TO COME BACK AGAIN.
O... OKAY...
I DON'T MEAN IN A PHYSICAL SENSE.
THIS IS PROBABLY...
...CLOSER TO AN EMOTIONAL ARGUMENT.
THAT'S...

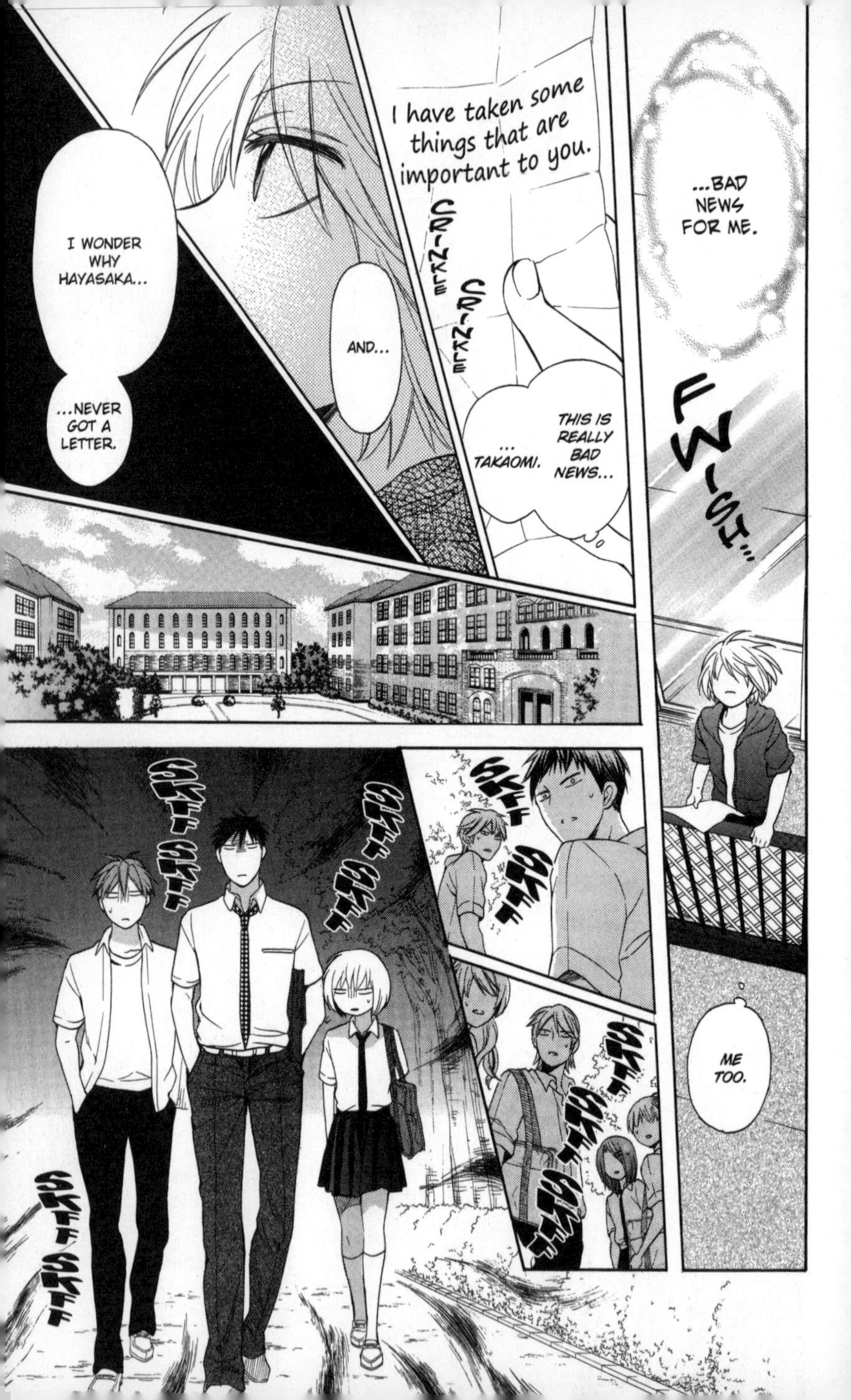

...BAD NEWS FOR ME.
FWISH...
ME TOO.
I have taken some things that are important to you.
CRINKLE
CRINKLE
THIS IS REALLY BAD NEWS...
... TAKAOMI.
AND...
I WONDER WHY HAYASAKA...
...NEVER GOT A LETTER.
SKFF SKFF
SKFF SKFF
SKFF SKFF SKFF
SKFF SKFF
SKFF SKFF
SKFF SKFF

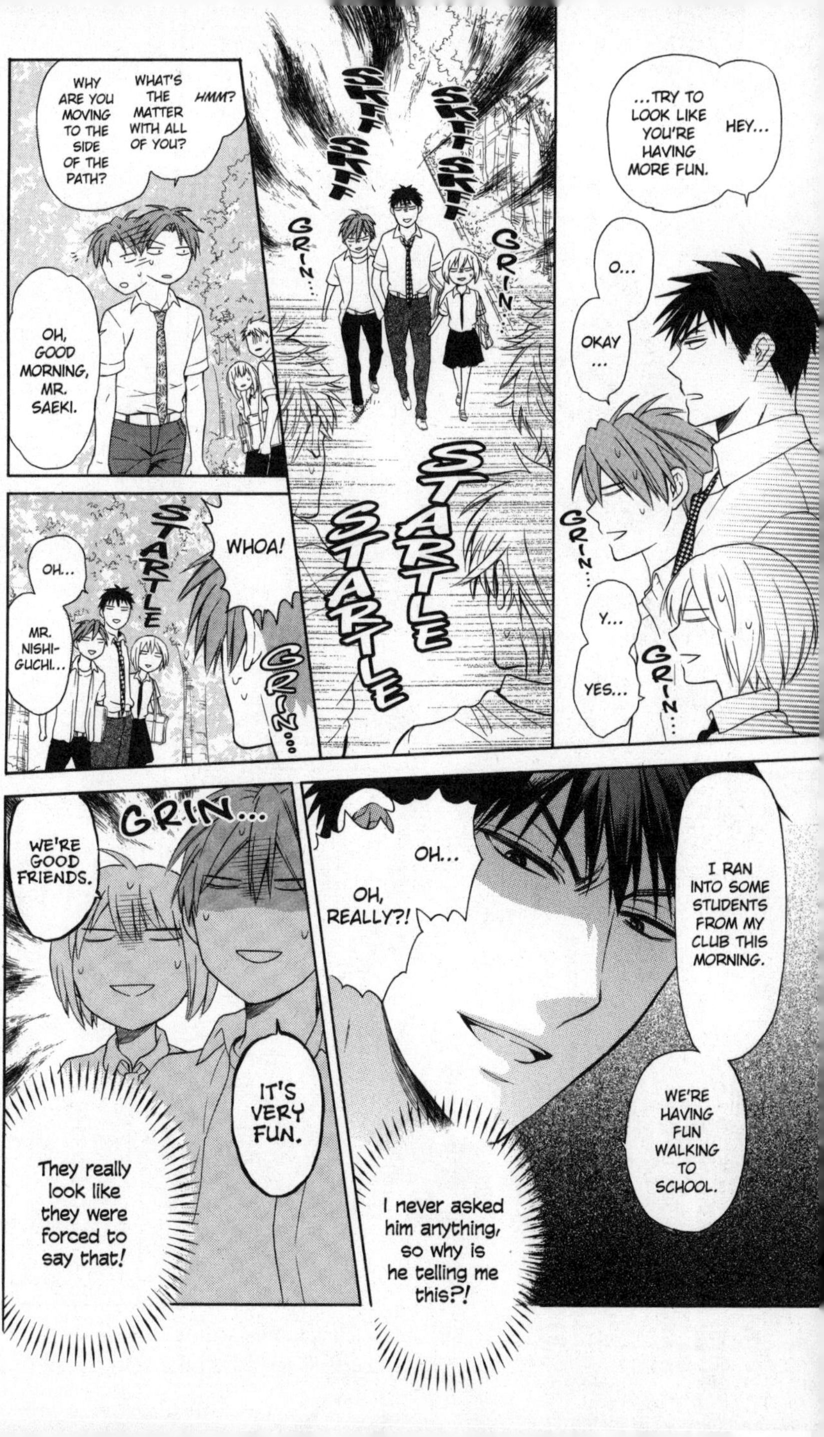
HEY...
...TRY TO LOOK LIKE YOU'RE HAVING MORE FUN.
O...
OKAY...
GRIN...
Y...
YES...
GRIN...
SKIT SKIT
SKIT SKIT
GRIN...
GRIN...
STARTLE
STARTLE
HMM?
WHAT'S THE MATTER WITH ALL OF YOU?
WHY ARE YOU MOVING TO THE SIDE OF THE PATH?
OH, GOOD MORNING, MR. SAEKI.
WHOA!
STARTLE
OH...
MR. NISHIGUCHI...
GRIN...
I RAN INTO SOME STUDENTS FROM MY CLUB THIS MORNING.
WE'RE HAVING FUN WALKING TO SCHOOL.
OH...
OH, REALLY?!
I never asked him anything, so why is he telling me this?!
GRIN...
WE'RE GOOD FRIENDS.
IT'S VERY FUN.
They really look like they were forced to say that!

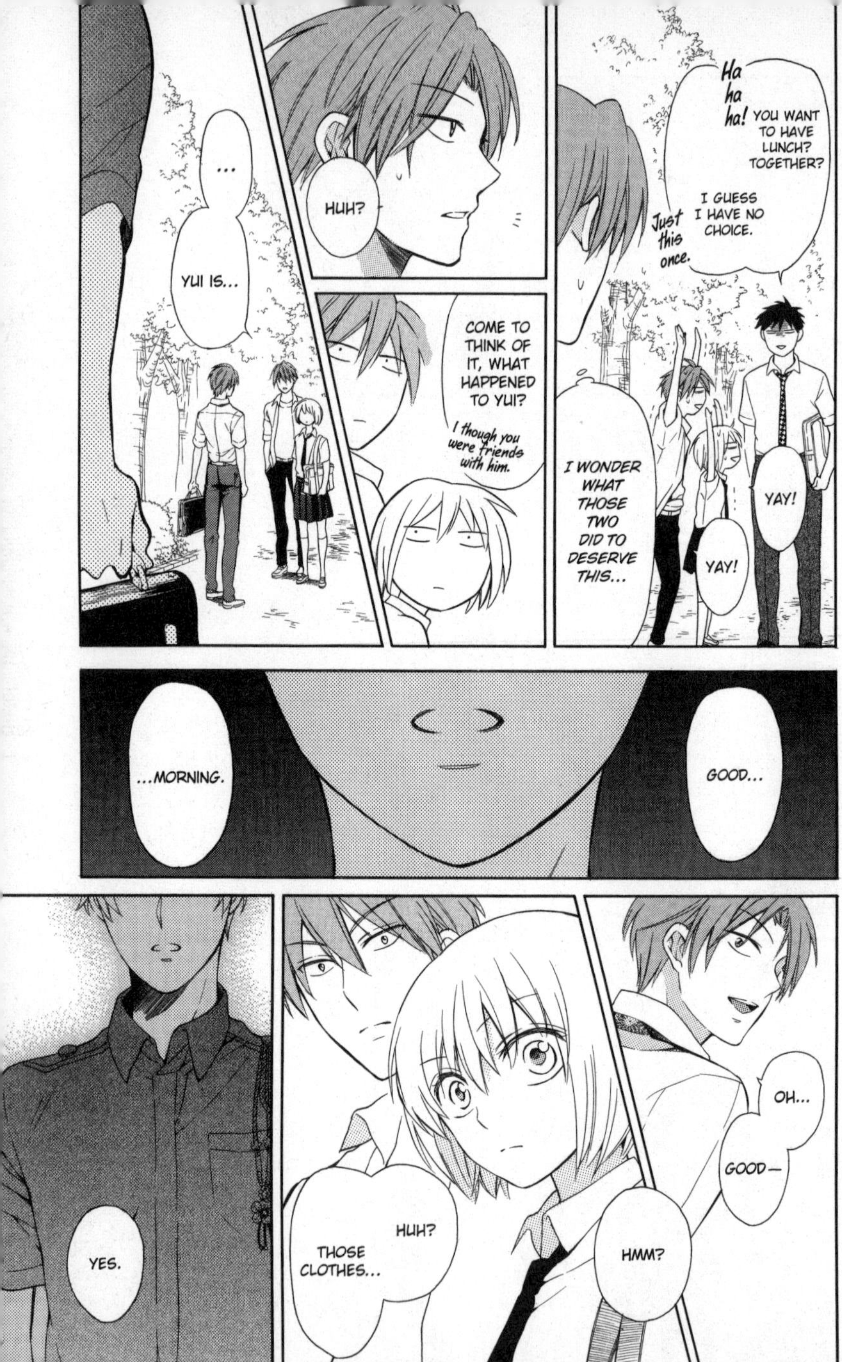
Ha ha ha! YOU WANT TO HAVE LUNCH? TOGETHER?
I GUESS I HAVE NO CHOICE.
Just this once.
YAY!
YAY!
I WONDER WHAT THOSE TWO DID TO DESERVE THIS...
HUH?
COME TO THINK OF IT, WHAT HAPPENED TO YUI?
I though you were friends with him.
...
YUI IS...
GOOD...
...MORNING.
OH...
GOOD—
HMM?
HUH?
THOSE CLOTHES...
YES.

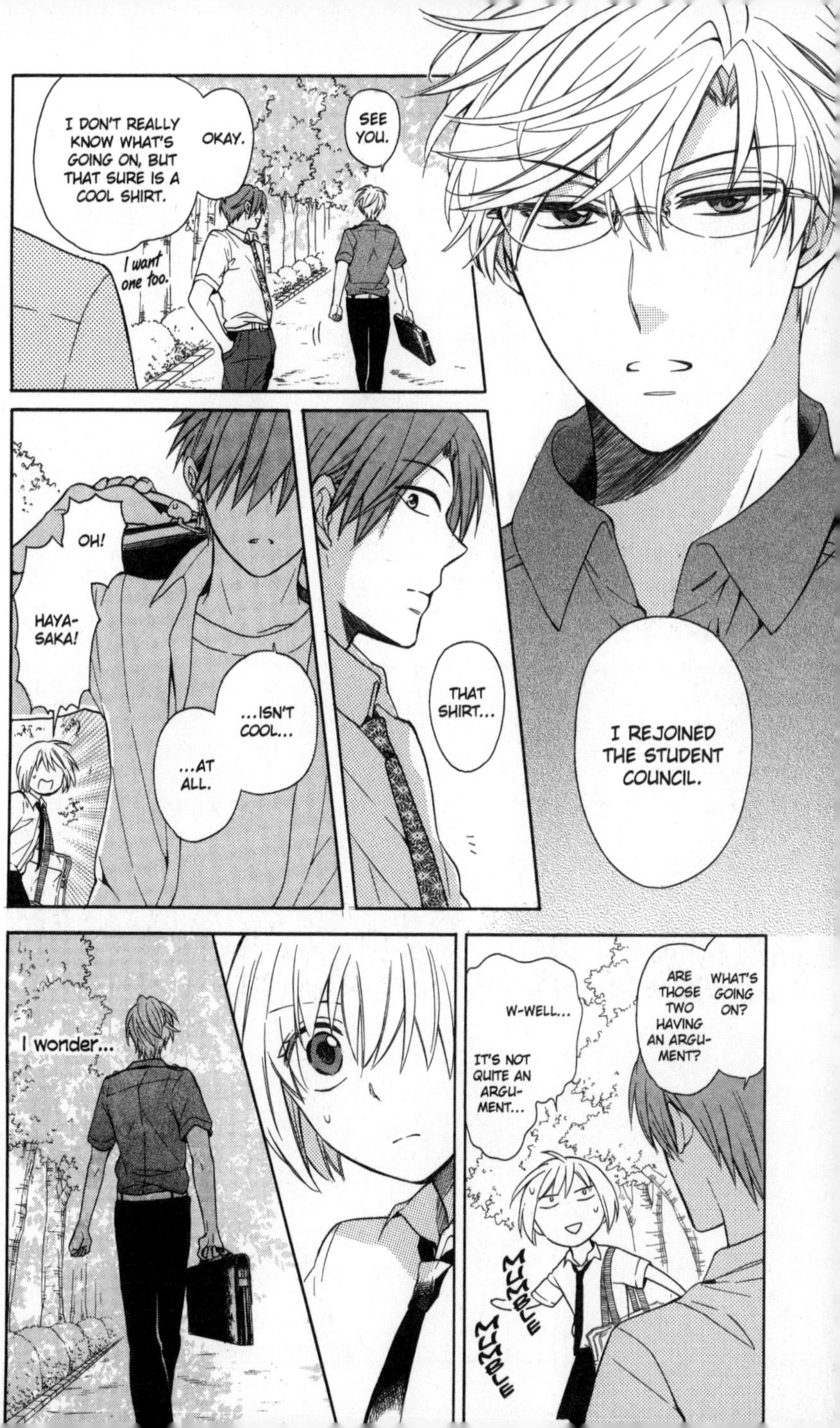
I REJOINED THE STUDENT COUNCIL.
SEE YOU.
OKAY.
I DON'T REALLY KNOW WHAT'S GOING ON, BUT THAT SURE IS A COOL SHIRT.
I want one too.
THAT SHIRT...
...ISN'T COOL...
...AT ALL.
OH!
HAYA-SAKA!
WHAT'S GOING ON?
ARE THOSE TWO HAVING AN ARGU-MENT?
W-WELL...
IT'S NOT QUITE AN ARGU-MENT...
MUMBLE MUMBLE
I wonder...

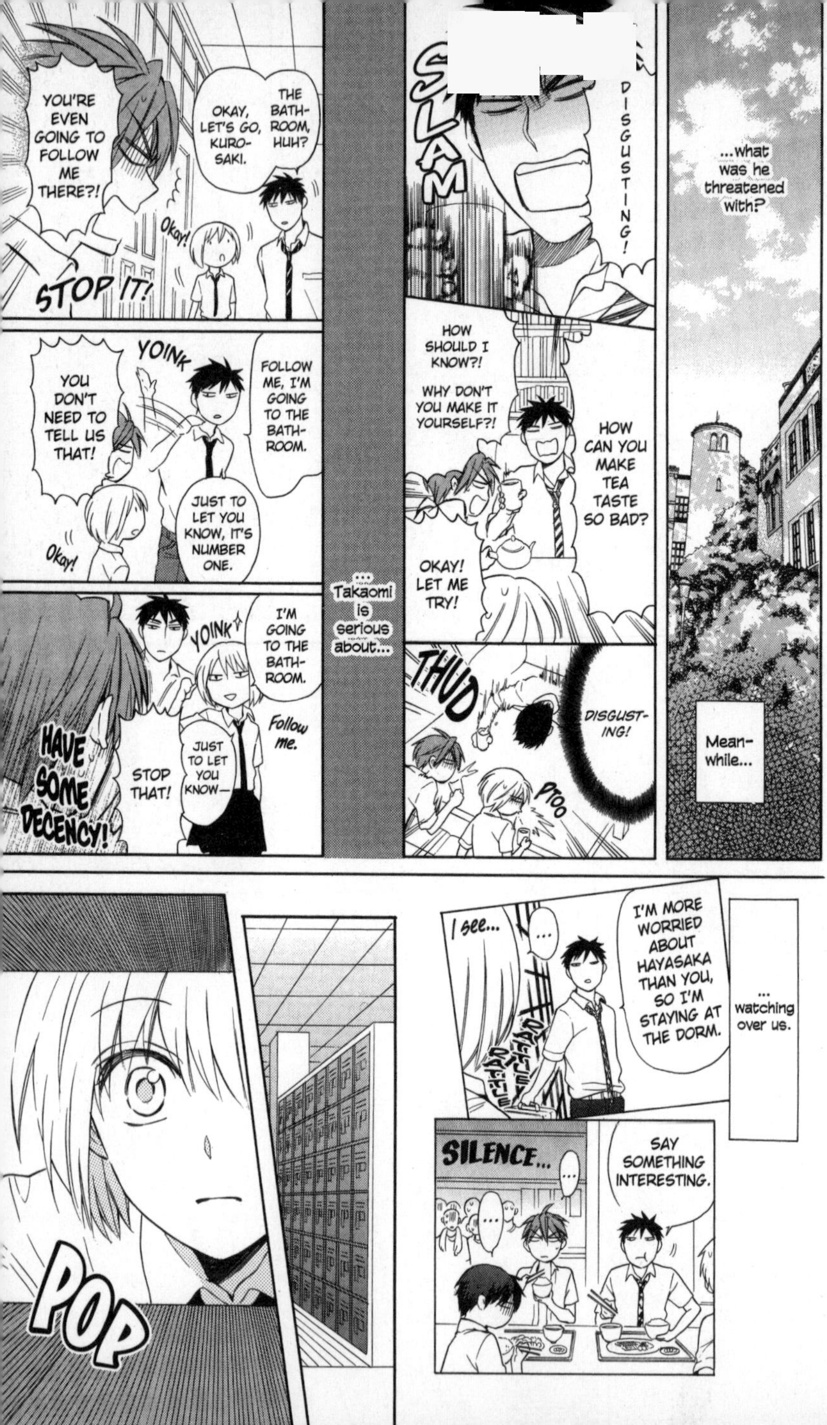
...what was he threatened with?
Mean-while...
DISGUSTING!
SLAM
HOW CAN YOU MAKE TEA TASTE SO BAD?
HOW SHOULD I KNOW?!
WHY DON'T YOU MAKE IT YOURSELF?!
OKAY! LET ME TRY!
DISGUST-ING!
THUD
PTOO
...Takaomi is serious about...
THE BATH-ROOM, HUH?
OKAY, LET'S GO, KURO-SAKI.
YOU'RE EVEN GOING TO FOLLOW ME THERE?!
Okay!
STOP IT!
FOLLOW ME, I'M GOING TO THE BATH-ROOM.
YOINK
JUST TO LET YOU KNOW, IT'S NUMBER ONE.
YOU DON'T NEED TO TELL US THAT!
Okay!
I'M GOING TO THE BATH-ROOM.
YOINK
Follow me.
JUST TO LET YOU KNOW—
STOP THAT!
HAVE SOME DECENCY!
...watching over us.
I'M MORE WORRIED ABOUT HAYASAKA THAN YOU, SO I'M STAYING AT THE DORM.
...
I see...
RATTLE RATTLE
SAY SOMETHING INTERESTING.
...
SILENCE...
...
POP

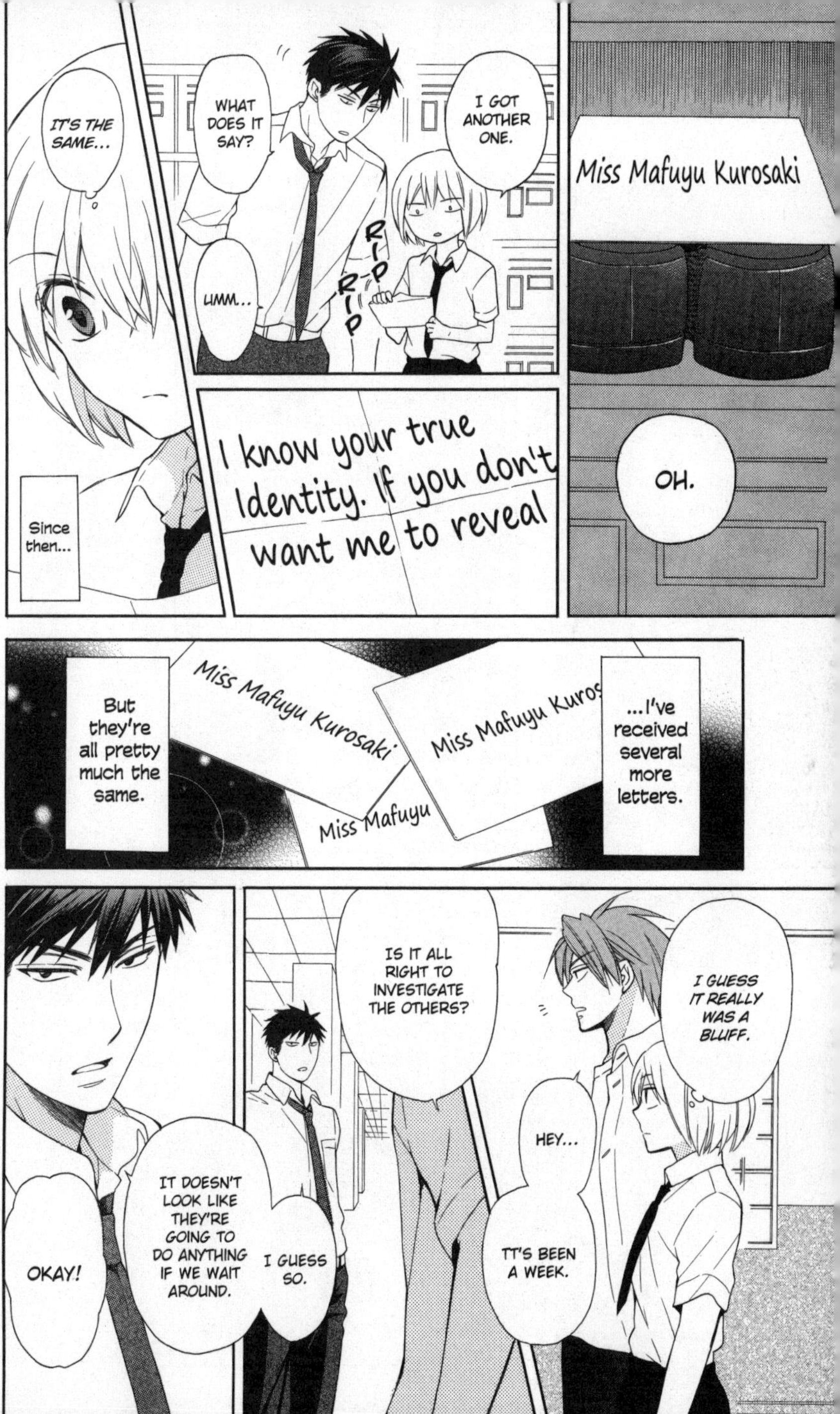
Miss Mafuyu Kurosaki
OH.
I GOT ANOTHER ONE.
WHAT DOES IT SAY?
RIP RIP
UMM...
I know your true Identity. If you don't want me to reveal
IT'S THE SAME...
Since then...
...I've received several more letters.
Miss Mafuyu Kuros
Miss Mafuyu Kurosaki
Miss Mafuyu
But they're all pretty much the same.
I GUESS IT REALLY WAS A BLUFF.
IS IT ALL RIGHT TO INVESTIGATE THE OTHERS?
HEY...
TT'S BEEN A WEEK.
I GUESS SO.
IT DOESN'T LOOK LIKE THEY'RE GOING TO DO ANYTHING IF WE WAIT AROUND.
OKAY!

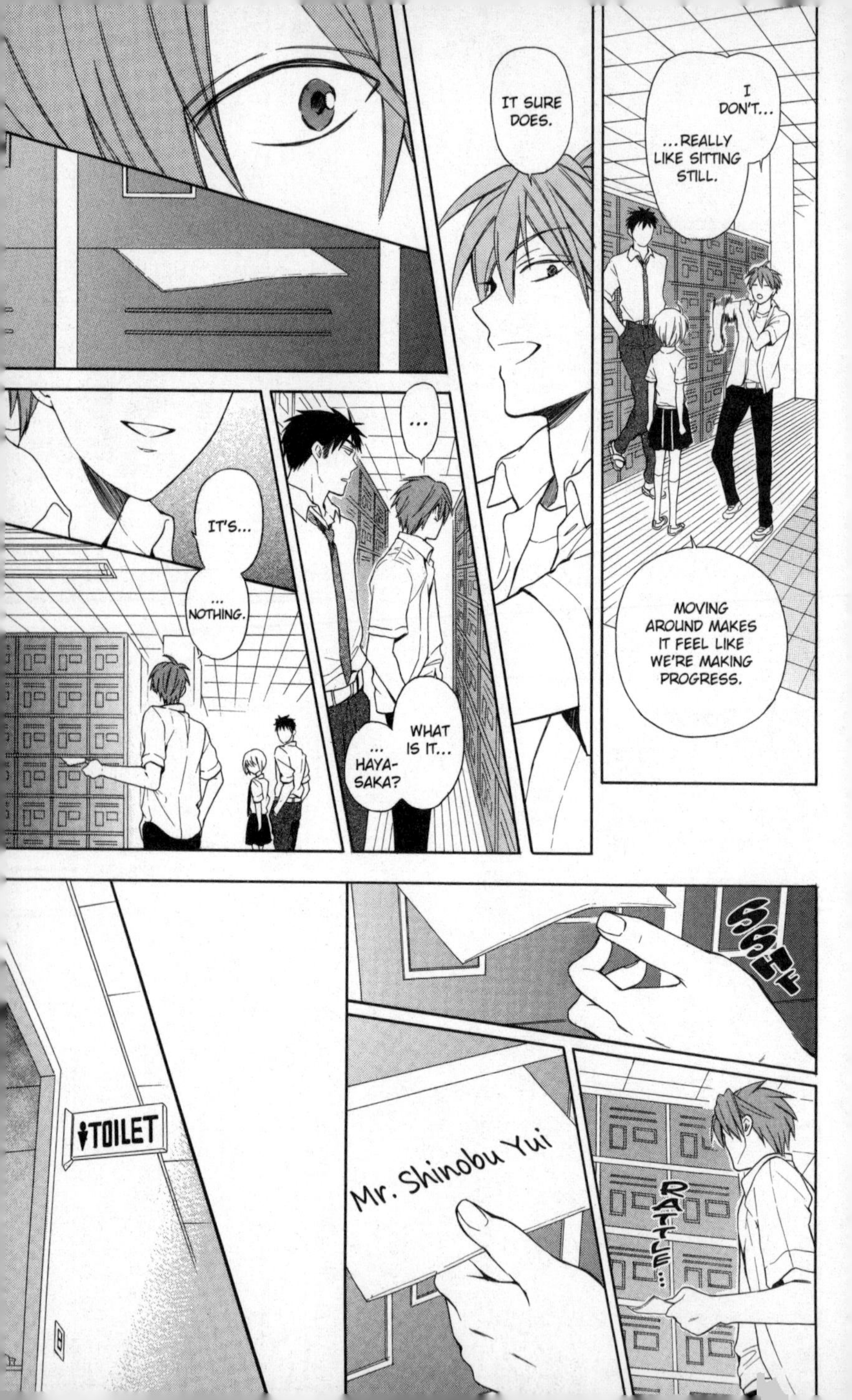

I DON'T...
...REALLY LIKE SITTING STILL.
MOVING AROUND MAKES IT FEEL LIKE WE'RE MAKING PROGRESS.
IT SURE DOES.
...
WHAT IS IT... ...HAYA-SAKA?
IT'S...
...NOTHING.
Mr. Shinobu Yui
RATTLE...
TOILET

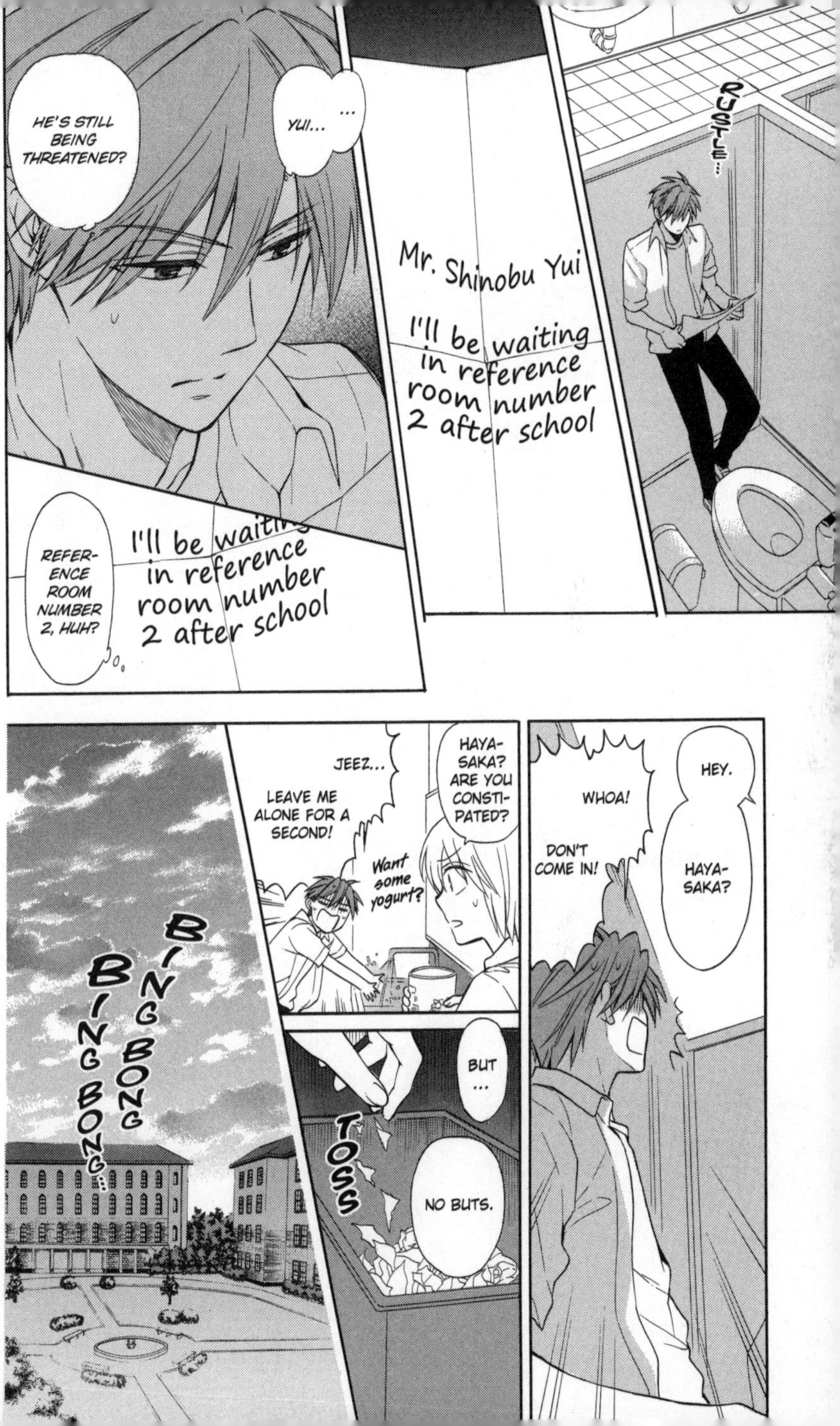
RUSTLE...
Mr. Shinobu Yui
I'll be waiting in reference room number 2 after school
...
YUI...
HE'S STILL BEING THREATENED?
I'll be waiting in reference room number 2 after school
REFERENCE ROOM NUMBER 2, HUH?
HEY.
HAYA-SAKA?
WHOA!
DON'T COME IN!
HAYA-SAKA? ARE YOU CONSTIPATED?
JEEZ...
LEAVE ME ALONE FOR A SECOND!
Want some yogurt?
BUT...
NO BUTS.
TOSS
BING BONG
BING BONG...

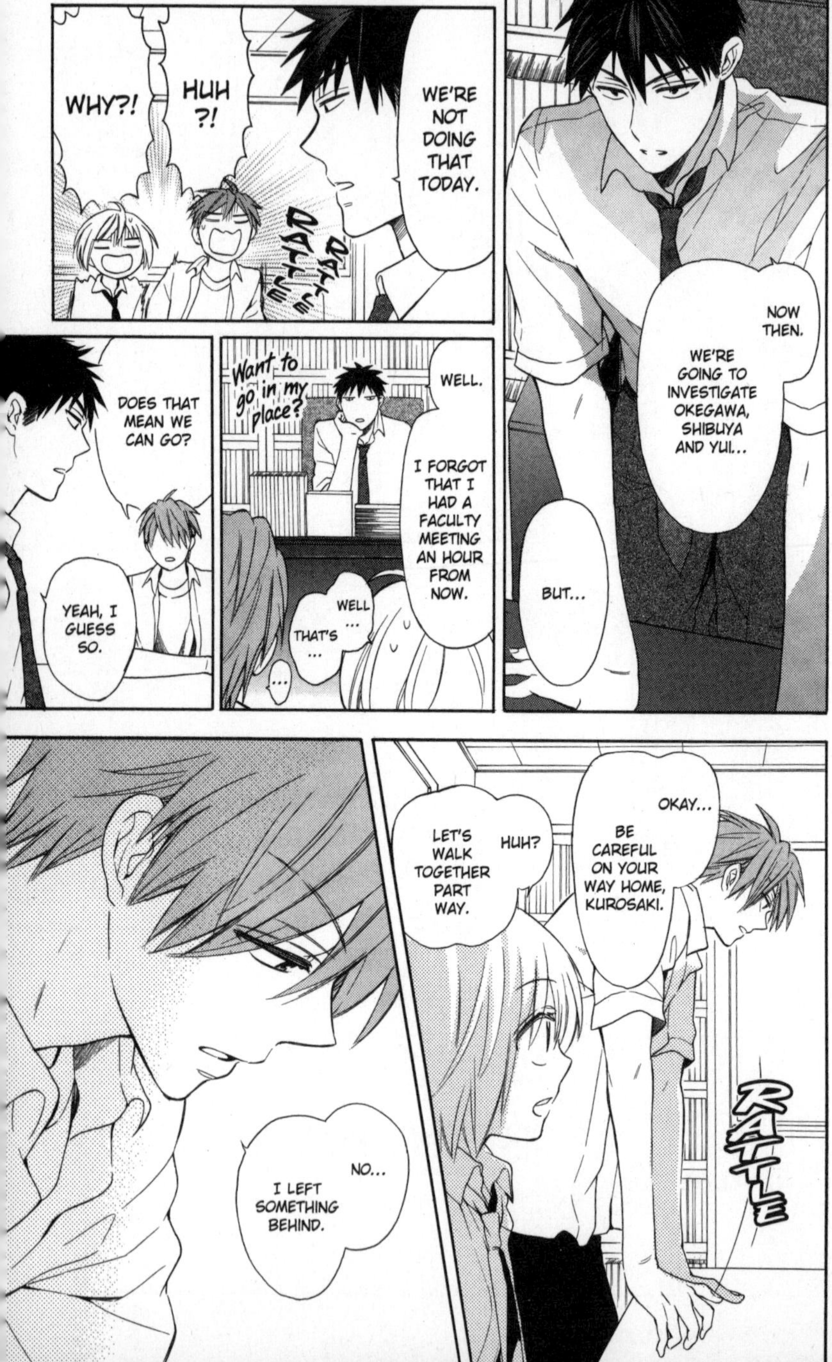
NOW THEN.
WE'RE GOING TO INVESTIGATE OKEGAWA, SHIBUYA AND YUI...
BUT...
WE'RE NOT DOING THAT TODAY.
HUH ?!
WHY?!
RATTLE RATTLE
WELL.
I FORGOT THAT I HAD A FACULTY MEETING AN HOUR FROM NOW.
Want to go in my place?
WELL...
THAT'S...
...
DOES THAT MEAN WE CAN GO?
YEAH, I GUESS SO.
OKAY...
BE CAREFUL ON YOUR WAY HOME, KUROSAKI.
HUH?
LET'S WALK TOGETHER PART WAY.
RATTLE
NO...
I LEFT SOMETHING BEHIND.

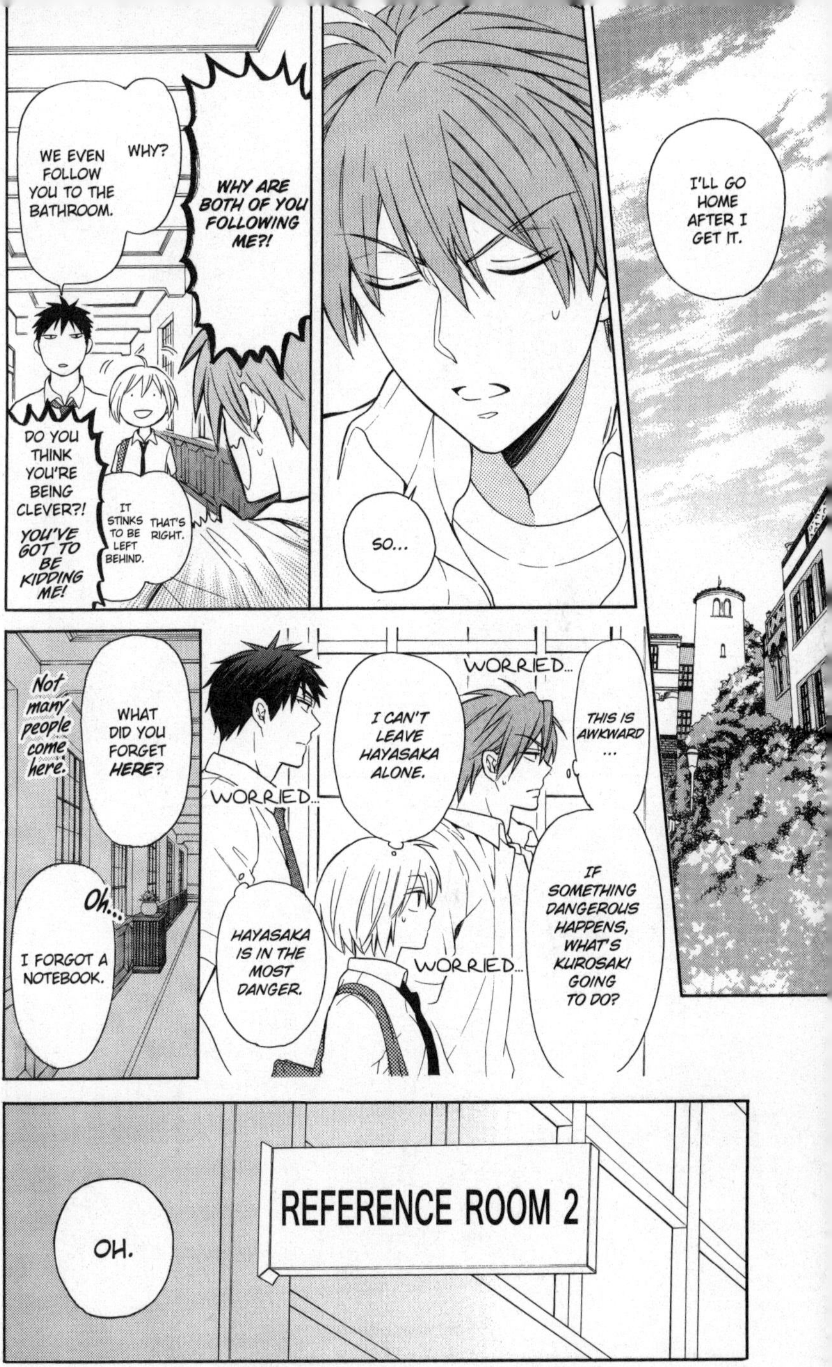
I'LL GO HOME AFTER I GET IT.
SO...
WHY ARE BOTH OF YOU FOLLOWING ME?!
WHY?
WE EVEN FOLLOW YOU TO THE BATHROOM.
DO YOU THINK YOU'RE BEING CLEVER?!
YOU'VE GOT TO BE KIDDING ME!
THAT'S RIGHT.
IT STINKS TO BE LEFT BEHIND.
THIS IS AWKWARD...
WORRIED...
IF SOMETHING DANGEROUS HAPPENS, WHAT'S KUROSAKI GOING TO DO?
I CAN'T LEAVE HAYASAKA ALONE.
WORRIED...
HAYASAKA IS IN THE MOST DANGER.
WORRIED...
WHAT DID YOU FORGET HERE?
Not many people come here.
Oh...
I FORGOT A NOTEBOOK.
REFERENCE ROOM 2
OH.

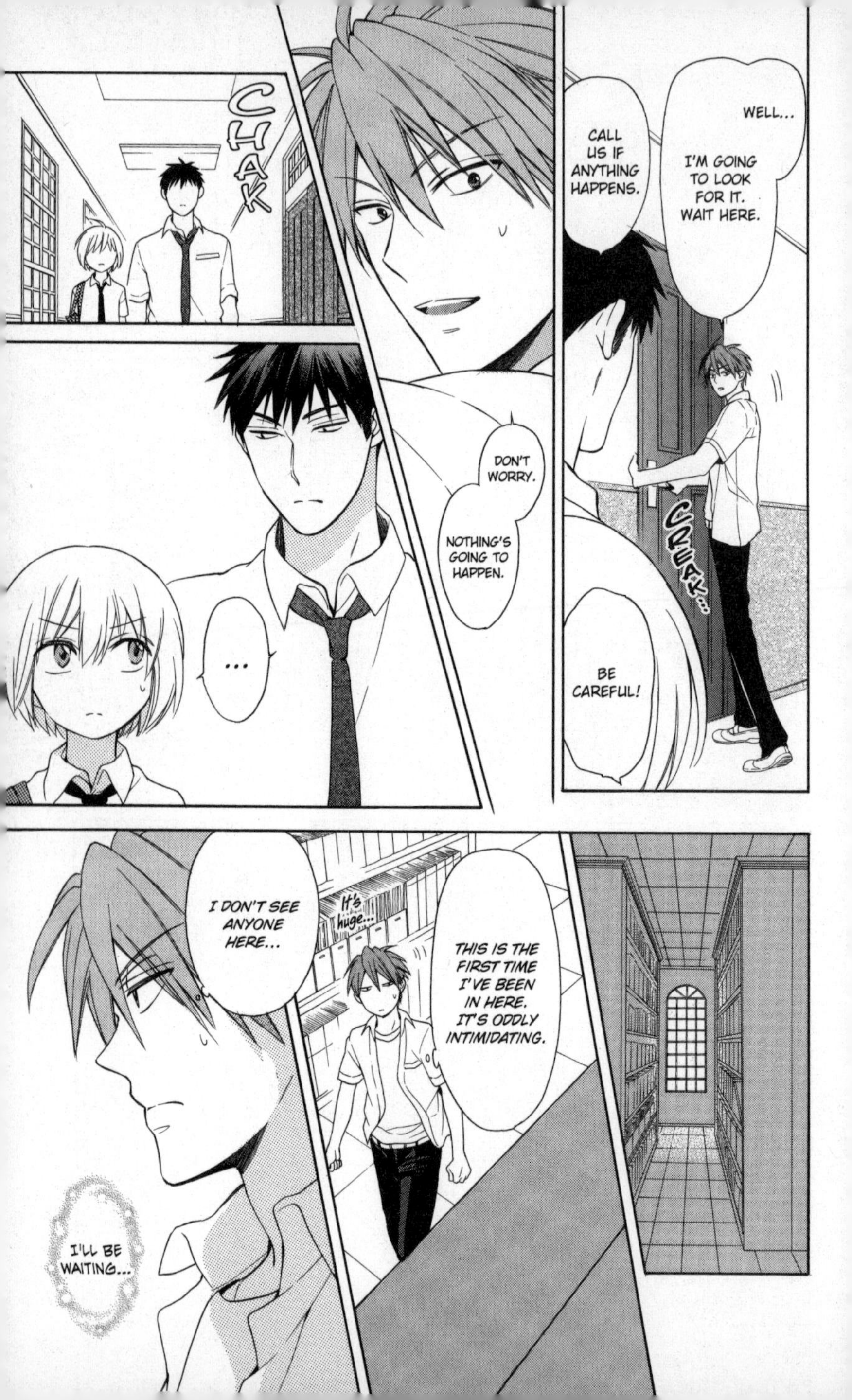
WELL...
I'M GOING TO LOOK FOR IT. WAIT HERE.
CALL US IF ANYTHING HAPPENS.
CREAK...
BE CAREFUL!
DON'T WORRY.
NOTHING'S GOING TO HAPPEN.
CHAK
...
THIS IS THE FIRST TIME I'VE BEEN IN HERE. IT'S ODDLY INTIMIDATING.
It's huge...
I DON'T SEE ANYONE HERE...
I'LL BE WAITING...

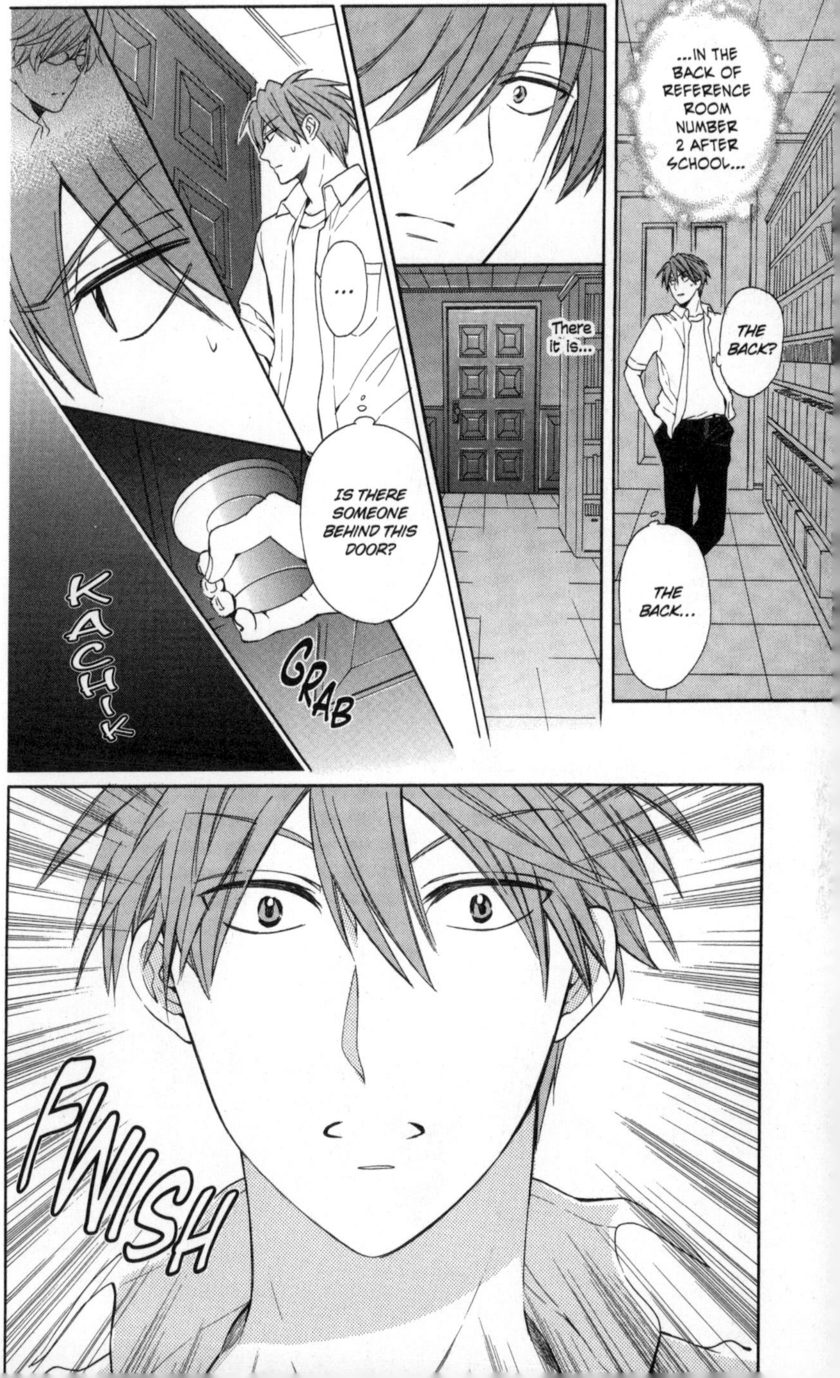
...IN THE BACK OF REFERENCE ROOM NUMBER 2 AFTER SCHOOL...
THE BACK?
THE BACK...
There it is...
...
IS THERE SOMEONE BEHIND THIS DOOR?
GRAB
KACHIK
FWISH

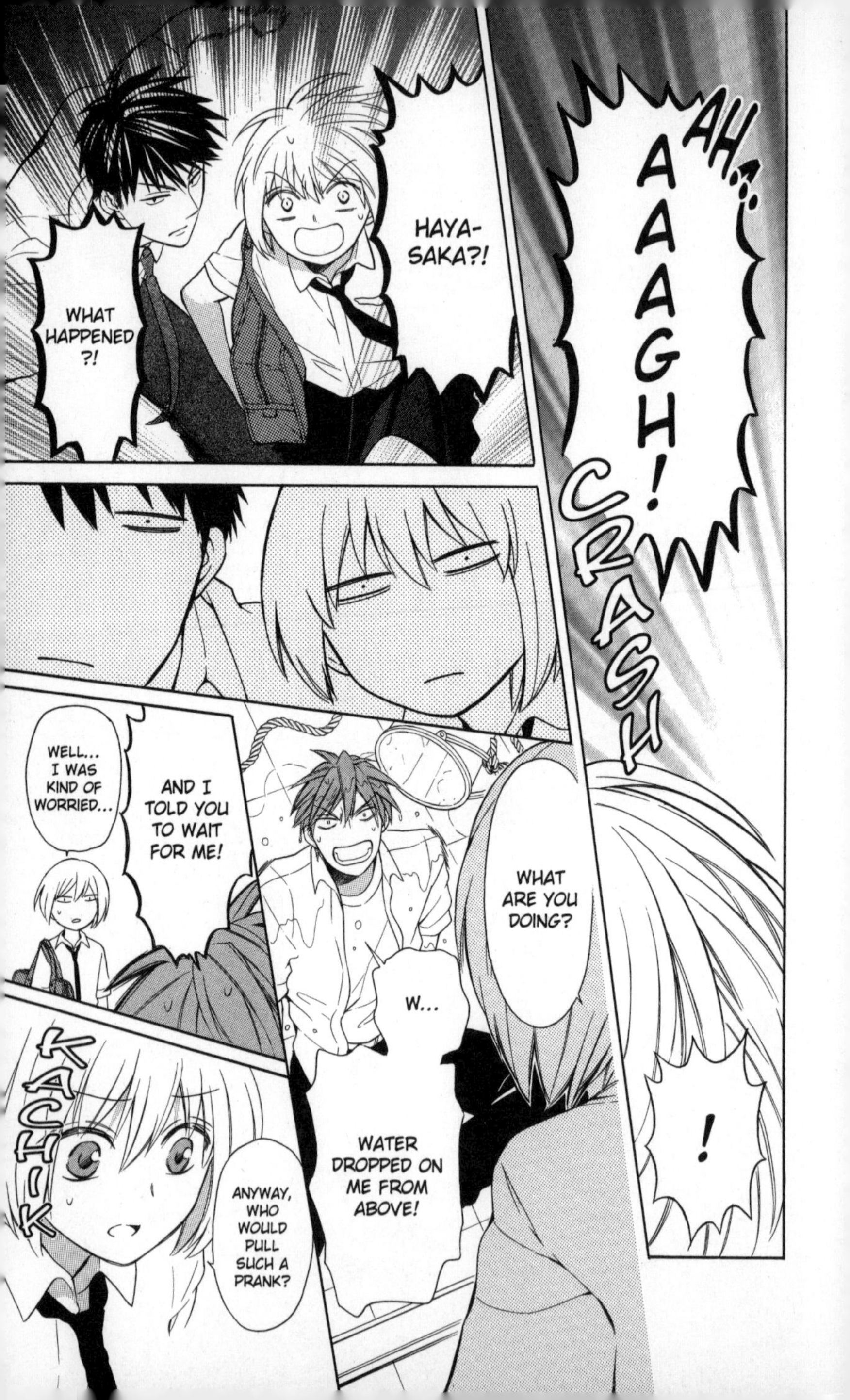
AH... AAAAGH!
CRASH
HAYA-SAKA?!
WHAT HAPPENED?!
!
WHAT ARE YOU DOING?
W...
WATER DROPPED ON ME FROM ABOVE!
AND I TOLD YOU TO WAIT FOR ME!
WELL... I WAS KIND OF WORRIED...
KACHIK
ANYWAY, WHO WOULD PULL SUCH A PRANK?

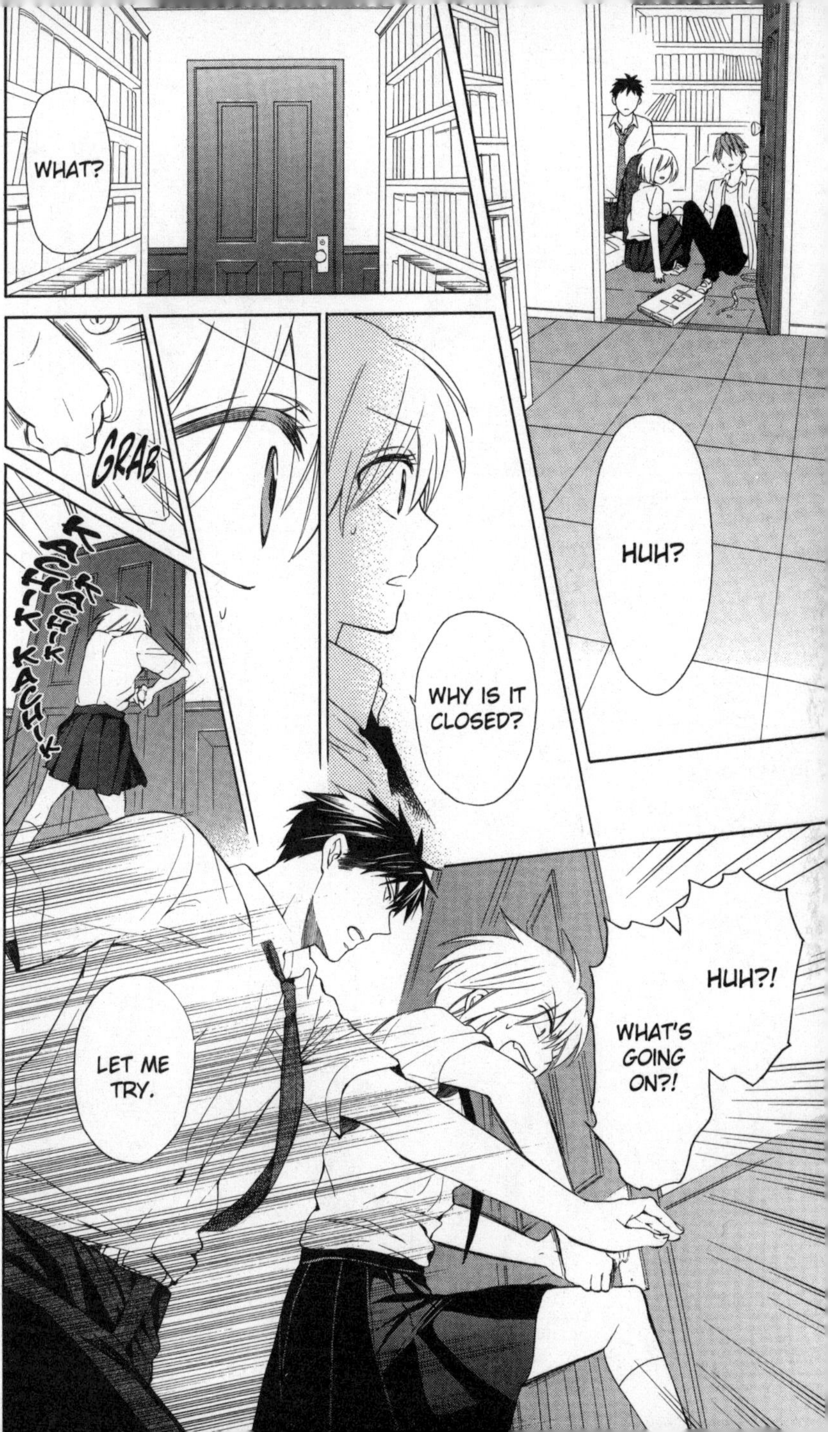
HUH?
WHAT?
WHY IS IT CLOSED?
GRAB
KACHIK KACHIK KACHIK
HUH?!
WHAT'S GOING ON?!
LET ME TRY.

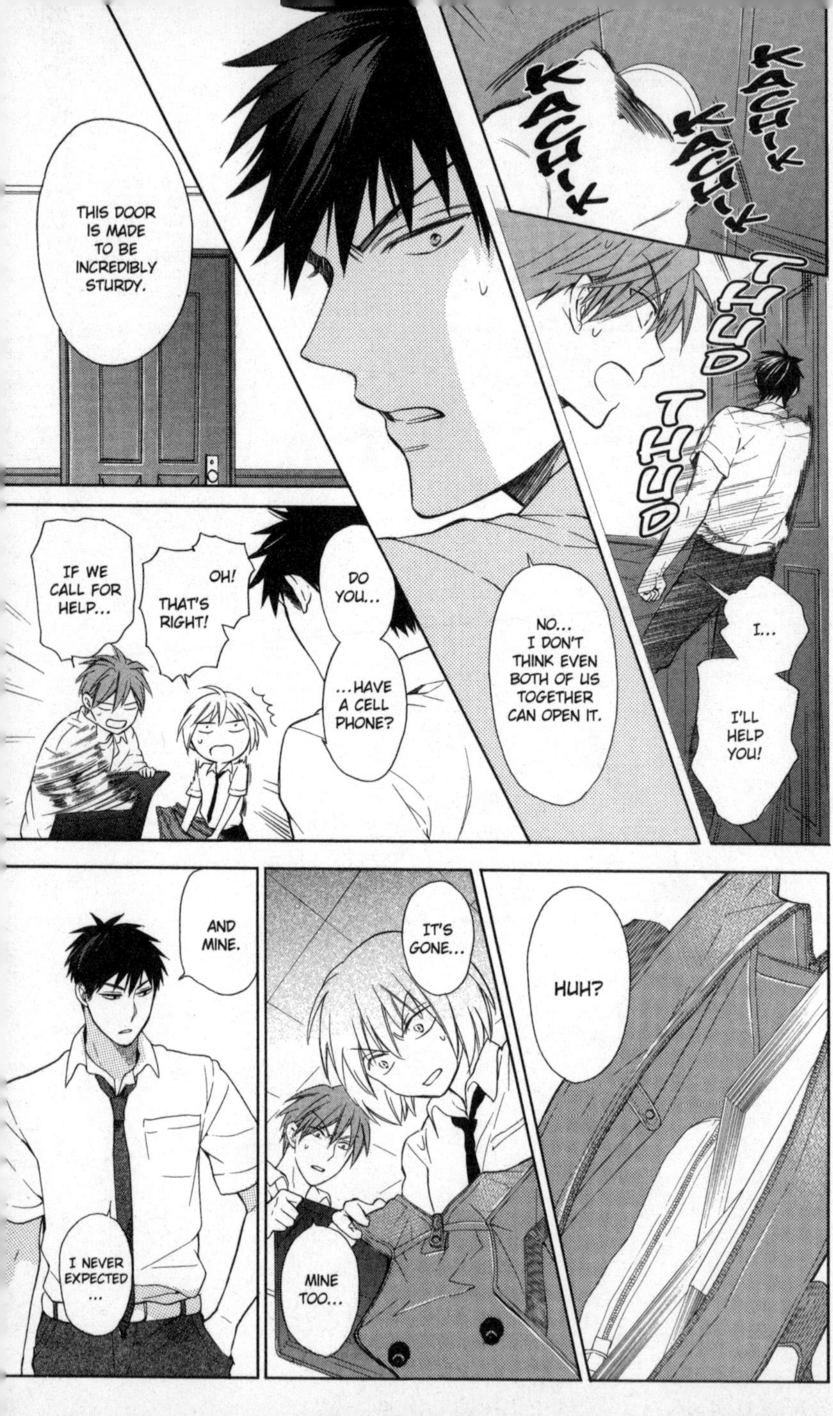
KACHIK
KACHIK
KACHIK
THUD
THUD
I...
I'LL HELP YOU!
NO... I DON'T THINK EVEN BOTH OF US TOGETHER CAN OPEN IT.
THIS DOOR IS MADE TO BE INCREDIBLY STURDY.
DO YOU...
...HAVE A CELL PHONE?
OH!
THAT'S RIGHT!
IF WE CALL FOR HELP...
HUH?
IT'S GONE...
MINE TOO...
AND MINE.
I NEVER EXPECTED ...

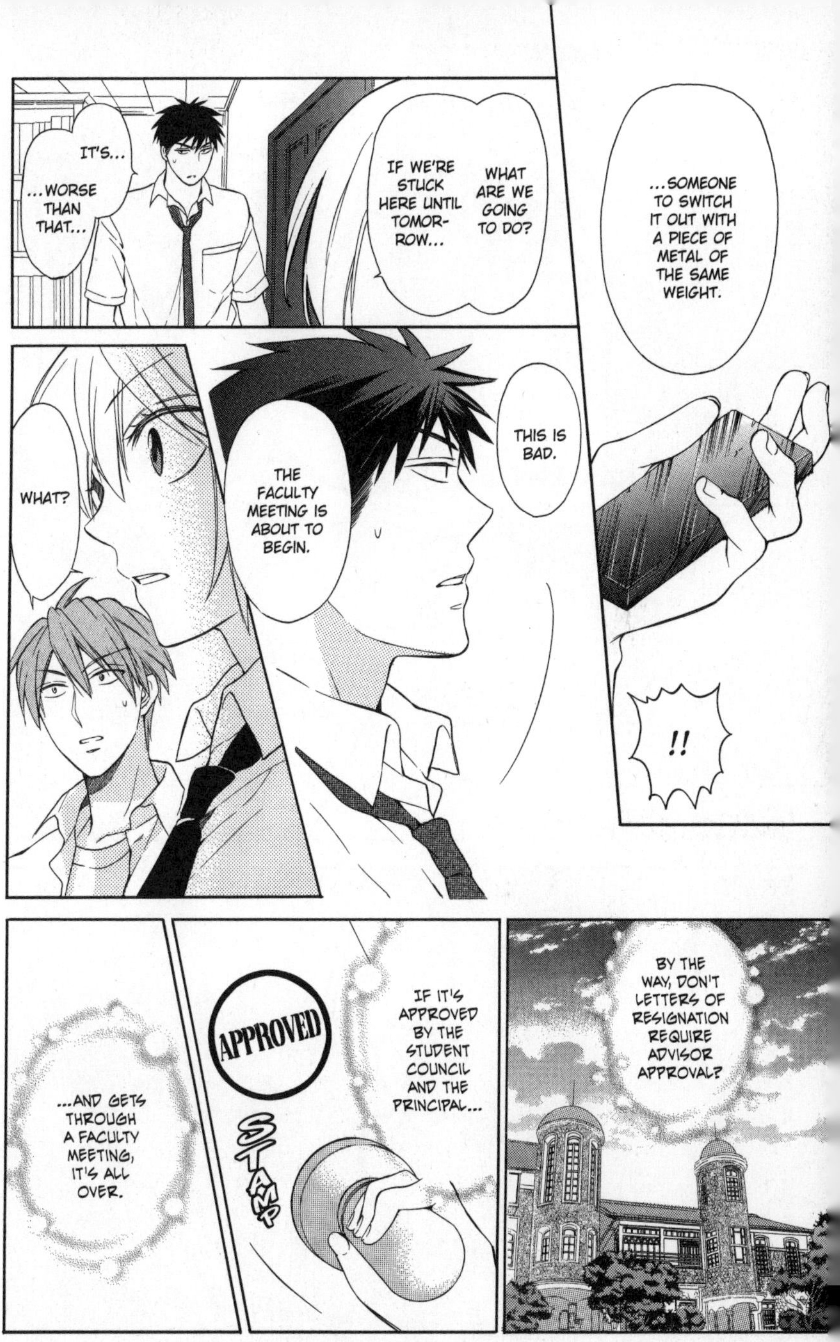
...SOMEONE TO SWITCH IT OUT WITH A PIECE OF METAL OF THE SAME WEIGHT.
!!
IF WE'RE STUCK HERE UNTIL TOMORROW... WHAT ARE WE GOING TO DO?
IT'S... ...WORSE THAN THAT...
THIS IS BAD.
THE FACULTY MEETING IS ABOUT TO BEGIN.
WHAT?
BY THE WAY, DON'T LETTERS OF RESIGNATION REQUIRE ADVISOR APPROVAL?
IF IT'S APPROVED BY THE STUDENT COUNCIL AND THE PRINCIPAL...
APPROVED
STAMP
...AND GETS THROUGH A FACULTY MEETING, IT'S ALL OVER.

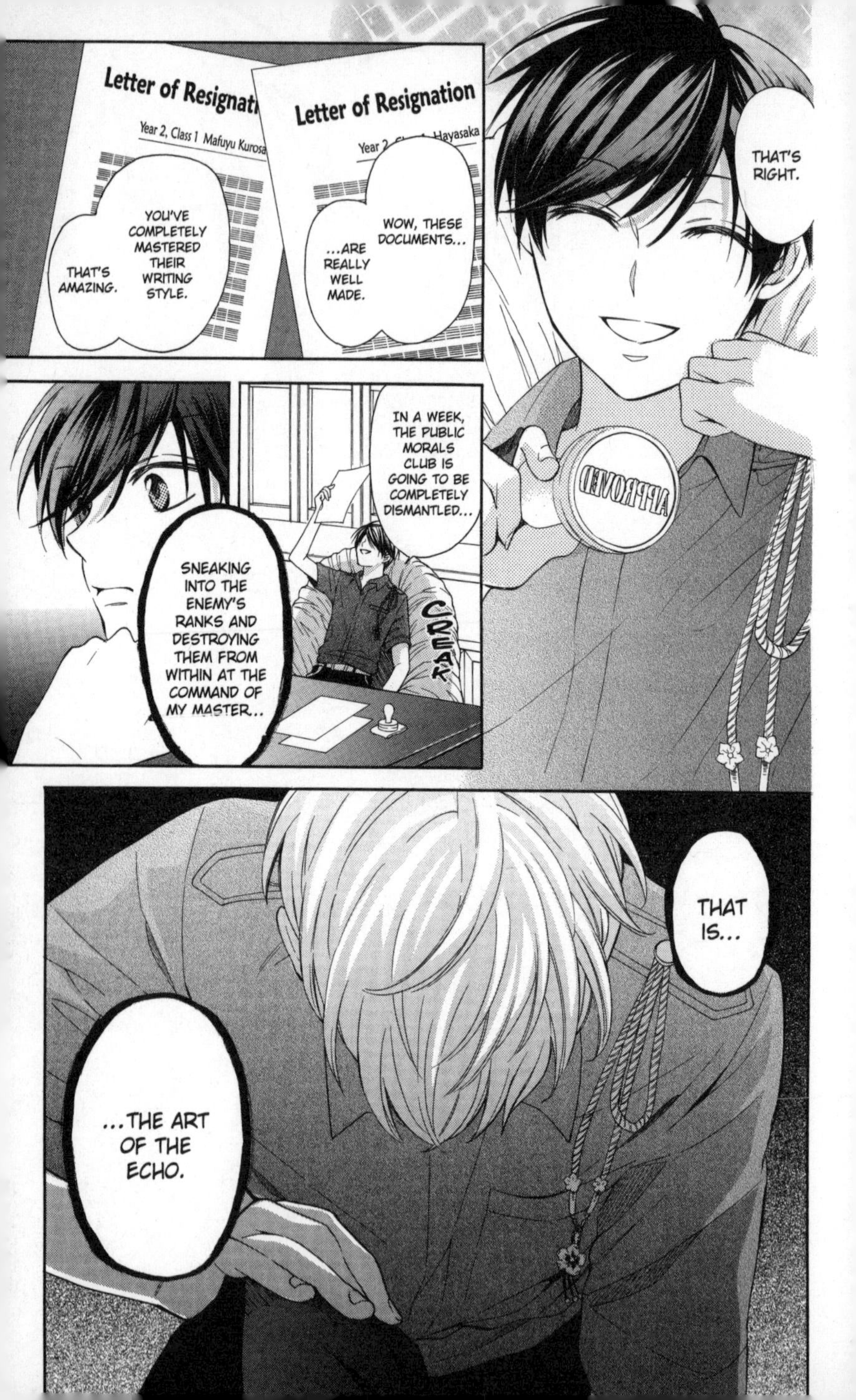
THAT'S RIGHT.
Letter of Resignation
Year 2
Hayasaka
WOW, THESE DOCUMENTS...
...ARE REALLY WELL MADE.
Letter of Resignati
Year 2, Class 1 Mafuyu Kurosa
YOU'VE COMPLETELY MASTERED THEIR WRITING STYLE.
THAT'S AMAZING.
APPROVED
IN A WEEK, THE PUBLIC MORALS CLUB IS GOING TO BE COMPLETELY DISMANTLED...
CREAK
SNEAKING INTO THE ENEMY'S RANKS AND DESTROYING THEM FROM WITHIN AT THE COMMAND OF MY MASTER...
THAT IS...
...THE ART OF THE ECHO.

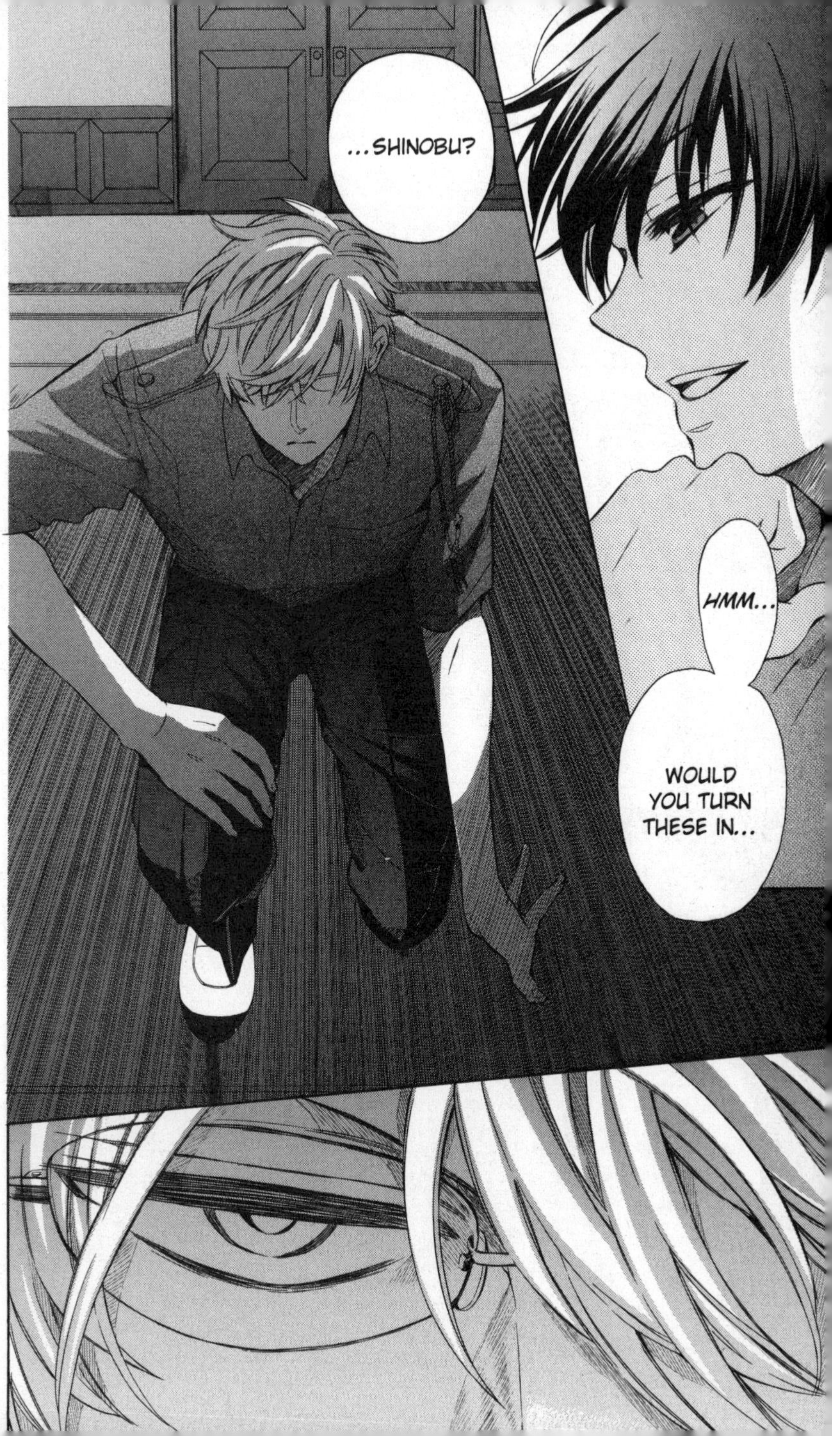
HMM...
WOULD YOU TURN THESE IN...
...SHINOBU?

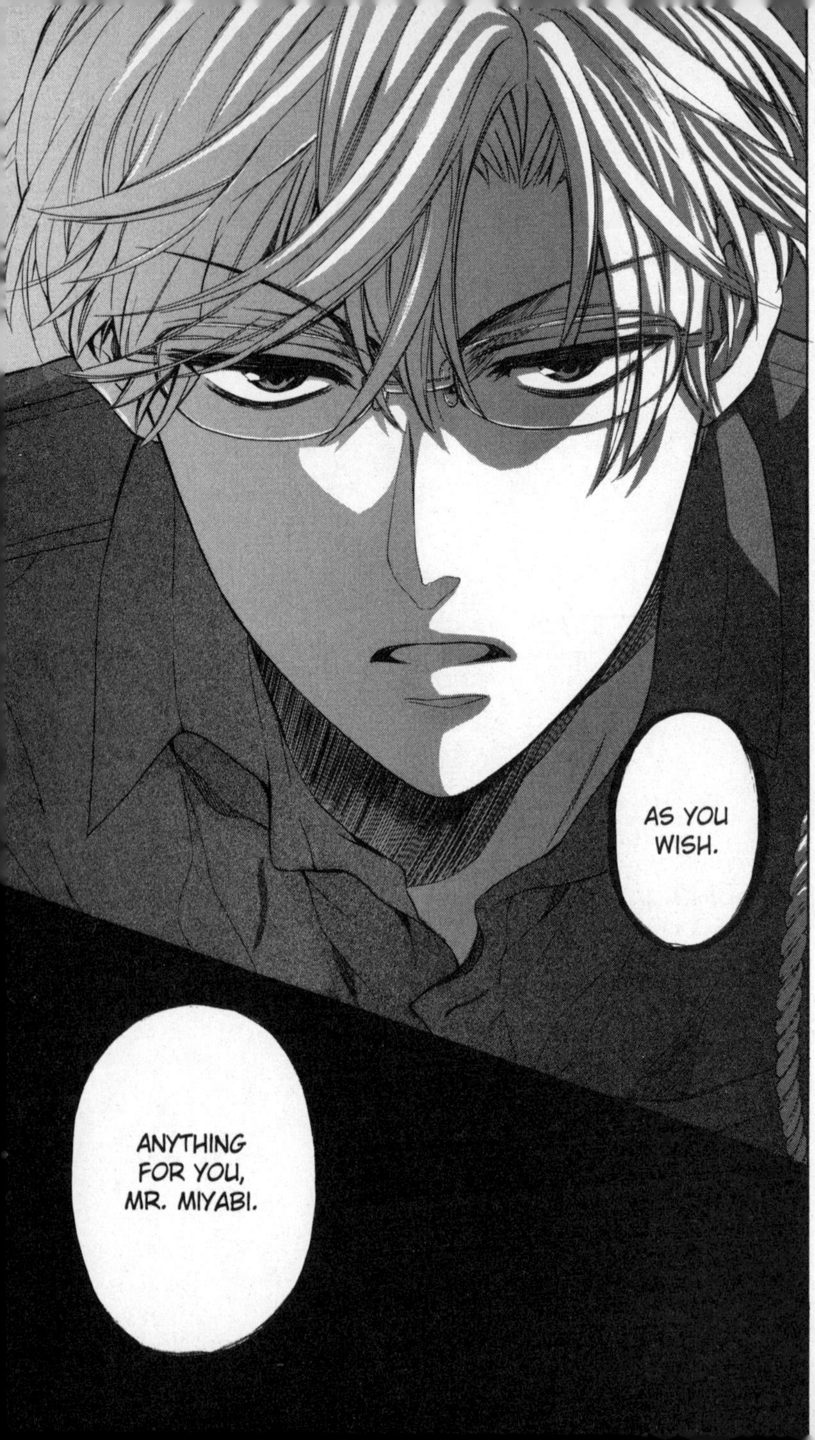
AS YOU WISH.
ANYTHING FOR YOU, MR. MIYABI.

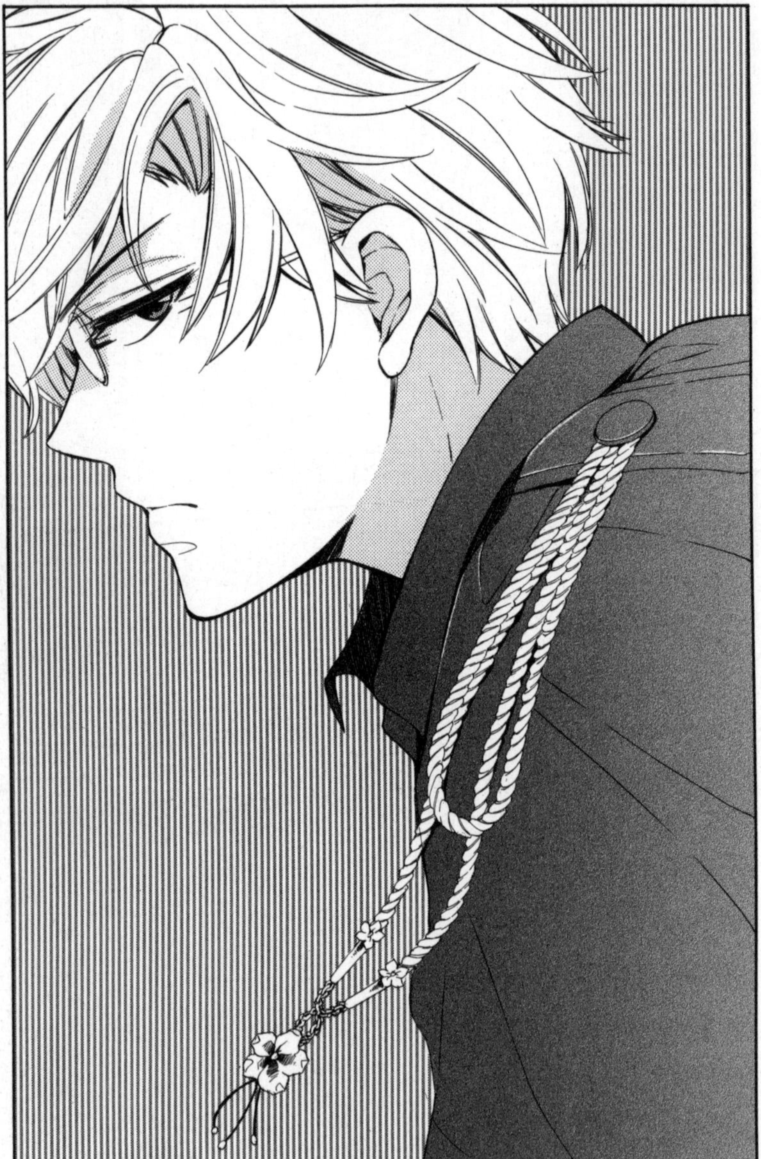

Chapter 92

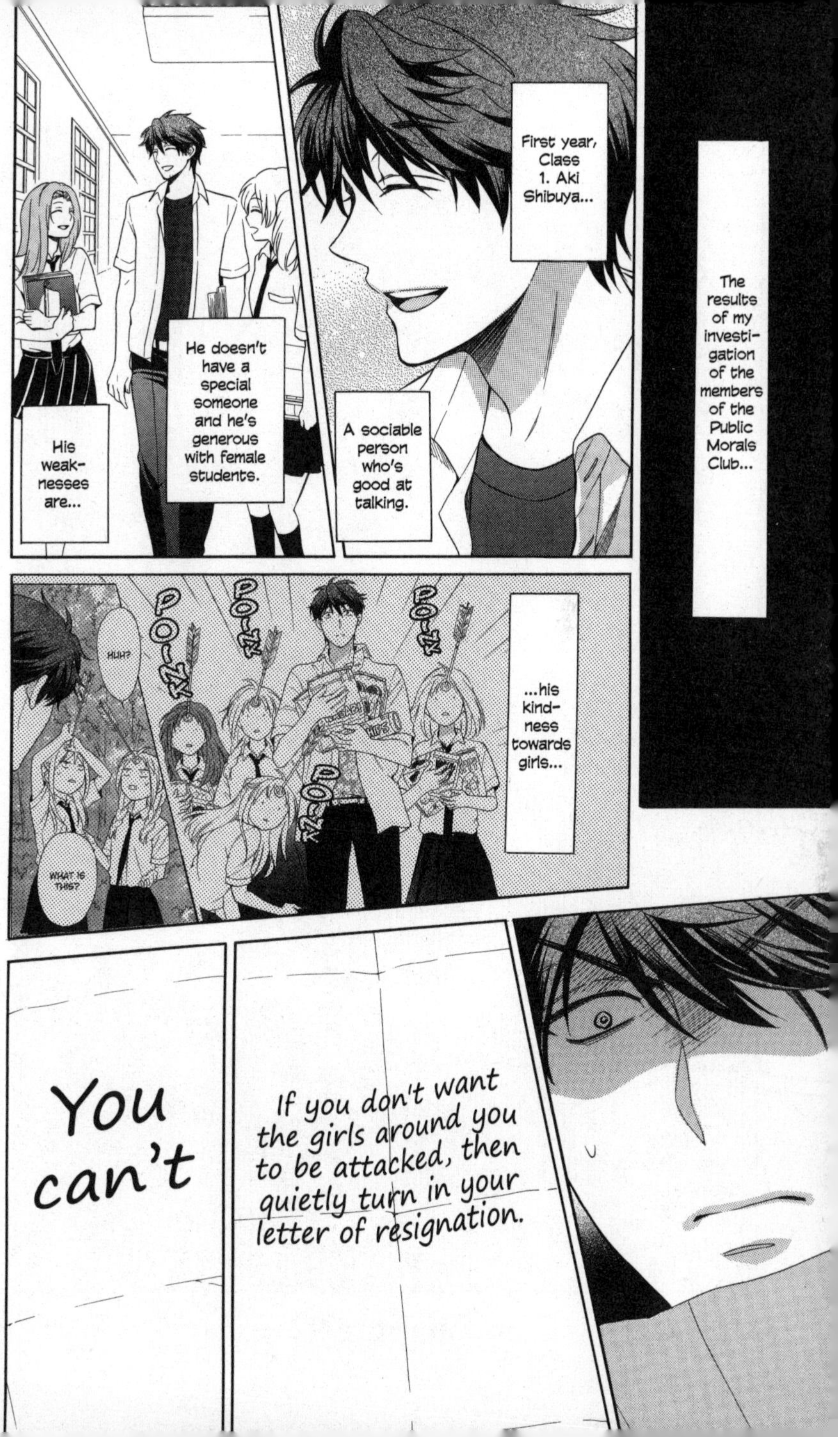
The results of my investigation of the members of the Public Morals Club...
First year, Class 1. Aki Shibuya...
A sociable person who's good at talking.
He doesn't have a special someone and he's generous with female students.
His weaknesses are...
...his kindness towards girls...
PO-IN
PO-IN
PO-IN
PO-IN
HUH?
WHAT IS THIS?
If you don't want the girls around you to be attacked, then quietly turn in your letter of resignation.
You can't

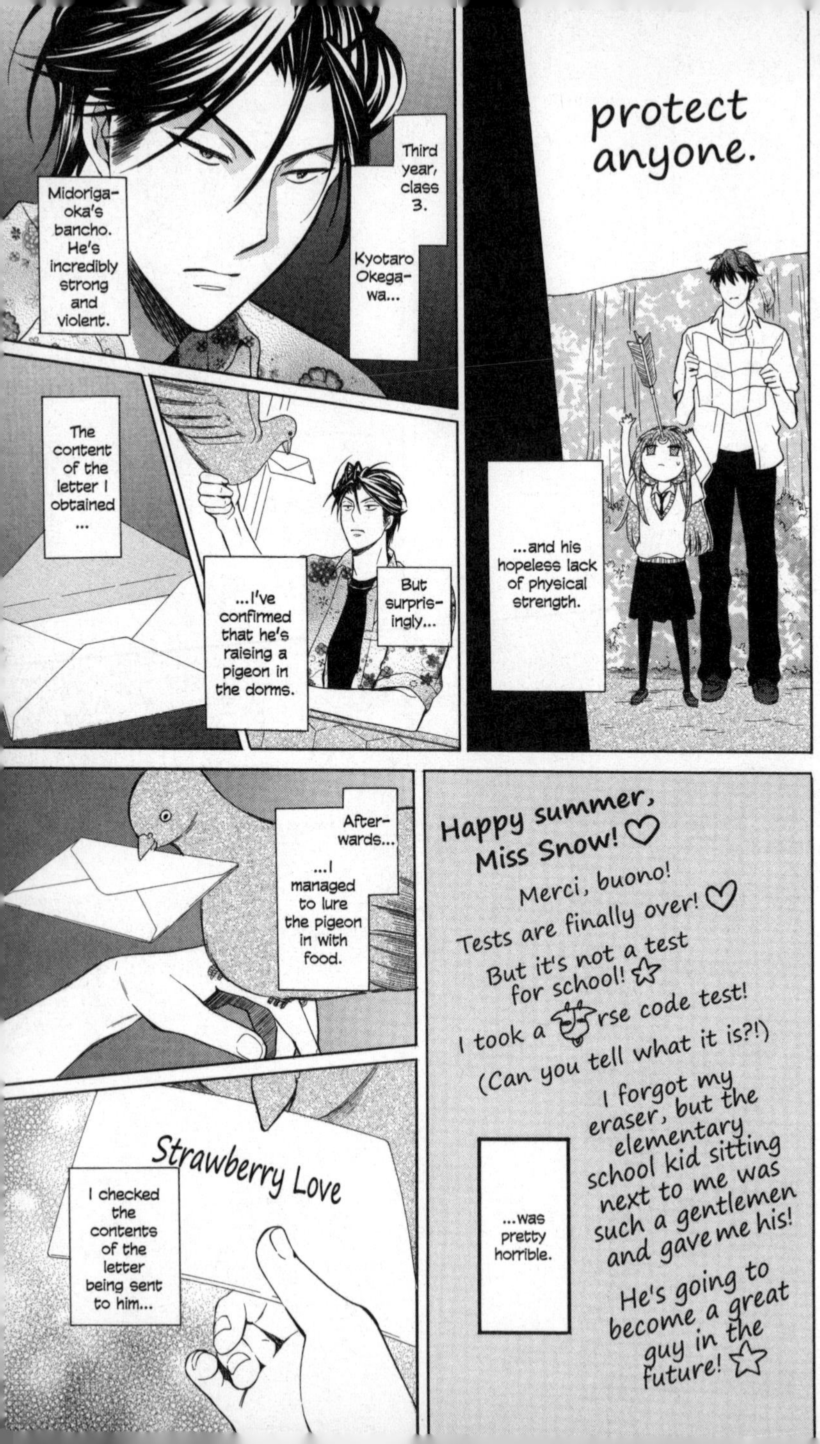
protect anyone.
...and his hopeless lack of physical strength.
Third year, class 3.
Kyotaro Okegawa...
Midorigaoka's bancho. He's incredibly strong and violent.
But surprisingly...
...I've confirmed that he's raising a pigeon in the dorms.
The content of the letter I obtained...
Happy summer, Miss Snow! ♡
Merci, buono!
Tests are finally over! ♡
But it's not a test for school! ☆
I took a [drawing]rse code test!
(Can you tell what it is?!)
I forgot my eraser, but the elementary school kid sitting next to me was such a gentlemen and gave me his!
He's going to become a great guy in the future! ☆
...was pretty horrible.
After-wards...
...I managed to lure the pigeon in with food.
Strawberry Love
I checked the contents of the letter being sent to him...

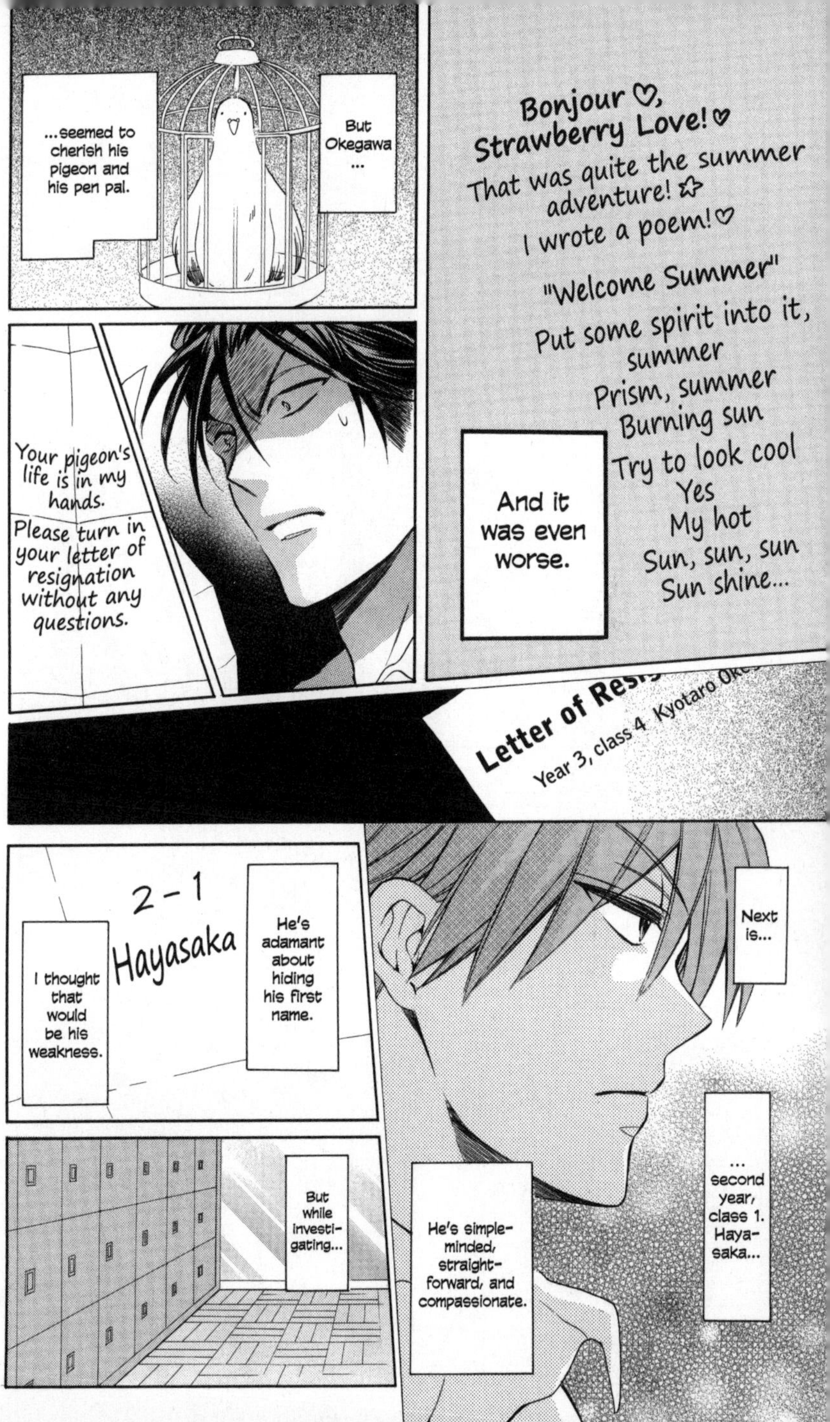
Bonjour ♡, Strawberry Love! ♡
That was quite the summer adventure! ☆
I wrote a poem! ♡
"Welcome Summer"
Put some spirit into it, summer
Prism, summer
Burning sun
Try to look cool
Yes
My hot
Sun, sun, sun
Sun shine...
And it was even worse.
But Okegawa...
...seemed to cherish his pigeon and his pen pal.
Your pigeon's life is in my hands.
Please turn in your letter of resignation without any questions.
Letter of Resi
Year 3, class 4 Kyotaro Oke
Next is...
...second year, class 1. Haya-saka...
He's simple-minded, straight-forward, and compassionate.
He's adamant about hiding his first name.
2 – 1
Hayasaka
I thought that would be his weakness.
But while investi-gating...

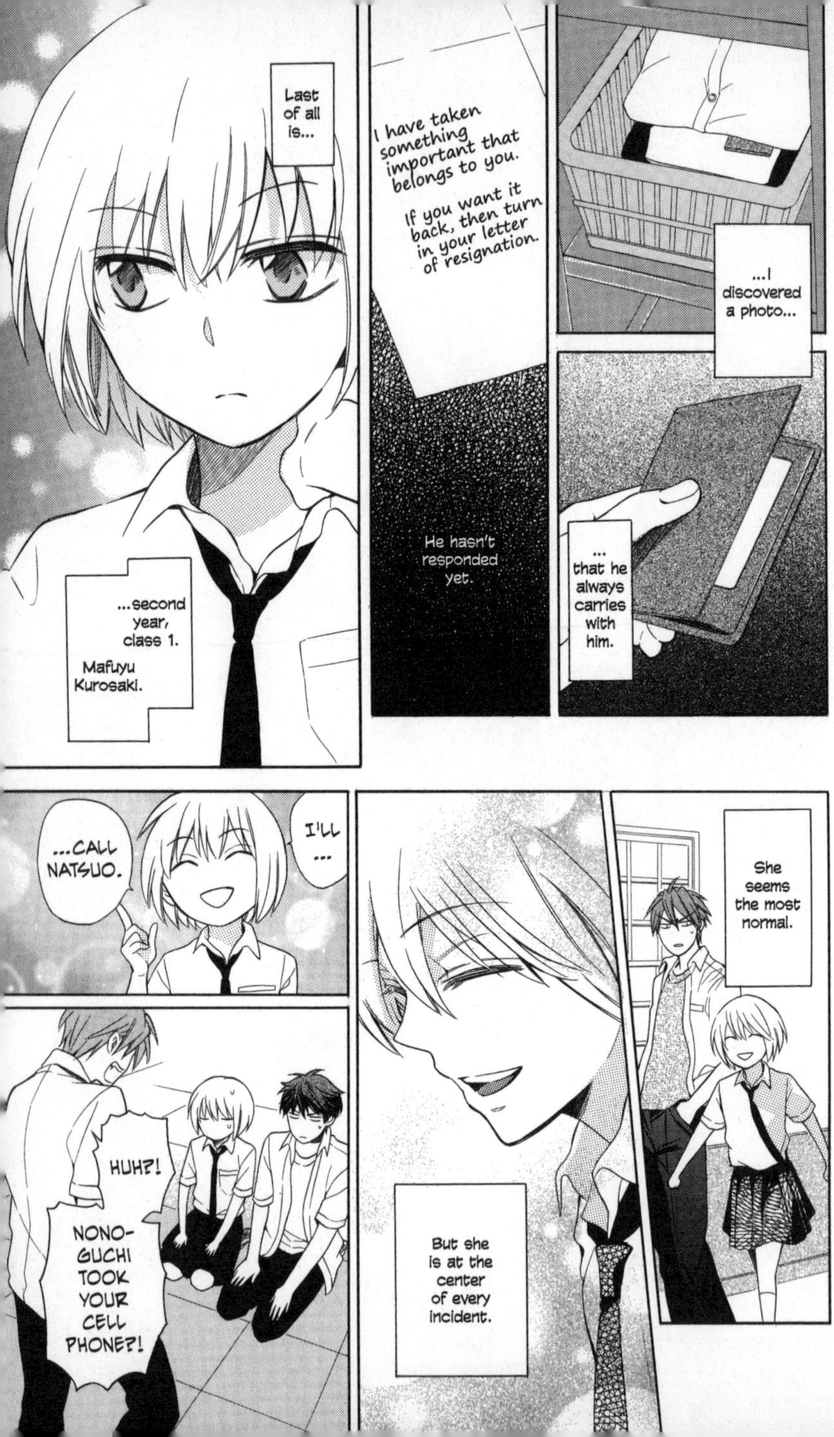
...I discovered a photo...
... that he always carries with him.
I have taken something important that belongs to you.
If you want it back, then turn in your letter of resignation.
He hasn't responded yet.
Last of all is...
...second year, class 1.
Mafuyu Kurosaki.
She seems the most normal.
But she is at the center of every incident.
I'LL ...
...CALL NATSUO.
HUH?!
NONO-GUCHI TOOK YOUR CELL PHONE?!

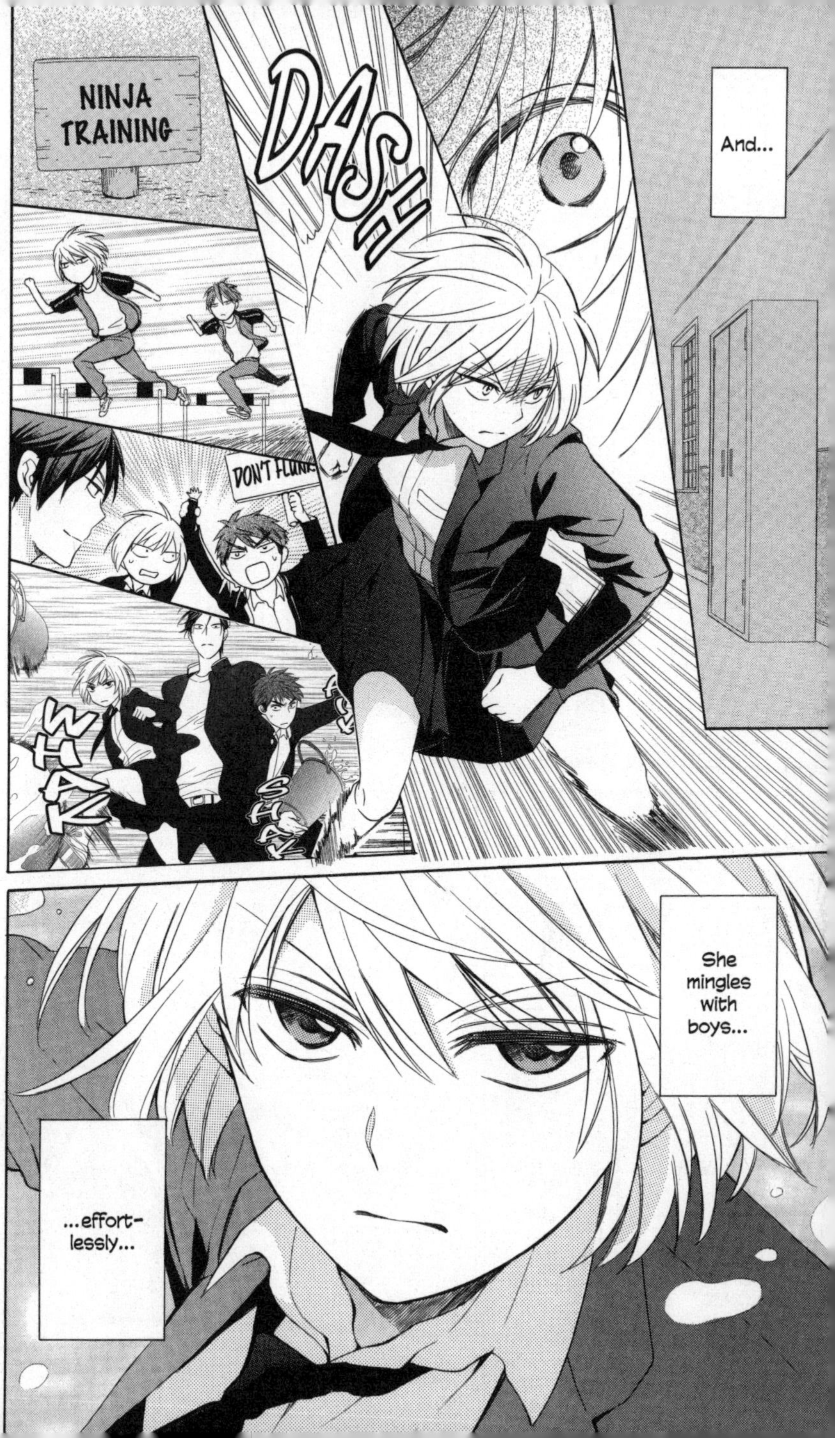

And...
DASH
NINJA TRAINING
DON'T FLUNK
ACK
SHAK
WHAK
She mingles with boys...
...effort-lessly...

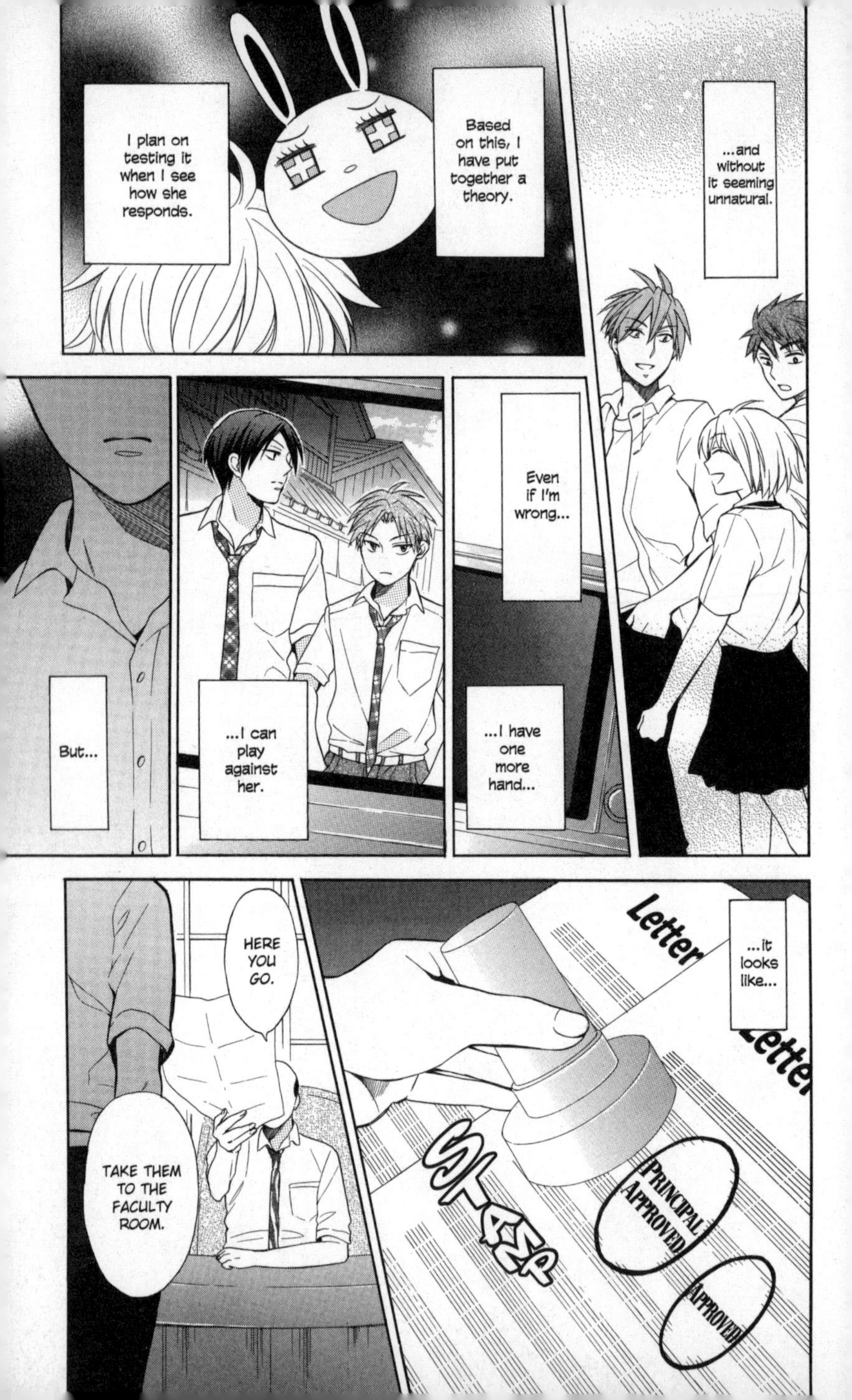
...and without it seeming unnatural.
Based on this, I have put together a theory.
I plan on testing it when I see how she responds.
Even if I'm wrong...
...I have one more hand...
...I can play against her.
But...
...it looks like...
Letter
Letter
PRINCIPAL APPROVED
APPROVED
HERE YOU GO.
TAKE THEM TO THE FACULTY ROOM.

THERE'S GOING TO BE...

Letter of Resignation

Year 2, class 1 Mafuyu Kurosaki

tter of Resignation

Year 2, class 1 Hayasaka

...A FACULTY MEETING.

...I won't have that chance.

YES, SIR.

That is all. —Shinobu Yui.

AAAAAGH!

AAAA-AGH!

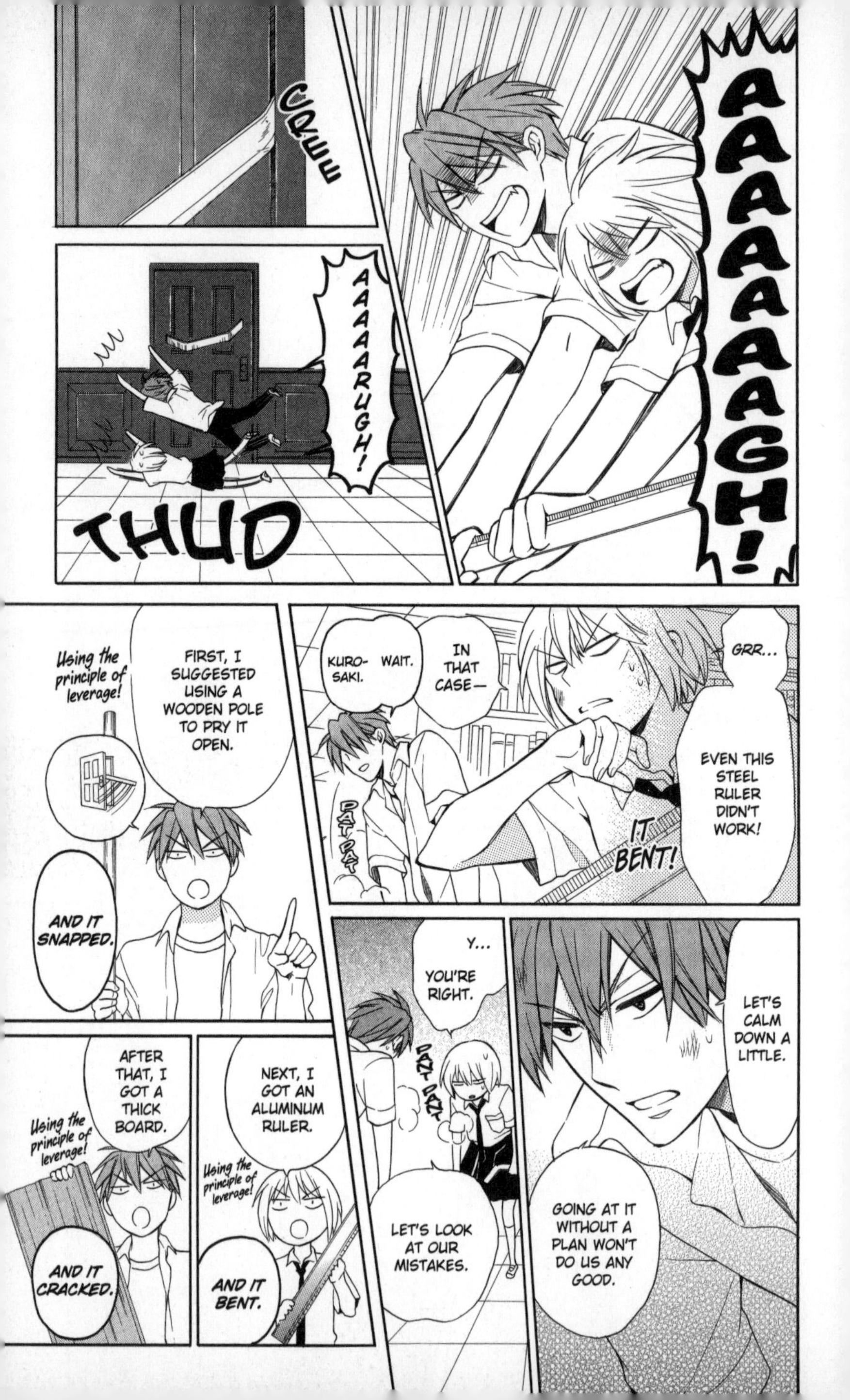
AAAAAAAGH!
CREEE
AAAAAARUGH!
THUD
GRR...
EVEN THIS STEEL RULER DIDN'T WORK!
IT BENT!
IN THAT CASE—
WAIT.
KURO-SAKI.
PAT PAT
LET'S CALM DOWN A LITTLE.
GOING AT IT WITHOUT A PLAN WON'T DO US ANY GOOD.
Y...
YOU'RE RIGHT.
PANT PANT
LET'S LOOK AT OUR MISTAKES.
FIRST, I SUGGESTED USING A WOODEN POLE TO PRY IT OPEN.
Using the principle of leverage!
AND IT SNAPPED.
AFTER THAT, I GOT A THICK BOARD.
Using the principle of leverage!
AND IT CRACKED.
NEXT, I GOT AN ALUMINUM RULER.
Using the principle of leverage!
AND IT BENT.

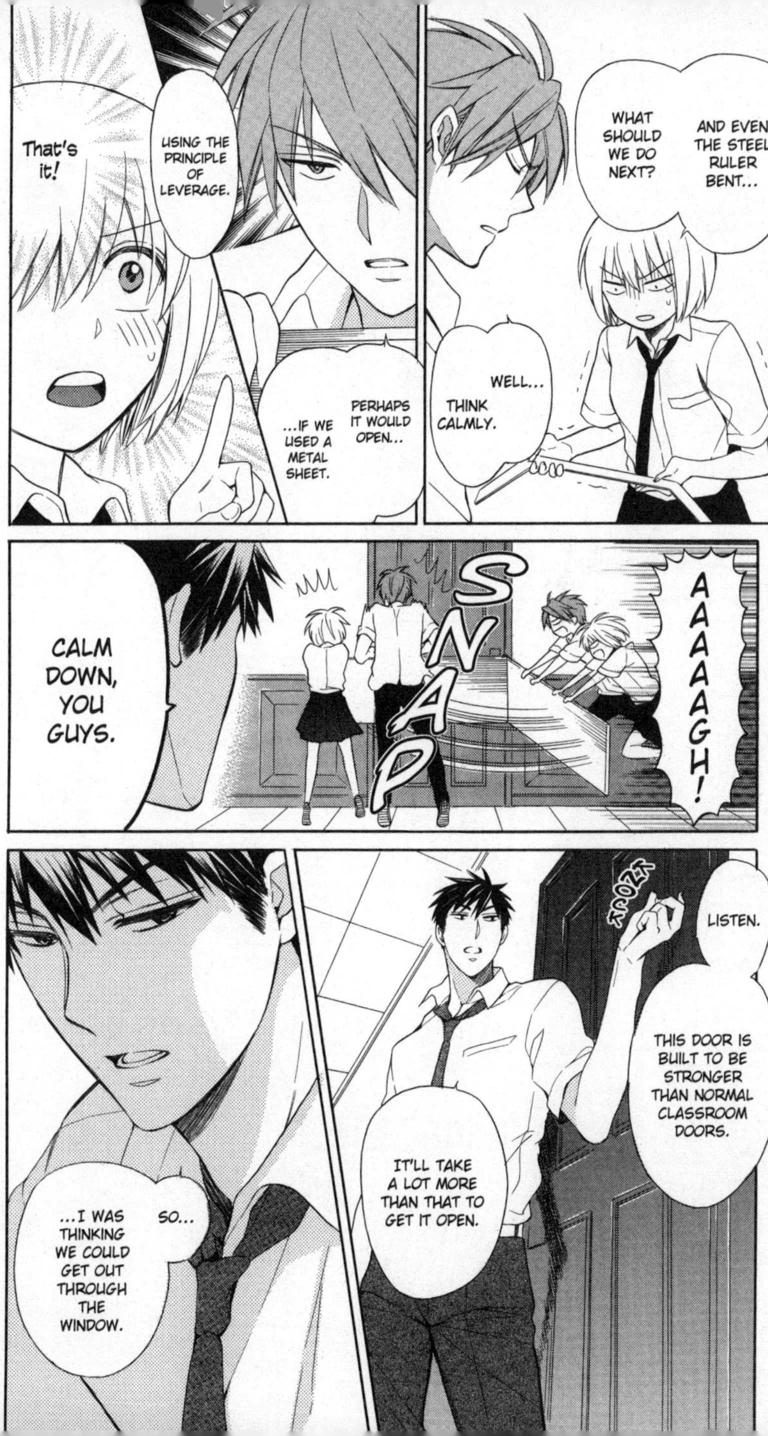
AND EVEN THE STEEL RULER BENT...
WHAT SHOULD WE DO NEXT?
WELL...
THINK CALMLY.
PERHAPS IT WOULD OPEN...
...IF WE USED A METAL SHEET.
USING THE PRINCIPLE OF LEVERAGE.
That's it!
AAAAAAGH!
SNAP
CALM DOWN, YOU GUYS.
LISTEN.
THIS DOOR IS BUILT TO BE STRONGER THAN NORMAL CLASSROOM DOORS.
IT'LL TAKE A LOT MORE THAN THAT TO GET IT OPEN.
SO...
...I WAS THINKING WE COULD GET OUT THROUGH THE WINDOW.

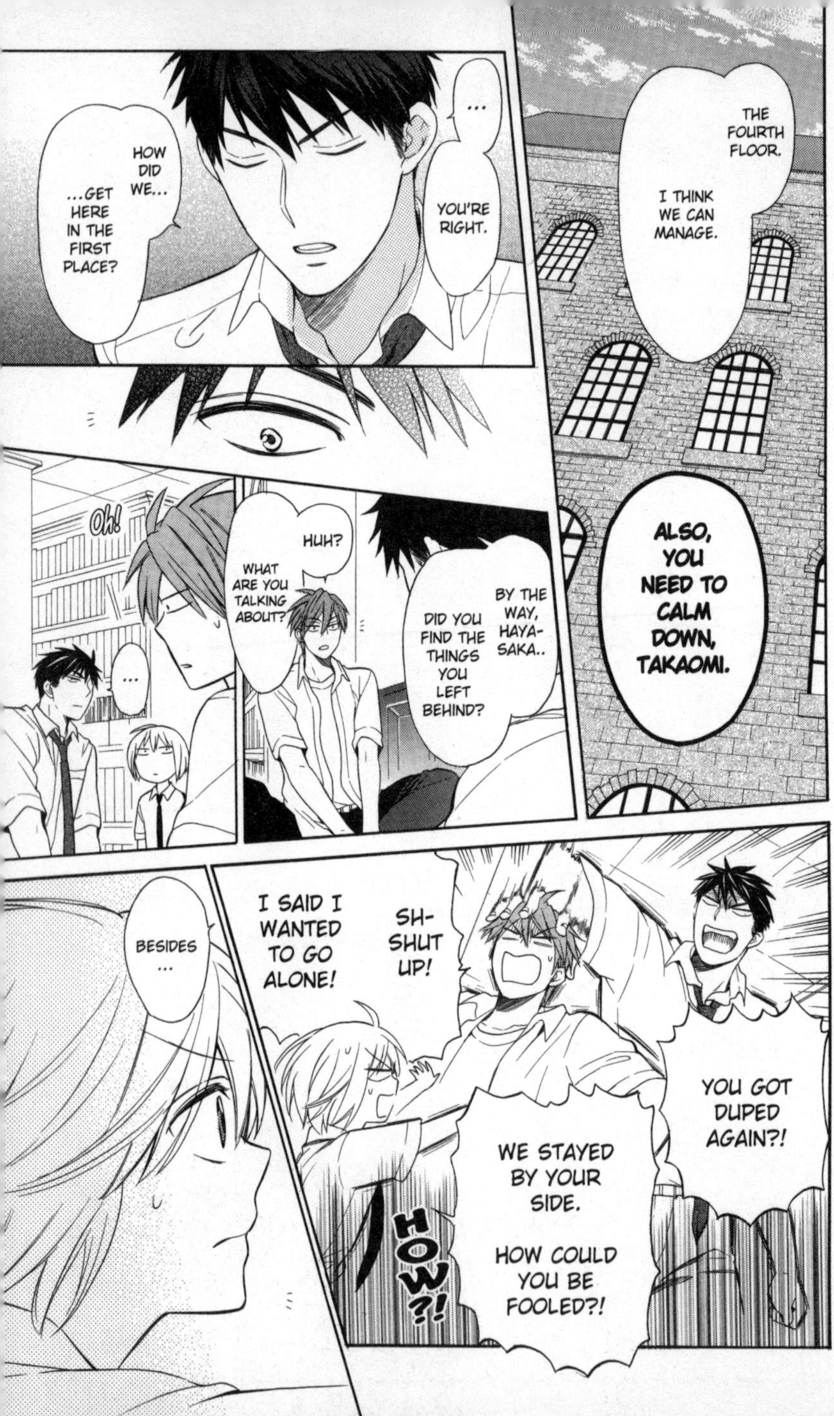
THE FOURTH FLOOR.
I THINK WE CAN MANAGE.
ALSO, YOU NEED TO CALM DOWN, TAKAOMI.
...
YOU'RE RIGHT.
HOW DID WE...
...GET HERE IN THE FIRST PLACE?
BY THE WAY, HAYA-SAKA..
DID YOU FIND THE THINGS YOU LEFT BEHIND?
HUH?
WHAT ARE YOU TALKING ABOUT?
Oh!
...
YOU GOT DUPED AGAIN?!
WE STAYED BY YOUR SIDE.
HOW COULD YOU BE FOOLED?!
HOW?!
SH-SHUT UP!
I SAID I WANTED TO GO ALONE!
BESIDES...

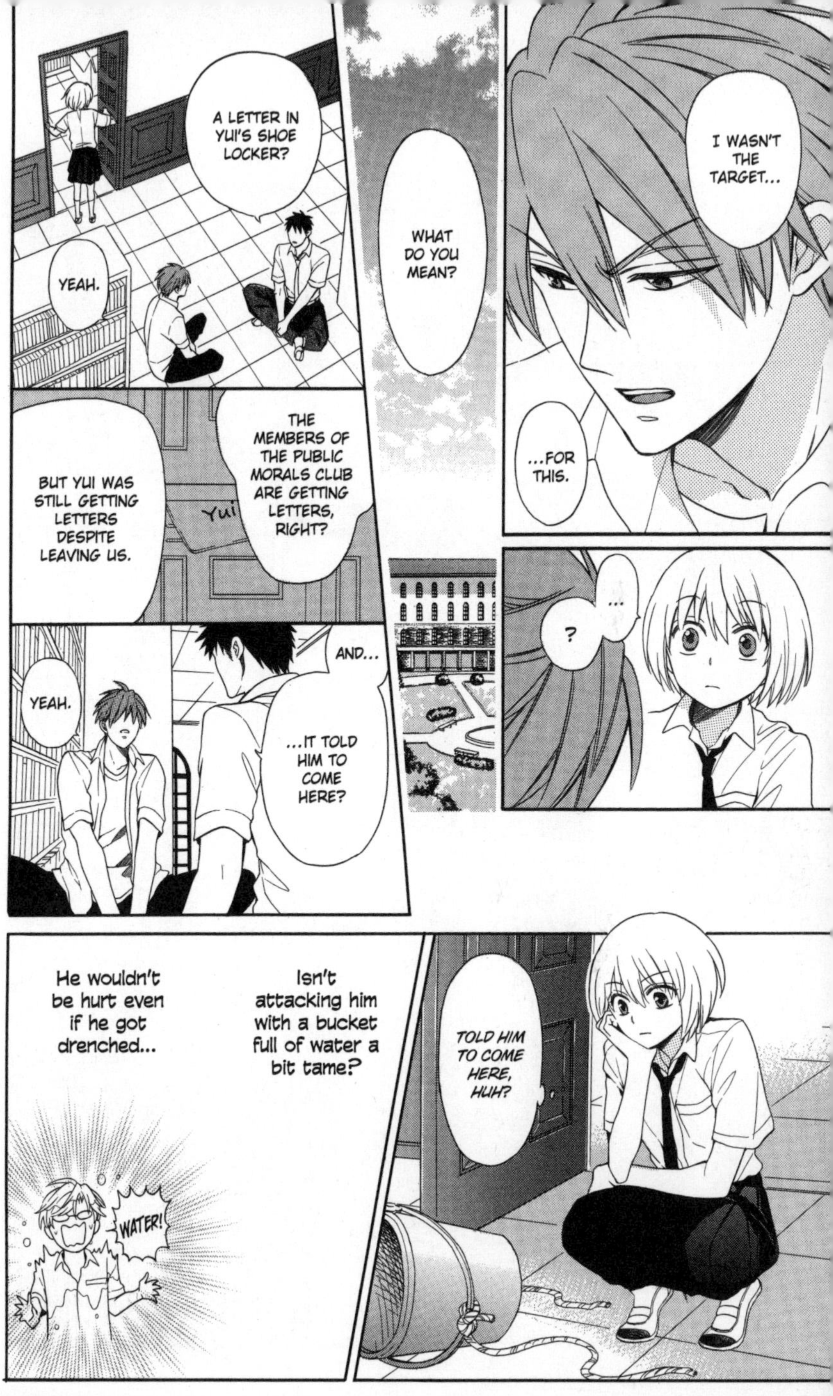

I WASN'T THE TARGET...
...FOR THIS.
WHAT DO YOU MEAN?
A LETTER IN YUI'S SHOE LOCKER?
YEAH.
...
?
THE MEMBERS OF THE PUBLIC MORALS CLUB ARE GETTING LETTERS, RIGHT?
Yui
BUT YUI WAS STILL GETTING LETTERS DESPITE LEAVING US.
AND...
...IT TOLD HIM TO COME HERE?
YEAH.
TOLD HIM TO COME HERE, HUH?
Isn't attacking him with a bucket full of water a bit tame?
He wouldn't be hurt even if he got drenched...
WATER!

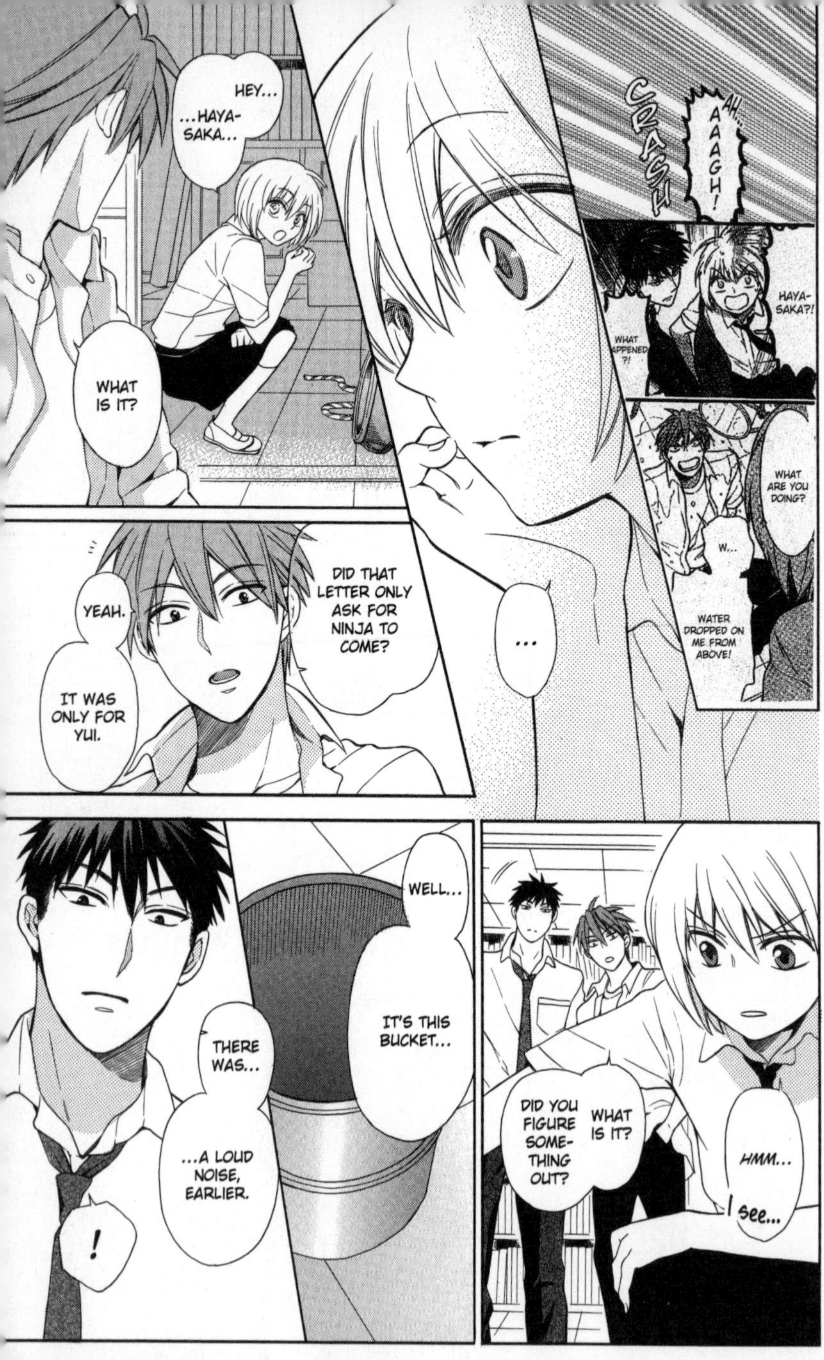
CRASH
AH... AAAGH!
HAYA-SAKA?!
WHAT HAPPENED ?!
WHAT ARE YOU DOING?
W...
WATER DROPPED ON ME FROM ABOVE!
...
HEY... ...HAYA-SAKA...
WHAT IS IT?
DID THAT LETTER ONLY ASK FOR NINJA TO COME?
YEAH.
IT WAS ONLY FOR YUI.
HMM...
I see...
WHAT IS IT?
DID YOU FIGURE SOME-THING OUT?
WELL...
IT'S THIS BUCKET...
THERE WAS...
...A LOUD NOISE, EARLIER.
!

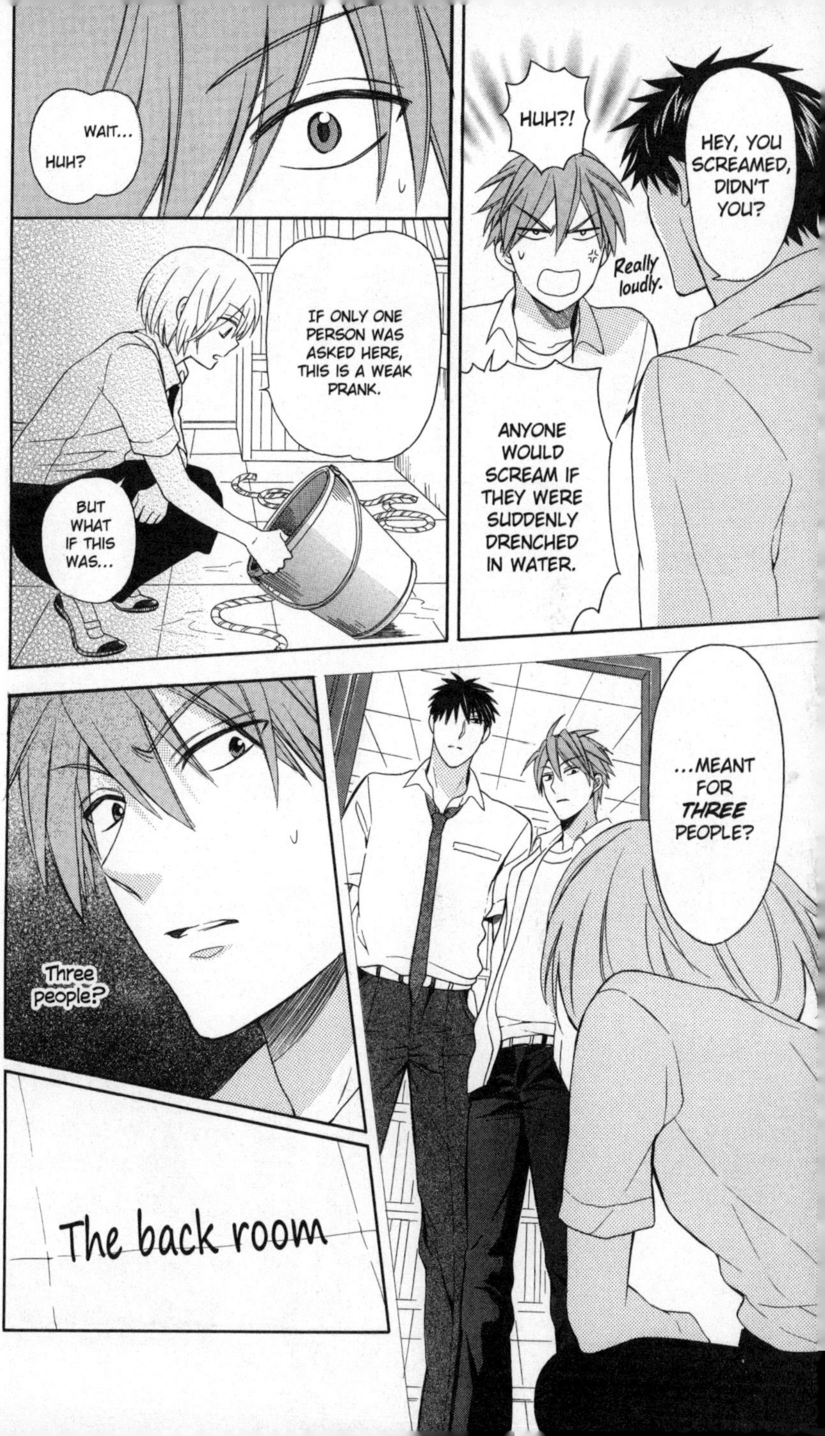

HEY, YOU SCREAMED, DIDN'T YOU?
HUH?!
Really loudly.
ANYONE WOULD SCREAM IF THEY WERE SUDDENLY DRENCHED IN WATER.
WAIT... HUH?
IF ONLY ONE PERSON WAS ASKED HERE, THIS IS A WEAK PRANK.
BUT WHAT IF THIS WAS...
...MEANT FOR *THREE* PEOPLE?
Three people?
The back room

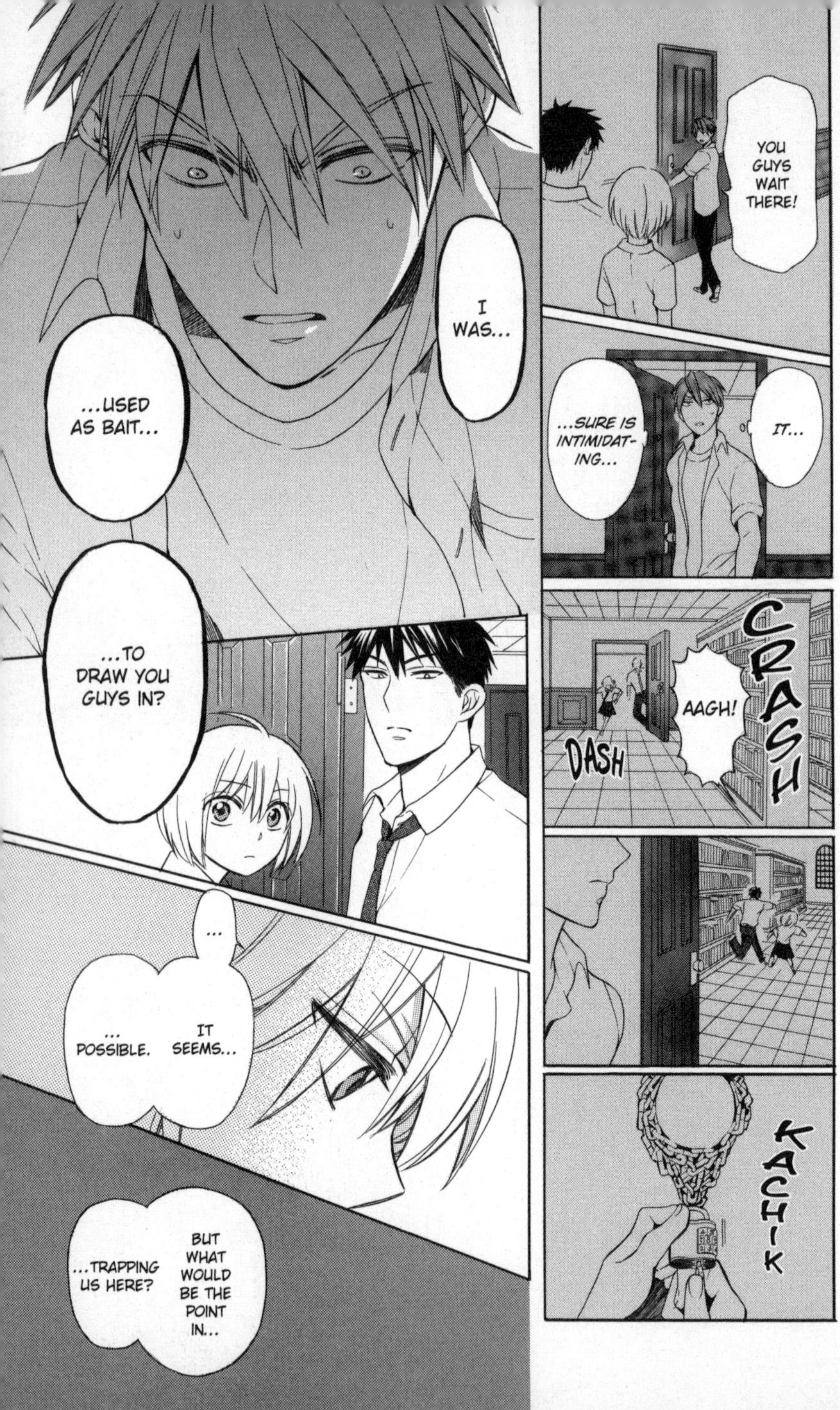
YOU GUYS WAIT THERE!
IT...
...SURE IS INTIMIDATING...
CRASH
AAGH!
DASH
KACHIK
I WAS...
...USED AS BAIT...
...TO DRAW YOU GUYS IN?
...
IT SEEMS...
...POSSIBLE.
BUT WHAT WOULD BE THE POINT IN...
...TRAPPING US HERE?

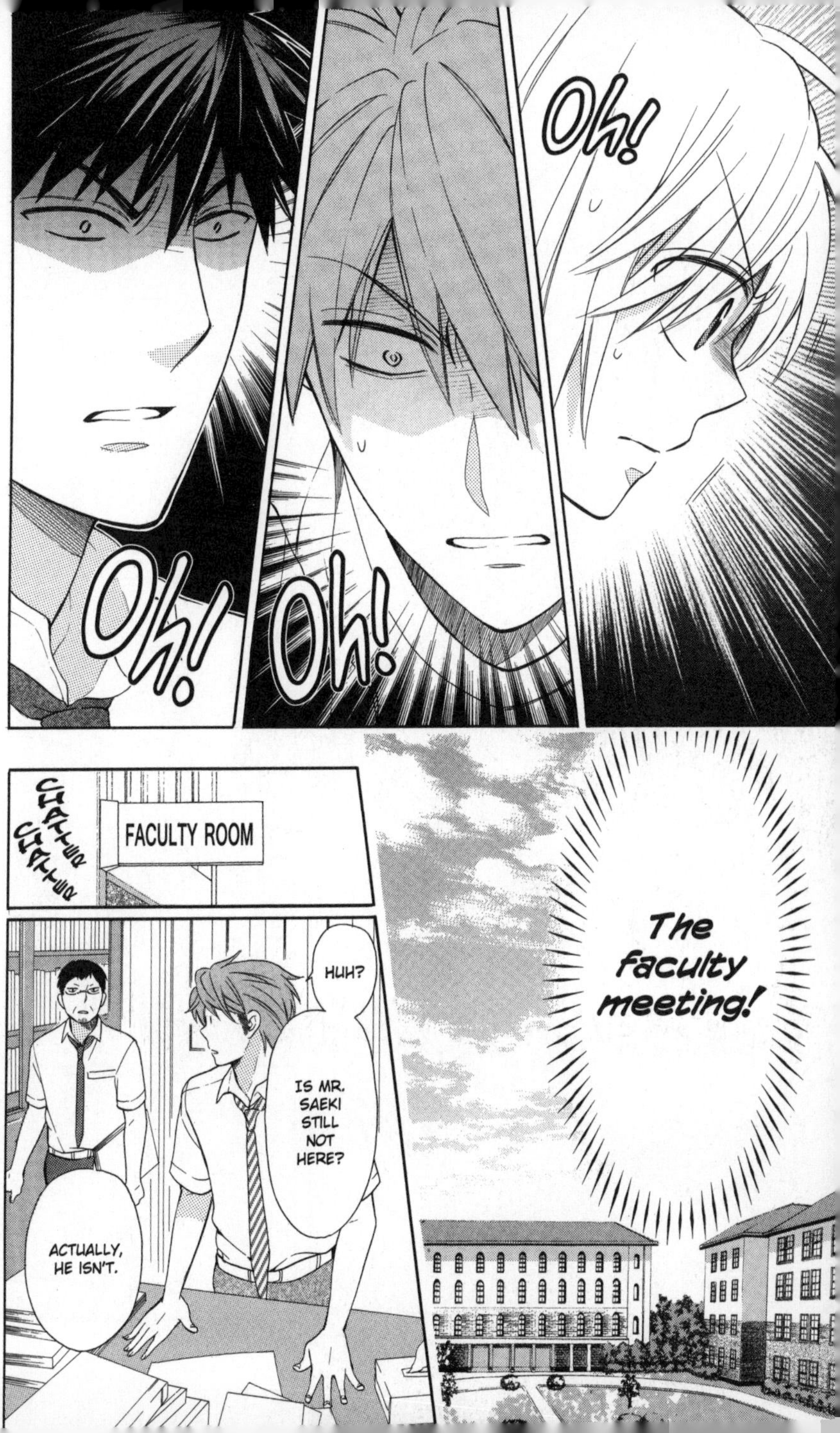
Oh!
Oh!
Oh!
The faculty meeting!
FACULTY ROOM
CHATTER CHATTER
HUH?
IS MR. SAEKI STILL NOT HERE?
ACTUALLY, HE ISN'T.

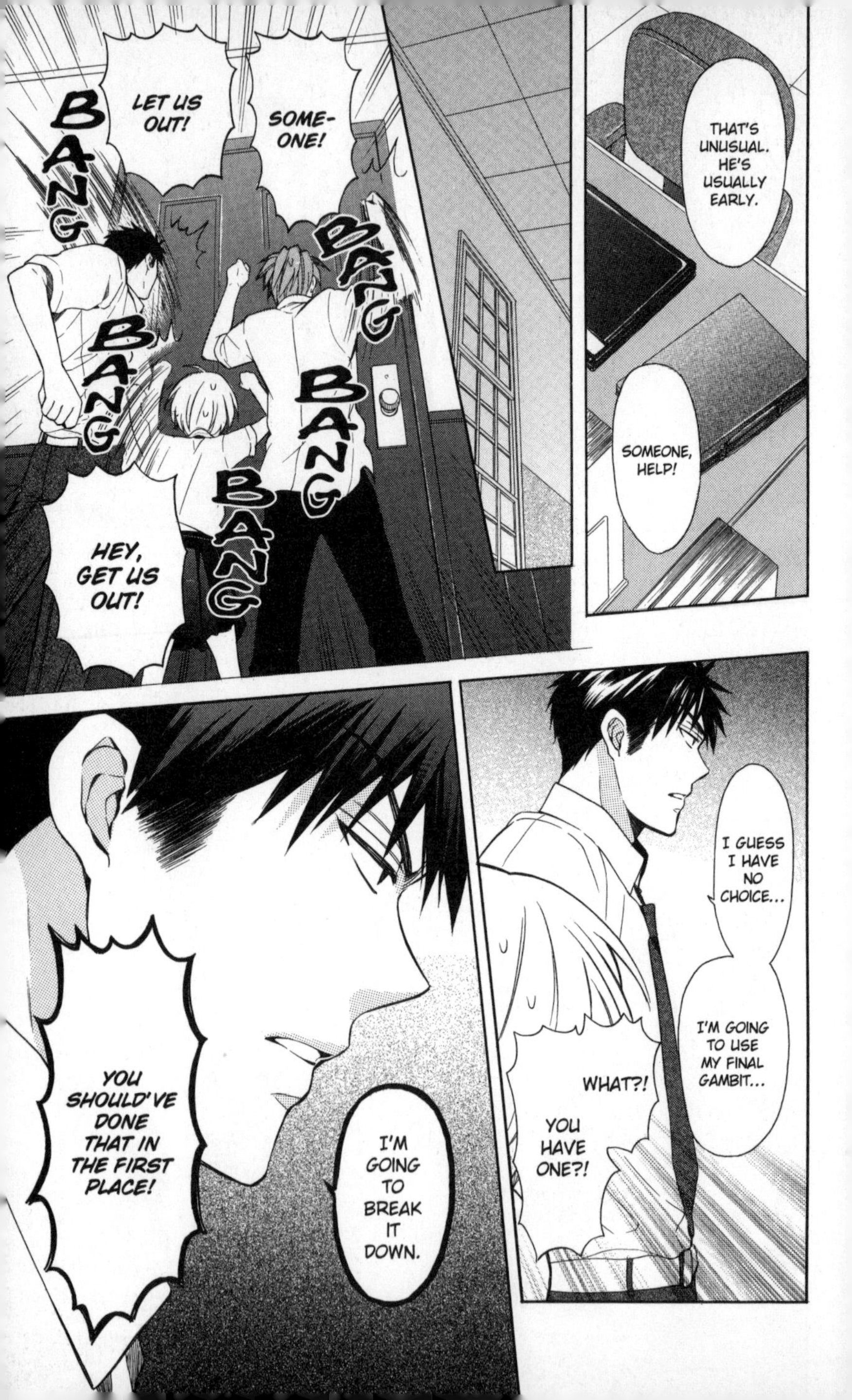
THAT'S UNUSUAL. HE'S USUALLY EARLY.
SOMEONE, HELP!
SOME-ONE!
LET US OUT!
BANG
BANG
BANG
BANG
BANG
HEY, GET US OUT!
I GUESS I HAVE NO CHOICE...
I'M GOING TO USE MY FINAL GAMBIT...
WHAT?!
YOU HAVE ONE?!
I'M GOING TO BREAK IT DOWN.
YOU SHOULD'VE DONE THAT IN THE FIRST PLACE!

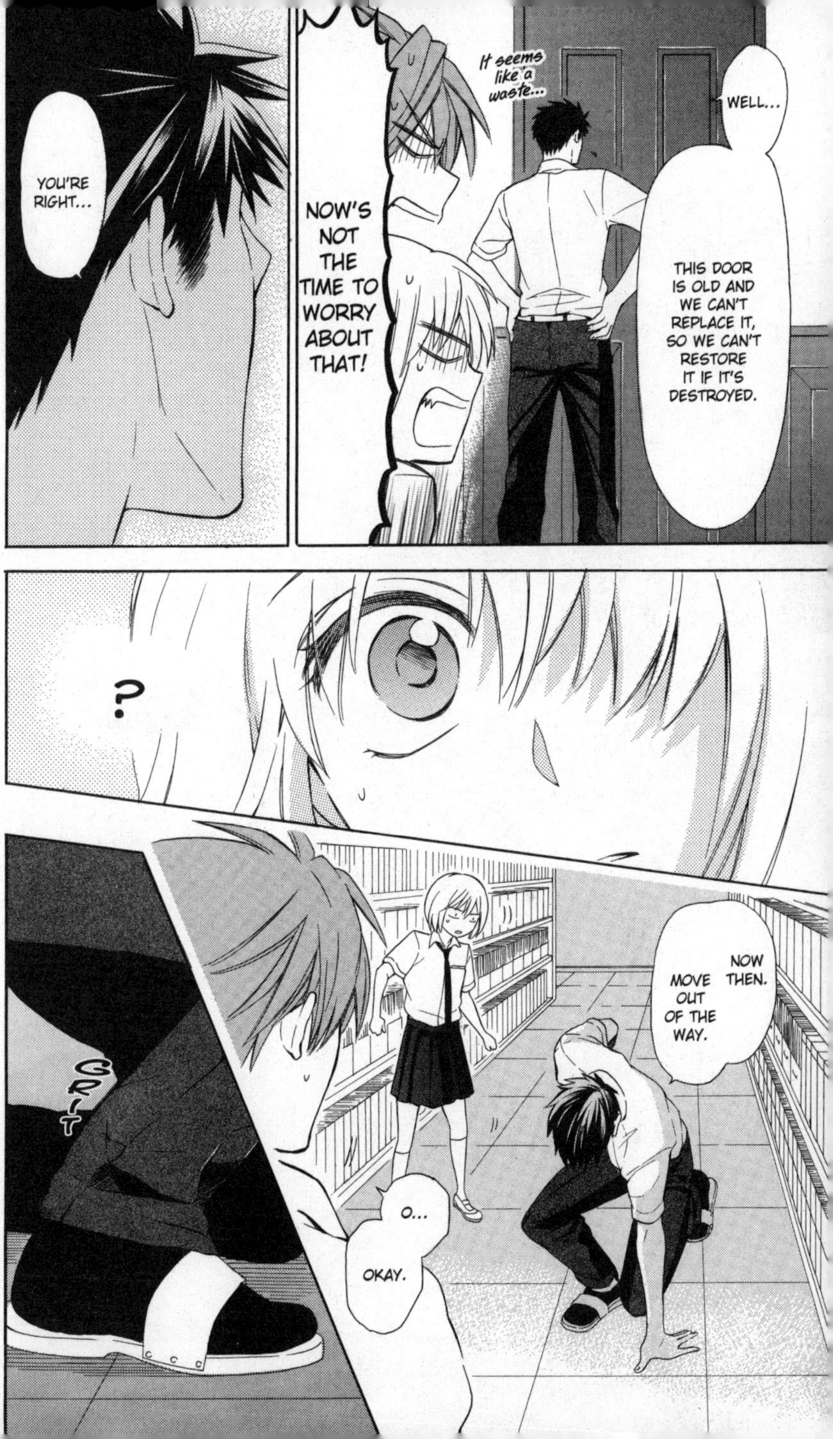
WELL...
THIS DOOR IS OLD AND WE CAN'T REPLACE IT, SO WE CAN'T RESTORE IT IF IT'S DESTROYED.
It seems like a waste...
NOW'S NOT THE TIME TO WORRY ABOUT THAT!
YOU'RE RIGHT...
?
NOW THEN. MOVE OUT OF THE WAY.
GRIT
O... OKAY.

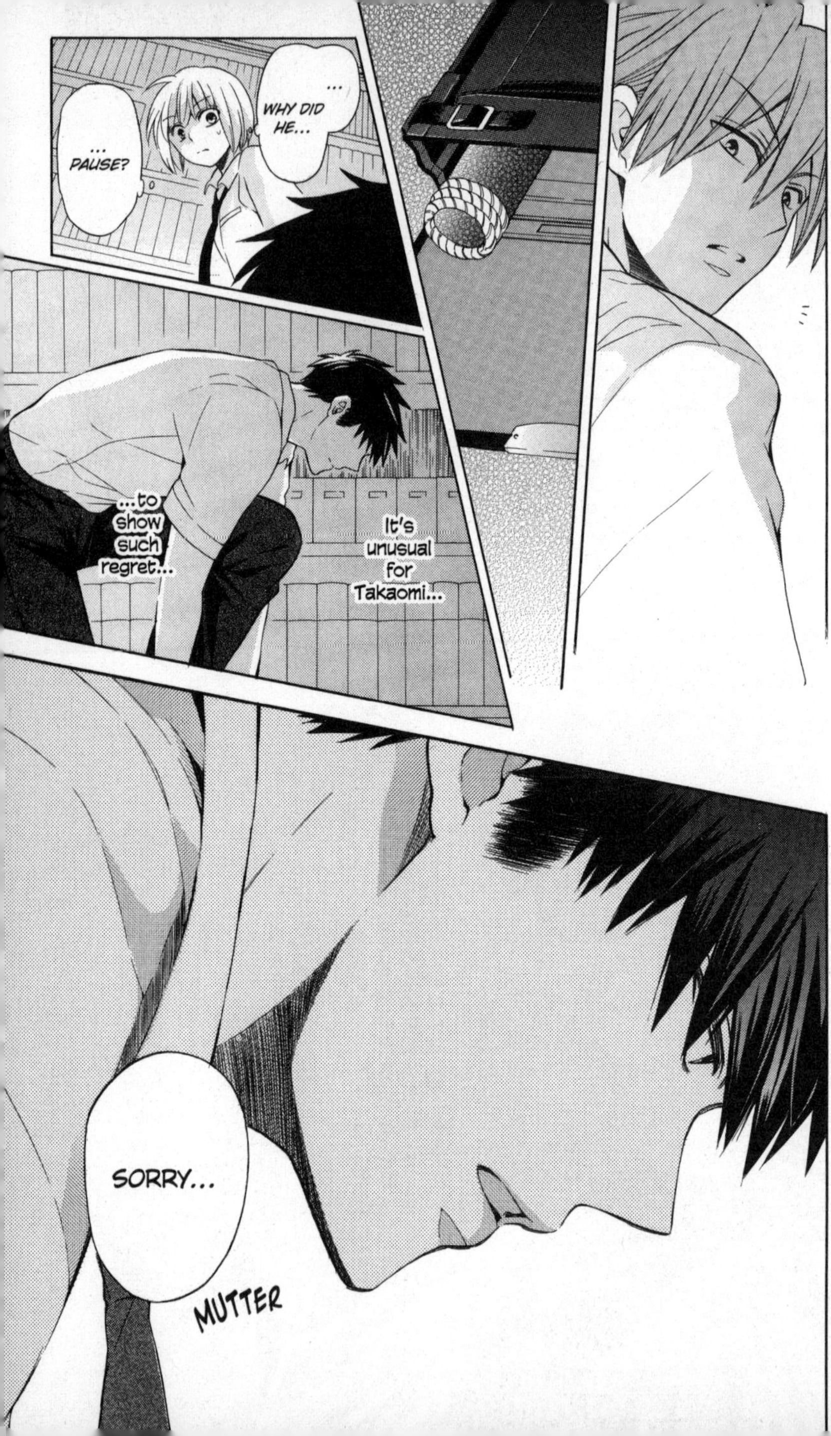

... WHY DID HE...
... PAUSE?
It's unusual for Takaomi...
...to show such regret...
SORRY...
MUTTER

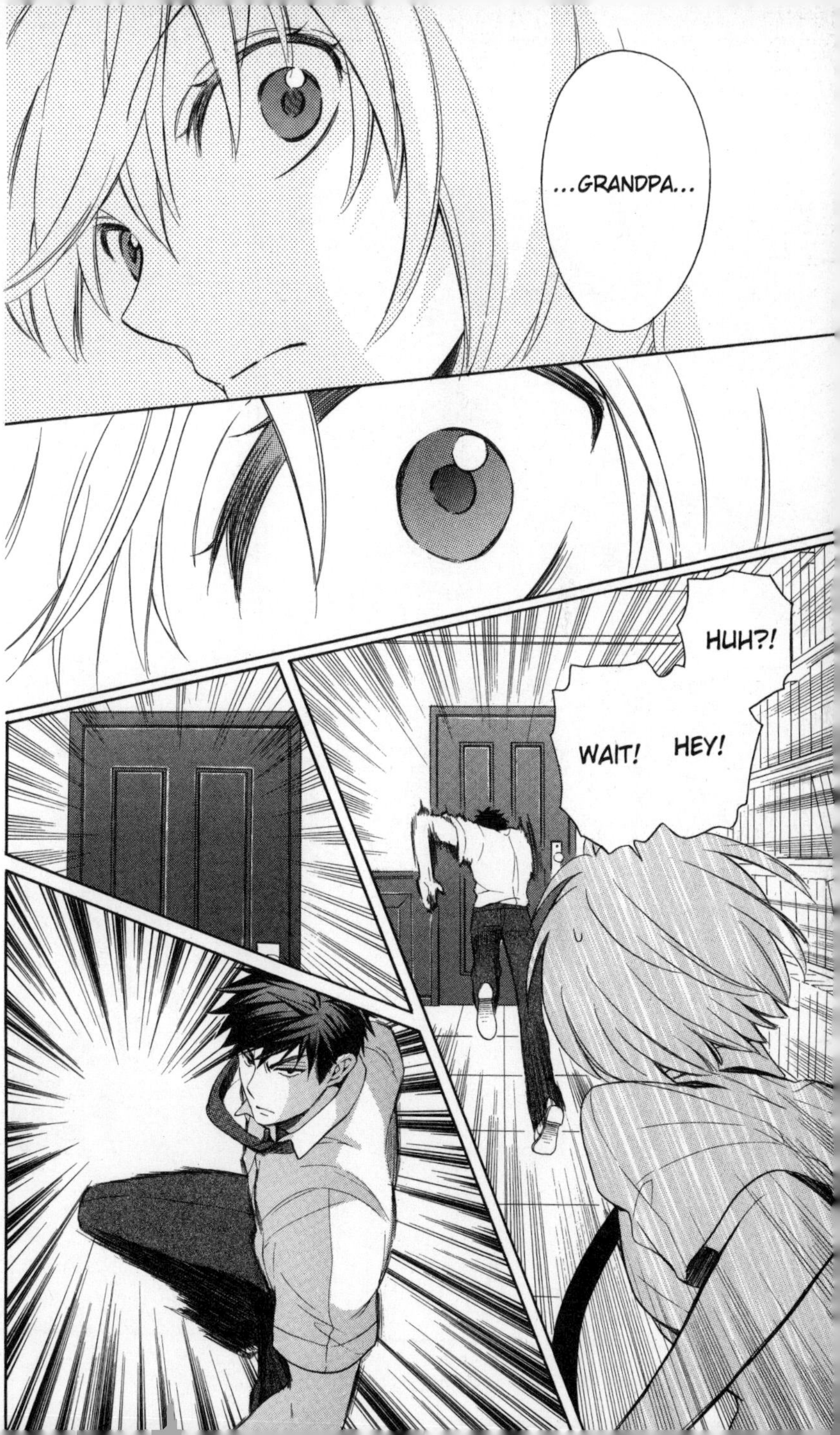
...GRANDPA...
HUH?!
HEY!
WAIT!

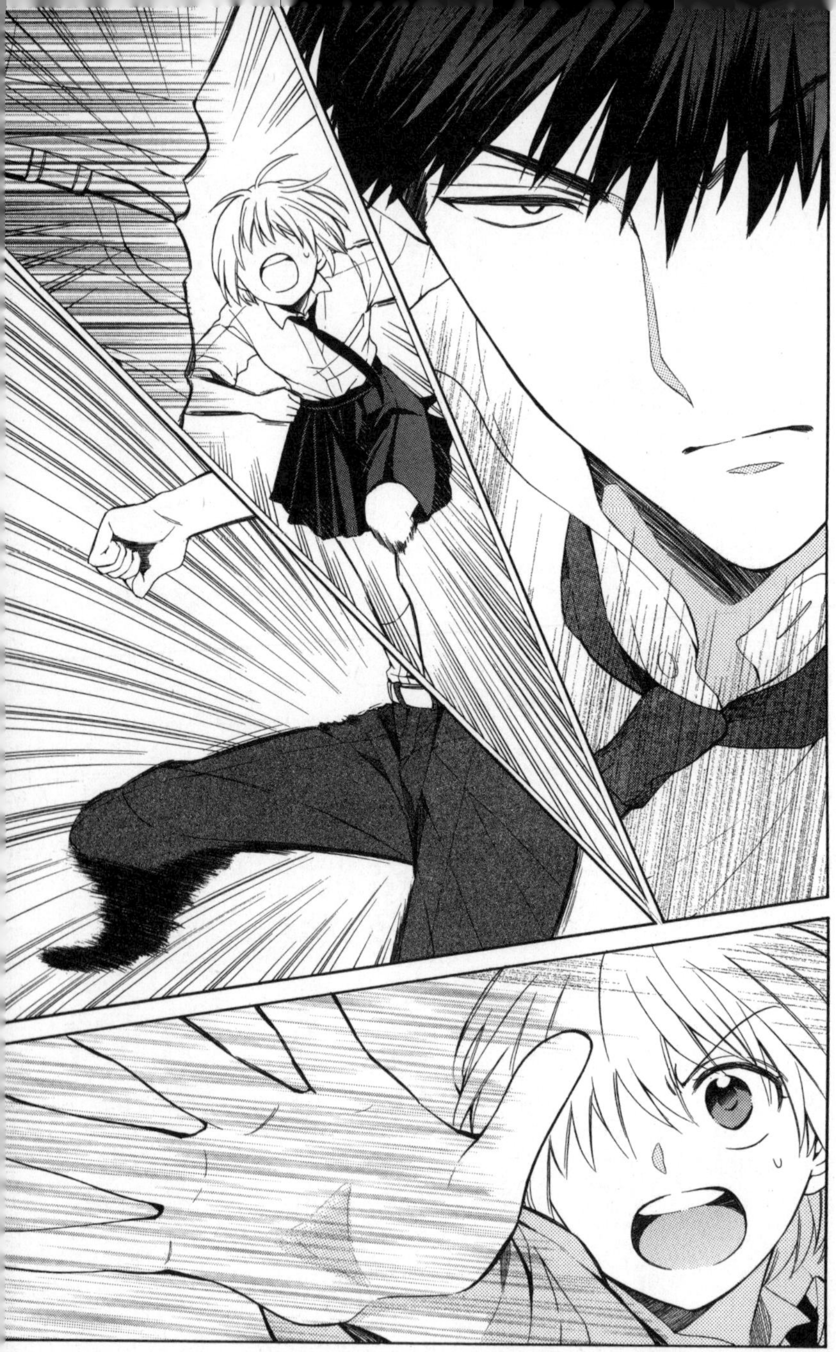

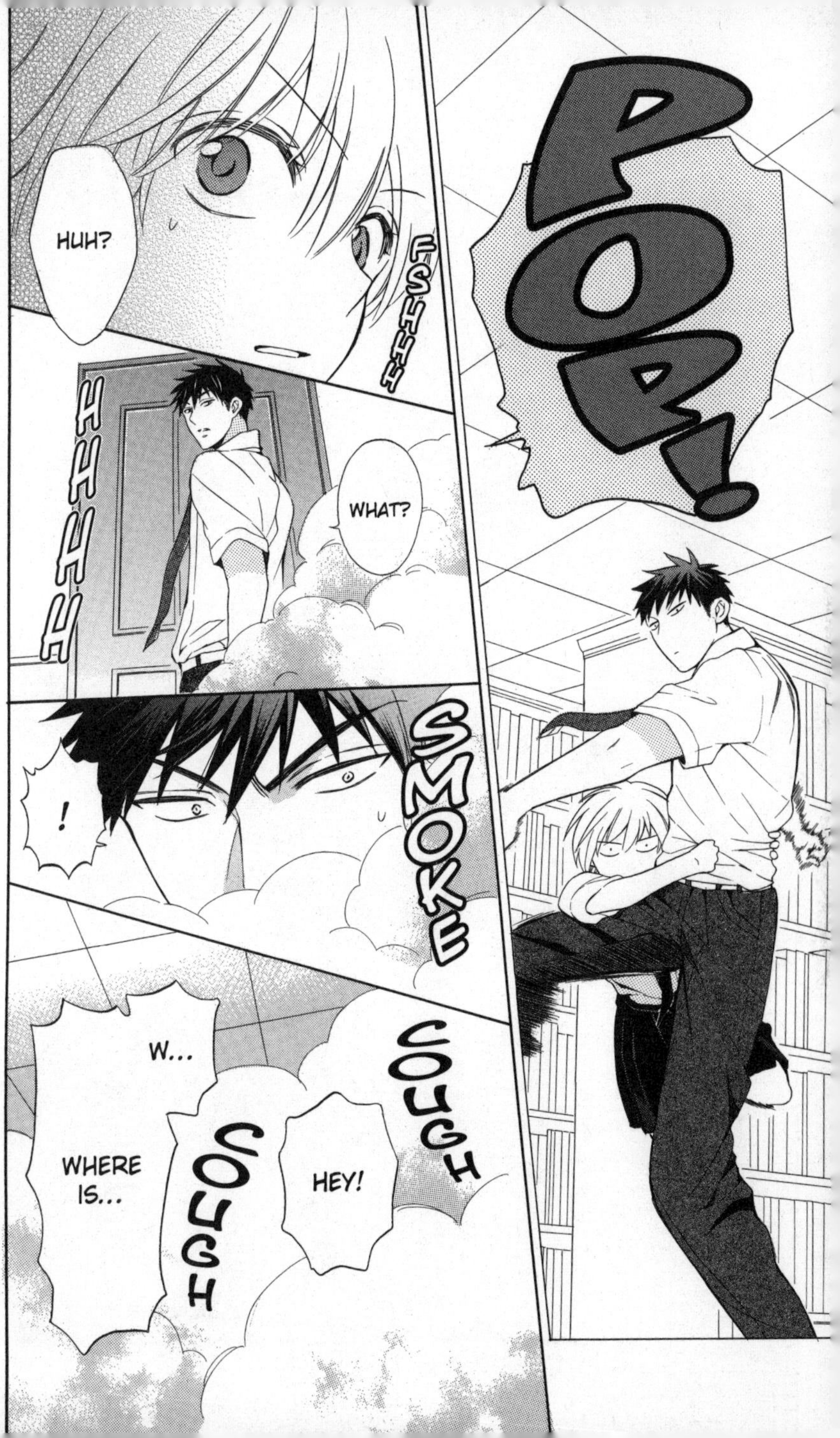
POP!
HUH?
FSHHHH
WHAT?
HHHHHH
!
SMOKE
COUGH
HEY!
COUGH
W...
WHERE IS...

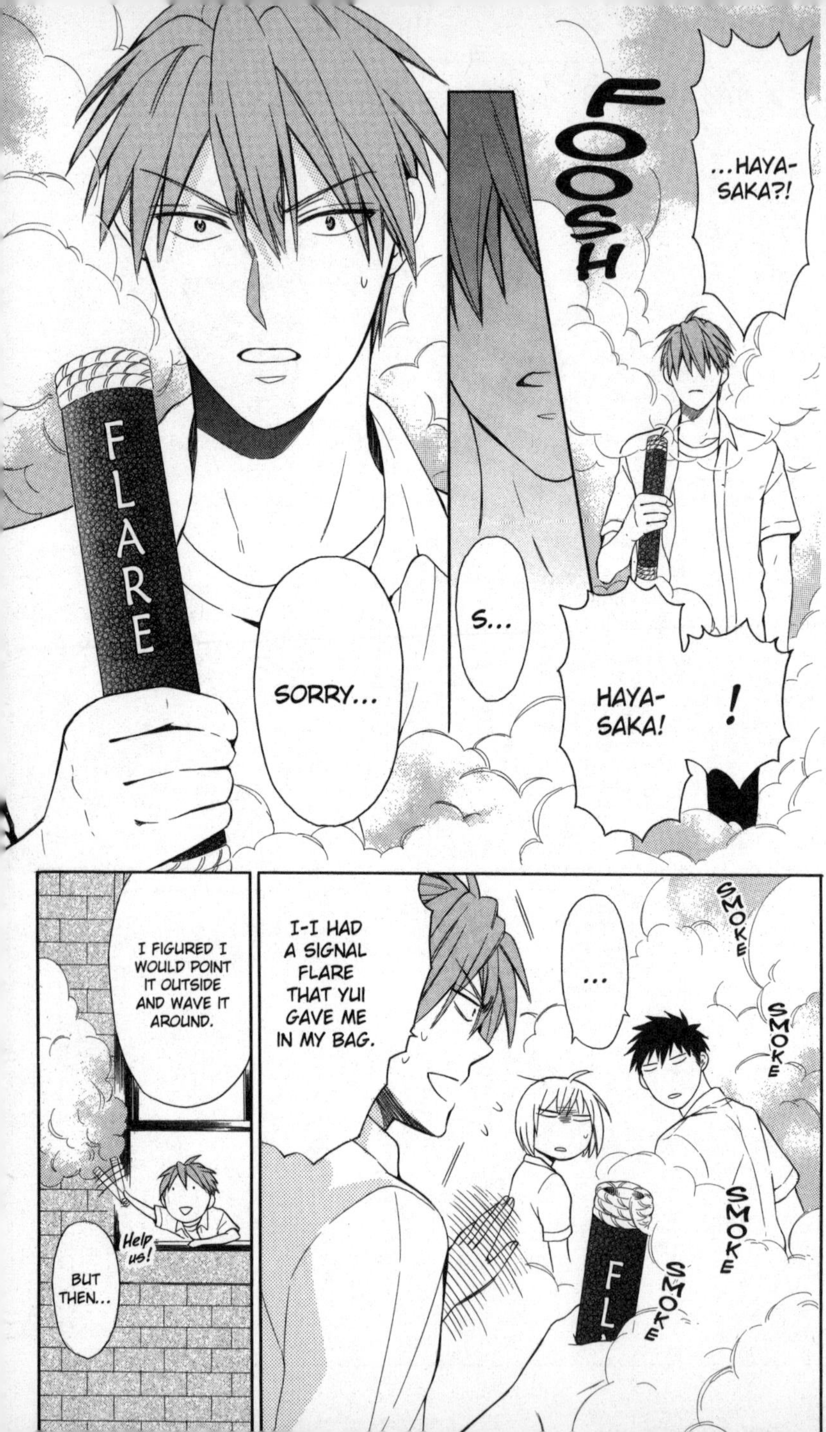
FOOSH
...HAYA-SAKA?!
HAYA-SAKA!
!
S...
FLARE
SORRY...
SMOKE SMOKE
SMOKE SMOKE
...
I-I HAD A SIGNAL FLARE THAT YUI GAVE ME IN MY BAG.
FL
I FIGURED I WOULD POINT IT OUTSIDE AND WAVE IT AROUND.
Help us!
BUT THEN...

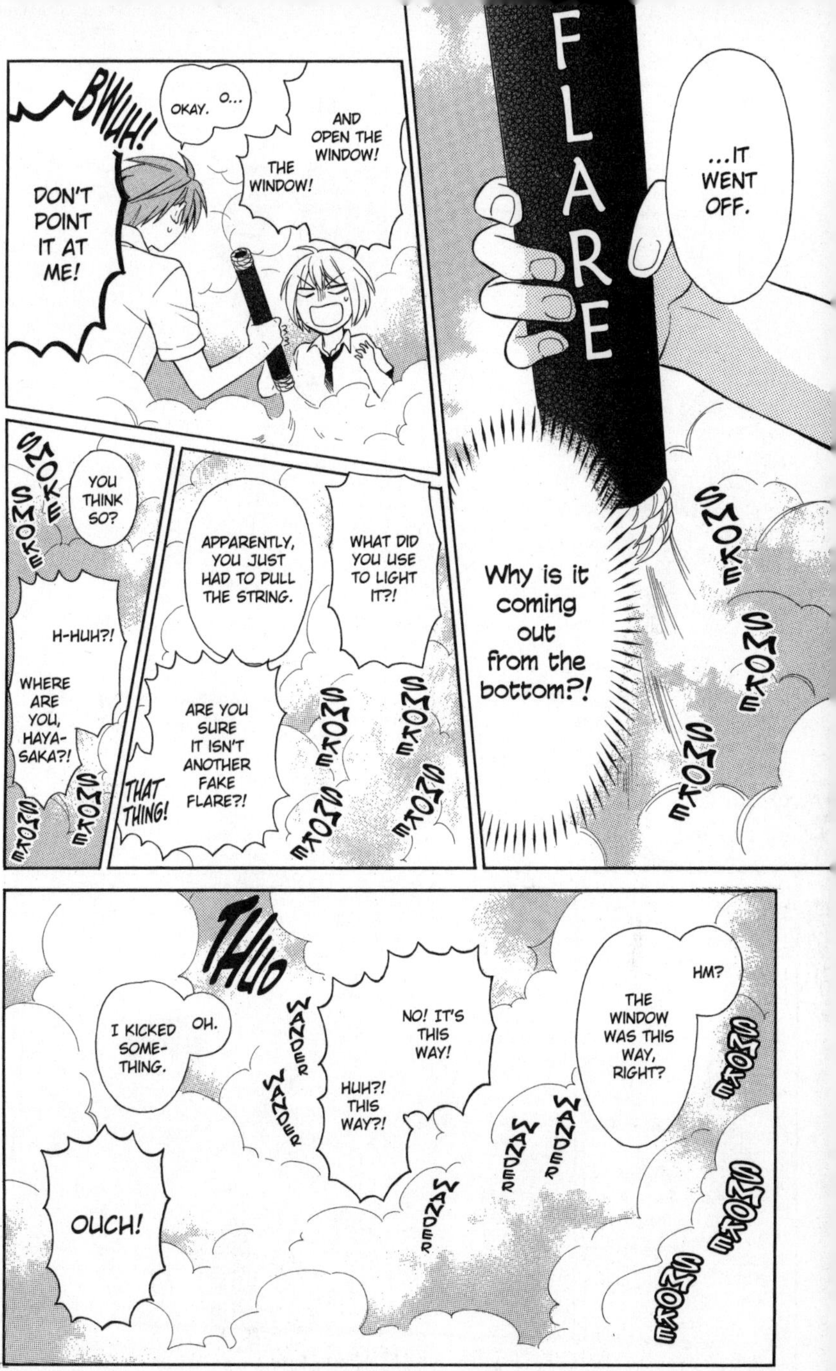

FLARE
...IT WENT OFF.
Why is it coming out from the bottom?!
SMOKE
SMOKE
SMOKE
BWUH!
AND OPEN THE WINDOW!
THE WINDOW!
OKAY. O...
DON'T POINT IT AT ME!
WHAT DID YOU USE TO LIGHT IT?!
APPARENTLY, YOU JUST HAD TO PULL THE STRING.
ARE YOU SURE IT ISN'T ANOTHER FAKE FLARE?!
THAT THING!
SMOKE
SMOKE
SMOKE
SMOKE
YOU THINK SO?
H-HUH?!
WHERE ARE YOU, HAYA-SAKA?!
SMOKE
SMOKE
SMOKE
SMOKE
HM?
THE WINDOW WAS THIS WAY, RIGHT?
SMOKE
SMOKE
SMOKE
WANDER
WANDER
WANDER
NO! IT'S THIS WAY!
HUH?! THIS WAY?!
WANDER
WANDER
THUD
OH.
I KICKED SOME-THING.
OUCH!

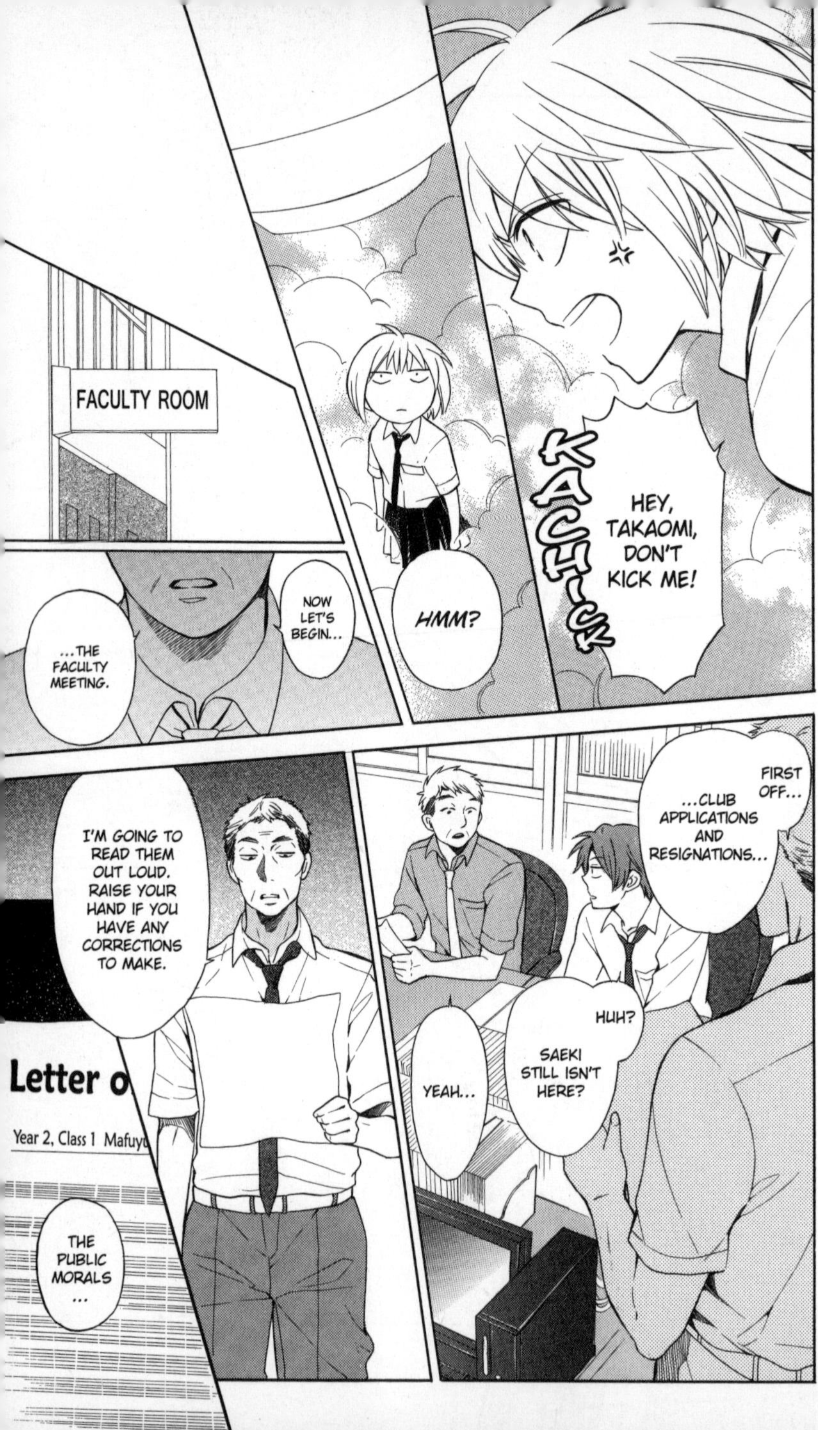
KACHICK
HEY, TAKAOMI, DON'T KICK ME!
HMM?
FACULTY ROOM
NOW LET'S BEGIN...
...THE FACULTY MEETING.
FIRST OFF...
...CLUB APPLICATIONS AND RESIGNATIONS...
HUH?
SAEKI STILL ISN'T HERE?
YEAH...
I'M GOING TO READ THEM OUT LOUD. RAISE YOUR HAND IF YOU HAVE ANY CORRECTIONS TO MAKE.
Letter o
Year 2, Class 1 Mafuyu
THE PUBLIC MORALS ...

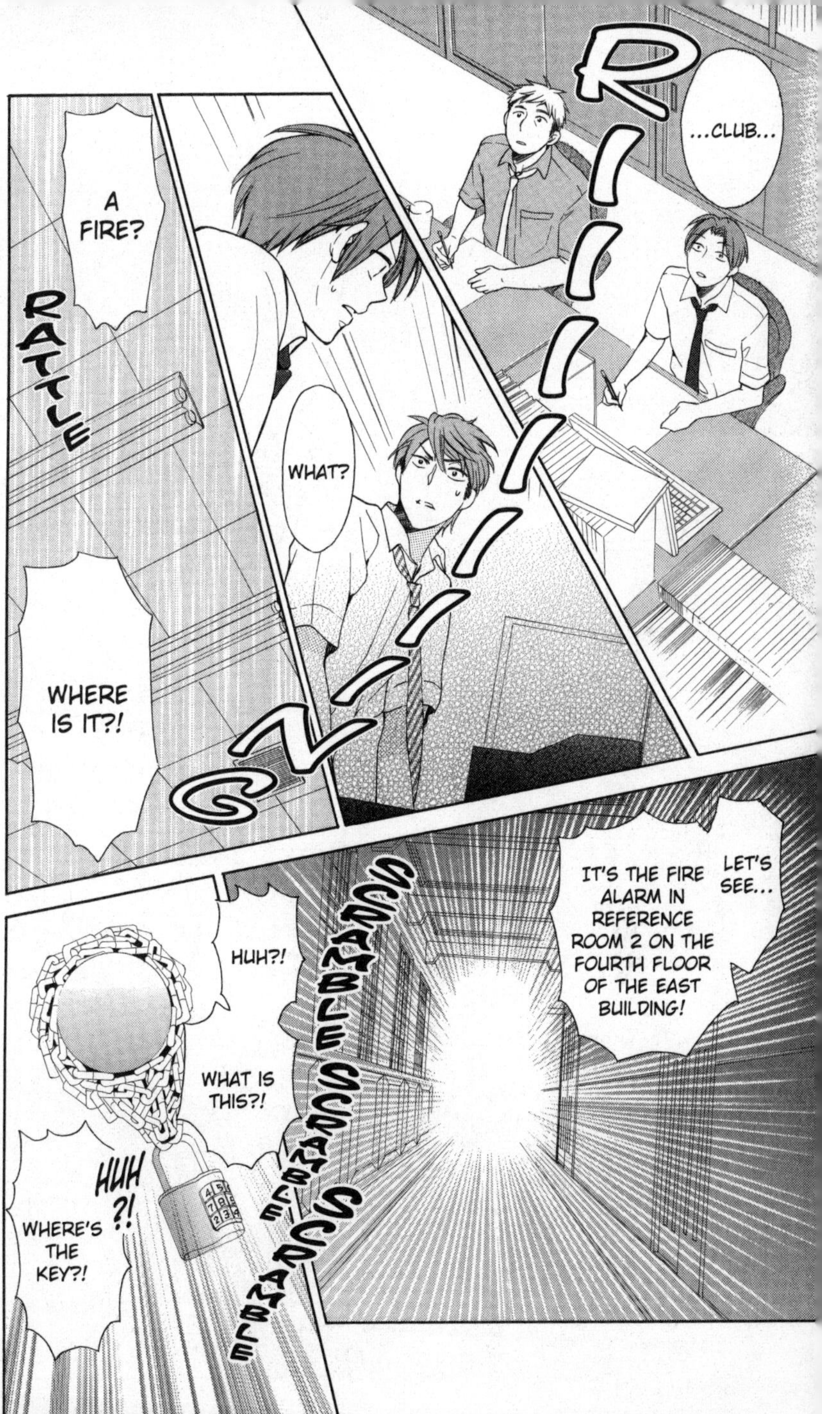
RIIIIIING
...CLUB...
WHAT?
A FIRE?
RATTLE
WHERE IS IT?!
LET'S SEE...
IT'S THE FIRE ALARM IN REFERENCE ROOM 2 ON THE FOURTH FLOOR OF THE EAST BUILDING!
SCRAMBLE SCRAMBLE SCRAMBLE
SCRAMBLE SCRAMBLE
HUH?!
WHAT IS THIS?!
HUH ?!
WHERE'S THE KEY?!

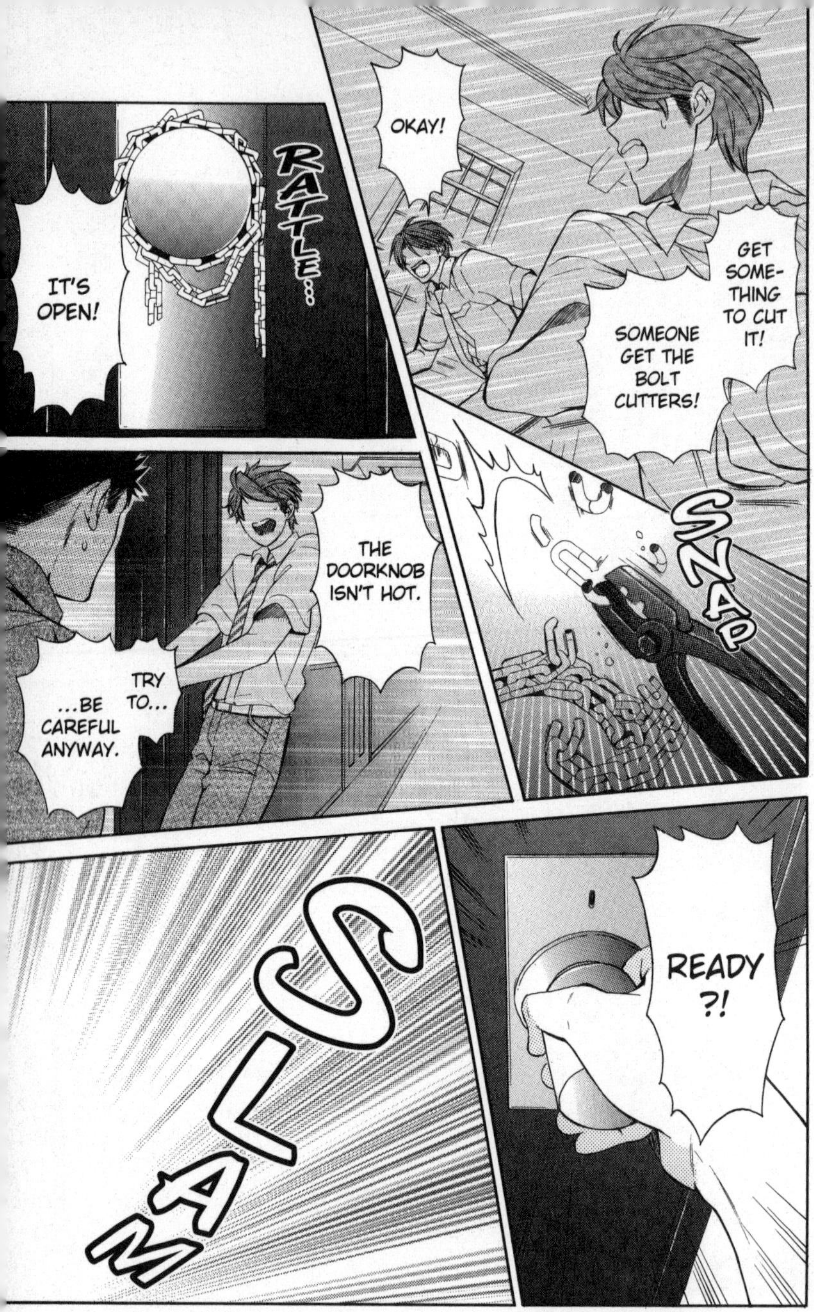
GET SOMETHING TO CUT IT!
SOMEONE GET THE BOLT CUTTERS!
OKAY!
RATTLE...
IT'S OPEN!
SNAP
THE DOORKNOB ISN'T HOT.
TRY TO...
...BE CAREFUL ANYWAY.
READY ?!
SLAM

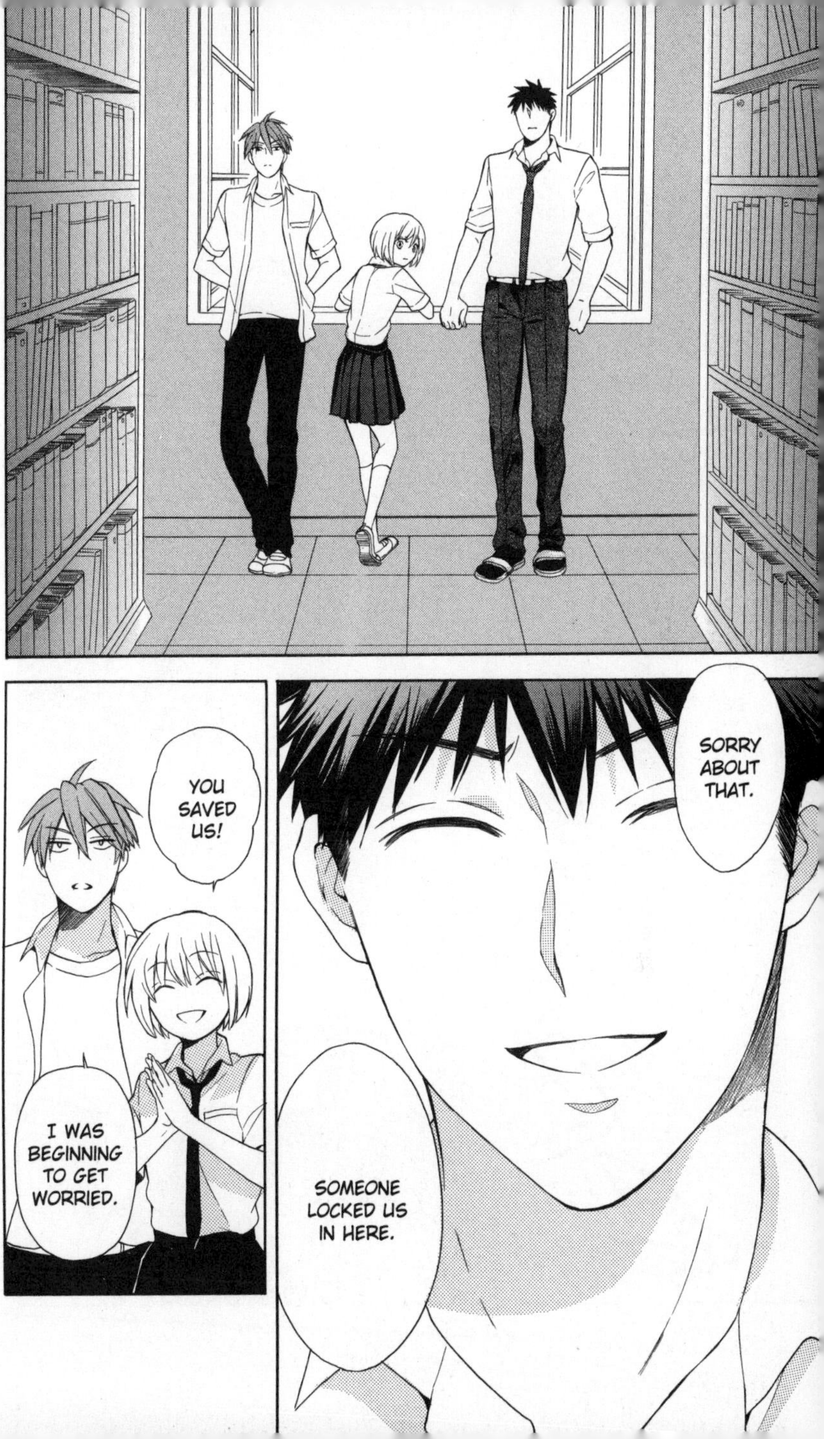
SORRY ABOUT THAT.
SOMEONE LOCKED US IN HERE.
YOU SAVED US!
I WAS BEGINNING TO GET WORRIED.

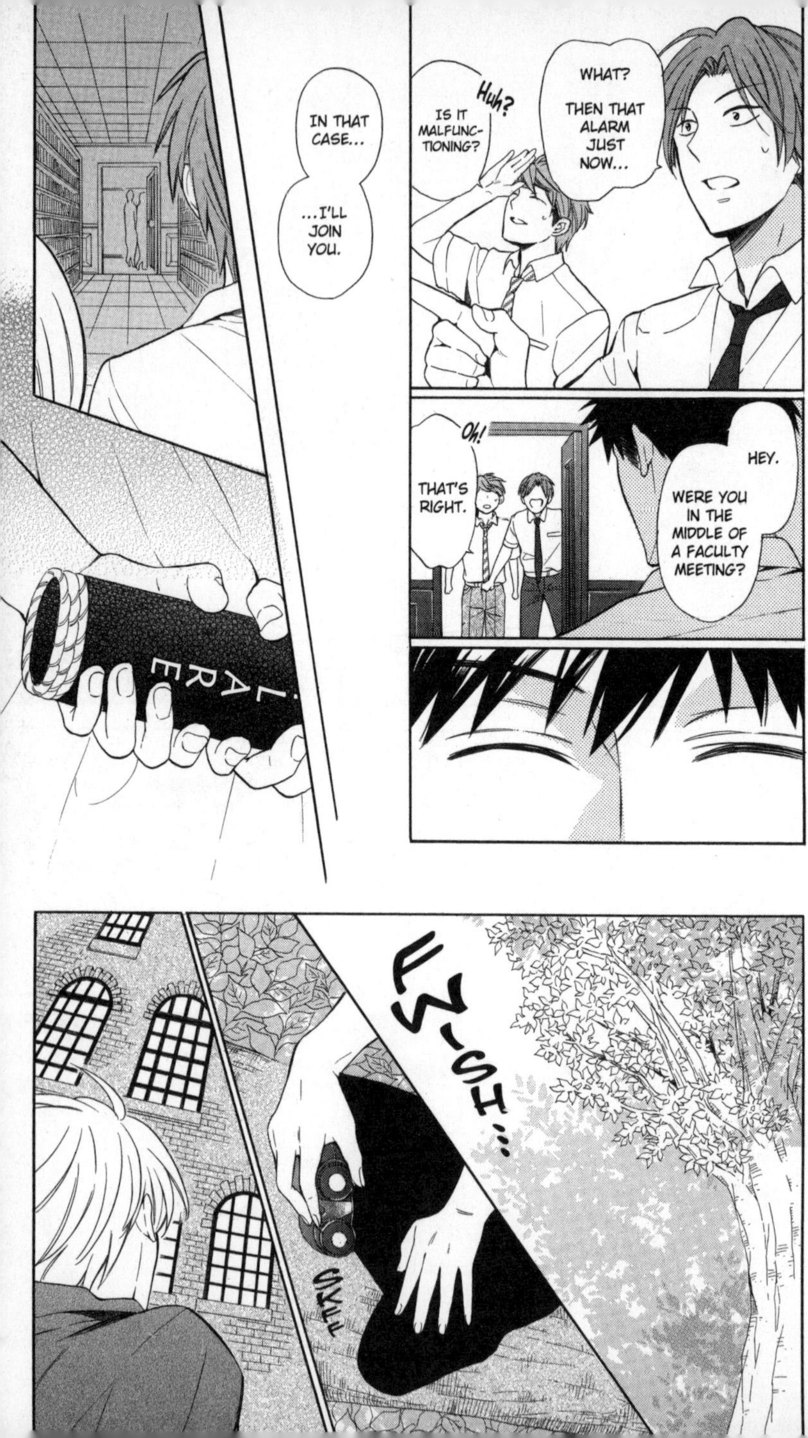
WHAT? THEN THAT ALARM JUST NOW...
Huh? IS IT MALFUNCTIONING?
HEY. WERE YOU IN THE MIDDLE OF A FACULTY MEETING?
Oh! THAT'S RIGHT.
IN THAT CASE...
...I'LL JOIN YOU.
ERAL
FWISH...
SKFF

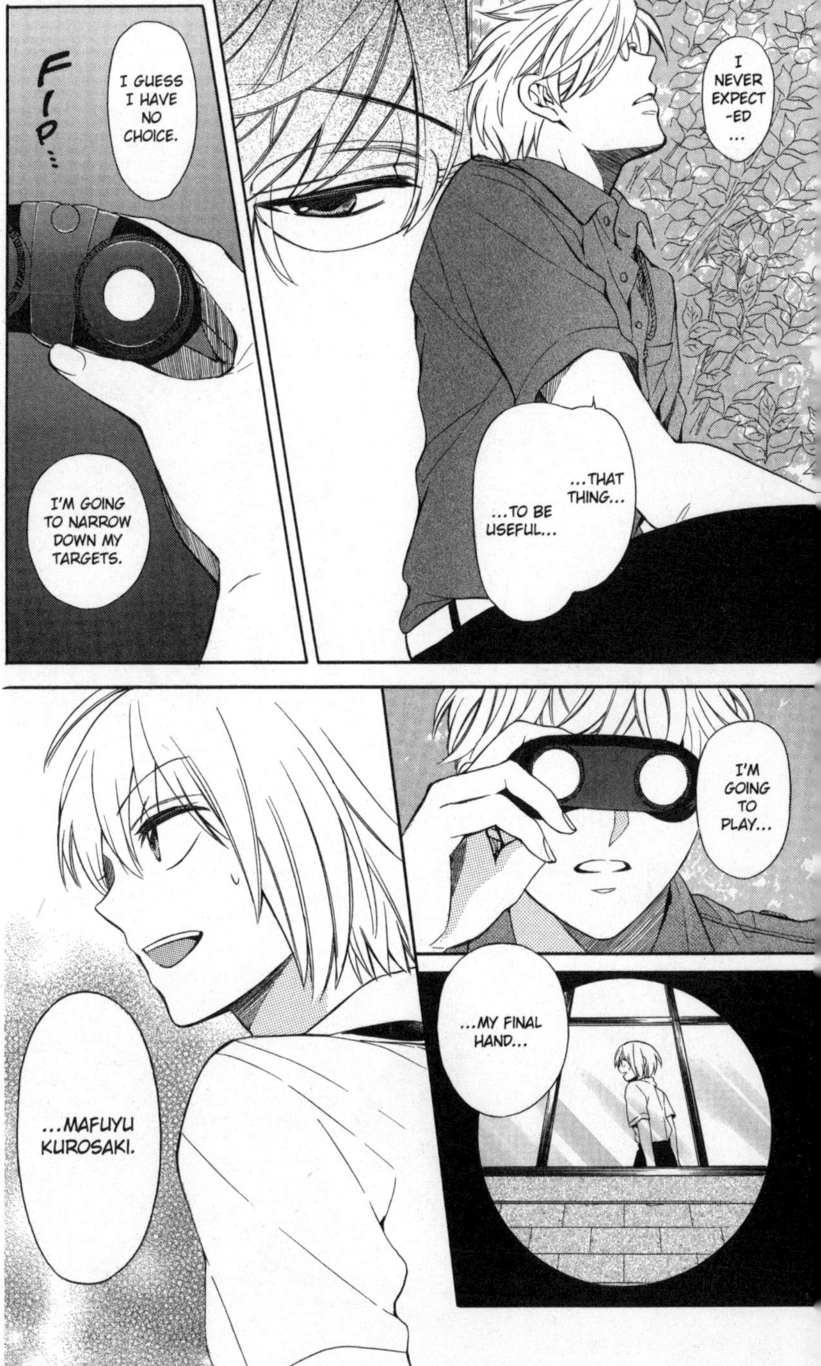
I NEVER EXPECT-ED...
...THAT THING...
...TO BE USEFUL...
I GUESS I HAVE NO CHOICE.
FLIP..
I'M GOING TO NARROW DOWN MY TARGETS.
I'M GOING TO PLAY...
...MY FINAL HAND...
...MAFUYU KUROSAKI.

HIS EXISTENCE

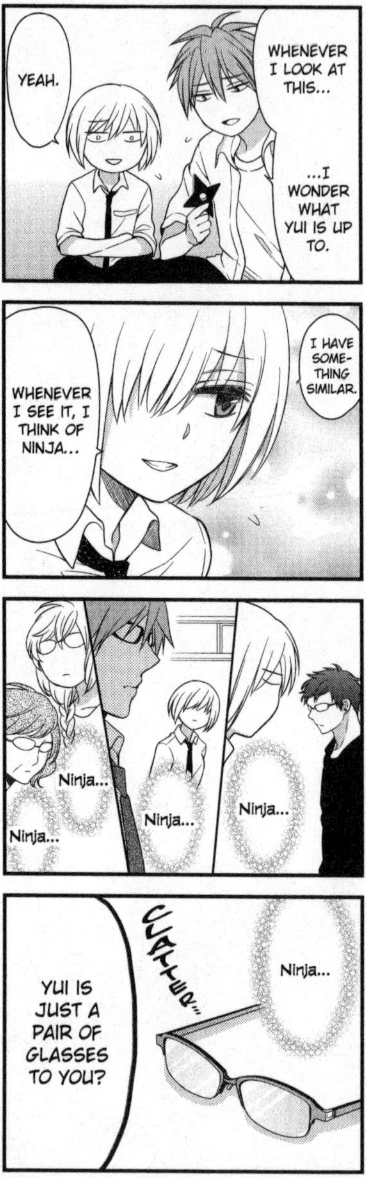
WHENEVER I LOOK AT THIS...
...I WONDER WHAT YUI IS UP TO.
YEAH.
I HAVE SOME-THING SIMILAR.
WHENEVER I SEE IT, I THINK OF NINJA...
Ninja...
Ninja...
Ninja...
Ninja...
Ninja...
CLATTER...
YUI IS JUST A PAIR OF GLASSES TO YOU?

HIS EXISTENCE 2

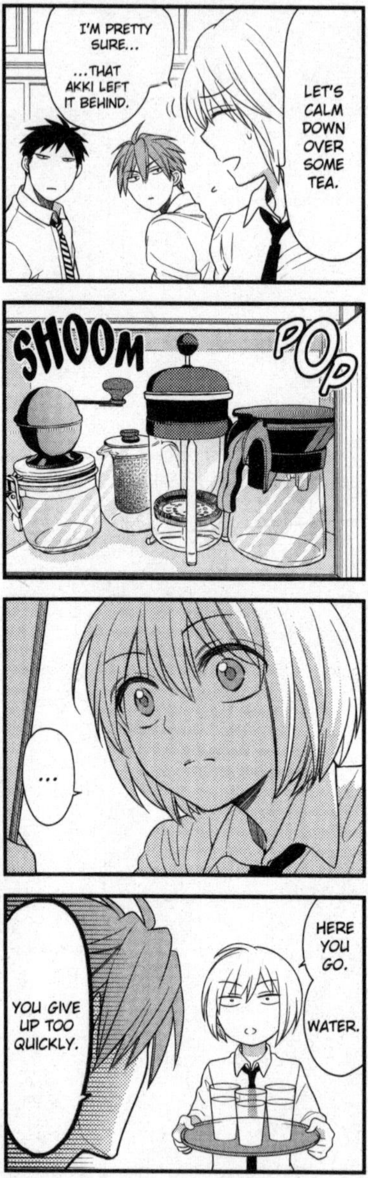
LET'S CALM DOWN OVER SOME TEA.
I'M PRETTY SURE...
...THAT AKKI LEFT IT BEHIND.
POP
SHOOM
...
HERE YOU GO.
WATER.
YOU GIVE UP TOO QUICKLY.

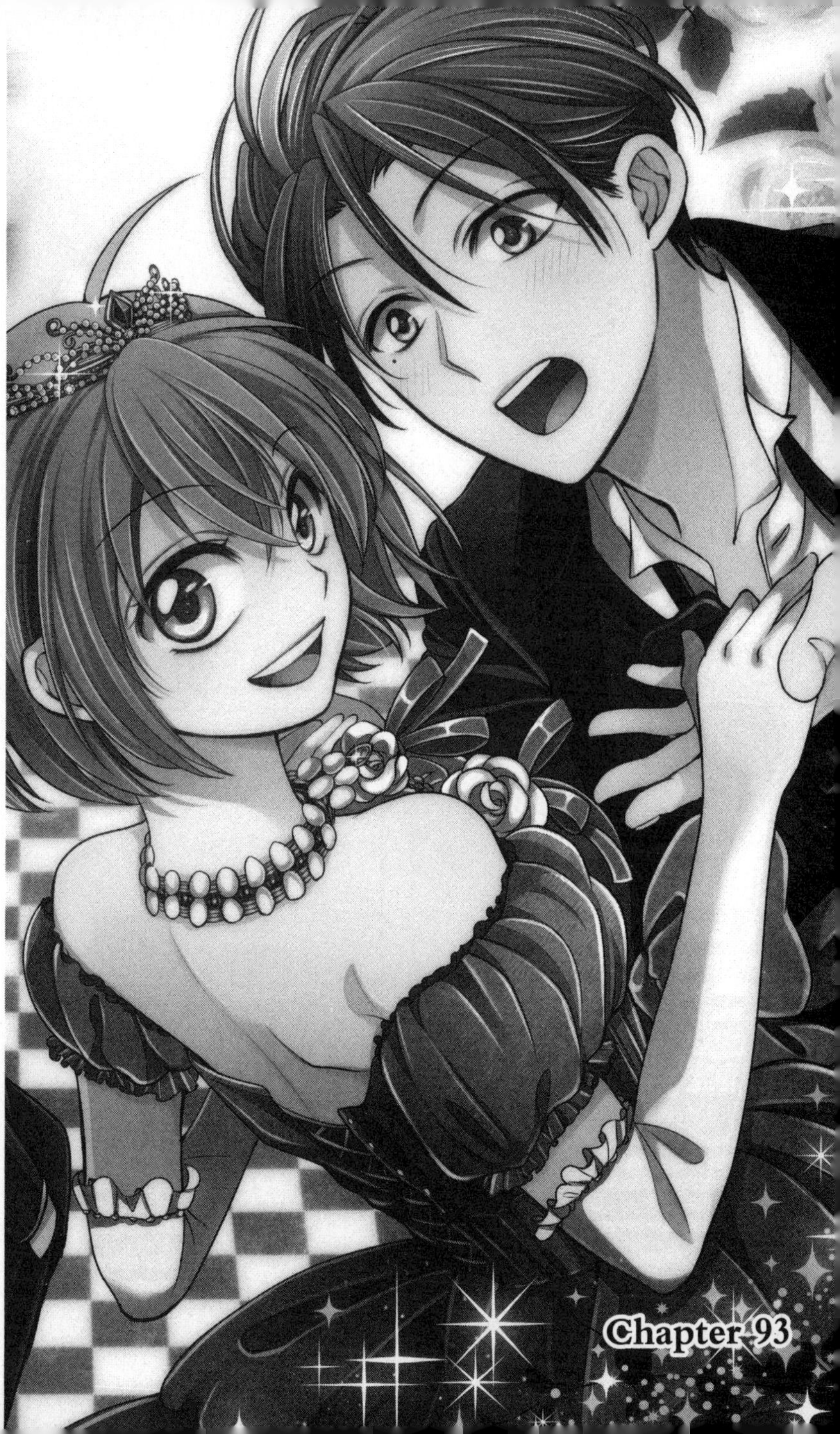
Chapter 93

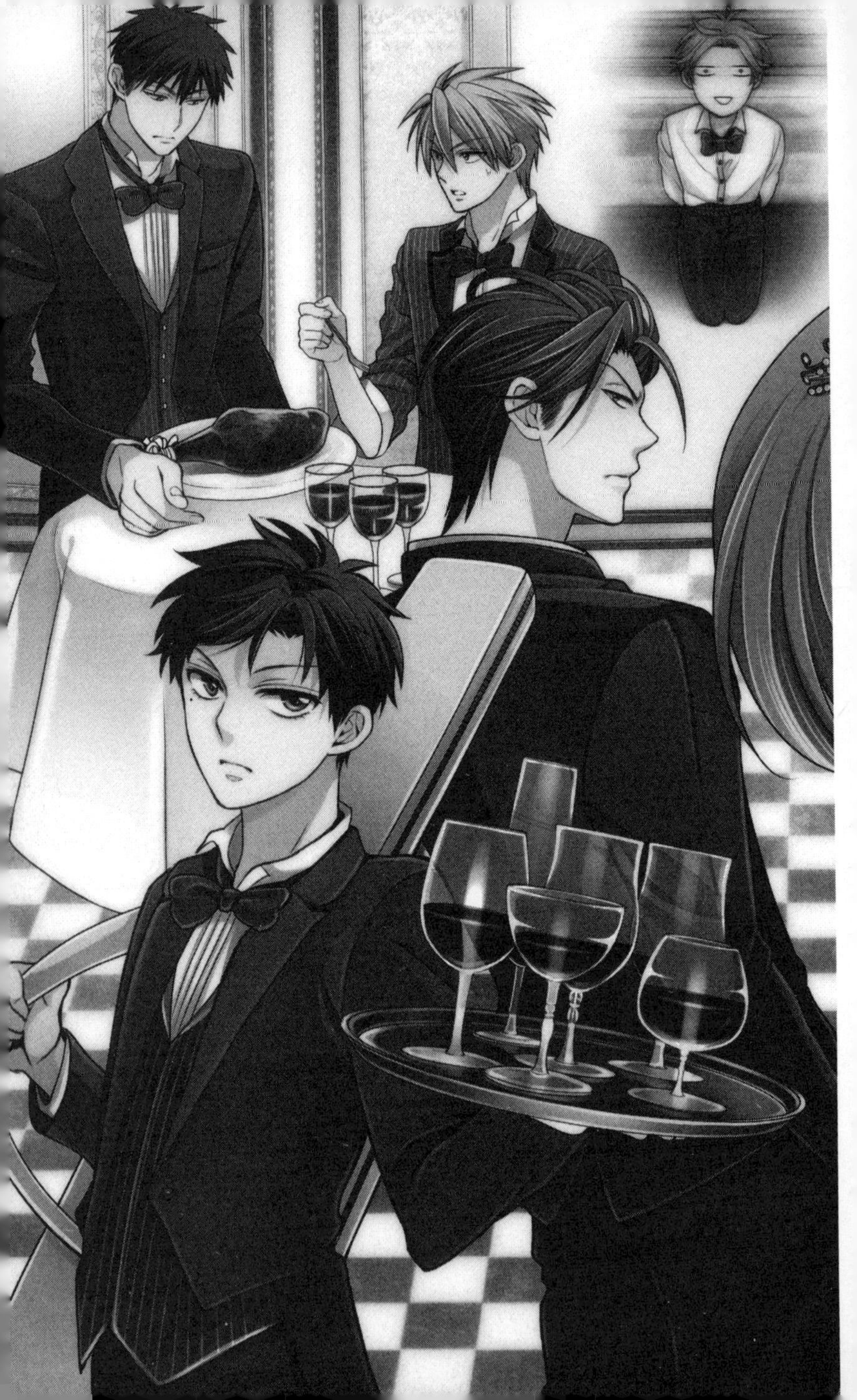

TEACHER'S EXISTENCE

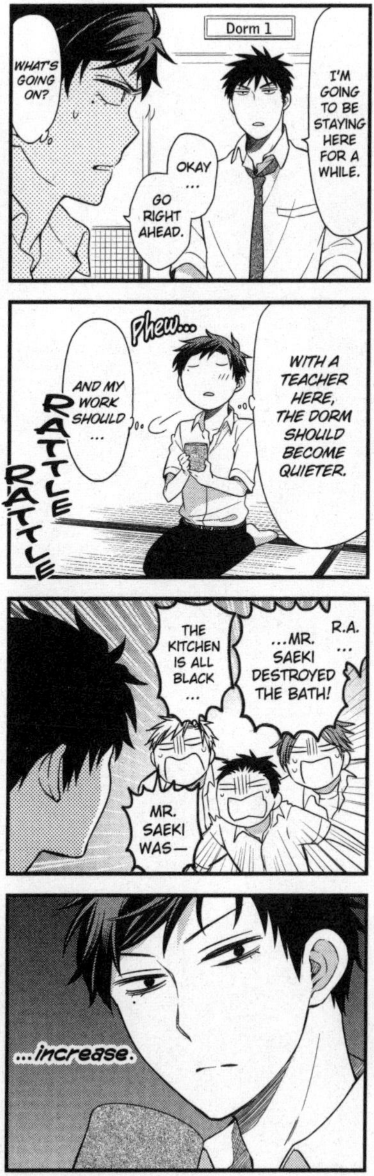
Dorm 1
I'M GOING TO BE STAYING HERE FOR A WHILE.
OKAY ... GO RIGHT AHEAD.
WHAT'S GOING ON?
WITH A TEACHER HERE, THE DORM SHOULD BECOME QUIETER.
Phew...
AND MY WORK SHOULD ...
RATTLE
RATTLE
R.A. ...
...MR. SAEKI DESTROYED THE BATH!
THE KITCHEN IS ALL BLACK ...
MR. SAEKI WAS—
...increase.

FOR EXAMPLE

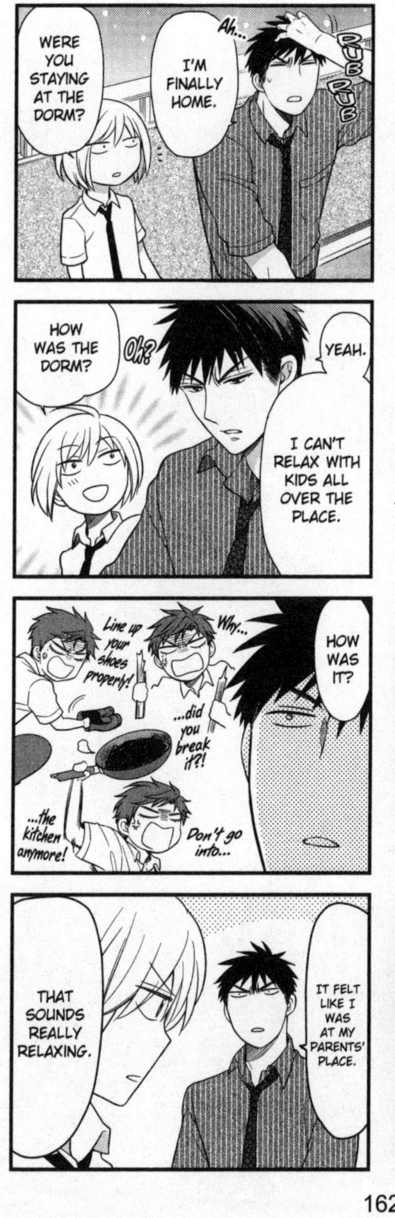
Ah...
RUB RUB
I'M FINALLY HOME.
WERE YOU STAYING AT THE DORM?
YEAH.
I CAN'T RELAX WITH KIDS ALL OVER THE PLACE.
Oh?
HOW WAS THE DORM?
HOW WAS IT?
Why...
...did you break it?!
Line up your shoes properly!
Don't go into...
...the kitchen anymore!
IT FELT LIKE I WAS AT MY PARENTS' PLACE.
THAT SOUNDS REALLY RELAXING.

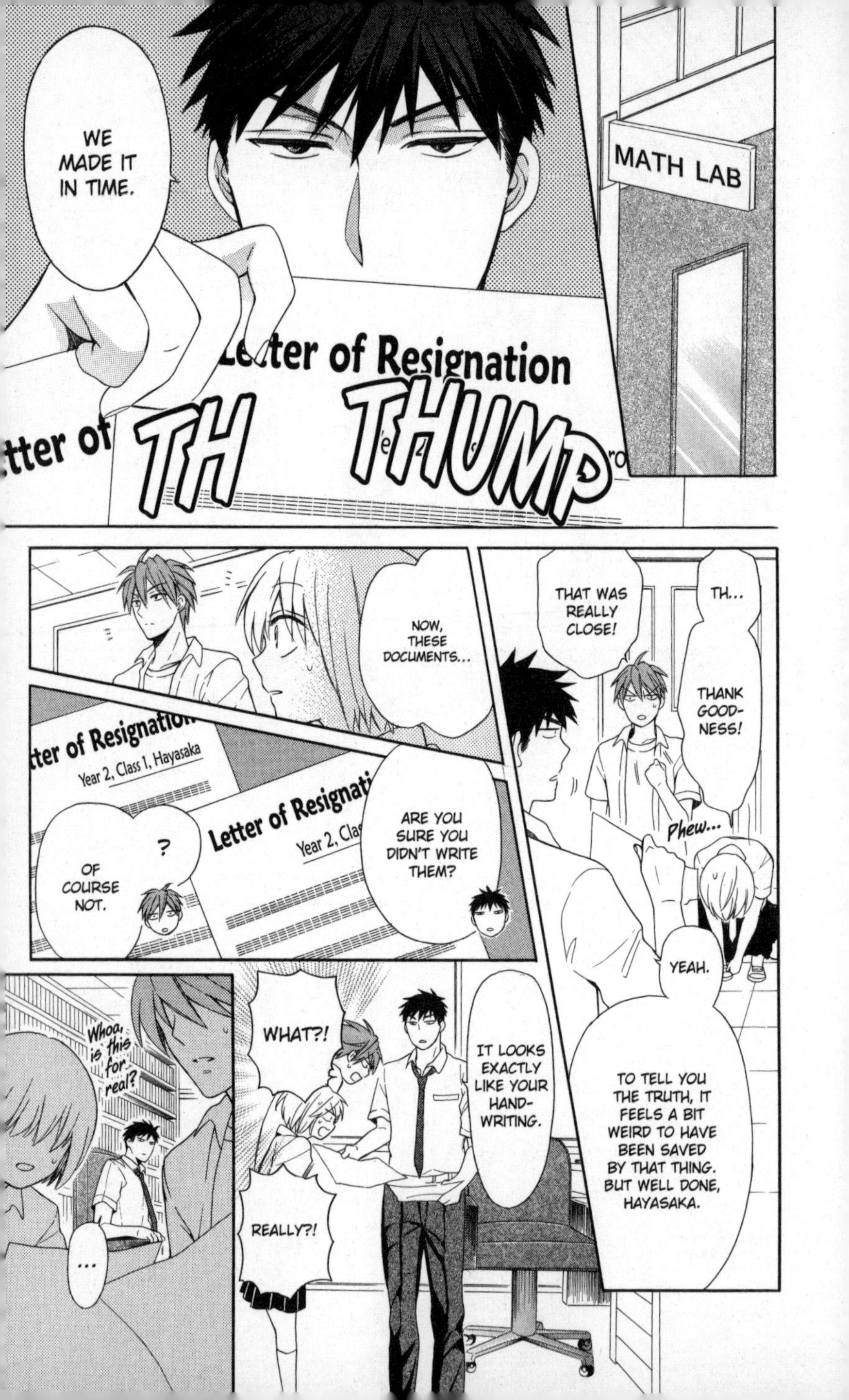
MATH LAB
WE MADE IT IN TIME.
Letter of Resignation
Letter of
TH THUMP
TH...
THAT WAS REALLY CLOSE!
THANK GOODNESS!
Phew...
YEAH.
TO TELL YOU THE TRUTH, IT FEELS A BIT WEIRD TO HAVE BEEN SAVED BY THAT THING. BUT WELL DONE, HAYASAKA.
NOW, THESE DOCUMENTS...
Letter of Resignation
Year 2, Class 1, Hayasaka
ARE YOU SURE YOU DIDN'T WRITE THEM?
Letter of Resignati
Year 2, Clas
?
OF COURSE NOT.
IT LOOKS EXACTLY LIKE YOUR HAND-WRITING.
WHAT?!
REALLY?!
Whoa, is this for real?
...

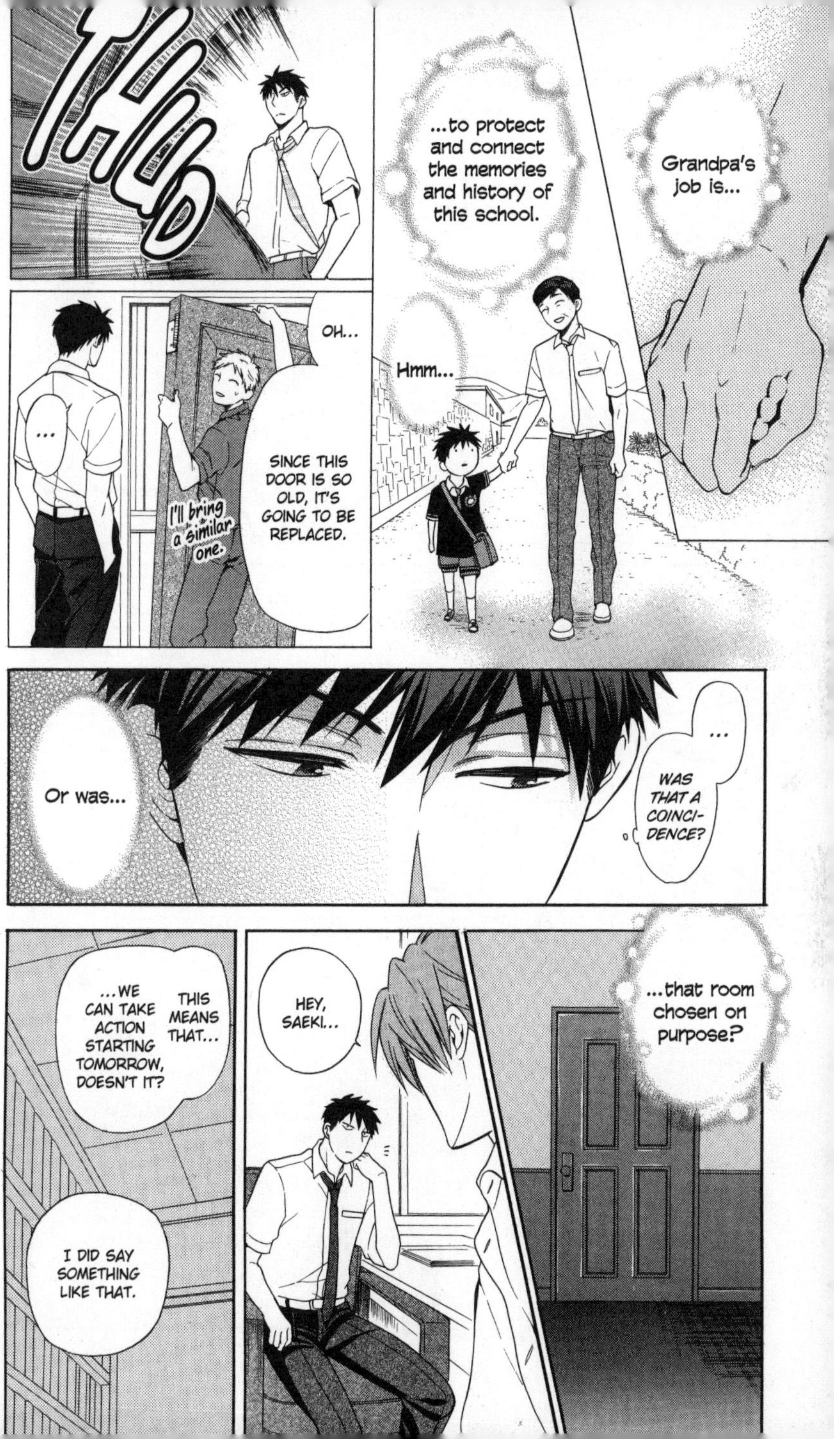
Grandpa's job is...
...to protect and connect the memories and history of this school.
Hmm...
THUD
OH...
SINCE THIS DOOR IS SO OLD, IT'S GOING TO BE REPLACED.
I'll bring a similar one.
...
...
WAS THAT A COINCIDENCE?
Or was...
...that room chosen on purpose?
HEY, SAEKI...
THIS MEANS THAT...
...WE CAN TAKE ACTION STARTING TOMORROW, DOESN'T IT?
I DID SAY SOMETHING LIKE THAT.

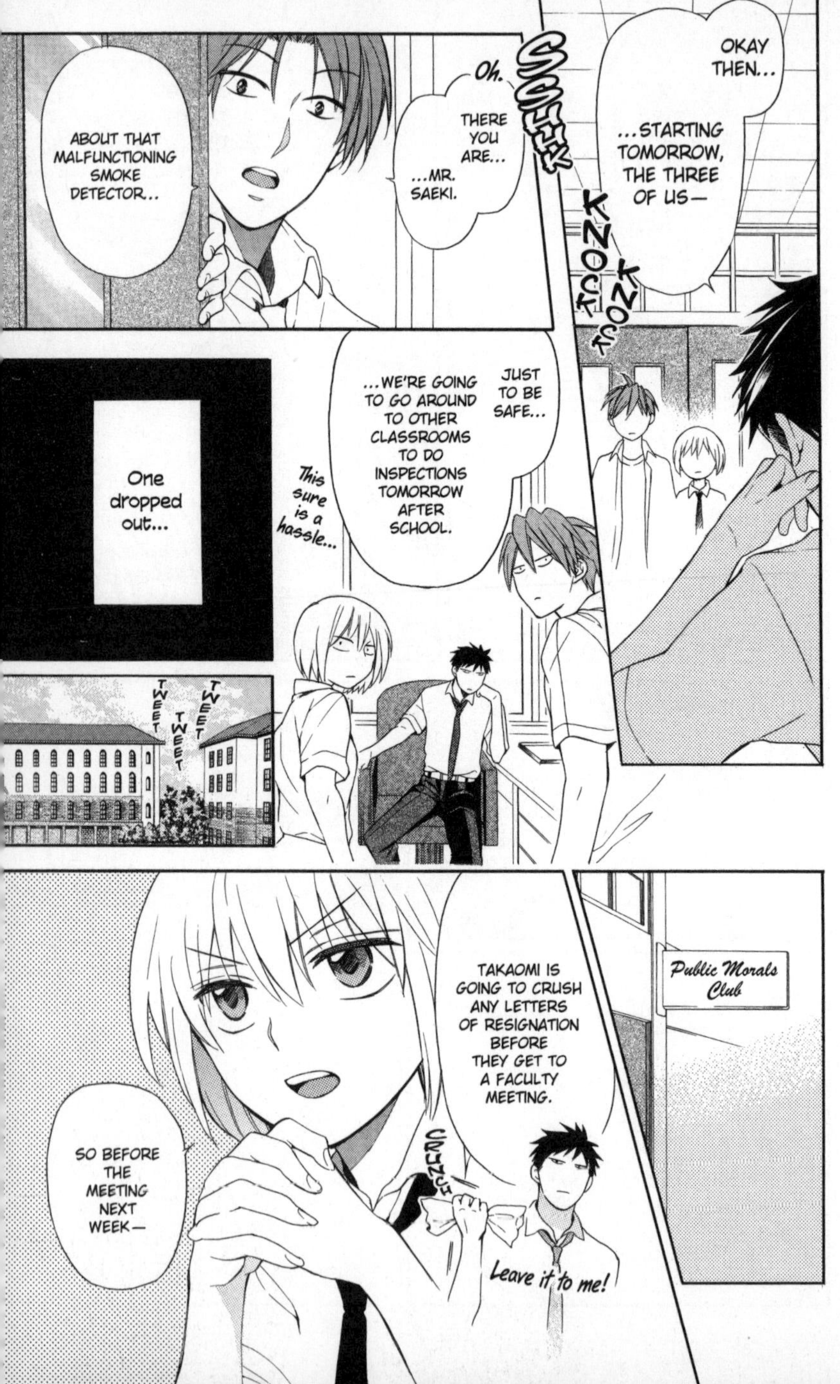
OKAY THEN...
...STARTING TOMORROW, THE THREE OF US—
KNOCK KNOCK
Oh.
THERE YOU ARE...
...MR. SAEKI.
ABOUT THAT MALFUNCTIONING SMOKE DETECTOR...
JUST TO BE SAFE...
...WE'RE GOING TO GO AROUND TO OTHER CLASSROOMS TO DO INSPECTIONS TOMORROW AFTER SCHOOL.
This sure is a hassle...
One dropped out...
TWEET TWEET TWEET
Public Morals Club
TAKAOMI IS GOING TO CRUSH ANY LETTERS OF RESIGNATION BEFORE THEY GET TO A FACULTY MEETING.
CRUNCH
Leave it to me!
SO BEFORE THE MEETING NEXT WEEK—

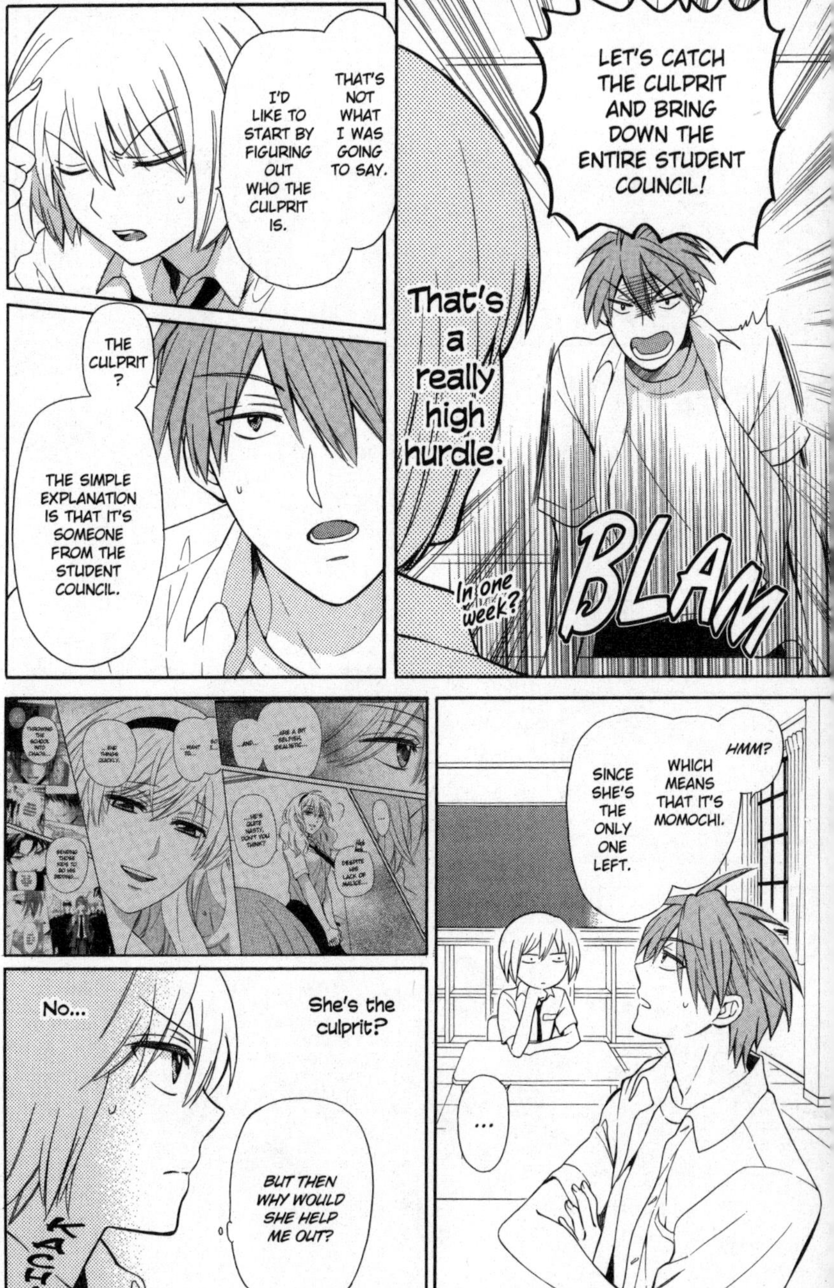
LET'S CATCH THE CULPRIT AND BRING DOWN THE ENTIRE STUDENT COUNCIL!
That's a really high hurdle.
In one week?
BLAM
THAT'S NOT WHAT I WAS GOING TO SAY.
I'D LIKE TO START BY FIGURING OUT WHO THE CULPRIT IS.
THE CULPRIT?
THE SIMPLE EXPLANATION IS THAT IT'S SOMEONE FROM THE STUDENT COUNCIL.
HMM?
WHICH MEANS THAT IT'S MOMOCHI.
SINCE SHE'S THE ONLY ONE LEFT.
...
...ARE A BIT SELFISH, IDEALISTIC...
...AND...
DESPITE HIS LACK OF MALICE...
...HE'S QUITE NASTY, DON'T YOU THINK?
...WANT TO...
...SHE THINKS QUICKLY.
THROWING THE SCHOOL INTO CHAOS...
SENDING THOSE KIDS TO DO HIS BIDDING...
She's the culprit?
No...
BUT THEN WHY WOULD SHE HELP ME OUT?
KACHI-K

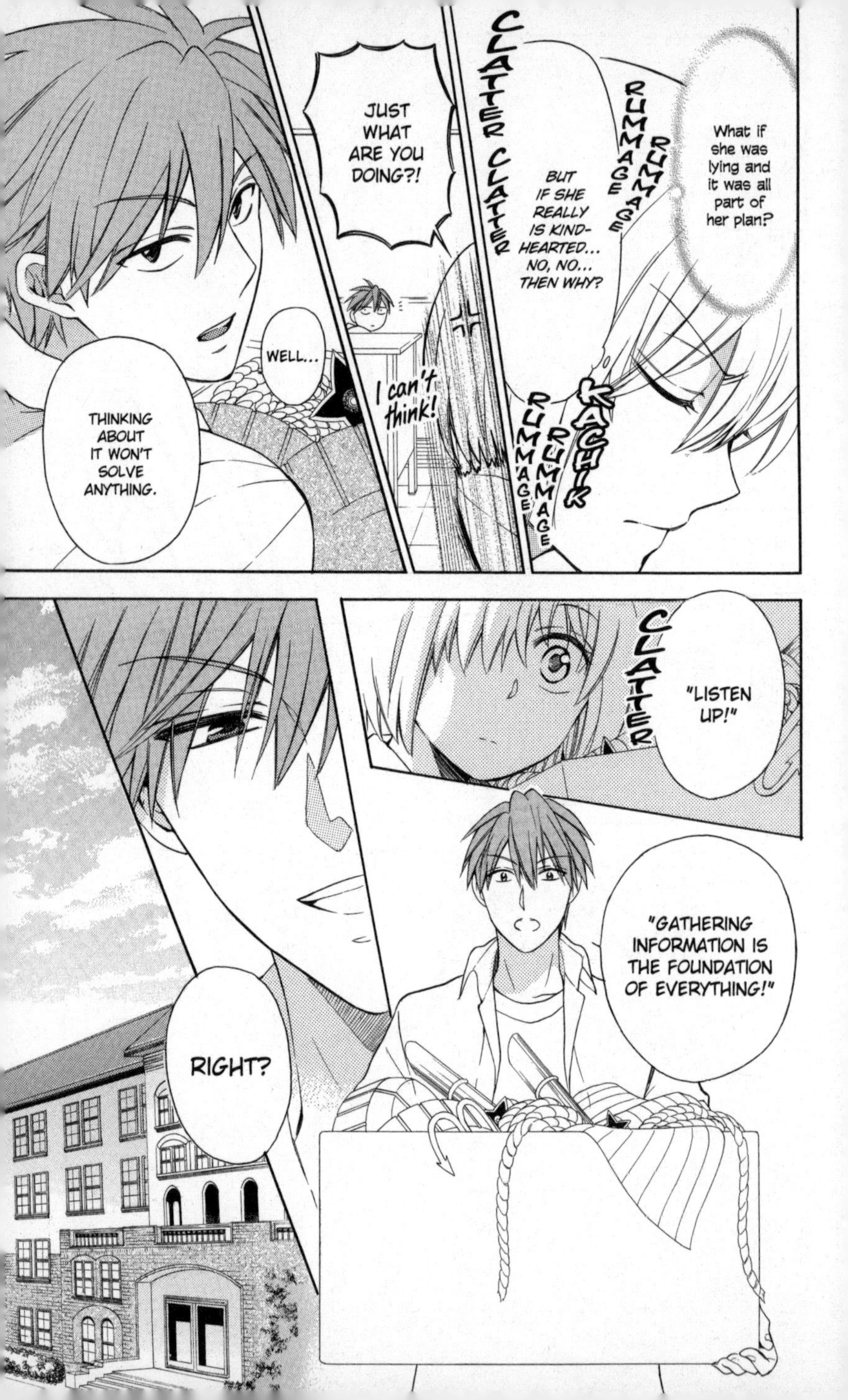
What if she was lying and it was all part of her plan?
RUMMAGE RUMMAGE
CLATTER CLATTER
BUT IF SHE REALLY IS KIND-HEARTED... NO, NO... THEN WHY?
KACHIK
RUMMAGE RUMMAGE
JUST WHAT ARE YOU DOING?!
I can't think!
WELL...
THINKING ABOUT IT WON'T SOLVE ANYTHING.
CLATTER
"LISTEN UP!"
"GATHERING INFORMATION IS THE FOUNDATION OF EVERYTHING!"
RIGHT?

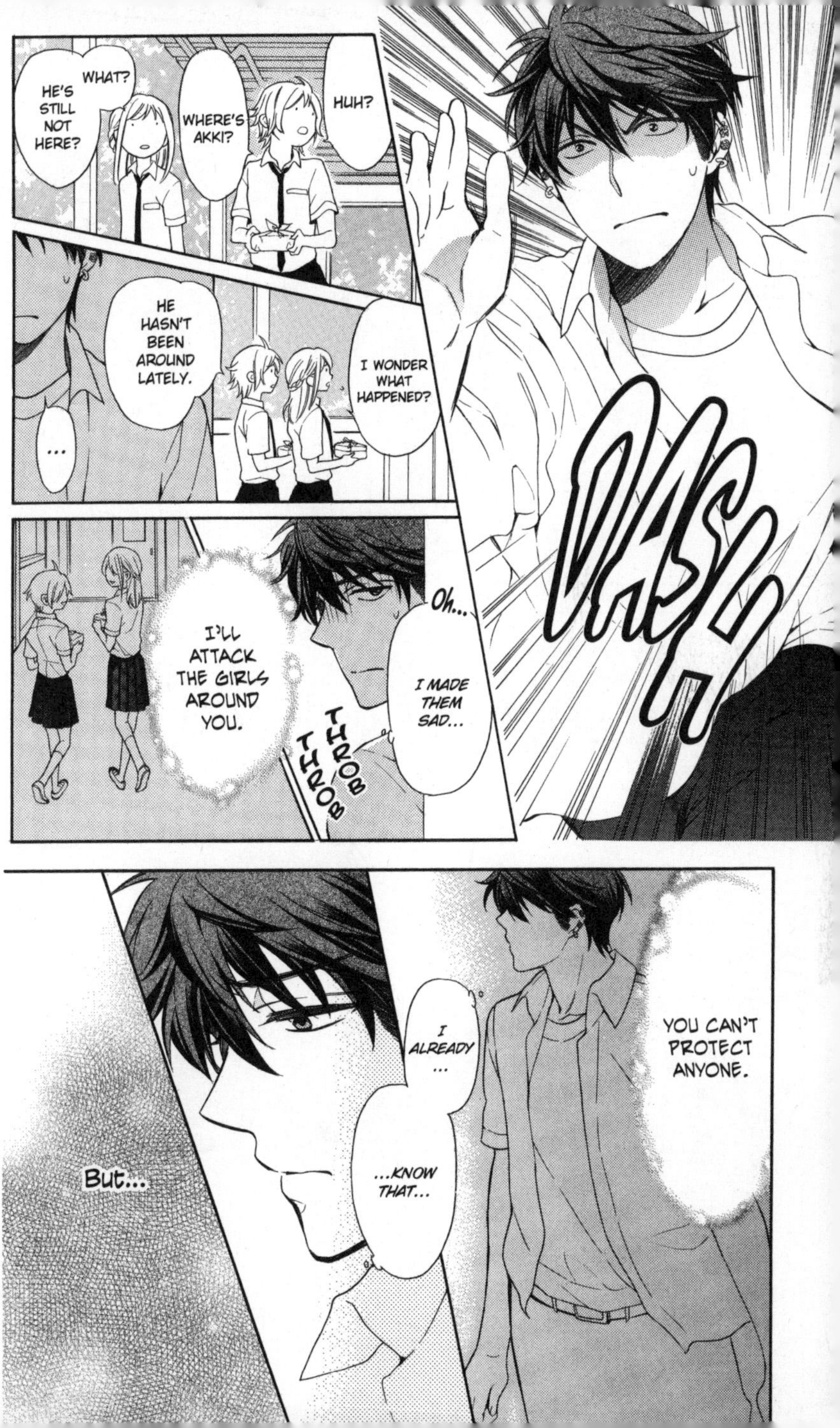
DASH
HUH?
WHERE'S AKKI?
WHAT?
HE'S STILL NOT HERE?
I WONDER WHAT HAPPENED?
HE HASN'T BEEN AROUND LATELY.
...
Oh...
I MADE THEM SAD...
THROB THROB
I'LL ATTACK THE GIRLS AROUND YOU.
YOU CAN'T PROTECT ANYONE.
I ALREADY...
...KNOW THAT...
But...

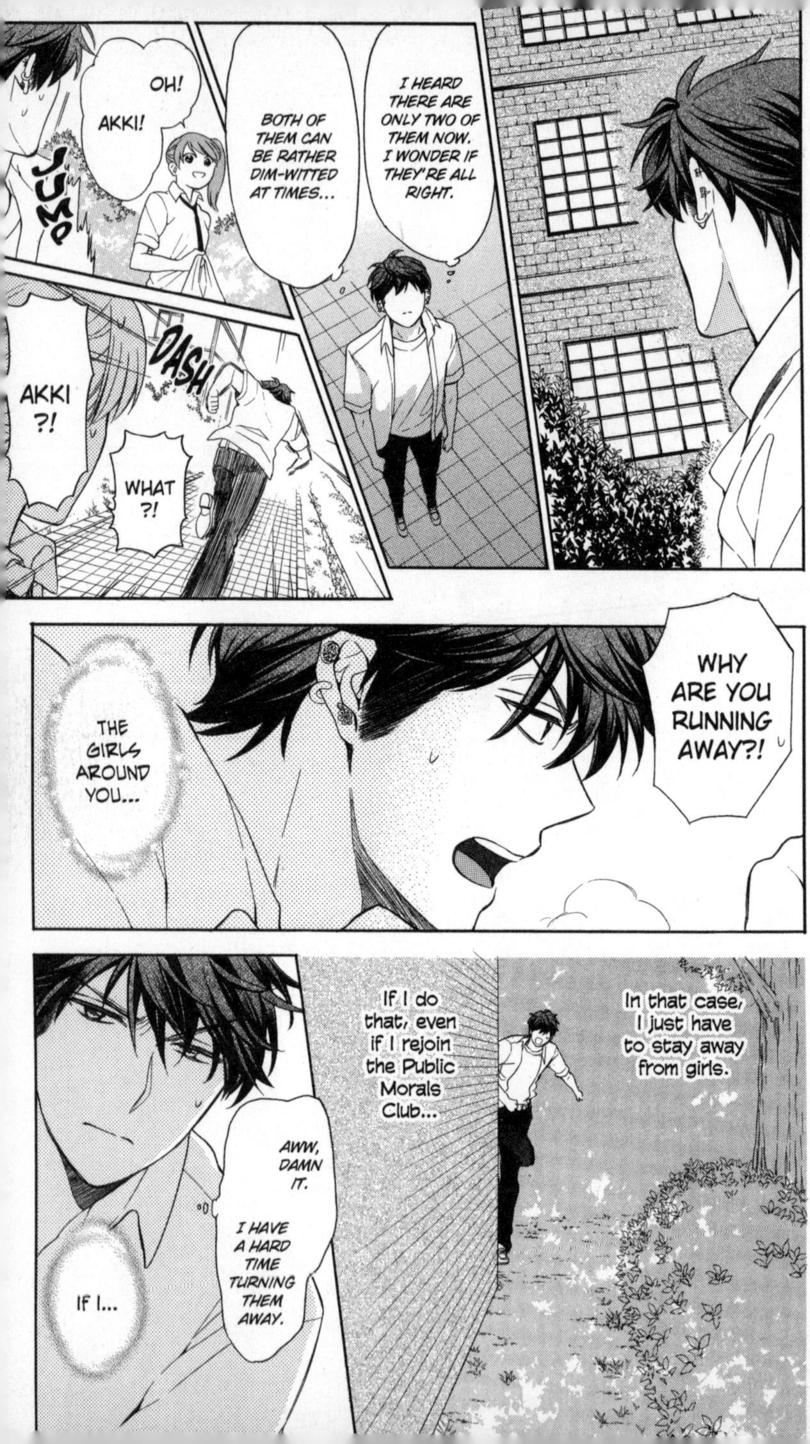
I HEARD THERE ARE ONLY TWO OF THEM NOW. I WONDER IF THEY'RE ALL RIGHT.
BOTH OF THEM CAN BE RATHER DIM-WITTED AT TIMES...
OH!
AKKI!
JUMP
DASH
AKKI ?!
WHAT ?!
WHY ARE YOU RUNNING AWAY?!
THE GIRLS AROUND YOU...
In that case, I just have to stay away from girls.
If I do that, even if I rejoin the Public Morals Club...
AWW, DAMN IT.
I HAVE A HARD TIME TURNING THEM AWAY.
If I...

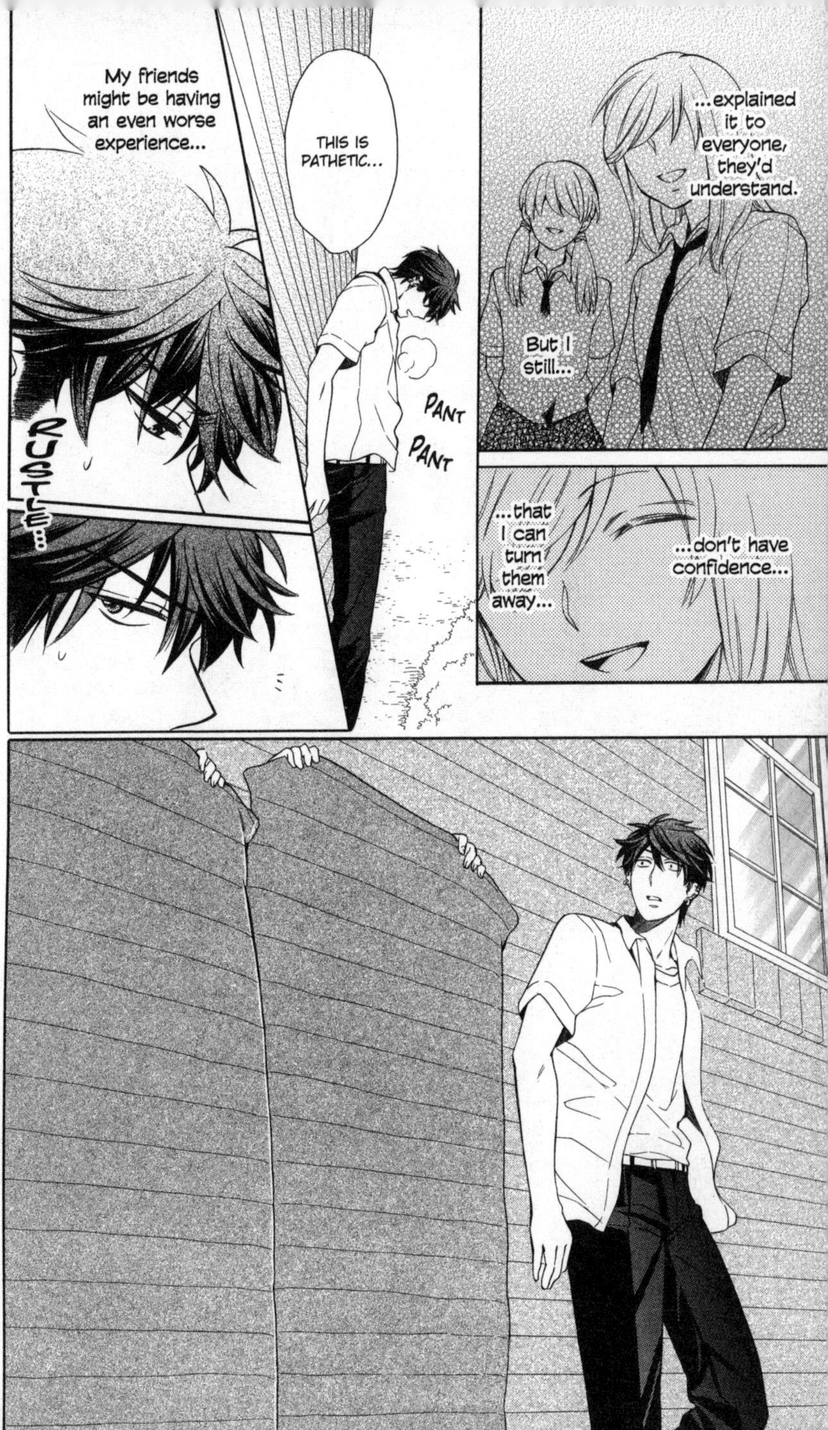
...explained it to everyone, they'd understand.
But I still...
...don't have confidence...
...that I can turn them away...
THIS IS PATHETIC...
PANT
PANT
My friends might be having an even worse experience...
RUSTLE...

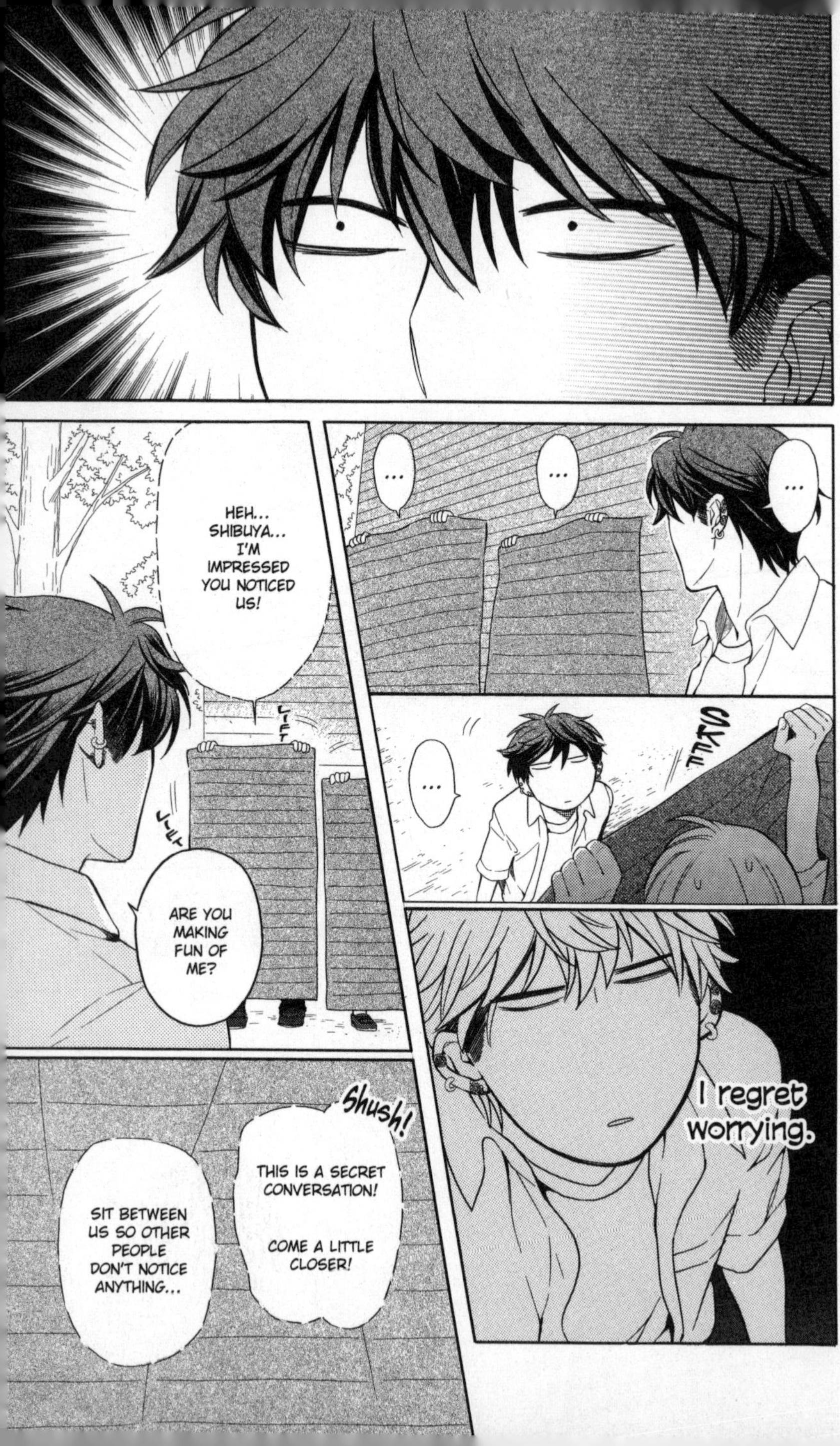
...
...
...
SKFF
...
HEH... SHIBUYA... I'M IMPRESSED YOU NOTICED US!
LIFT
LIFT
ARE YOU MAKING FUN OF ME?
I regret worrying.
Shush!
THIS IS A SECRET CONVERSATION!
COME A LITTLE CLOSER!
SIT BETWEEN US SO OTHER PEOPLE DON'T NOTICE ANYTHING...

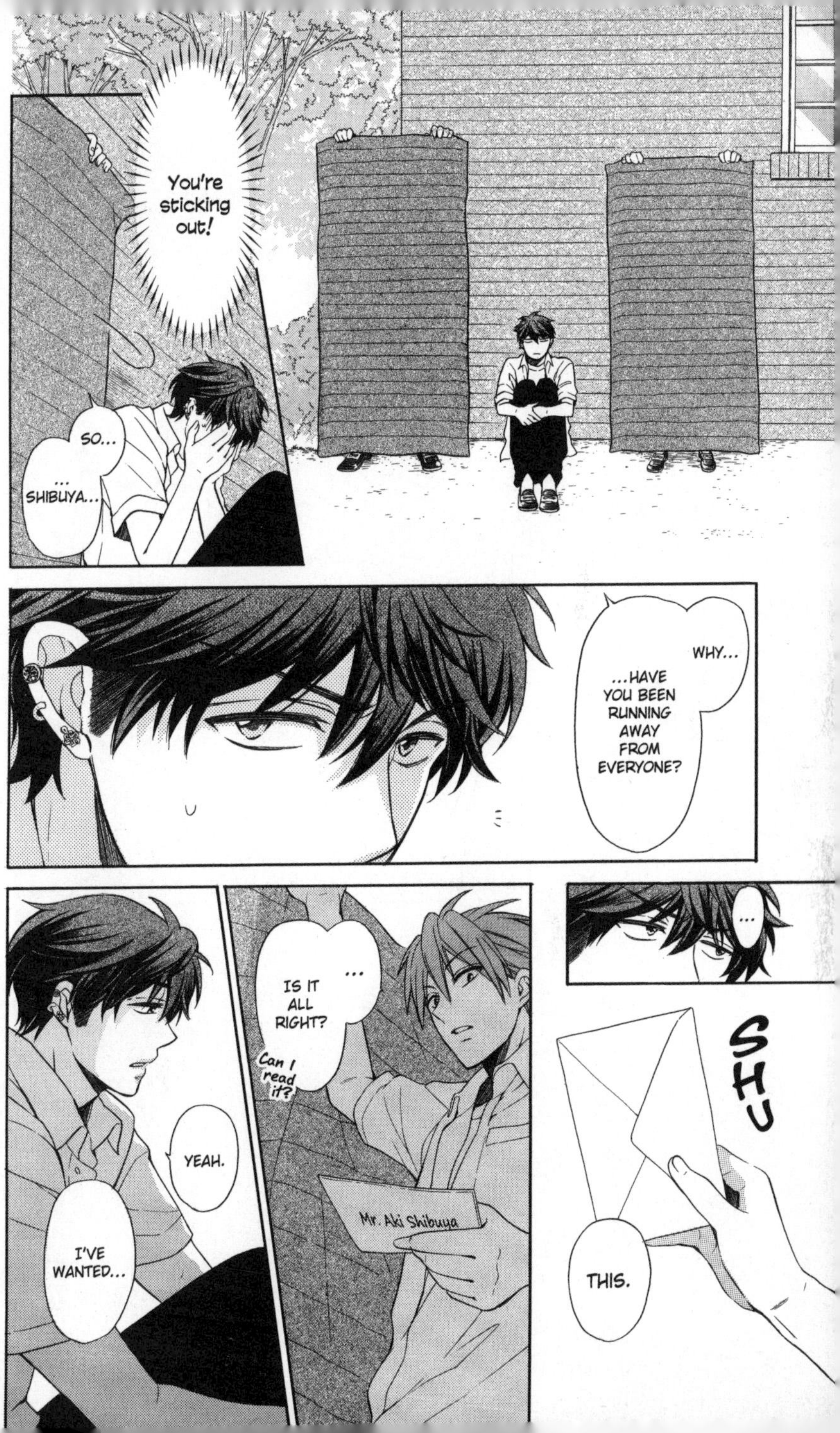
You're sticking out!
SO...
...SHIBUYA...
WHY...
...HAVE YOU BEEN RUNNING AWAY FROM EVERYONE?
...
SHU
THIS.
...
IS IT ALL RIGHT?
Can I read it?
Mr. Aki Shibuya
YEAH.
I'VE WANTED...

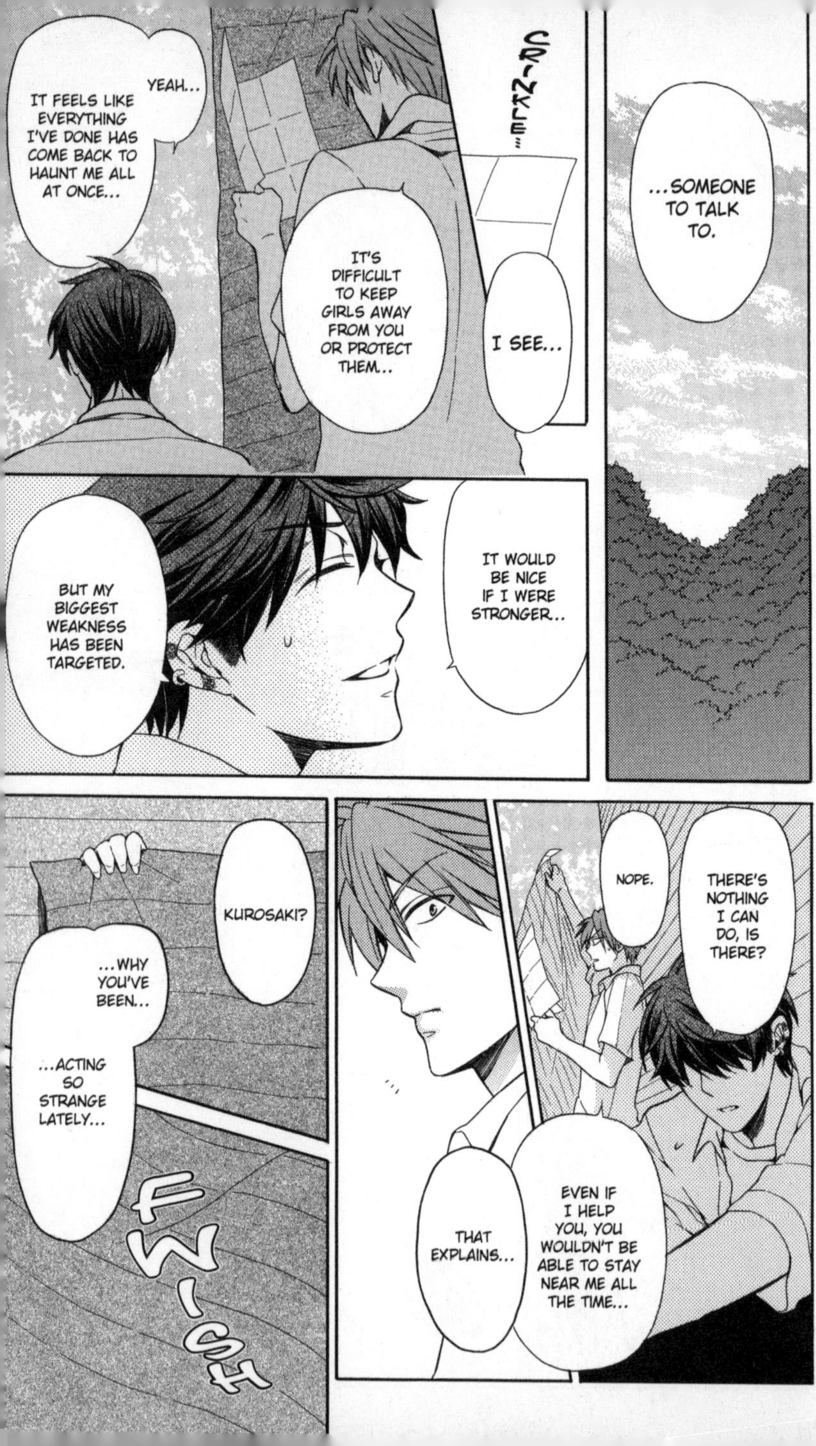
...SOMEONE TO TALK TO.
CRINKLE...
I SEE...
IT'S DIFFICULT TO KEEP GIRLS AWAY FROM YOU OR PROTECT THEM...
YEAH...
IT FEELS LIKE EVERYTHING I'VE DONE HAS COME BACK TO HAUNT ME ALL AT ONCE...
IT WOULD BE NICE IF I WERE STRONGER...
BUT MY BIGGEST WEAKNESS HAS BEEN TARGETED.
THERE'S NOTHING I CAN DO, IS THERE?
NOPE.
EVEN IF I HELP YOU, YOU WOULDN'T BE ABLE TO STAY NEAR ME ALL THE TIME...
...
THAT EXPLAINS...
KUROSAKI?
...WHY YOU'VE BEEN...
...ACTING SO STRANGE LATELY...
FWISH

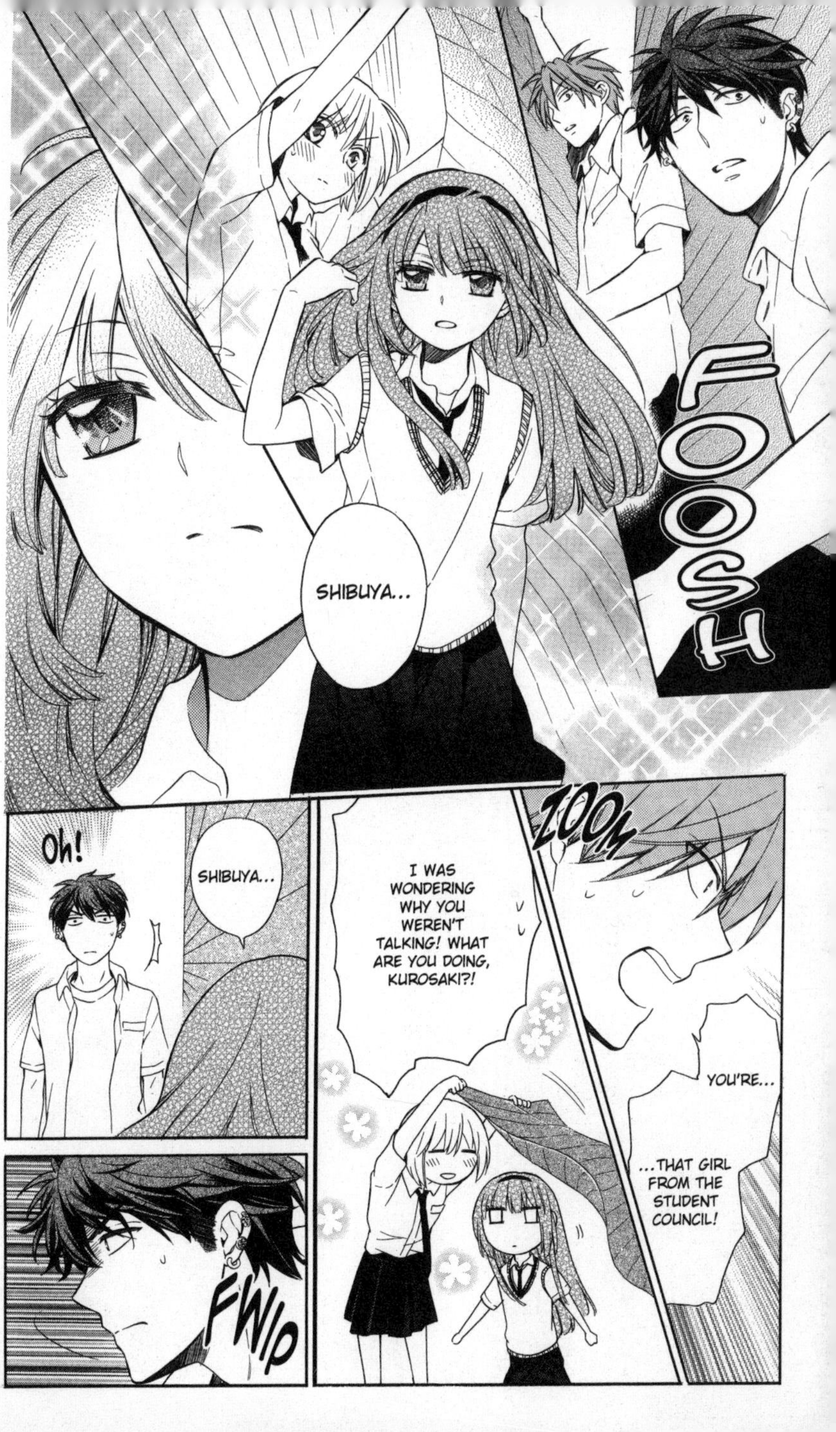
FOOSH
SHIBUYA...
ZOOM
YOU'RE...
...THAT GIRL FROM THE STUDENT COUNCIL!
I WAS WONDERING WHY YOU WEREN'T TALKING! WHAT ARE YOU DOING, KUROSAKI?!
Oh!
SHIBUYA...
FWIP

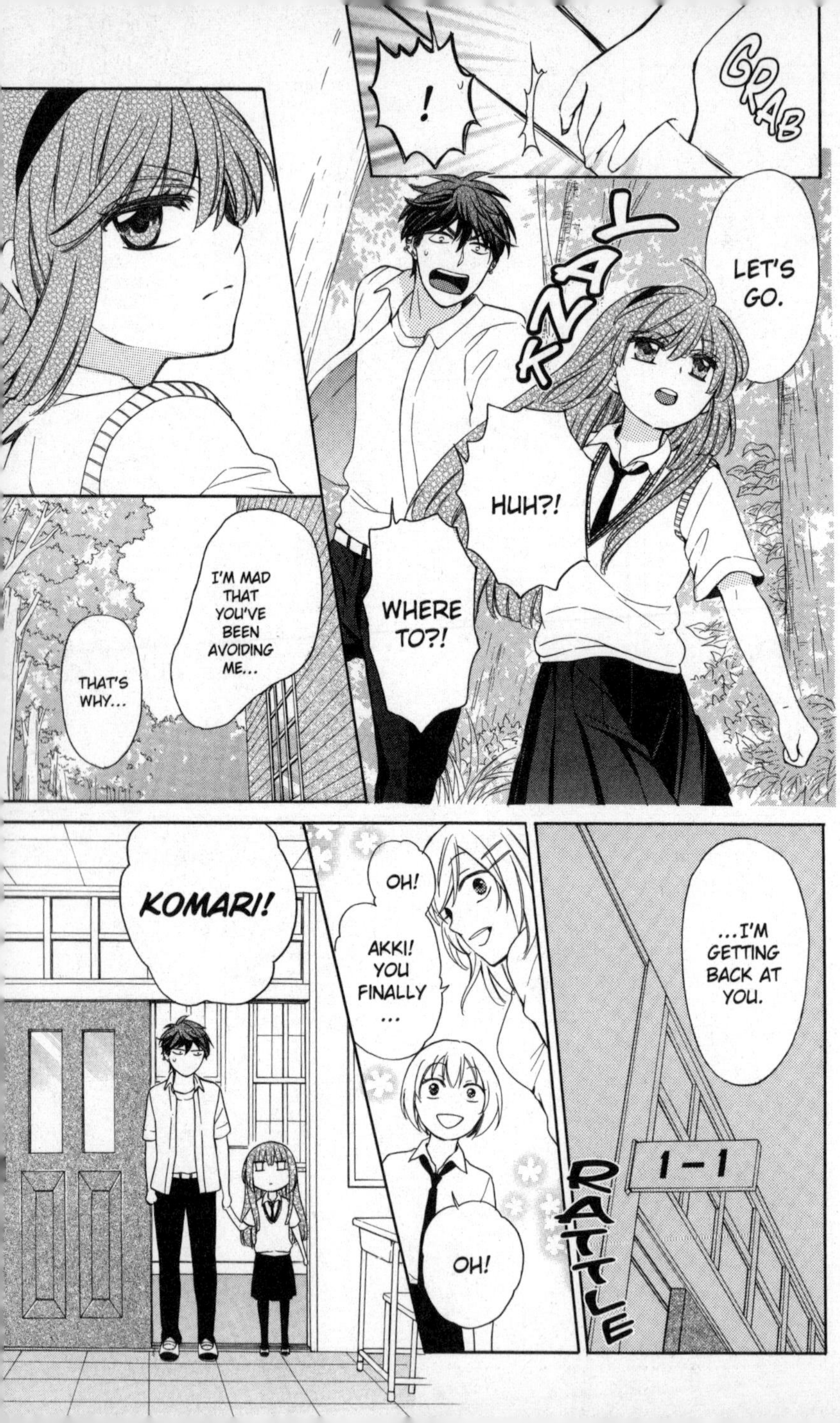

!
GRAB
LET'S GO.
KZAY
HUH?!
WHERE TO?!
I'M MAD THAT YOU'VE BEEN AVOIDING ME...
THAT'S WHY...
...I'M GETTING BACK AT YOU.
1-1
RATTLE
OH!
AKKI! YOU FINALLY ...
OH!
KOMARI!

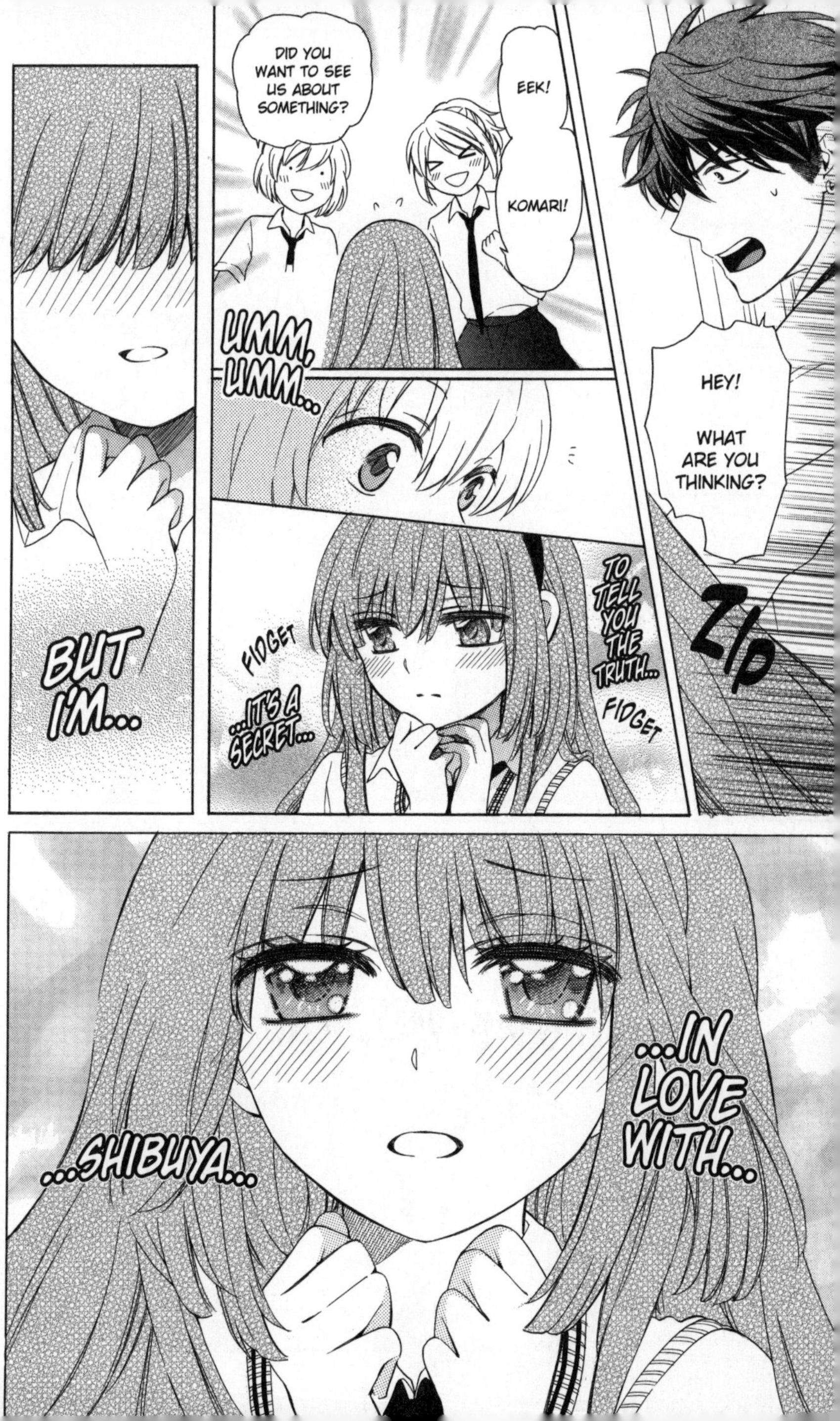
HEY!
WHAT ARE YOU THINKING?
ZIP
EEK!
KOMARI!
DID YOU WANT TO SEE US ABOUT SOMETHING?
UMM, UMM...
TO TELL YOU THE TRUTH...
FIDGET
FIDGET
...IT'S A SECRET...
BUT I'M...
...IN LOVE WITH...
...SHIBUYA...

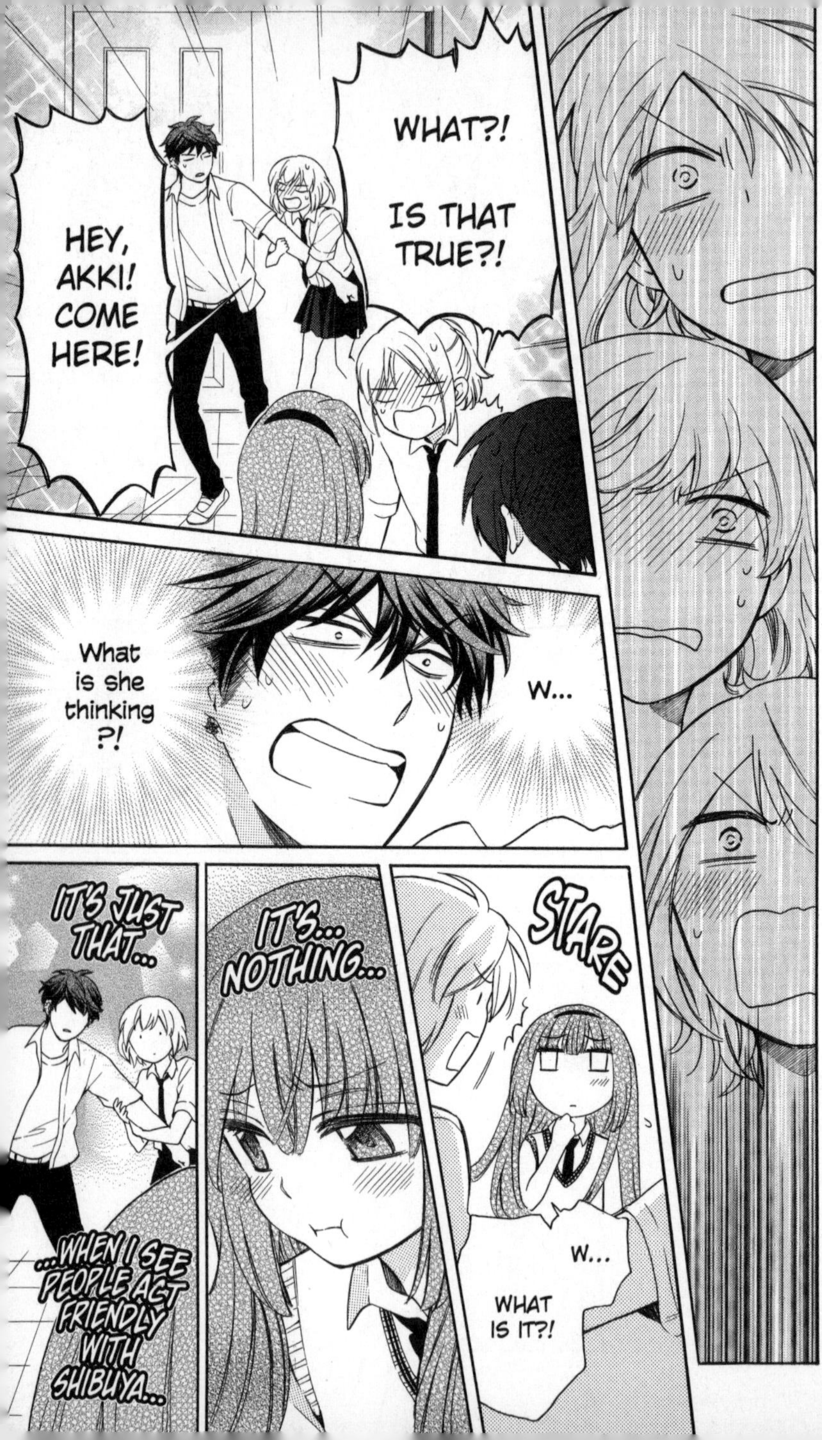
WHAT?!
IS THAT TRUE?!
HEY, AKKI! COME HERE!
W...
What is she thinking ?!
STARE
W...
WHAT IS IT?!
IT'S... NOTHING...
IT'S JUST THAT...
...WHEN I SEE PEOPLE ACT FRIENDLY WITH SHIBUYA...

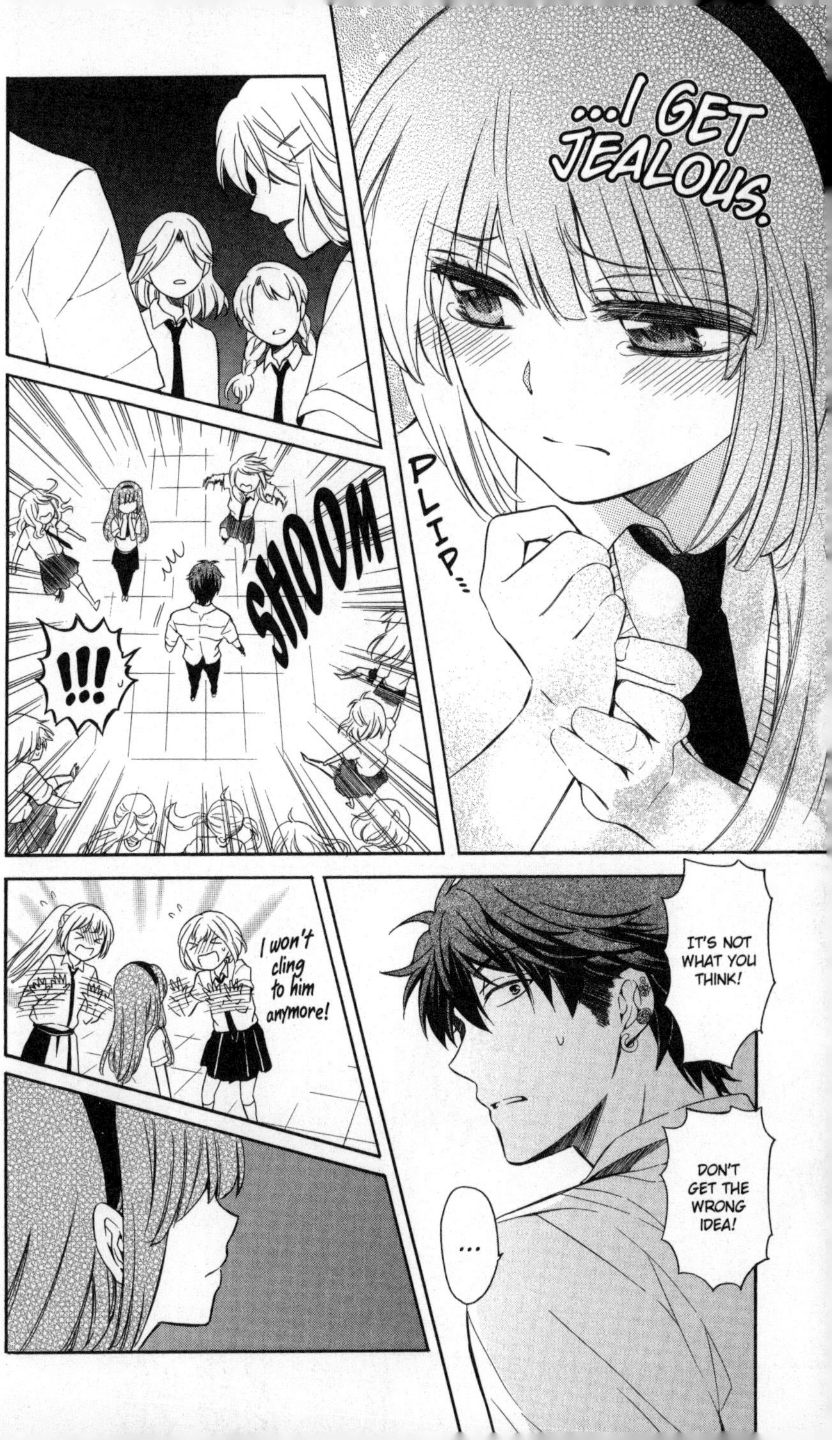
...I GET JEALOUS.
PLIP...
SHOOM
!!!
IT'S NOT WHAT YOU THINK!
DON'T GET THE WRONG IDEA!
...
I won't cling to him anymore!

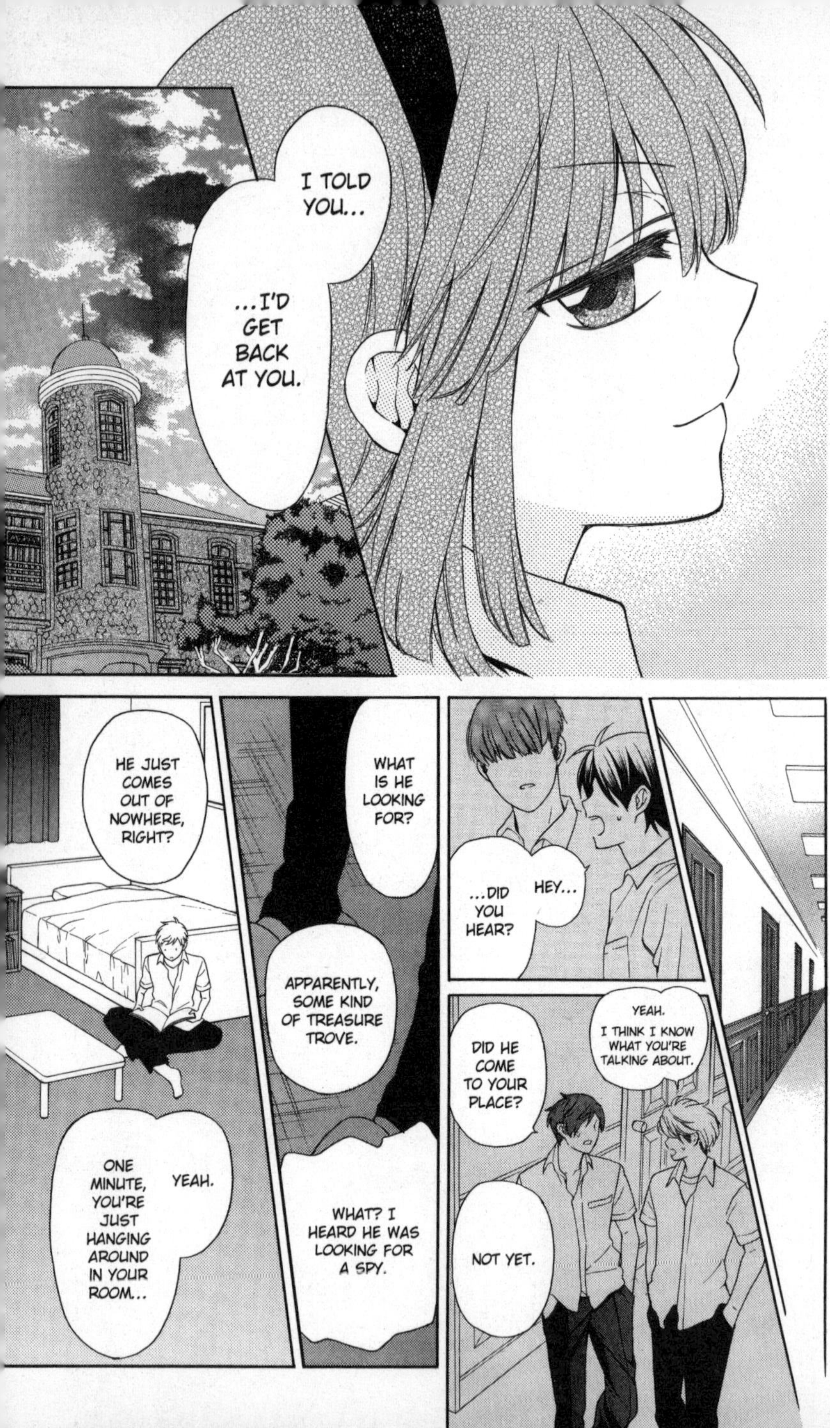
I TOLD YOU...
...I'D GET BACK AT YOU.
HEY...
...DID YOU HEAR?
YEAH. I THINK I KNOW WHAT YOU'RE TALKING ABOUT.
DID HE COME TO YOUR PLACE?
NOT YET.
WHAT IS HE LOOKING FOR?
APPARENTLY, SOME KIND OF TREASURE TROVE.
WHAT? I HEARD HE WAS LOOKING FOR A SPY.
HE JUST COMES OUT OF NOWHERE, RIGHT?
YEAH.
ONE MINUTE, YOU'RE JUST HANGING AROUND IN YOUR ROOM...

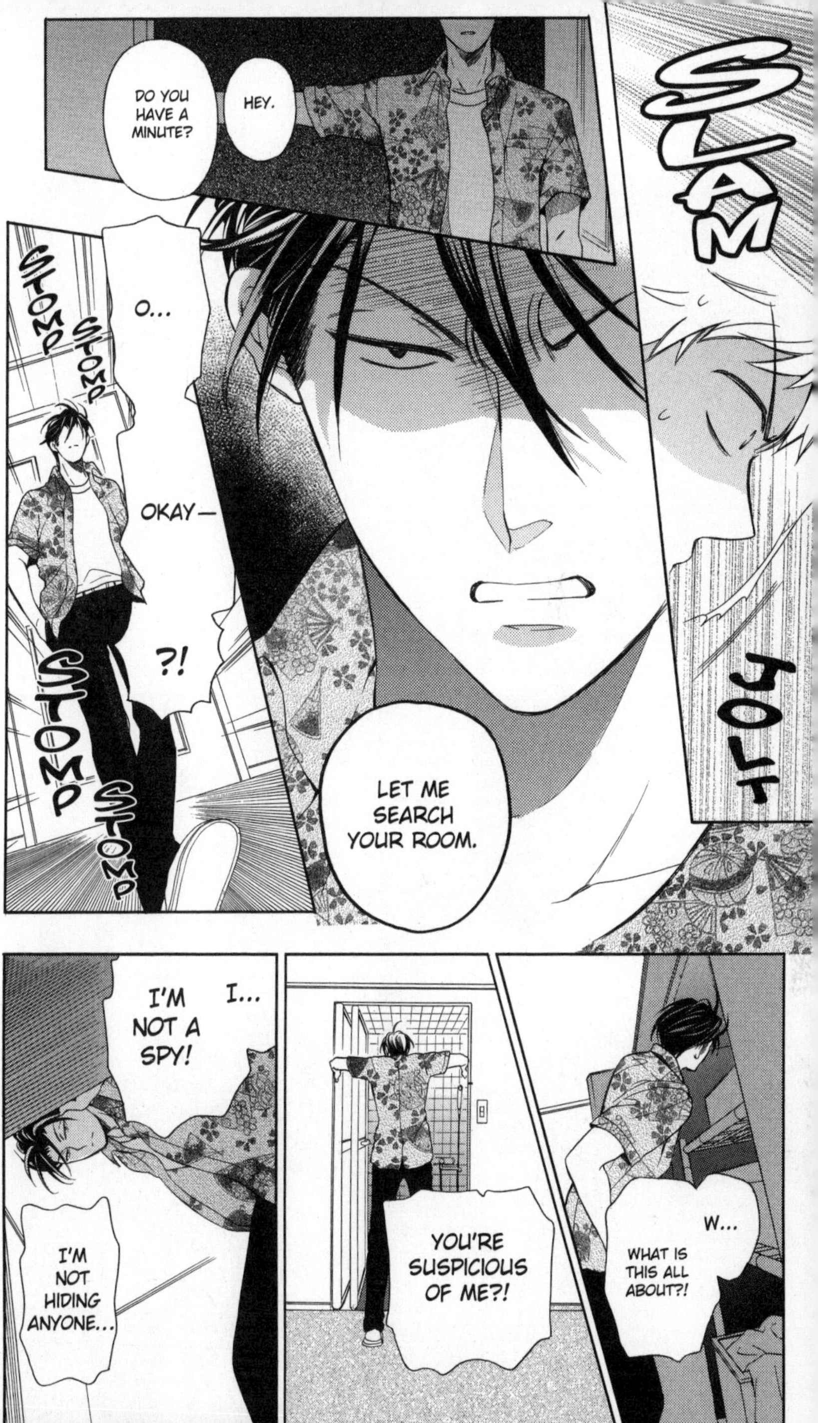
SLAM
JOLT
HEY.
DO YOU HAVE A MINUTE?
LET ME SEARCH YOUR ROOM.
O...
OKAY—
?!
STOMP STOMP
STOMP STOMP
W...
WHAT IS THIS ALL ABOUT?!
YOU'RE SUSPICIOUS OF ME?!
I...
I'M NOT A SPY!
I'M NOT HIDING ANYONE...

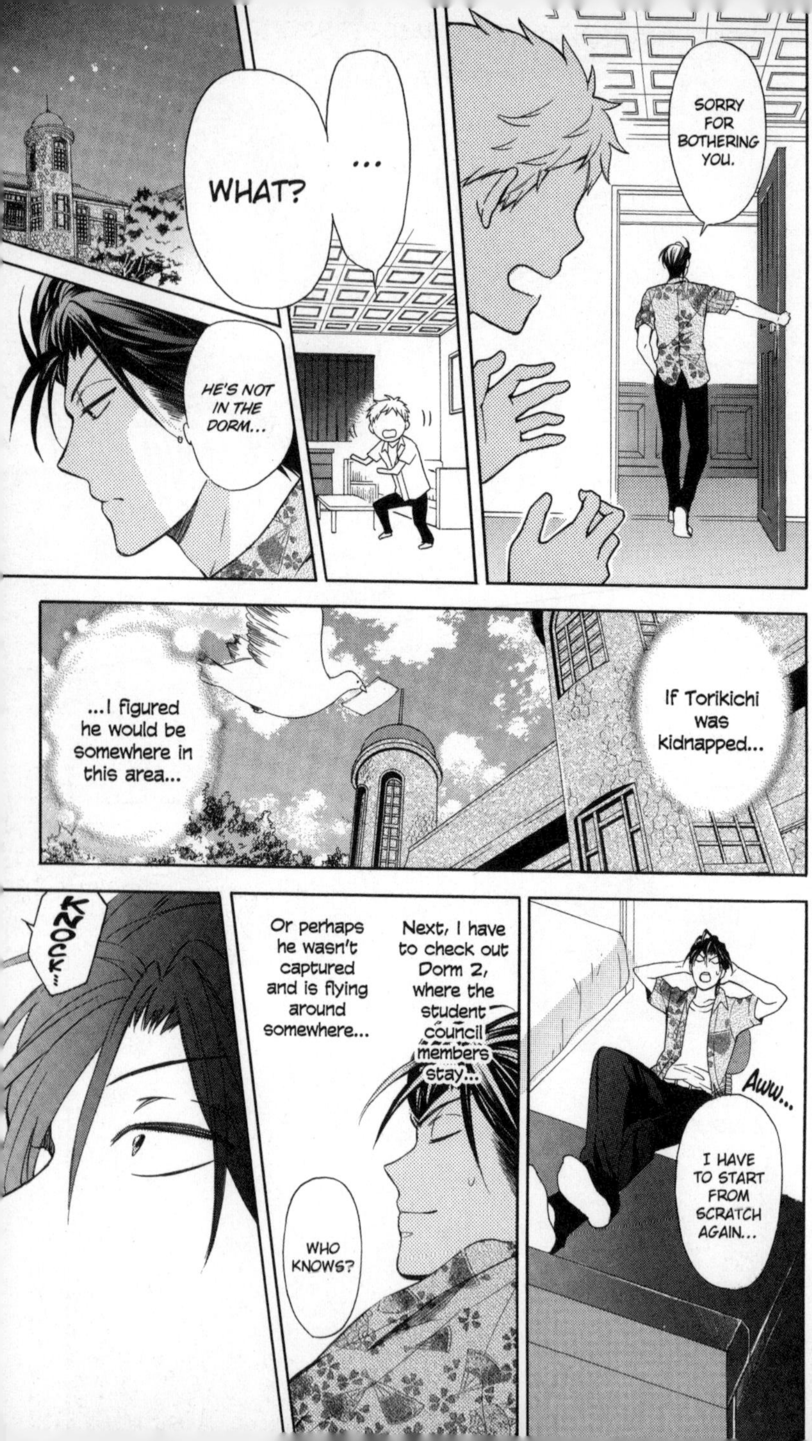
SORRY FOR BOTHERING YOU.
...
WHAT?
HE'S NOT IN THE DORM...
If Torikichi was kidnapped...
...I figured he would be somewhere in this area...
Aww...
I HAVE TO START FROM SCRATCH AGAIN...
Next, I have to check out Dorm 2, where the student council members stay...
Or perhaps he wasn't captured and is flying around somewhere...
WHO KNOWS?
KNOCK...

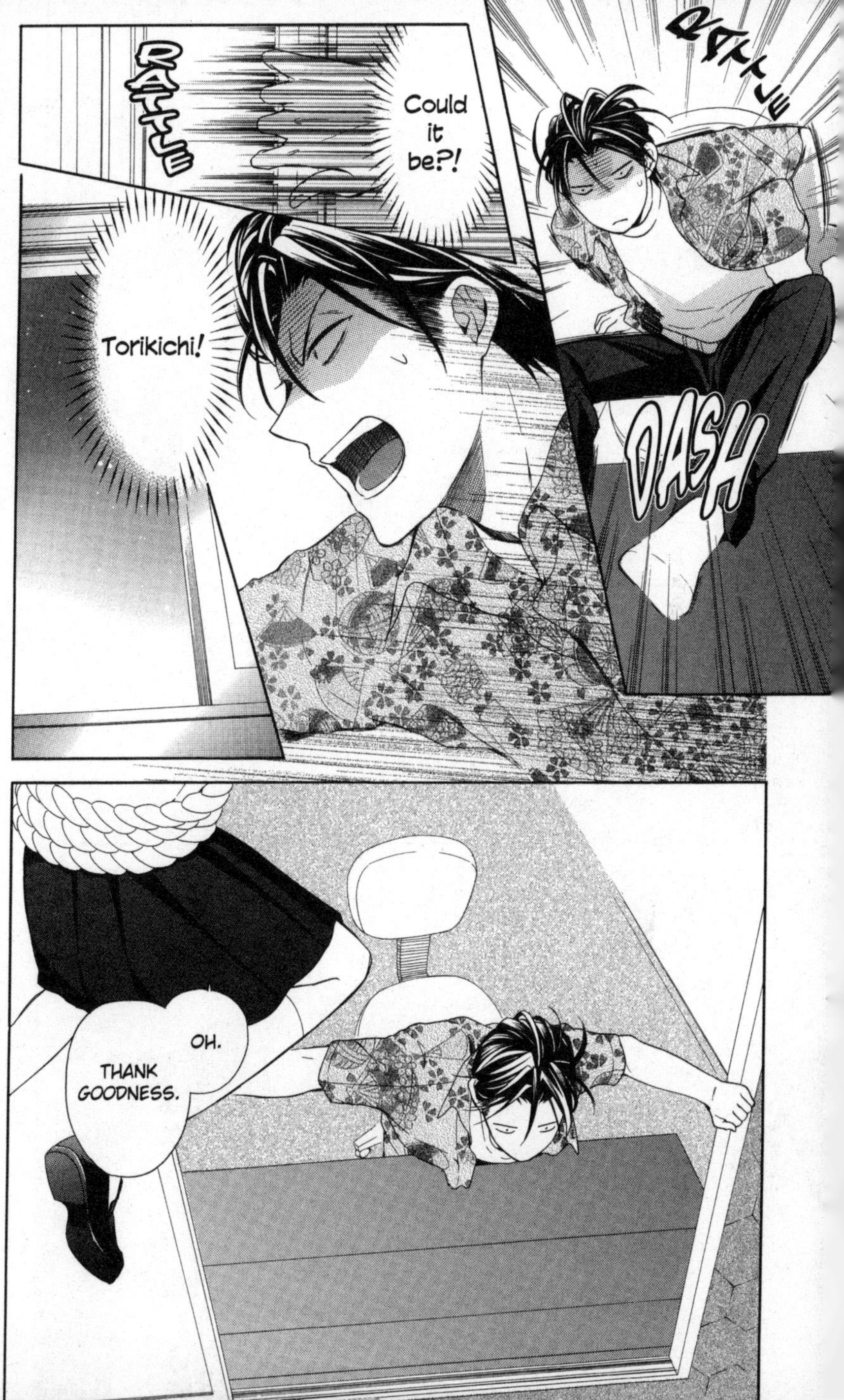
RATTLE
DASH
RATTLE
Could it be?!
Torikichi!
OH.
THANK GOODNESS.

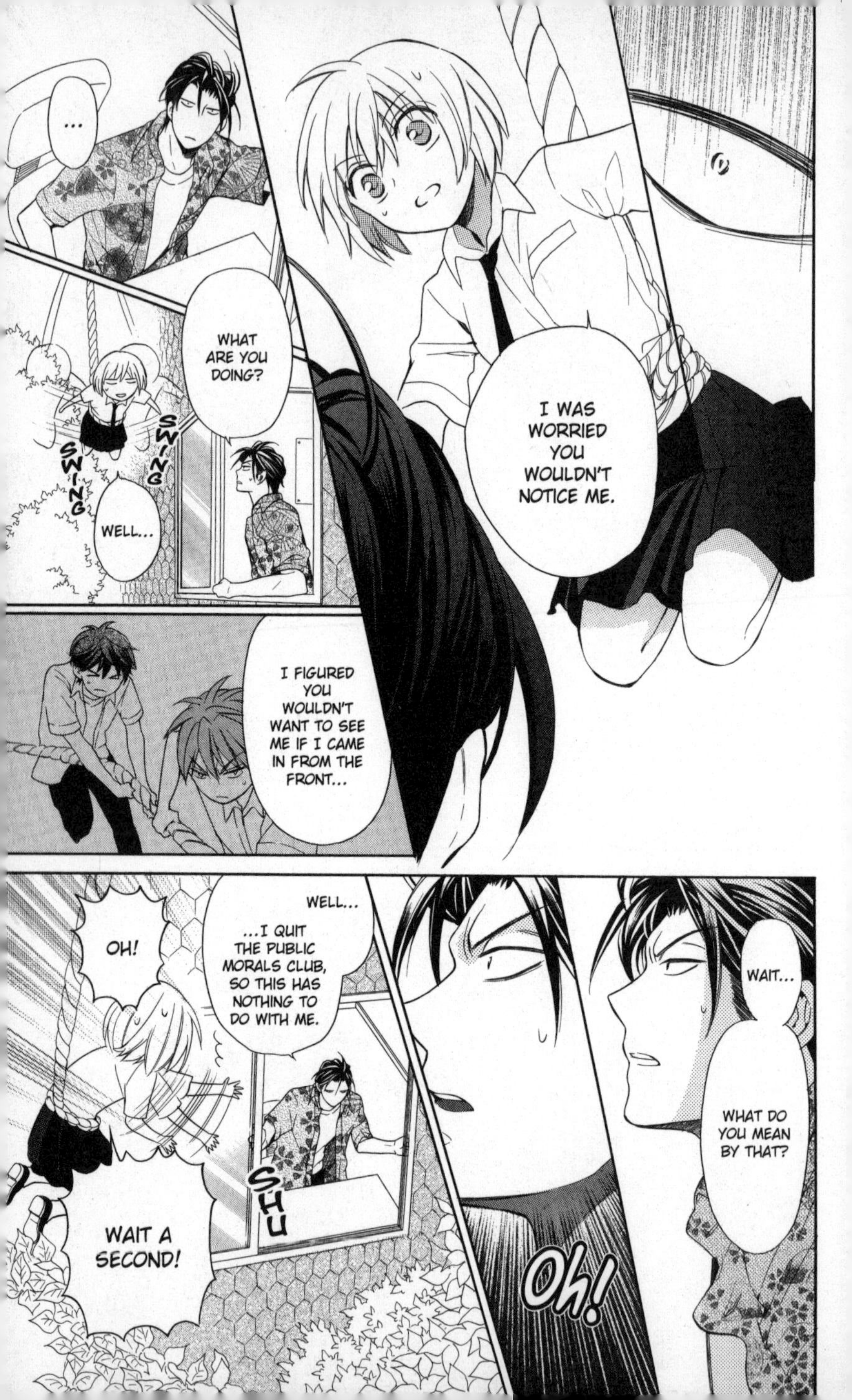
I WAS WORRIED YOU WOULDN'T NOTICE ME.
...
WHAT ARE YOU DOING?
SWING
SWING
WELL...
I FIGURED YOU WOULDN'T WANT TO SEE ME IF I CAME IN FROM THE FRONT...
WAIT...
WHAT DO YOU MEAN BY THAT?
Oh!
WELL...
...I QUIT THE PUBLIC MORALS CLUB, SO THIS HAS NOTHING TO DO WITH ME.
OH!
SHU
WAIT A SECOND!

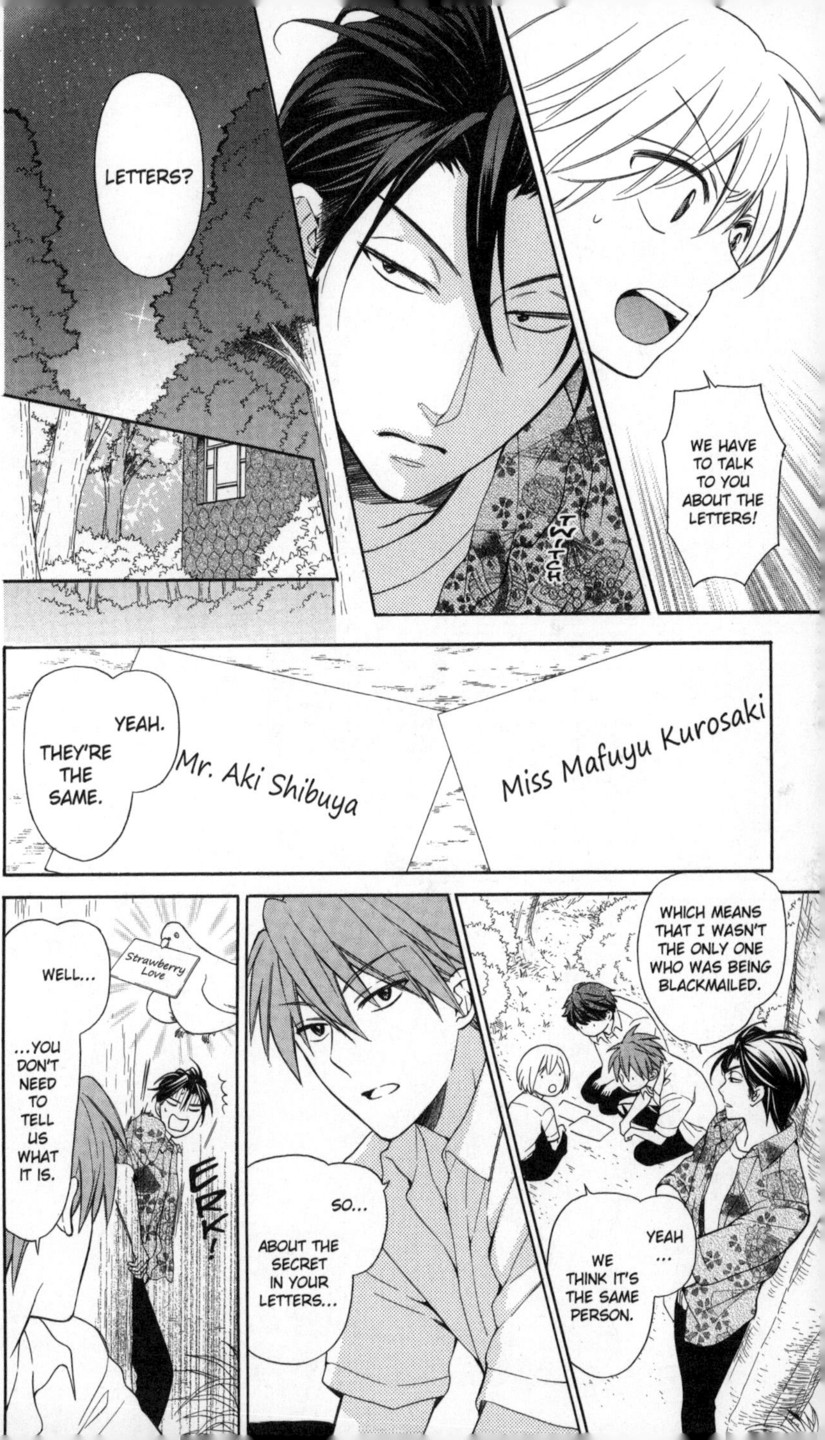
WE HAVE TO TALK TO YOU ABOUT THE LETTERS!
TWITCH
LETTERS?
Miss Mafuyu Kurosaki
Mr. Aki Shibuya
YEAH. THEY'RE THE SAME.
WHICH MEANS THAT I WASN'T THE ONLY ONE WHO WAS BEING BLACKMAILED.
YEAH ...
WE THINK IT'S THE SAME PERSON.
SO...
ABOUT THE SECRET IN YOUR LETTERS...
WELL...
Strawberry Love
...YOU DON'T NEED TO TELL US WHAT IT IS.
ERK!

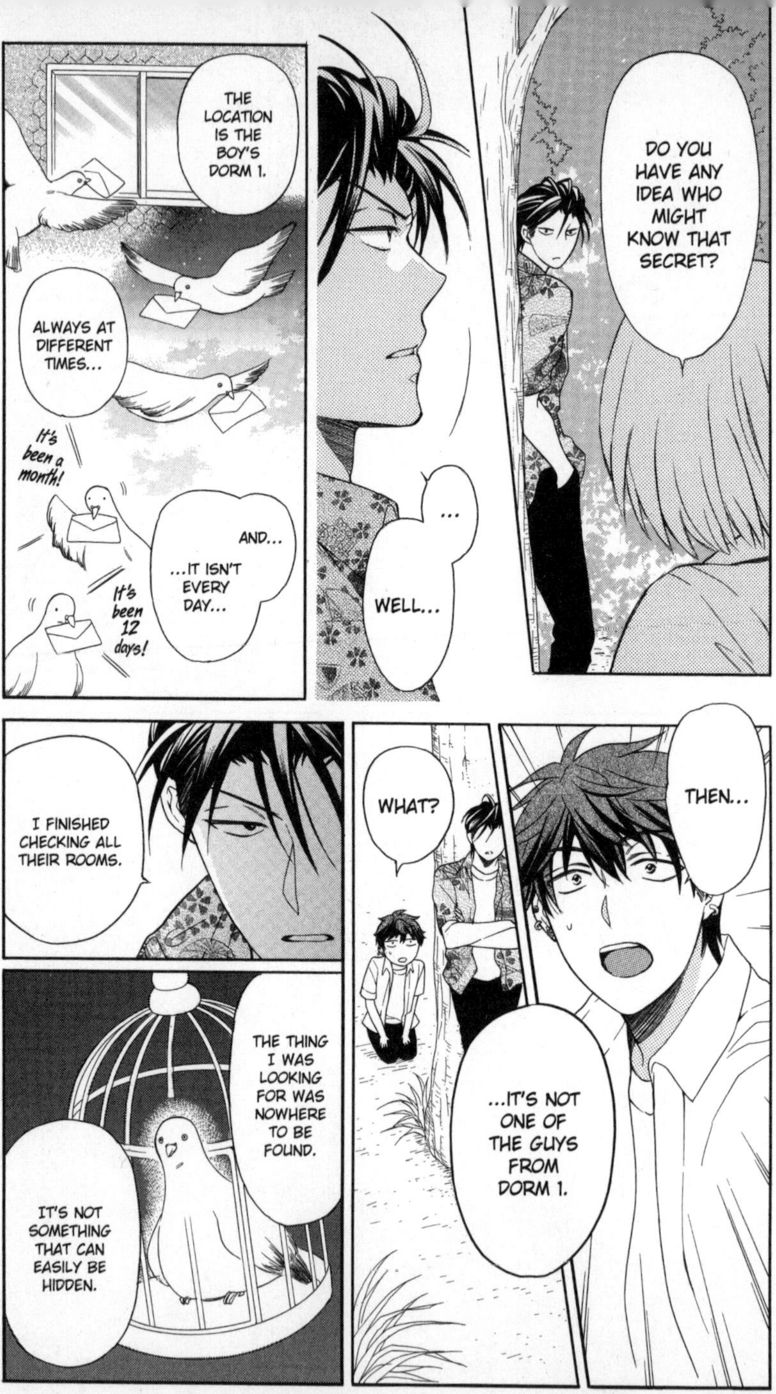
DO YOU HAVE ANY IDEA WHO MIGHT KNOW THAT SECRET?
...
WELL...
THE LOCATION IS THE BOY'S DORM 1.
ALWAYS AT DIFFERENT TIMES...
AND...
...IT ISN'T EVERY DAY...
It's been a month!
It's been 12 days!
THEN...
...IT'S NOT ONE OF THE GUYS FROM DORM 1.
WHAT?
I FINISHED CHECKING ALL THEIR ROOMS.
THE THING I WAS LOOKING FOR WAS NOWHERE TO BE FOUND.
IT'S NOT SOMETHING THAT CAN EASILY BE HIDDEN.

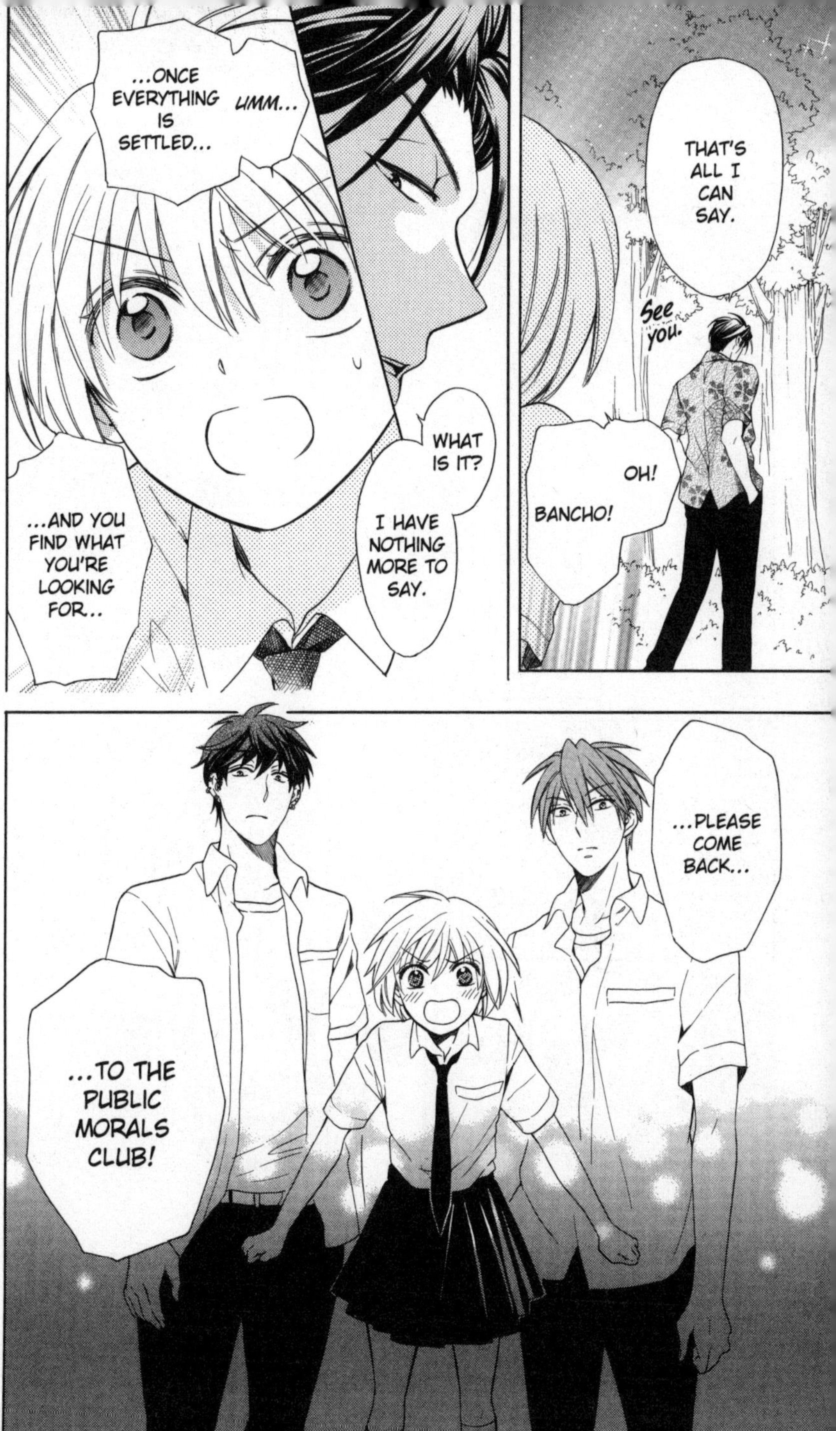
THAT'S ALL I CAN SAY.
See you.
OH!
BANCHO!
UMM...
WHAT IS IT?
I HAVE NOTHING MORE TO SAY.
...ONCE EVERYTHING IS SETTLED...
...AND YOU FIND WHAT YOU'RE LOOKING FOR...
...PLEASE COME BACK...
...TO THE PUBLIC MORALS CLUB!

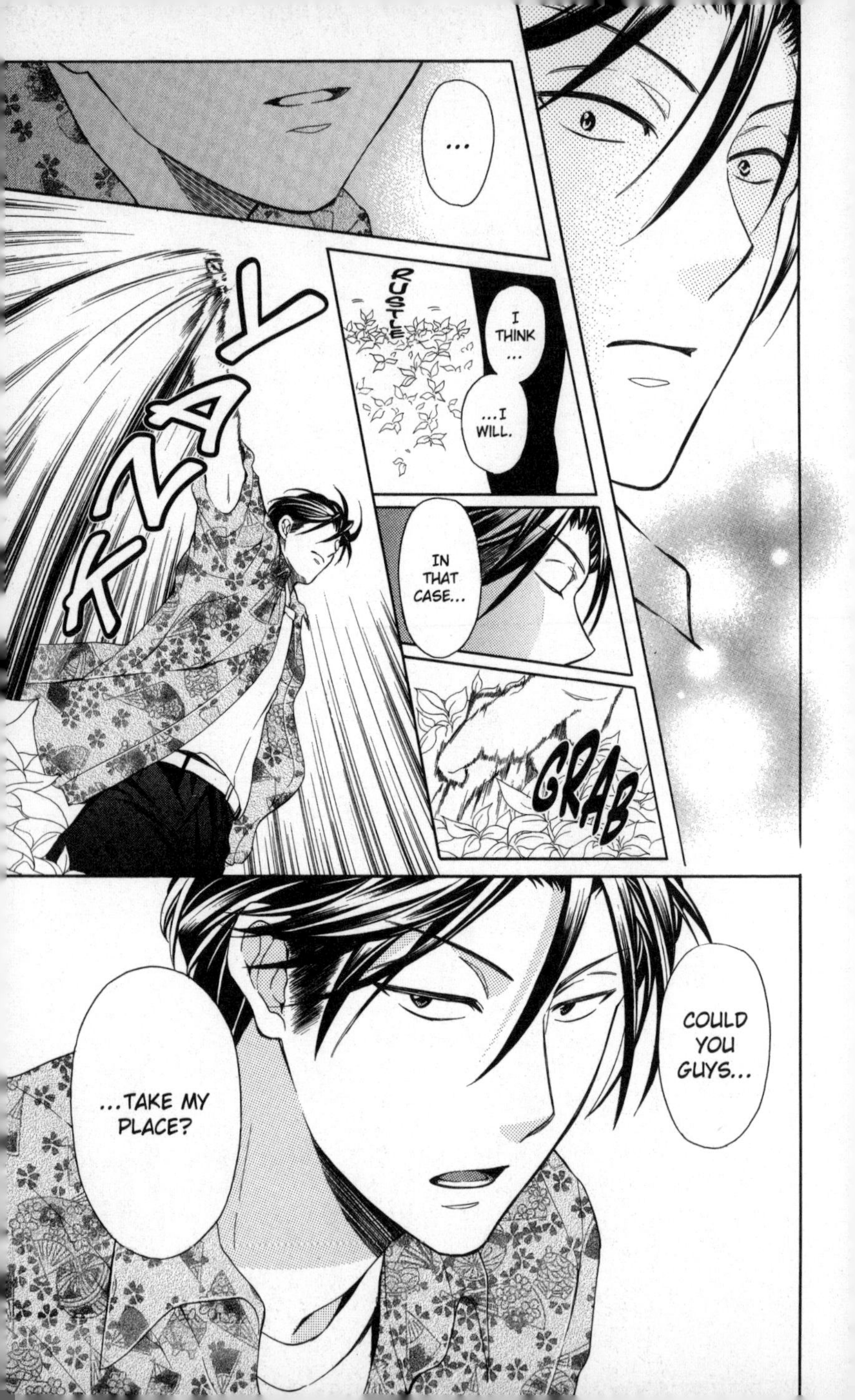
...
RUSTLE
I THINK...
...I WILL.
IN THAT CASE...
GRAB
KZAY
COULD YOU GUYS...
...TAKE MY PLACE?

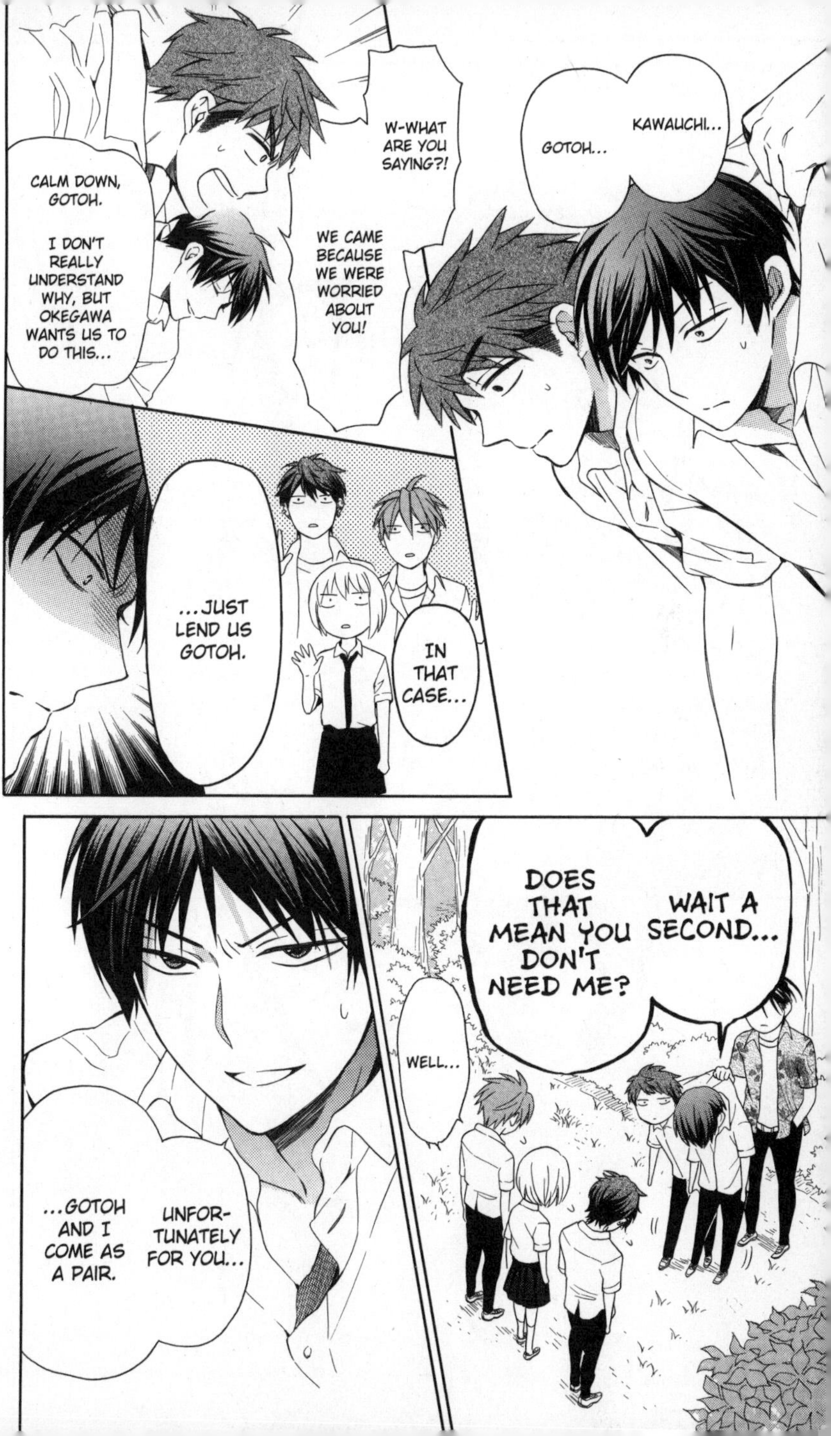
KAWAUCHI...
GOTOH...
W-WHAT ARE YOU SAYING?!
WE CAME BECAUSE WE WERE WORRIED ABOUT YOU!
CALM DOWN, GOTOH.
I DON'T REALLY UNDERSTAND WHY, BUT OKEGAWA WANTS US TO DO THIS...
IN THAT CASE...
...JUST LEND US GOTOH.
WAIT A SECOND...
DOES THAT MEAN YOU DON'T NEED ME?
WELL...
UNFOR-TUNATELY FOR YOU...
...GOTOH AND I COME AS A PAIR.

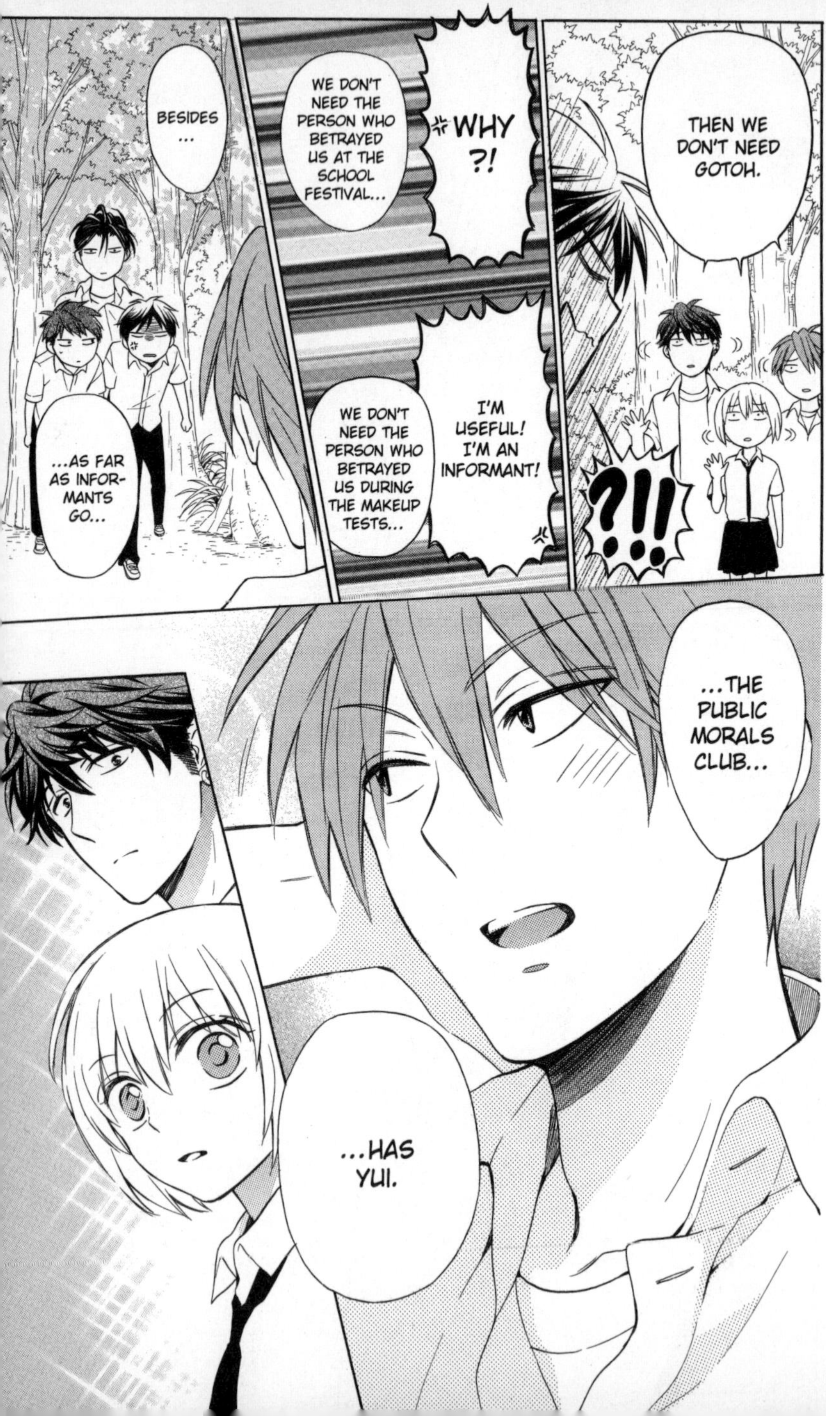
THEN WE DON'T NEED GOTOH.
?!!
WHY ?!
WE DON'T NEED THE PERSON WHO BETRAYED US AT THE SCHOOL FESTIVAL...
I'M USEFUL! I'M AN INFORMANT!
WE DON'T NEED THE PERSON WHO BETRAYED US DURING THE MAKEUP TESTS...
BESIDES...
...AS FAR AS INFOR-MANTS GO...
...THE PUBLIC MORALS CLUB...
...HAS YUI.

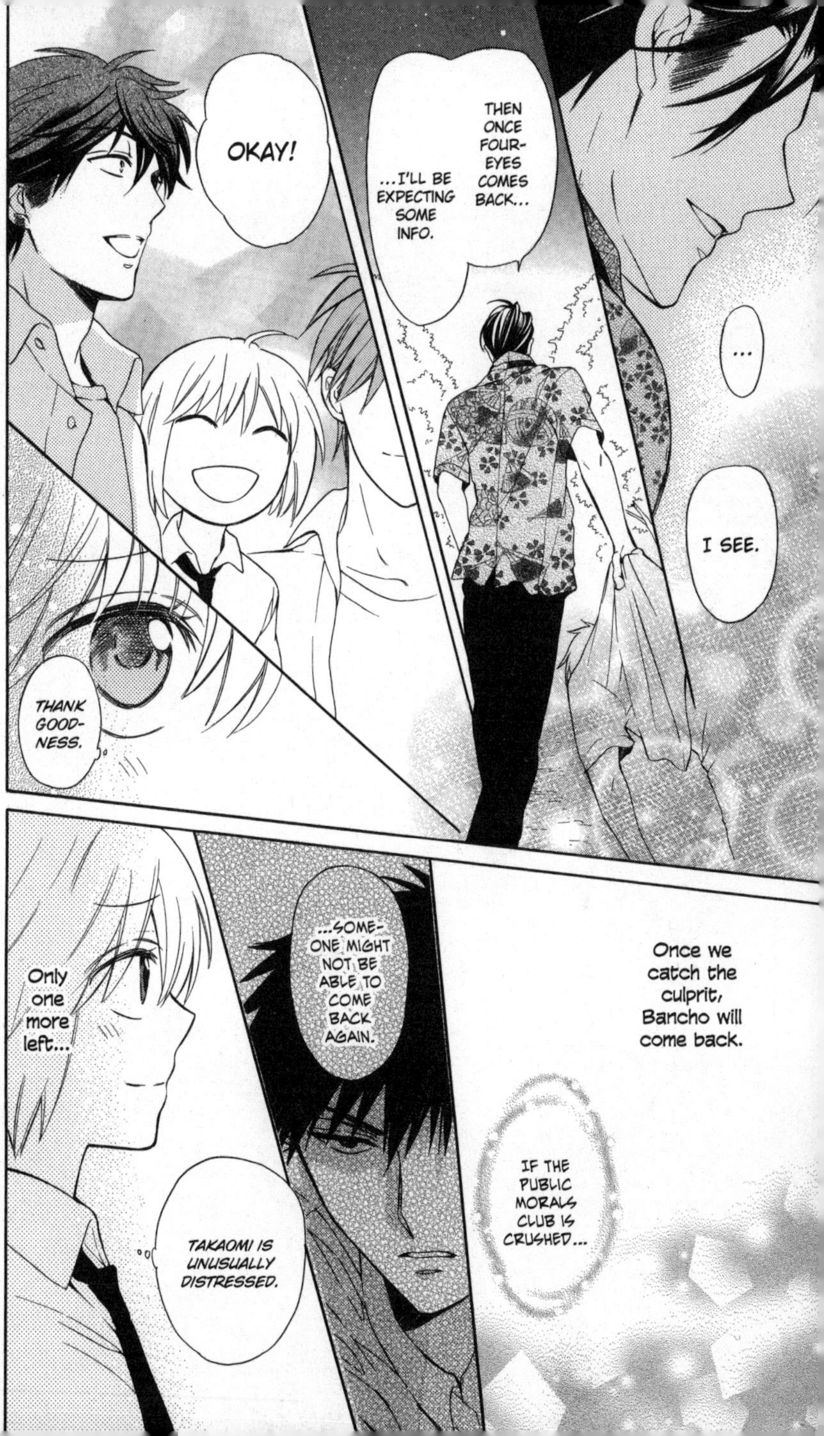
...
I SEE.
THEN ONCE FOUR-EYES COMES BACK...
...I'LL BE EXPECTING SOME INFO.
OKAY!
THANK GOODNESS.
Once we catch the culprit, Bancho will come back.
IF THE PUBLIC MORALS CLUB IS CRUSHED...
...SOME-ONE MIGHT NOT BE ABLE TO COME BACK AGAIN.
Only one more left...
TAKAOMI IS UNUSUALLY DISTRESSED.

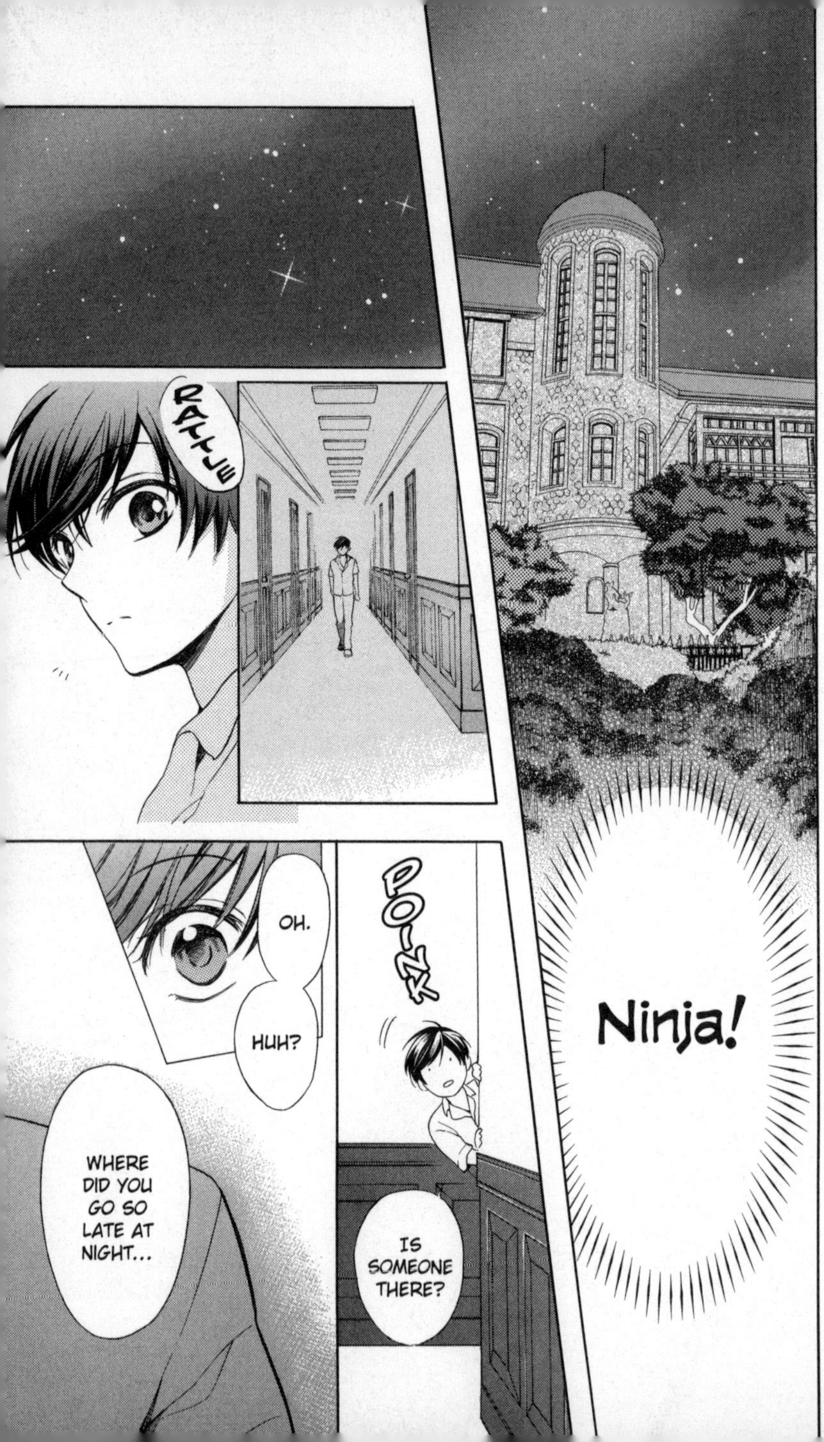
Ninja!
RATTLE
POINK
IS SOMEONE THERE?
OH.
HUH?
WHERE DID YOU GO SO LATE AT NIGHT...

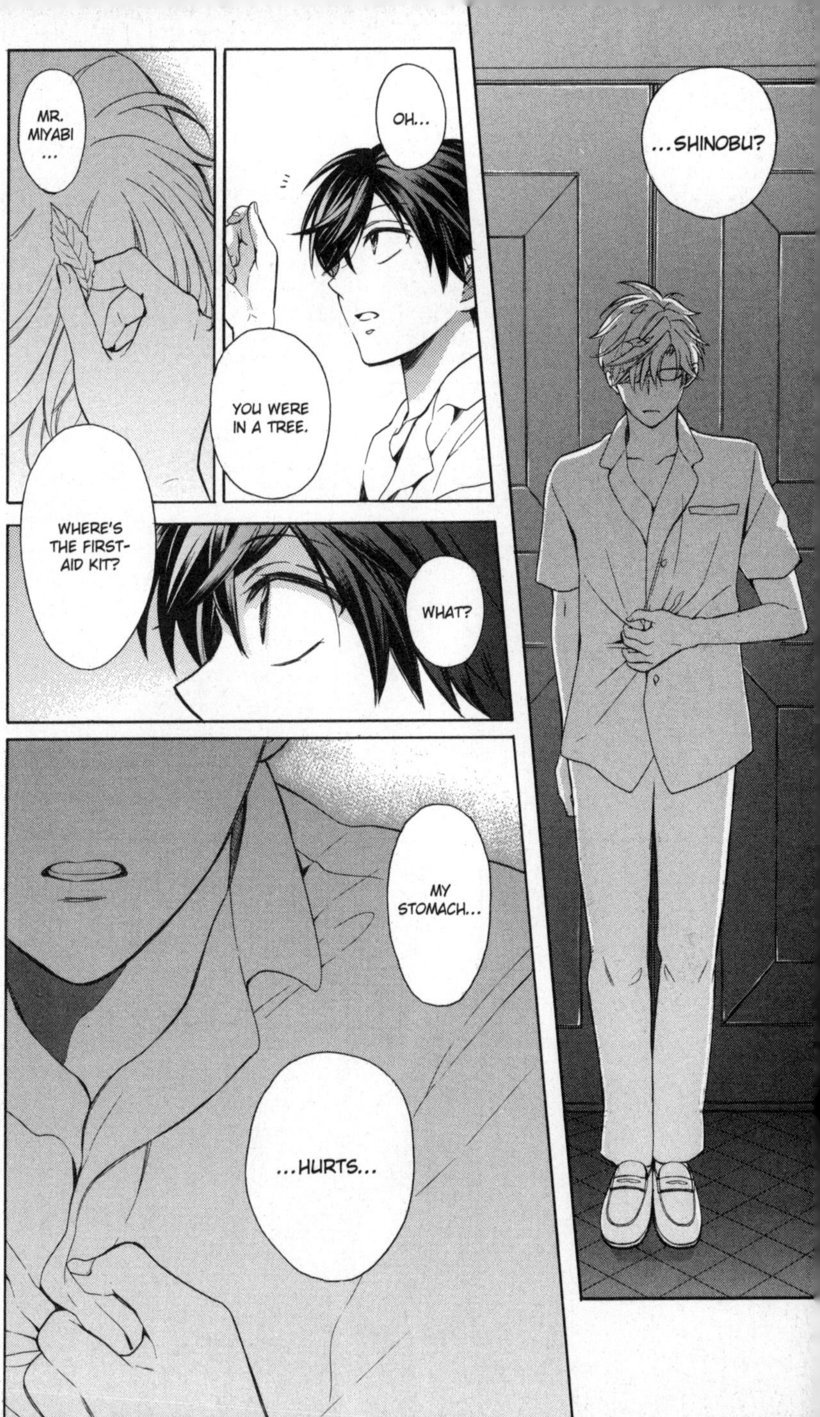
...SHINOBU?
OH...
YOU WERE IN A TREE.
MR. MIYABI ...
WHERE'S THE FIRST-AID KIT?
WHAT?
MY STOMACH...
...HURTS...

FIRST ORESAMA TEACHER CHARACTER CONTEST RESULTS!

THE RESULTS OF THE FIRST CHARACTER CONTEST WERE REVEALED IN *HANA TO YUME* VOLUME 5 (FEBRUARY 5, 2013), BUT DUE TO SPACE CONSTRAINTS, WE COULD ONLY SHOW THE TOP 20, SO WE'RE REVEALING THE FULL RESULTS HERE! CHECK OUT HOW WELL YOUR FAVORITE CHARACTERS DID! ☆

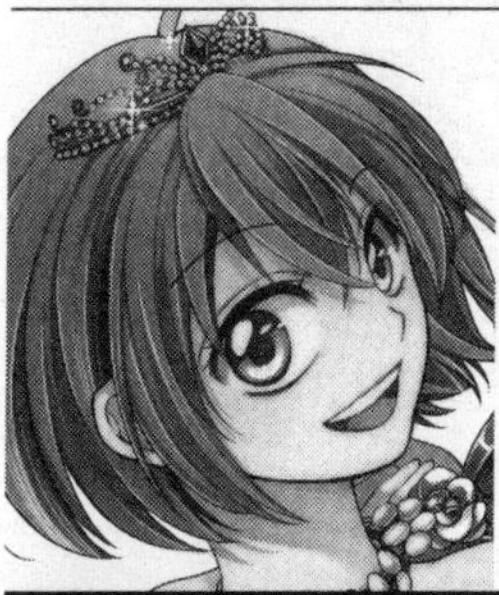

1st Place

7576 Points

MAFUYU KUROSAKI

(Natsuo 1682 Points / Super Bun 106 Points)

THE HEROINE IS AT THE TOP! I'M REALLY HAPPY! THANK YOU VERY MUCH! I THOUGHT THAT NATSUO WOULD GET MOST OF HER POINTS, BUT MAFUYU GOT THEM ON HER OWN. LOOKING AT THE RESULTS MAKES ME GLAD I DID A POLL!

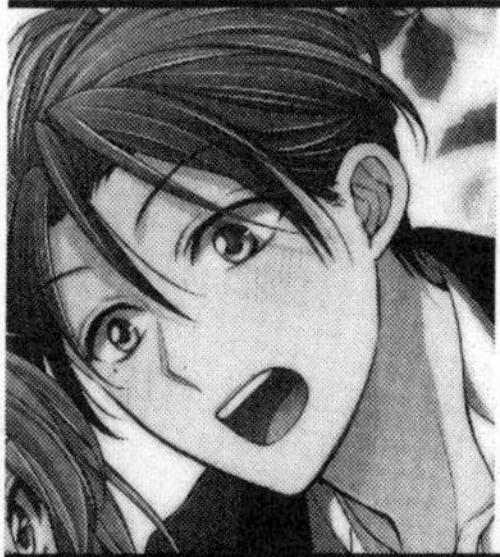

2nd Place

4454 Points

KOHEI KANGAWA

WHY IS HE IN SECOND PLACE WITH SO FEW APPEARANCES?! HE MAY NOT APPEAR VERY OFTEN, BUT KANGAWA IS VERY POPULAR IN THE LETTERS I RECEIVE, SO I FIGURED THIS MIGHT HAPPEN. IT'S AMAZING! PEOPLE KEEP CALLING HIM CUTE, SO I THINK I SHOULD SHOW A MANLY SIDE TO HIM!

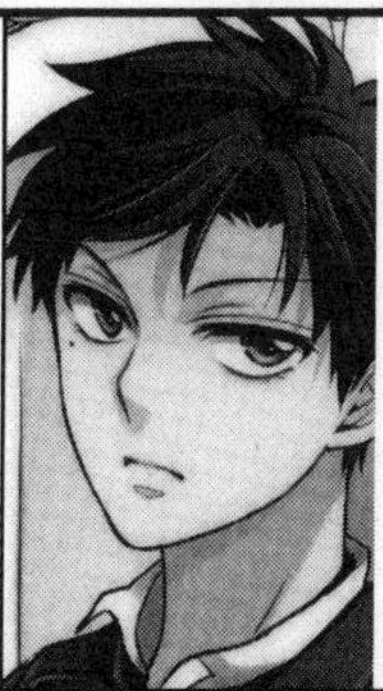

3rd Place

3159 Points

REITO AYABE

HE'S LIKE EVERYONE'S BIG BROTHER, SO HE EASILY GOT POINTS. IT WAS AMUSING TO SEE THAT HIS FANS WERE SPLIT BETWEEN HIS CLEANING PERSONALITY AND BIG BROTHER PERSONALITY. THERE WAS ALSO THE MOLE UNDER HIS EYE. THAT MOLE UNDER HIS EYE WAS A PRETTY STRONG FACTOR!

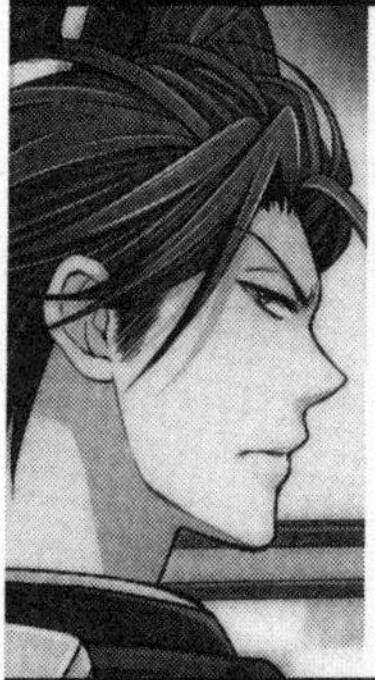

4th Place

3022 Points

KYOTARO OKEGAWA

OVERALL, HE HAD AN OVERWHELMING NUMBER OF VOTES FOR FIRST CHOICE, WHICH GAVE HIM A LOT OF POINTS. HE'S THE KIND OF PERSON YOU GIVE YOUR TRUE-LOVE CHOCOLATE TO ON VALENTINE'S DAY! A LOT OF PEOPLE CHOSE HIM ALONG WITH MAFUYU, NEKOMATA AND KAWAUCHI.

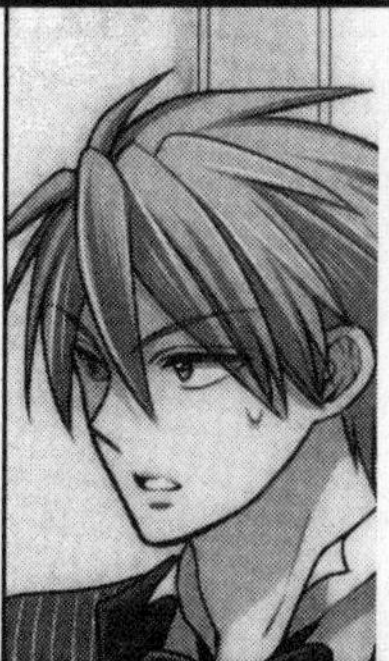

5th Place

2423 Points

HAYASAKA

HE GOT A LOT OF POSTCARDS THAT SEEMED LIKE THEY CAME FROM PROFESSIONALS. HOW INTENSE! HE PROBABLY HAS THE MOST FULL COLOR ILLUSTRATIONS. HAYASAKA'S ARC IS COMING SOON, SO STAY TUNED FOR THAT!

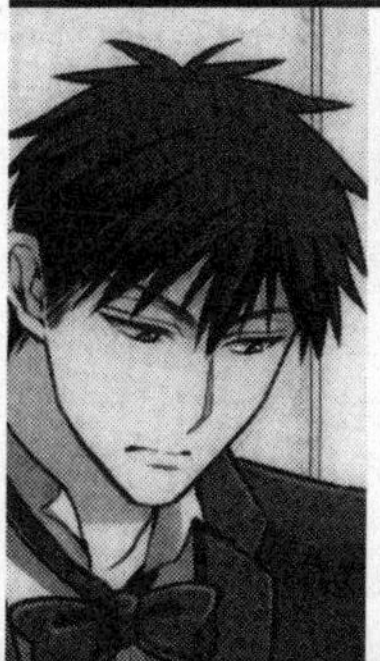

6th Place

2097 Points

TAKAOMI SAEKI

I KNEW HE WAS THE KIND OF PERSON WHO PEOPLE EITHER LOVED OR HATED, SO GETTING SIXTH PLACE IS PRETTY AMAZING! HE HAS MORE VOTES FROM ADULT WOMEN THAN STUDENTS. I THINK HE'D APPRECIATE THAT.

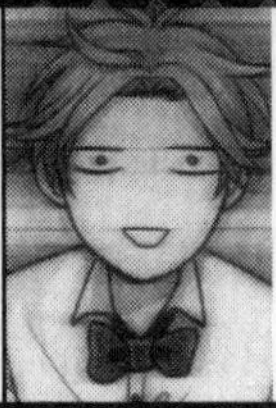

7th Place — **YUTO MAIZONO** — 1595 Points

A LOT OF PEOPLE VOTED FOR HIM ALONG WITH MAFUYU AND KANGAWA, THE OTHER TWO MEMBERS OF THE EAST HIGH TRIO. IT WAS AMUSING TO SEE HOW PASSIONATE THE PEOPLE WHO PICKED HIM AS THEIR FIRST CHOICE WERE.

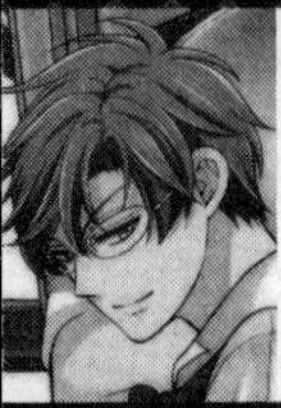

8th Place — **SHINOBU YUI** — 755 Points

BECAUSE OF THINGS THAT HAPPENED IN THIS VOLUME, I COULDN'T PUT HIM ON THE COVER, BUT YUI DID WELL! IF THIS HAPPENED A LITTLE LATER, I THINK HE WOULD HAVE LOST A LOT OF POINTS, SO HE JUST BARELY GOT BY! THANK GOODNESS!

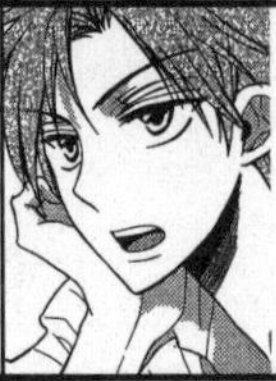

9th Place — **ASAHI SAKURADA** — 711 Points

WHY SAKURADA?! SAKURADA HAS SOME ENTHUSIASTIC FANS SINCE HE FIRST APPEARED. WHENEVER HE APPEARS, I ALWAYS WONDER IF I SHOULD HAVE HIM CROSS-DRESS OR DRESS AS A BANCHO. OR IN HIS UNDERWEAR.

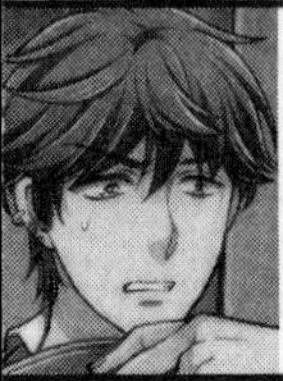

10th Place — **AKI SHIBUYA** — 476 Points

THE CHARACTER POLL WAS BEING RUN DURING THE AKKI ARC, SO HE GOT A LOT OF POINTS WITH KOMARI. HE'S LAZY AND HAS A WEAK PERSONALITY, SO I WAS WORRIED WHAT WOULD HAPPEN IF I SHOWED HIS INNER SELF, BUT I'M RELIEVED.

11th Place — **KOTOBUKI OKUBO** — 438 Points

OKUBO WAS POPULAR AMONGST THE READERS OF THE GRAPHIC NOVELS! I WAS GLAD THAT MANY PEOPLE VOTED FOR HIM WITH MINATO. THERE WERE A FEW PEOPLE WHO VOTED FOR HIM WITH MAIZONO AND YAMASHITA AS WELL.

12th Place — **KOMARI YUKIOKA** — 318 Points

SHE'S ACTUALLY THE SECOND HIGHEST-RANKING FEMALE CHARACTER. SHE ONLY APPEARED RECENTLY, BUT I WAS SURPRISED AT HOW MANY POINTS SHE GOT. SHE WAS MORE POPULAR AFTER SHE REVEALED HER TRUE NATURE. I HAVE MY EDITOR CHECK HER ACCENT!

13th Place — **TOMOHIRO KAWAUCHI** — 305 Points

WHY KAWAUCHI?! I HONESTLY QUESTION WHY HE'S IN THIS POSITION, BUT WELL DONE, KAWAUCHI! COME TO THINK OF IT, BECAUSE OF THE THINGS THAT HAPPENED WITH KOMARI, I'VE BEEN ASKED WHETHER HE HAS A LOLITA COMPLEX, BUT KAWAUCHI LIKES MANLY MEN AND DAINTY GIRLS WHO NEED PROTECTING. HE HAS PRETTY OLD-FASHIONED PREFERENCES. IN REALITY, BOTH ARE A MISTAKE. HE HAS BAD TASTE!

14th Place — **KANON NONOGUCHI** — 289 Points

THERE WERE A LOT OF COMMENTS ABOUT HER PIGTAILS (*LAUGH*). KANON'S HAIR IS PROBABLY THE MOST DIFFICULT TO CARE FOR. I WAS WONDERING WHETHER TO GIVE HER ARC A ROMANTIC FOCUS, BUT I ENDED UP FOCUSING ON THE BATTLES. IT BECAME THE BIGGEST DISTURBANCE SO FAR.

15th Place — **MINATO KANGAWA** — 173 Points

HER VOTES CAME COMPLETELY FROM THE READERS OF THE GRAPHIC NOVELS! IT'S AMAZING THAT THE MAGAZINE READERS DON'T KNOW HER AT ALL. I'D LIKE TO DO ANOTHER NORTH SOUTH EAST WEST.

16th Place — **WAKANA HOJO** — 136 Points

SHE WAS OFTEN PAIRED WITH YUI. AT THE SAME TIME, THERE WERE A LOT OF PEOPLE WHO THOUGHT SHE SHOULDN'T GO AFTER HIM.

17th Place — **TAKUMI YAMASHITA** — 133 Points

IT WAS AMUSING TO SEE A REALLY DEVOTED FAN OF HIS ONCE IN A WHILE. IT'S ALL ABOUT MEN WHO CAN COOK!

18th Place — **ARISUGAWA** — 114 Points

HE WASN'T LISTED IN THE MAGAZINE-AN UNEXPECTED PRINTING MISTAKE. YOU PLACED PRETTY HIGH, ARISU-CHAN! HIS IS THE LEADER OF CLASS 2, YUI'S CLASS, SO I HOPE I CAN HAVE HIM SHOW UP IN THE FUTURE.

19th Place — **NEKOMATA** — 208 Points

NOW THAT I THINK OF IT, ALL OF THE MASCOT RELATED THINGS—SUPER BUN, NEKOMATA-SAN, TORIKICHI—ARE ALL FOCUSED ON MAFUYU AND BANCHO.

20th Place — **MIYABI HANABUSA** — 88 Points

HE'S THE MOST POPULAR AT MY HOUSE.

21st Place DAIKICHI GOTOH 62 Points	22nd Place KENTO NOGAMI 44 Points	23rd Place SHUNTARO KOSAKA 33 Points
24th Place IZUMI TSUBAKI 28 Points	25th Place RYUNOSUKE HIMEJI 16 Points	26th Place KAKIMOTO 13 Points
27th Place JOSEPHINE 11 Points	28th Place RUNA MOMOCHI 10 Points	29th Place KOZUE AYABE 8 Points
30th Place MITSUBAYASHI 7 Points	31st Place UMINO 6 Points	32nd Place YOTSUYA 6 Points
33rd Place HORTICULTURE CLUB'S MAN-EATING FLOWER 3 Points	34th Place CRAFT CLUB'S MACHO MEN 3 Points	35th Place UMETSUGU AYABE 2 Points
36th Place DELINQUENT WHO BETRAYED THE BANCHO 1 Points		

THANK YOU TO EVERYONE WHO VOTED!

MEMBERS OF OTHER CLUBS

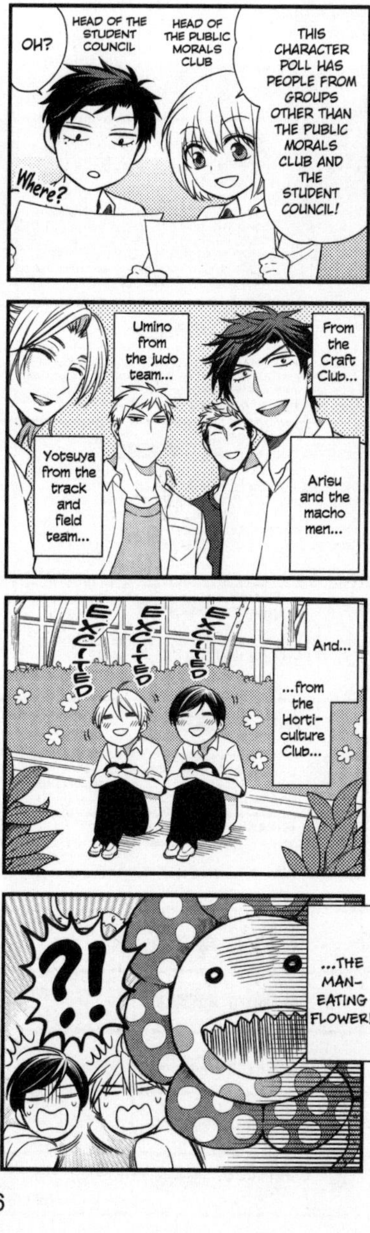
THIS CHARACTER POLL HAS PEOPLE FROM GROUPS OTHER THAN THE PUBLIC MORALS CLUB AND THE STUDENT COUNCIL!
HEAD OF THE PUBLIC MORALS CLUB
HEAD OF THE STUDENT COUNCIL
OH?
Where?
From the Craft Club...
Arisu and the macho men...
Umino from the judo team...
Yotsuya from the track and field team...
And...
...from the Horti-culture Club...
EXCITED
EXCITED
EXCITED
...THE MAN-EATING FLOWER!
?!

36TH PLACE

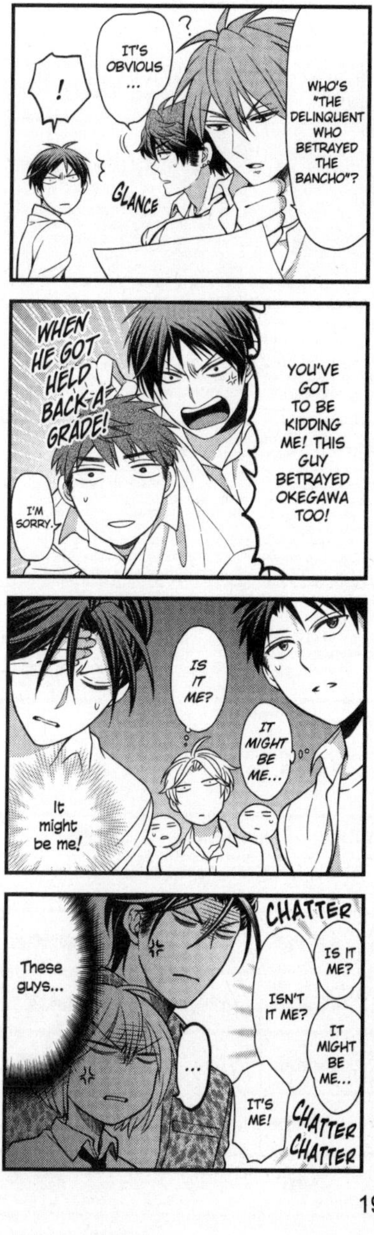
WHO'S "THE DELINQUENT WHO BETRAYED THE BANCHO"?
?
IT'S OBVIOUS ...
!
GLANCE
YOU'VE GOT TO BE KIDDING ME! THIS GUY BETRAYED OKEGAWA TOO!
WHEN HE GOT HELD BACK A GRADE!
I'M SORRY.
IS IT ME?
IT MIGHT BE ME...
It might be me!
CHATTER
IS IT ME?
ISN'T IT ME?
IT MIGHT BE ME...
IT'S ME!
CHATTER CHATTER
...
These guys...

MASCOT BATTLE

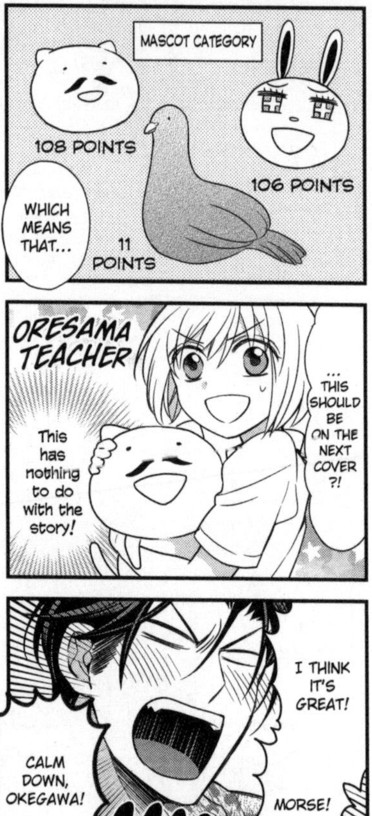
MASCOT CATEGORY
106 POINTS
108 POINTS
11 POINTS
WHICH MEANS THAT...
ORESAMA TEACHER
...THIS SHOULD BE ON THE NEXT COVER?!
This has nothing to do with the story!
I THINK IT'S GREAT!
MORSE!
CALM DOWN, OKEGAWA!
AAAGH!
YOU'VE GOT TO BE KIDDING ME, YOU JERK!
?!
YOU CALM DOWN TOO, HAYASAKA!
GRAB

AN EVEN HIGHER MASCOT

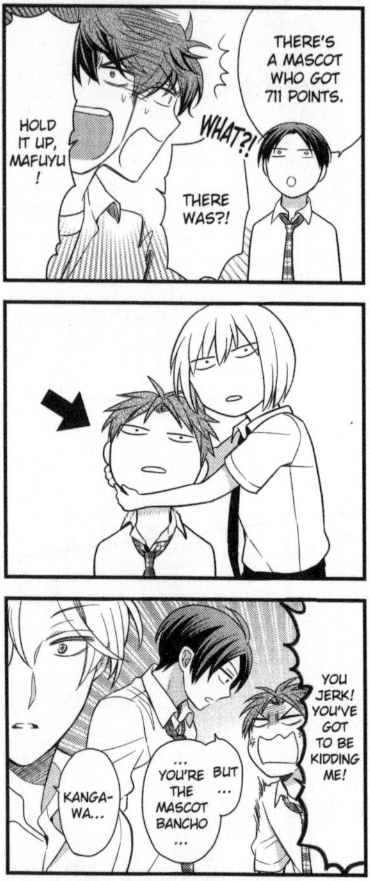
THERE'S A MASCOT WHO GOT 711 POINTS.
WHAT?!
THERE WAS?!
HOLD IT UP, MAFUYU!
YOU JERK! YOU'VE GOT TO BE KIDDING ME!
BUT...
...YOU'RE THE MASCOT BANCHO...
KANGAWA...
DO YOU WANT TO BECOME A MASCOT?
TWITCH

CHARACTER RELATIONSHIPS

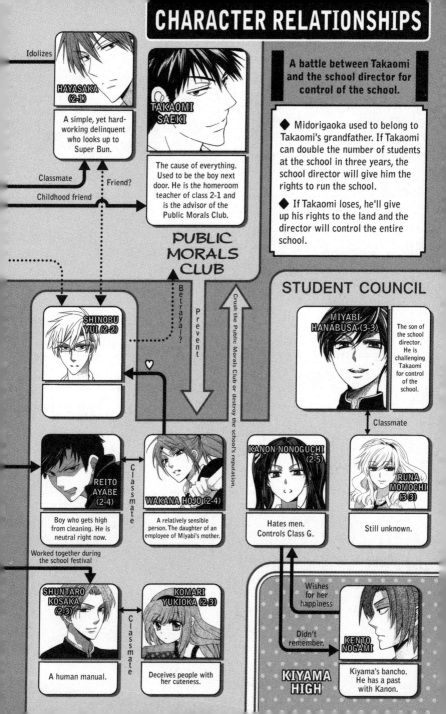

Idolizes

HAYASAKA (2-1)

A simple, yet hard-working delinquent who looks up to Super Bun.

Classmate

Childhood friend

Friend?

TAKAOMI SAEKI

The cause of everything. Used to be the boy next door. He is the homeroom teacher of class 2-1 and is the advisor of the Public Morals Club.

A battle between Takaomi and the school director for control of the school.

◆ Midorigaoka used to belong to Takaomi's grandfather. If Takaomi can double the number of students at the school in three years, the school director will give him the rights to run the school.

◆ If Takaomi loses, he'll give up his rights to the land and the director will control the entire school.

PUBLIC MORALS CLUB

Betrayal?

Prevent

Crush the Public Morals Club or destroy the school's reputation.

SHINOBU YUI (2-2)

STUDENT COUNCIL

MIYABI HANABUSA (3-3)

The son of the school director. He is challenging Takaomi for control of the school.

Classmate

REITO AYABE (2-4)

Boy who gets high from cleaning. He is neutral right now.

Classmate

WAKANA HOJO (2-4)

A relatively sensible person. The daughter of an employee of Miyabi's mother.

KANON NONOGUCHI (2-5)

Hates men. Controls Class G.

RUNA MOMOCHI (3-3)

Still unknown.

Worked together during the school festival

SHUNTARO KOSAKA (2-3)

A human manual.

Classmate

KOMARI YUKIOKA (2-3)

Deceives people with her cuteness.

Wishes for her happiness

Didn't remember.

KENTO NOGAMI

Kiyama's bancho. He has a past with Kanon.

KIYAMA HIGH

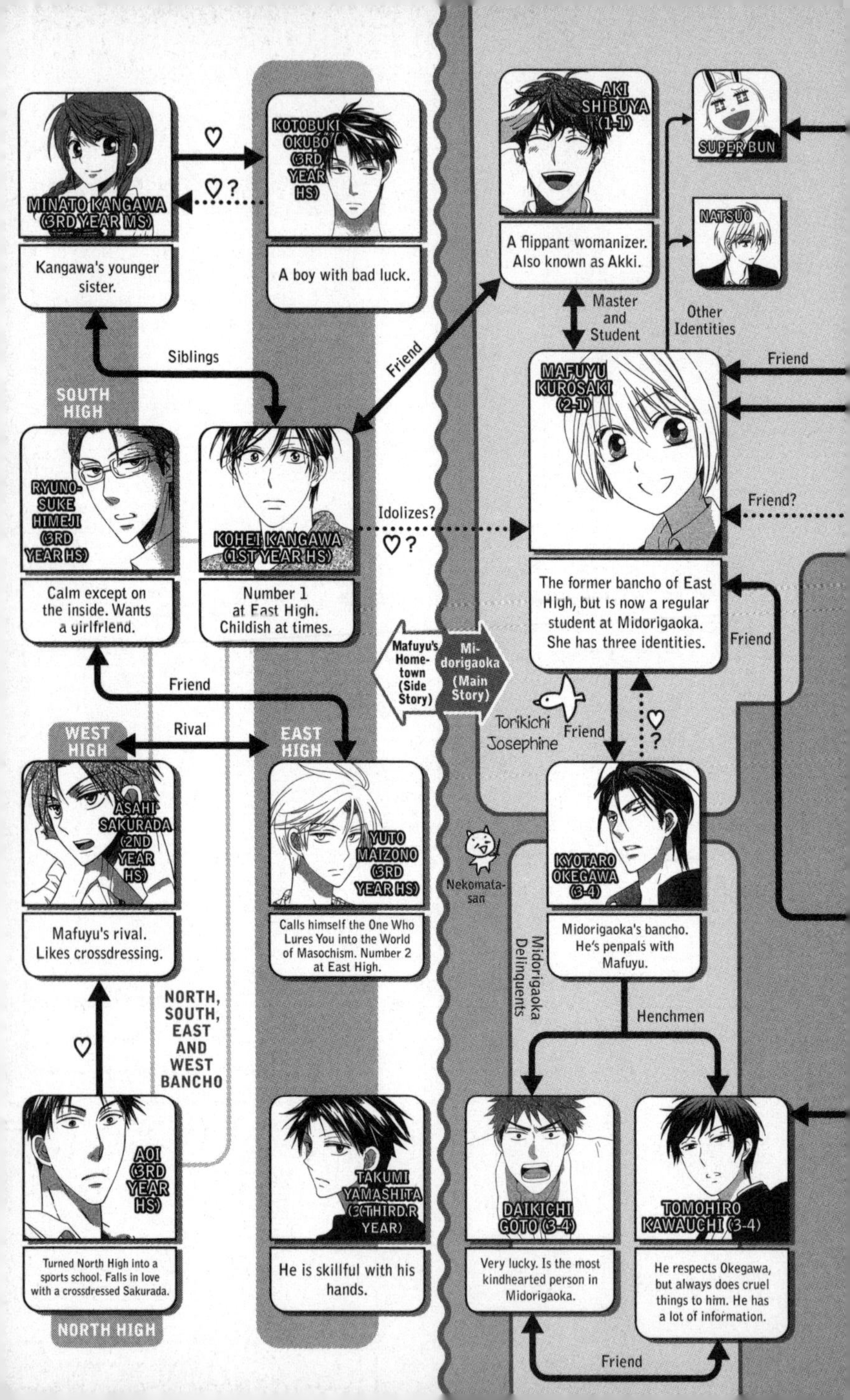
MINATO KANGAWA (3RD YEAR MS)
Kangawa's younger sister.
KOTOBUKI OKUBO (3RD YEAR HS)
A boy with bad luck.
♡
♡?
Siblings
SOUTH HIGH
RYUNO-SUKE HIMEJI (3RD YEAR HS)
Calm except on the inside. Wants a girlfriend.
KOHEI KANGAWA (1ST YEAR HS)
Number 1 at East High. Childish at times.
Friend
Idolizes?
♡?
Friend
Rival
WEST HIGH
EAST HIGH
Mafuyu's Home-town (Side Story)
Mi-dorigaoka (Main Story)
ASAHI SAKURADA (2ND YEAR HS)
Mafuyu's rival. Likes crossdressing.
YUTO MAIZONO (3RD YEAR HS)
Calls himself the One Who Lures You into the World of Masochism. Number 2 at East High.
NORTH, SOUTH, EAST AND WEST BANCHO
♡
AOI (3RD YEAR HS)
Turned North High into a sports school. Falls in love with a crossdressed Sakurada.
NORTH HIGH
TAKUMI YAMASHITA (3THIRD.R YEAR)
He is skillful with his hands.
AKI SHIBUYA (1-1)
A flippant womanizer. Also known as Akki.
SUPER BUN
NATSUO
Master and Student
Other Identities
Friend
MAFUYU KUROSAKI (2-1)
Friend?
The former bancho of East High, but is now a regular student at Midorigaoka. She has three identities.
Friend
Torikichi Josephine
Friend
♡?
Nekomata-san
KYOTARO OKEGAWA (3-4)
Midorigaoka's bancho. He's penpals with Mafuyu.
Midorigaoka Delinquents
Henchmen
DAIKICHI GOTO (3-4)
Very lucky. Is the most kindhearted person in Midorigaoka.
TOMOHIRO KAWAUCHI (3-4)
He respects Okegawa, but always does cruel things to him. He has a lot of information.
Friend

Izumi Tsubaki began drawing manga in her first year of high school. She was soon selected to be in the top ten of *Hana to Yume*'s HMC (*Hana to Yume* Mangaka Course), and subsequently won *Hana to Yume*'s Big Challenge contest. Her debut title, *Chijimete Distance* (Shrink the Distance), ran in 2002 in *Hana to Yume* magazine, issue 17. Her other works include *The Magic Touch* (*Oyayubi kara Romance*) and *Oresama Teacher*, which she is currently working on.